I Will Surely Multiply Your Offspring

I Will Surely Multiply Your Offspring

An Old Testament Theology of the Blessing of Progeny with Special Attention to the Latter Prophets

JAMIE VIANDS

With a Foreword by Richard Schultz

☙PICKWICK *Publications* • Eugene, Oregon

I WILL SURELY MULTIPLY YOUR OFFSPRING
An Old Testament Theology of the Blessing of Progeny with Special Attention to the Latter Prophets

Copyright © 2014 Jamie Viands. All rights reserved. Except for brief quotations in critical publications or reviews, no part of this book may be reproduced in any manner without prior written permission from the publisher. Write: Permissions, Wipf and Stock Publishers, 199 W. 8th Ave., Suite 3, Eugene, OR 97401.

Pickwick Publications
An Imprint of Wipf and Stock Publishers
199 W. 8th Ave., Suite 3
Eugene, OR 97401

www.wipfandstock.com

ISBN 13: 978-1-62032-485-1

Cataloguing-in-Publication data:

Viands, Jamie.

I will surely multiply your offspring : an Old Testament theology of the blessing of progeny with special attention to the latter prophets / Jamie Viands ; with a foreword by Richard Schultz.

xviii + 356 pp. ; 23 cm. Includes bibliographical references and index.

ISBN 13: 978-1-62032-485-1

1. Bible. Prophets—Criticism, interpretation, etc. 2. Bible. Isaiah—Criticism, interpretation, etc. 3. Bible. Jeremiah—Criticism, interpretation, etc. 4. Bible. Ezekiel—Criticism, interpretation, etc. 5. Bible. Minor Prophets—Criticism, interpretation, etc. I. Title.

BS1505.52 V415 2014

Manufactured in the U.S.A.

For Kim

*You are a blessing from the Lord.
It is pure joy to experience the blessing of children with you.*

Contents

Foreword by Richard Schultz   ix
Preface   xiii
Acknowledgements   xv
Abbreviations   xvii

1. Introduction   1
2. The Progeny Blessing in the Old Testament Outside the Latter Prophets   21
3. The Progeny Blessing in the Book of Isaiah   108
4. The Progeny Blessing in the Book of Jeremiah   171
5. The Progeny Blessing in the Book of Ezekiel   204
6. The Progeny Blessing in the Book of the Twelve   232
7. A Synthesis of the Progeny Blessing in the Latter Prophets   270

Appendix A: Progeny Blessing Texts   289
Appendix B: OT Distribution of the Terminology of the Progeny Blessing   297
Bibliography   299
Ancient Document Index   321

Foreword

PSALM 127:3, 5 PROCLAIMS: "Children are a heritage from the LORD, offspring a reward from him.... Blessed is the man whose quiver is full of them" (NIV). In an age when committed individuals campaign against the overpopulation of the world and the resultant depletion of its natural resources, when a number of Western nations are experiencing negative population growth, and when childbearing has become a postponed priority for many couples for various reasons, a *quiver* full of children hardly sounds like a blessing! At the same time, couples struggling with the heartache of infertility may wonder why they are not also enjoying this *reward*. Nevertheless, procreation is a basic human need if family life is to be continued, culture passed on, and the species preserved.

It is unsurprising, then, as Jamie Viands points out in this monograph, that God's first recorded blessing after creating man and woman is "Be fruitful and increase in number." Someone has commented, half jokingly, that this may be the only command in the Bible that people have obeyed consistently—at least until recently! But it is not just about bearing babies—it is about divine blessing—since both the biblical narrative and personal experience confirm that divine enablement must accompany human desire in producing offspring. For this reason, the following work focuses on the progeny *promise* as well as its converse—the curse of barrenness. *I Will Surely Multiply Your Offspring* traces this foundational theme through the Hebrew Bible, analyzing every pertinent text, considering intertextual relationships and influences, and synthesizing the resultant theological findings. This first comprehensive study examines the roots of the progeny promise in the creational and covenantal blessings of the Pentateuch and follows its development in the Former Prophets and Writings before highlighting its creative employment by the Latter Prophets.

The author makes two unexpected discoveries in the course of his journey through the Hebrew Bible. First of all, he realizes the difficulty of determining with any degree of certainty to which pentateuchal version of the progeny promise a specific text might be referring. It certainly could be drawing on the initial occurrence of the promise given to the newly-created human pair in Gen 1:28 which, somewhat surprisingly, echoes quite closely the similar promissory charge given to sea creatures and birds in Gen 1:22. It even utilizes the same three Hebrew verbs to express the reproductive abundance, although the former are then instructed to rule over the latter. Species multiplication is the stated divine goal for all animals following the great flood, according to Gen 8:17, while the progeny promise is issued twice to Noah and his sons in 9:1 and 7 when God's covenant is reestablished with his creatures. The latter immediately follows the prohibition of and punitive measures in response to the taking of human life (vv. 5–6), as if to counter the resultant diminution of the human race.[1] Recent studies exploring the possible cultural or cultic implications of the command to "fill the earth and subdue it" cannot remove the primary connotation of numerical growth, as confirmed by the recurrence of the key "multiplication" verbs in Exod 1:7.

In electing Abraham and his descendants to become conduits through whom divine blessings would flow to all of the peoples on earth (Gen 12:3), God granted them both material benefits (offspring and land) and spiritual benefits (a personal relationship with the self-revealing God), ultimately turning a landless and barren immigrant couple into a "great nation" (Gen 12:1–2). The fullest expression of the progeny promise to Abraham is included among the covenantal promises in Genesis 17:4–6, which, in turn, could supply the basis for Isaac's parting words to his son Jacob in Gen 28:3 as the latter prepares to flee from his cheated and enraged brother Esau: "May God Almighty bless you and make you fruitful and increase your numbers until you become a community of peoples." The promise is also bestowed upon Abraham's son Ishmael at his father's request (Gen 17:20).

With the establishment of the Israelite nation at Mount Sinai, especially in light of God's promise to make Abraham into a great nation, it is not unexpected that the progeny promise would be incorporated into the provisions of the national covenant, though contingent upon their obedience to the covenantal stipulations, as recorded in Lev 26:9: "I will look on you with favor and make you fruitful and increase your numbers, and I will keep my covenant with you" (cf. Deut 28:4, 11). The converse, population decimation, will also certainly accompany national disobedience (cf. especially Lev 26:38 and Deut 28:18–22).

---

1. Waltke, *Genesis*, 144, notes that, unlike in the Mesopotamian Atrahasis Epic's account of the flood, "Genesis 1–11 presents human life as an unqualified good."

Foreword

Jamie Viands exercises appropriate caution in seeking to determine whether the creational, ancestral, or national iteration of the progeny promise is being invoked primarily in a given text. Since the various divine covenants are fundamentally in continuity, building on those which precede them, it may be unnecessary to make such a distinction. God's plan to fill the earth with his image bearers will not be thwarted ultimately by human sinfulness, though the focus of that blessing is first narrowed to one family and then broadened to encompass one people who constitute an elect nation among the peoples of the world.

The author's second surprising discovery is the degree of rhetorical diversity which the Latter Prophets employ in expressing the progeny promise, as they offer various metaphors rather than merely echoing the formulation of the foundational pentateuchal texts. Each of the prophetic books of Isaiah, Jeremiah, and Ezekiel offers its own distinctive emphases, although within the Book of the Twelve the promise is limited to a few verses in Hosea and Zechariah. Most fascinating is the development within the final section of Isaiah, in which the biological growth of the nation is supplemented by the inclusion of foreigners within the worshipping community, as described, for example, in Isa 56:6–8.[2] This anticipates the inclusion of Gentiles within the initially Jewish-dominated church as the book of Acts progresses and culminates in the vision in Rev 7:9 of "a great multitude that no one could count, from every nation, tribe, people and language, standing before the throne and before the Lamb." Such is the biblical-theological scope and import of the progeny promise that Jamie Viands insightfully expounds in the following book.

Richard Schultz
Blanchard Professor of Old Testament
Wheaton College

---

2. See Schultz, "Nationalism and Universalism," 140.

Preface

THE BLESSING OF CHILDREN is one of the most fundamental and common experiences of life. Thus, it is not surprising that God's determination to bless humanity with children (or threaten decimation or barrenness as judgment) surfaces dozens of times throughout the Old Testament. Furthermore, this blessing is a component of every major covenant God creates with humanity. However, this theme has often been neglected altogether in Old Testament and Biblical Theologies. This study seeks to fill this gap by tracing the progeny motif throughout the Old Testament, with a special emphasis on its use in the Latter Prophets, where the disparity between its prominence and its treatment in scholarship is particularly acute.

A secondary goal of our analysis is to make a contribution to studies in intertextuality. We will demonstrate that the prophets depend on prior Old Testament progeny blessing texts and traditions for their own understanding of the blessing, although each prophet tends to emphasize a different tradition. The prophets make unique contributions to this motif as well, including the implication in Isaiah and Zechariah that the inclusion of foreign converts to Yahwism may contribute to the future expansion of the people of God, anticipating the (partial?) reinterpretation of this blessing in the New Testament.

Throughout Jewish and Christian history, God's people have debated whether "be fruitful and multiply" (Gen 1:28) is an obligatory command or a blessing that all should inherently desire. This study addresses this question through a thorough exegesis of the relevant texts in Genesis and by synthesizing the testimony of Scripture elsewhere regarding the progeny blessing. Furthermore, many today wrestle with a host of ethical questions that relate to this fundamental blessing. For example: How should we think about or practice birth control? How should we view reproductive and fertility technologies? Is overpopulation a significant threat and what should be done about it? Scripture may not directly answer such questions, but these issues can and should be framed within a strong exegetical and biblical-theological worldview. This foundation must include the biblical perspective concerning human proliferation, the subject of this book.

The following is a slightly revised and expanded version of my doctoral dissertation submitted to Wheaton College in December 2009 under the guidance of Dr. Richard Schultz and Dr. Daniel Block.

Acknowledgments

THE COMPLETION OF MY doctoral dissertation and its revision into the present manuscript have been possible only because of the support and work of many others. First and foremost, I am grateful to my parents, Donald and Janice Viands, who have funded the majority of my education. What a tremendous blessing it is to complete doctoral studies debt-free! This is not the result of my own hard work, but is a gift from generous and loving parents. It is my parents who fueled my interest in the study of Scripture from a young age and modeled it in their own lives. I continue to admire my father for his diligent personal study, including learning Greek and Hebrew almost entirely on his own. I remain grateful for their encouragement and support each step along the way.

I am thankful to those who made Wheaton's PhD program in Biblical and Theological Studies possible. In particular, I owe a debt of gratitude to Mr. and Mrs. Dale Kemp, who generously funded my doctoral studies, and have continued to demonstrate interest in my life and ministry in Africa.

Many instructors have had an impact on my thinking and personal development over the years. The passion for biblical theology that Dr. Scott Hafemann and Dr. G. K. Beale consistently display has been infectious. Dr. Hafemann's fervor for overseas theological education was the first "spark" the Lord used to lead my family overseas to assist in the training of pastors and leaders for the East African church. I continue to envy the pedagogical skill of Dr. Douglas Stuart and seek to emulate him in my own teaching.

None have had such a sustained effect on my academic and personal development as Dr. Richard Schultz, my doctoral mentor. We first met in the Summer of 1999 on Wheaton's "Holy Lands" trip, when I became one of the few ever to witness Dr. Schultz without a beard, foreshadowing and symbolizing our close relationship in the years to come. His hospitality and desire to support and be involved in the lives of his students remains a compelling example of Christ-like love. He has prioritized me whenever I need to see him and can always be counted on for thorough and helpful feedback. In recent years he has counseled me concerning career options, ministry, and relationships, and has prayed with me countless times. He had joked that I should not be able to defend my dissertation prior to experiencing the very blessing that I had been studying. Sadly, I failed him in this regard, but I have since satisfied this "requirement" within the five-year extension he had granted me.

I am also grateful to Dr. Daniel Block, my second reader. His careful reading and suggestions have undoubtedly improved the quality of this work. His pastoral encouragements have often come at just the right time. In addition, I have greatly appreciated the thoughtful and helpful feedback of my external reader, Dr. Elmer Martens.

My wife, Kimberly Joy Viands ("KJV"), was merely a special friend when I defended my dissertation three years ago. Now she is my companion through life, a constant source of joy, and the mother of our daughter, Eliya. I am continually amazed at the grace and patience she displays toward me—and toward everyone. How precious it is to have a Christ-like wife who models the gospel.

Finally, I give thanks and praise to God, the source of all life, who blessed my parents with progeny, the sole explanation for my existence. I am blessed beyond measure in Christ Jesus.

Abbreviations

Ag. Ap.	*Against Apion* (Josephus)
b.	*Babylonian Talmud*
B. Bat.	*Baba Batra*
BHS	*Biblia Hebraica Stuttgartensia.* Edited by K. Elliger and W. Rudolph. Stuttgart, 1983
CCSL	Corpus Christianorum: Series Latina. Turnhout, 1953–
DCD	Augustine, *De civitate Dei*
DtH	Deuteronomistic History
'Ed.	*'Eduyyot*
ESV	English Standard Version
GCS	Die griechischen christlichen Schriftsteller
Gen. Rab.	*Genesis Rabbah*
Git.	*Gittin*
GKC	*Gesenius' Hebrew Grammar.* Edited by E. Kautzsch. Translated by A. E. Cowley. 2nd. ed. Oxford, 1910.
Hag.	*Hagigah*
HALOT	Koehler, L., W. Baumgartner, and J. J. Stamm, *The Hebrew and Aramaic Lexicon of the Old Testament.* Translated and edited under the supervision of M. E. J. Richardson. 4 vols. Leiden, 1994–99
Hev	Nahal Hever (Dead Sea Scrolls)

Abbreviations

KJV	King James Version
LXX	Septuagint
m.	*Mishnah*
Meg.	*Megillah*
Mm	Masorah magna
Mp	Masorah parva
Ms	one Hebrew manuscript
Mss	multiple Hebrew manuscripts
MT	Masoretic Text
Mur	Murabba'at (Dead Sea Scrolls)
NASB	New American Standard Bible
NCB	New Century Bible
NEB	New English Bible
NIV	New International Version
NRSV	New Revised Standard Version
NT	New Testament
OT	Old Testament
Pesah.	*Pesahim*
Q	Qumran
Sanh.	*Sanhedrin*
t.	*Tosefta*
Yebam.	*Yebamot*

1

Introduction

IN HIS FIRST WORDS to humankind, as recorded in Genesis, God blesses them: "Be fruitful and multiply and fill the earth . . ." (Gen 1:28). This blessing of human proliferation is a prominent theme in Genesis, and is a crucial component of God's promises to Abraham and his descendants.[1] Despite fulfillment of this initial promise in Exod 1:7, God pledges to continue to bless Israel with progeny in the context of the covenant. It then plays a significant role in the Latter Prophets in the restoration oracles of future prosperity for Israel beyond exile, as anticipated in Deut 30:5, 9. The blessing of children garners attention in the Psalms and Wisdom Literature as well.

Most scholarly discussions of this blessing focus on Genesis and on Gen 1:28 in particular.[2] Elsewhere in the OT it has generally been neglected. This may be due to a perceived lack of biblical-theological or exegetical significance to this theme. Or perhaps this inattention is a result of the general tendency in OT studies to emphasize God's historical salvific acts (i.e., deliverance) to the neglect of God's sustaining work for humankind's well-being (i.e., blessing).[3] However, given 1) the foundational role of Gen 1:28 in the OT, 2) the acknowledged importance of this theme in Genesis,

---

1. See Appendix A for a comprehensive list of texts related to the progeny blessing in the OT, demonstrating the pervasiveness of this theme.

2. Nearly all of the literature specifically devoted to the multiplication of humankind from a biblical perspective focuses on Gen 1:28 and is usually concerned with discerning whether it functions as an obligatory command (along with its contemporary ethical implications). See, for example, Daube, *Duty of Procreation*; Lohfink, "Seid fruchtbar," 77–82; Magnuson, "Marriage," 26–42; Novak, "Be Fruitful," 12–31; Shapiro, "Be Fruitful," 59–79; Van Leeuwen, "Be Fruitful," 58–61.

3. See Westermann, *Blessing in the Bible*. This is a central concern that pervades and motivates Westermann's work.

3) its presence among the blessings of the Sinai covenant, and 4) the regular occurrence of the progeny blessing throughout the OT, this dearth of attention is somewhat puzzling and certainly unwarranted.

Although a few studies have treated the progeny blessing in greater detail, none have done so comprehensively, synthesizing all relevant texts. G. K. Beale views the multiplication and spread of humankind as integral to a theology of the temple since it is the means by which the temple-presence of God spreads.[4] Accordingly, he examines Gen 1:28 and similar passages, but his attention to "multiplication texts" in the Latter Prophets is limited to twenty pages[5] due to the broad scope of the work. Jeremy Cohen thoroughly examines the history of the interpretation of Gen 1:28, with particular attention to Jewish sources, but he devotes little attention to the inner-biblical development of the theme.[6] Stephen G. Dempster structures his OT theology around the twin themes of dominion/geography and dynasty/genealogy, based on Gen 1:28.[7] However, he almost entirely abandons the role of the corporate blessing of progeny after Genesis, content to focus solely on the individual "seed of the woman" to be traced through Judah and David to Christ (as suggested by his "dynasty" word choice). Andrew J. Schmutzer conducts an exegetical-theological study of the "Creation Mandate" texts of Gen 1:22, 28, 8:17, and 9:1, 7.[8] He considers the progeny element to be the "core charge" in the mandate, which consists of "endowment" for reproduction and "commission" for ruling,[9] concluding that "[t]he Creation Mandate (1:28) is God's functional blessing, a vitality of relationship, status, and capability for both propagation and governance."[10] Carol M. Kaminski seeks to demonstrate that the "command" of Gen 1:28 was not fulfilled by the nations in Gen 10–11.[11] It has been fulfilled in Israel in Exod 1:7, but it still awaits worldwide fulfillment for the nations through Israel. Unfortunately, Kaminski never ventures beyond Exod 1:7. David Anthony Yegerlehner covers the history of

---

4. Beale, *The Temple*.
5. Ibid., 110–13, 129–44.
6. Cohen, *Be Fertile and Increase*.
7. Dempster, *Dominion and Dynasty*.
8. Schmutzer, *Be Fruitful and Multiply*.
9. Ibid., 93, 106–8, 146–47.
10. Ibid., 226.
11. Kaminski, *From Noah to Israel*.

interpretation of fifteen key multiplication texts, only one of which is from the Latter Prophets (Isa 54:1).[12]

The Focus of This Study

The present study provides a comprehensive examination of the progeny motif in the Hebrew Bible.[13] Yet the use of the progeny blessing in the Latter Prophets is the *primary* focus of this study for the following reasons: 1) Inattention to the progeny blessing is most glaring in the four works that comprise the Latter Prophets, where the motif is frequent, yet commentators often have little or nothing to say about it. 2) It is here that we are best able to explore the richness of the growth of the tradition of the progeny blessing in Israel's Scriptures. 3) The Latter Prophets emphasize Yahweh's future blessing of progeny following exilic judgment. As a result, these texts are especially relevant for our understanding of the blessing in the NT. 4) The prophetic progeny texts are also some of the most difficult to understand.

We focus on texts that explicitly address the collective multiplication of humankind (see Appendix A). Both within and outside the Latter Prophets, most of these texts pertain to the promise or possibility of future multiplication. References to present or past expansion—typically as fulfillment of prior promises—are crucial for our study as well (e.g., Exod 1:7; 1 Kgs 4:20; Isa 48:19).

In addition, we treat some ancillary themes in order to provide the proper context for our examination of the progeny blessing in each prophetic book: 1) We summarize the traditions and OT texts to which each prophetic book most closely corresponds. 2) We locate the progeny blessing within the context of each prophet's portrayal of future restoration. 3) We consider whether texts concerning the conversion of Gentiles or the influx of the nations[14] indicate that foreigners contribute to the numerical expansion of Israel. Where appropriate, we also consider 4) census and battle figures that help us trace the growth of the population, 5) accounts of individual fertility and infertility, such as those that drive the patriarchal narratives, demonstrating the localized experience or non-experience

---

12. Yegerlehner, "Be Fruitful and Multiply."

13. The canonical Hebrew Scriptures will serve as the basis for the study, although it will not always be assumed that the MT preserves the best text.

14. E.g., Isa 2:2–3; 14:1; 19:24–25; 56:6–8; 66:18–23; Mic 4:1–2; Zech 2:15[11]; 8:20–23; and 14:16.

of the universal blessing, and 6) texts that explain or qualify the blessedness of children.

We cannot adequately treat the motif of population expansion without some treatment of the negation and frustration of this blessing as a result of the curse as well. Clearly human history—and the OT account of Israel's history—does not consist of ever-increasing blessing and expansion, but of multiplication and decimation in tension. Families, tribes, and nations come and go as they experience the ebb and flow of blessing through the centuries. It is not possible for us to examine the curses of decimation as thoroughly as we will treat the progeny blessing. This is especially the case in the Latter Prophets, where prophetic judgment oracles, consisting largely of the reversal of the multiplication of Israel, vastly outnumber restoration oracles anticipating proliferation following exile. However, within the following study we frequently return to this theme and its relationship to the blessing. Even prior to our focus on the Latter Prophets, we examine the effect of Gen 3:16 on the blessing, significant decimations in humankind's and Israel's history noted in the OT, and the function of the covenant curses of decimation (e.g., war, famine, illness, and infertility) in the Sinai covenant and their relationship to the blessings. For each book in the Latter Prophets, our detailed treatment of texts pertaining to the progeny blessing is preceded by a summary of decimation texts and themes.

Methodology

Analysis of Progeny Texts outside the Latter Prophets

Texts that introduce significant progeny blessing traditions and are recognized for their biblical-theological significance are the basis for our identification of progeny texts elsewhere. Genesis 1:28 is foremost among these since there we find the initial blessing of human proliferation, both historically and canonically. God's subsequent promise to Abraham that he will multiply his seed is foundational for Israel's unique experience of human proliferation. A small set of verbs and similes is repeatedly employed to denote the progeny blessing in these texts (e.g., פָּרָה, רָבָה, כְּכוֹכְבֵי הַשָּׁמַיִם, כַּחוֹל אֲשֶׁר עַל־שְׂפַת הַיָּם; see below). As a result, it is relatively easy to identify other occurrences of human proliferation that may echo these texts. However, a few seldom-used verbs and images are employed to express the blessing as well (e.g., שָׁרַץ, עָצַם, פָּרַץ, פְּרִי + בֶּטֶן, לֹא תִהְיֶה מְשַׁכֵּלָה

וְעֲקָרָה). In addition, in some cases related themes, such as the Abrahamic promise of land, aid us in our identification of the blessing. Furthermore, in our analysis we incorporate texts that explain the blessedness of children and describe those whom God blesses (e.g., Ps 107:38, 41; 113:9; 127; Prov 10:1). In chapter 2 of our study, our aim is to trace the development of the progeny blessing through Israel's narrative, to identify the major manifestations of the blessing, and to understand their interrelationships. Therefore, our attention to each occurrence of the progeny blessing varies, based on its perceived importance. For example, we devote much attention to the first occurrence of a new manifestation of the blessing (e.g., Gen 1:28; 12:2) or to the fulfillment of a prior promise (e.g., Exod 1:7; 1 Kgs 4:20). Repeated restatements of prior promises, such as we find throughout the Patriarchal narratives, are treated briefly and together rather than separately. This analysis in chapter two is valuable in its own right in order to grasp the OT progeny theme in its fullness, but is necessary background for our subsequent analysis of prophetic texts as well.

Analysis of Prophetic Progeny Texts

Within the Latter Prophets, we examine in detail each text that denotes the corporate numerical expansion of humanity, regardless of time, scope, or place.[15] In addition, we treat texts that employ the proliferation of humanity as a metaphor to depict a different reality (e.g., the return from exile in Isa 49:19–21). In the majority of its occurrences, the same vocabulary used elsewhere in the OT to denote the blessing is employed. In other cases, the proliferation of people is described apart from this standard vocabulary. In these instances, usually in poetry, we first study the language itself in its literary context to determine whether it refers to the multiplication of humanity. We give less attention to texts where the presence of the blessing is not certain but only possible or likely.

For each text in the Latter Prophets, we describe the function of the progeny blessing in its literary context. We give attention to a number of dimensions of the blessing, including its articulation, timing, place, scope, purpose, agent, means of realization, and relationship to other blessings in the text, although the presentation does not necessarily cover each of these aspects systematically. The extent to which we treat each of these facets of

---

15. We do not discuss instances in which the prophets note individual experiences of the progeny blessing, such as the birth of sons to a king or the children of Isaiah the prophet.

the progeny blessing varies depending on the specific contours of each text. In addition, some texts require unique exegetical inquiries (e.g., text-critical, historical, lexical, etc.) in order to determine adequately how the blessing functions there. Finally, we seek to correlate each prophetic use of the progeny blessing with one or more prior progeny traditions.

The Prophets' Indebtedness to Prior Tradition

Contrary to the biblical portrayal, twentieth-century historical-critical scholars typically viewed the pre-exilic prophets as radical innovators who laid the groundwork for the development of the concept of the covenant. Von Rad was one of the first to reject this thesis, basing the second volume of his *Old Testament Theology* on the claim that the prophets "were in greater or lesser degree conditioned by old traditions which they reinterpreted and applied to their own times."[16] Clements claimed that it was the *people of Israel* who were "innovators" who had left their traditions, while the prophets were urging them to return to them.[17] Similarly, Zimmerli maintained that the prophets were in substantial continuity with prior traditions, noting that "[i]n their preaching [tradition] becomes the accuser of the present."[18]

The exact content of these traditions may be impossible to define, and it is unlikely that each prophet was familiar with or embraced the same set of traditions.[19] However, covenant was certainly central. According to Clements, the "unifying tendency" in prophecy is "an overall concern with the covenant as the basis and explanation of Israel's existence,"[20] so that "[w]ithout the prior fact of the covenant the prophets would not be intelligible to us."[21] The prophets are thus "interpreters of history" and of the present situation in light of the covenant which had been forgotten or distorted by the populace.[22] The prophets call them back to the covenant and urge them to reorient their lives in accordance with it. It must not be thought, however, that the prophets simply reiterated inherited traditions

---

16. Von Rad, *Old Testament Theology: Prophetic Traditions*, 4.
17. See Clements, *Prophecy and Covenant*, 16.
18. Zimmerli, *Fiery Throne*, 20; see 1–17. Each of these scholars also affirms, however, that the prophets modified and transformed some inherited traditions.
19. See Clements, *Prophecy and Tradition*, 87–89.
20. Clements, *Prophecy and Covenant*, 8.
21. Ibid., 126. See also Stuart, *Hosea–Jonah*, xxxii.
22. See Clements, *Prophecy and Covenant*, 26, 124.

concerning the covenant. Regardless of the dating of Deut 29–30, prophetic descriptions of future hope certainly go beyond and expand prior traditions. Nevertheless, the future is portrayed through the lens of Israel's prior experiences (e.g., new creation, new exodus, new covenant, new Davidic king, new kingdom on Zion).

Some of the clearest conceptual correspondences between the covenant traditions as recorded in the Pentateuch and the prophets are between the covenant curses and the prophetic oracles of judgment and the covenant blessings and the prophetic oracles of restoration. Since most of the covenant curses and blessings of the Pentateuch are not unique to Israel but are common to other ancient Near Eastern cultures, it is difficult to establish conclusively based on the language of the prophets that they are consciously drawing exclusively from the OT covenant curses and blessings.[23] However, since the basic framework of the prophets is indebted to the Sinai covenant, there is good reason to believe that such dependence exists. Stuart thus rightly claims that "[n]early all of the content of the classical (writing) prophets' oracles revolve [sic] around the announcement of the near-time fulfillment of covenantal curses and the end-time fulfillment of covenantal restoration blessings."[24] We see evidence of this in a number of prophetic texts that refer to the progeny blessing.

Therefore, although we cannot prove that the prophets possessed Deuteronomy and the other Pentateuchal documents in their present form and that they alluded specifically to them as literary works, we do maintain that they were familiar with the covenant traditions. This certainly includes the progeny blessing, especially given its centrality in the covenants. We do not assume that each prophet knew the progeny blessing in each of its universal, Abrahamic, and Sinaitic manifestations. However, we remain attentive to textual evidence that may indicate such familiarity based on literary correspondences between Pentateuchal and prophetic texts, seeking to relate each prophetic text to prior traditions, whether written or oral. This appeal to common traditions places us on firmer ground than arguing for specific textual dependence, since the study of compositional dependence is notoriously complex, riddled with uncertainties and characterized by multiple explanations.[25] We do, how-

---

23. See Clements, *Prophecy and Tradition*, 16–19. However, the correspondences are fairly strong in some cases. The language of Jeremiah, for example, is often quite close to that of Deuteronomy.

24. Stuart, *Hosea–Jonah*, xxxii.

25. See, for example, Schultz, *Search for Quotation*, 62–71.

ever, give attention to the clearest and most significant instances of textual dependence.

Presentation

Narrative Framework

According to Goldingay, "[t]he fact that the Old Testament opens with narrative and is dominated by narrative makes narrative form the appropriate starting point for Old Testament theology."[26] A narrative approach is especially appropriate for the study of the progeny blessing, since the development of this theme is tied to the unfolding narrative of the nation of Israel. Therefore, prior to the Latter Prophets, we trace the development of the progeny blessing based on the narrative plotline of the Bible rather than according to the compositional history of Israelite literature. For the Pentateuch and Former Prophets, this corresponds to the Hebrew canonical order. The Psalms and Wisdom Literature (Job, Proverbs, Ecclesiastes) do not relate the progeny blessing to Israel's narrative (except Ps 105:24) and will therefore be discussed thereafter. Thus our ordering of 1) books containing Israel's narrative, 2) Psalms and Wisdom Literature, and 3) the Latter Prophets groups the OT books into broad genre categories and permits the most helpful understanding of the blessing in the OT, culminating in our detailed work in the prophets, while approximating the chronological order of the events related in these books.[27]

The Literary Final Form as Interpretive Context

In his recent monograph, *Prophecy and Hermeneutics*, Christopher Seitz advocates an approach to the prophets that is adopted here. In his words, "[t]he main thesis of the present work is that theological reading of the prophets means reading them in such a way that history is properly appreciated, on the terms of its own biblical presentation."[28] This entails taking seriously the canonical form of each book and the Latter Prophets as a unified corpus. Methodologically, it also entails treating the prophets in

---

26. Goldingay, *Old Testament Theology: Israel's Gospel*, 32; see also 28.

27. John Goldingay employs a similar three-fold division for his three-volume *Old Testament Theology*, although his rationale differs.

28. Seitz, *Prophecy*, 247.

the order of their literary presentation in the canon rather than breaking up the Twelve and Isaiah based on hypothetical compositional histories.[29] In addition, Seitz rightly states that it is better to "give way to a model that is more interested in the final form of witnesses and the way the prophetic figures *have been presented* in the mature form of the witness" than to have "an interest in original settings due to [the historical paradigm's] preoccupation with the prophetic consciousness and individuality."[30] Seitz's proposal is based on the work of Brevard Childs, who long ago recognized that "a major literary and theological force was at work in shaping the present form of the Hebrew Bible,"[31] a force that ought to be considered decisive in interpretation over against historical-critical hypotheses regarding sources, redactions, and original settings.

Although more interested in literary theory and reading strategies than in theology, Edgar Conrad adopts a similar approach, seeking for each prophetic book "the intention of the work" as composed by the implied author for the implied reader.[32] Without neglecting the historical context, he rightly identifies the world of the text (i.e., the "intertext") as the primary interpretive context for understanding individual texts and books.[33] Clements[34] and Rendtorff[35] are other prominent voices encouraging the shift within prophetic scholarship to a focus on the final form of the text.

This approach obviously has exegetical ramifications. Occasionally we explore the possible historical contexts in which individual texts containing the progeny blessing were composed or orally delivered. Our focus, however, is upon the literary and theological contexts of each text, seeking to locate it within the book and within the theology of the Latter

---

29. See ibid., 59.
30. Ibid., 95, emphasis original.
31. Childs, "Canonical Shape," 47.
32. Conrad, *Reading the Latter Prophets*, 26; see 23–30. On the "implied" or "model" author and reader, see also Longman III, *Literary Approaches*, 84–85. Although we will consider extra-biblical information concerning the real author(s) and the original audience(s), this focus is simply an acknowledgment that our knowledge of both author(s)/editor(s) and audience(s) is based almost exclusively on the text and is best sought there. As Longman notes, there is often little practical distinction between the "implied author" and the "narrator" (85–87).
33. See ibid., 27–28.
34. See Clements, *Old Testament Prophecy*, 11–14.
35. See Rendtorff, *Old Testament*.

Prophets as a whole.[36] The meaning of an oracle and its perlocutionary effect in its original historical context may be transformed and made relevant in new or fresh ways for later generations in the context of a written corpus.[37] Both dimensions are worthy of exploration, but it is the latter that is our primary focus since the text now functions in the context of a written canon and since the former is often uncertain.[38] Moreover, each book in its final form (viewing the Twelve as one book) now contains both judgment and future hope.[39] Clements thus observes that the Latter Prophets exhibit a unified voice "centered on the death and rebirth of Israel, interpreted theologically as acts of divine judgment and salvation," attesting to the unity of Yahweh's character and purposes.[40] We aim to hear the prophets together as mutually interpreting witnesses without losing the distinct voice of each book.[41]

Conclusion

Therefore, our method combines diachronic and synchronic approaches. Outside the Latter Prophets, we trace the diachronic development of the progeny motif through Israel's history as it is presented in the biblical

---

36. As a result, secondary historical causes for population growth and related archaeological evidence play, at most, a supporting role.

37. According to Clements, prophetic oracles "have acquired further meanings in the extended context which the canonical portrayal provided" (*Old Testament Prophecy*, 194; see also 197–99). For example, salvation oracles delivered by pre-exilic prophets were likely thought by the prophet and/or the audience to apply to a time in the near future. In their present context, juxtaposed with the other prophetic writings, they describe a distant, future hope beyond exile.

38. Both Seitz (*Prophecy*, 196) and Clements (*Old Testament Prophecy*, 207) express an interest in both aspects but with a preference for the latter.

39. John H. Walton explains that this thematic emphasis common in the Latter Prophets is unique among extant ancient Near Eastern prophetic texts. Ancient Near Eastern prophetic oracles contained very little judgment and predicted near-term support and blessing since their aim was the legitimation of the current king. In the OT, salvation and blessing are typically long-term since the short-term generally does not promise blessing but rather judgment (*Ancient Near Eastern Thought*, 252–53, 268).

40. Clements, *Old Testament Prophecy*, 200, 207. This unity is recognized, for example, in 2 Kgs 17:13–15 and Acts 3:24 (see Clements 192–93).

41. As we examine the theme of population growth within the context of the final literary form of each book we will rely on previous descriptions of literary unity. See Childs, "Canonical Shape," 46–55; Conrad, *Reading Isaiah*; McConville, *Judgment and Promise*; Renz, *Rhetorical Function of Ezekiel*; House, *Unity of the Twelve*; Nogalski and Sweeney, *Reading and Hearing*.

Introduction

texts. Furthermore, we describe the influence of these prior traditions on the prophetic texts. However, we treat the progeny blessing in each prophetic book synchronically, concluding each chapter with a synthesis of the presentation of the blessing in the book. In the process, we consider whether the contours of the blessing change in the course of the final form of the book. Thus, our synchronic treatment of the prophetic books both contributes to and is rooted in our diachronic treatment of the progeny blessing. These dimensions come together most fully in the conclusion of our study.

The canonical approach we have adopted for the Latter Prophets highlights the unique contribution of each prophetic book, thus mirroring the Bible's own presentation of the progeny motif, and facilitates helpful comparisons between the prophetic books. We are then in a better place to note unity within diversity as we combine these diverse presentations into a topical synthesis in concluding our study.[42]

Purpose

Thus, the aim of this study is to trace the development of the progeny blessing through the OT, to understand its function within each stage of redemptive history, and to relate diverse portrayals of the blessing to one another, as a contribution to biblical theology.

We seek to answer a number of interrelated questions pertaining to the progeny blessing in the Latter Prophets: Do the purpose, scope, location, attendant circumstances, and realization of the blessing in redemptive history differ within or between the individual prophetic books? Do the prophets appear to be at odds with or in continuity with the other OT

---

42. This represents only one possible method and manner of presentation for an OT theology of the progeny blessing. For example, we could organize our treatment of the blessing in the Latter Prophets hierarchically around its individual, national, and universal manifestations rather than around the development of the blessing in each book. However, such a categorization is of limited value since the prophets are almost exclusively concerned with the national blessing and since individual experiences of the blessing are not our focus. Our data could be arranged in some other topical fashion (e.g., purpose, scope, and correlations to prior traditions), but a sense of the progress of the blessing throughout Israel's history and the development of this motif within individual books would be lost. In any case, we accomplish this in our synthetic sections. Alternatively, we could employ a fuller diachronic approach and analyze prophetic texts chronologically. However, the date of each text often has little bearing on the interpretation of the progeny blessing itself since most will be realized following exile.

texts on these matters? Specifically, how do the prophets cohere with the testimony of the OT with respect to past, present, and future fulfillment(s) of the blessing? How does the blessing of multiplication relate to other blessings in the prophets? Does this blessing pertain only to ethnic Israel or to the nations as spiritual progeny of Yahweh as well? Does it merely refer to increased birth rates and lower mortality rates among the people, or more broadly to life-sustaining processes or even to return from exile? What are God's ultimate aims in blessing his people and humankind with numerous children?

Blessing in the Old Testament

Due to the dominant emphasis on Yahweh's mighty acts of deliverance in Old Testament Theology over the last century, his sustaining work in blessing humanity has often been overlooked. However, although it often appears to be mundane and ordinary, blessing pervades the pages of the Old Testament. In fact, as Goldingay states, "Israel's story (the world's story) is not ultimately about deliverance but about blessing. When things have gone wrong (e.g., the people are slaves in Egypt), then God needs to take some emergency measures to put them right by delivering them. But normal life is then about blessing."[43] Westermann helpfully describes blessing as "a quiet, continuous, flowing, and unnoticed work of God which cannot be captured in moments and dates. Blessing is realized in a gradual process, as in the process of growing, maturing, and fading."[44]

The OT presupposes that all blessing stems from Yahweh. These blessings include a wide array of processes and gifts that sustain and enhance individual and corporate life: agricultural abundance, the fertility of cattle and flocks, fruitfulness of the womb, health, prosperity, security, and power over enemies. Yahweh alone is the provider of offspring and he alone has the power to open and close the womb (e.g., Gen 15:3; 16:1–2; 20:17–18; 21:1–2; 25:21; 29:31; 30:2, 22; Deut 1:10–11; 7:13–14; 10:22; 30:5, 9).[45]

43. Goldingay, *Old Testament Theology: Israel's Gospel*, 471.

44. Westermann, *Elements*, 103. Westermann has emphasized the role of blessing in the OT more than any other recent scholar. See especially his work devoted to tracing blessing through the Bible, *Blessing in the Bible*.

45. Under the influence of the history-of-religions school and its indebtedness to evolutionary thinking, early twentieth-century scholars posited a primitive notion of blessing that lies behind some of the earliest OT texts. In his influential work, *Israel: Its Life and Culture*, Pedersen describes blessing as a "force," a "power of the soul" (1:182),

The Terminology of the Progeny Blessing in the Old Testament

In the prophetic texts, Yahweh's blessing of human proliferation is expressed in a variety of ways, in part because many such texts are poetic. However, in the OT as a whole and in the Pentateuch in particular where the progeny blessing is most conspicuous, certain verbs and expressions are employed repeatedly to denote it. A brief study of this vocabulary will better enable us to trace the trajectories of the progeny blessing as it unfolds in the OT. Therefore, we will examine verbs denoting increase in order of frequency as well as similes that express population growth.

רָבַב and רָבָה

Based on the broad semantic range and frequency of רָבָה in the OT, רָבָה appears to have been the most common Hebrew term for increase of any sort. It can refer either to quantitative or qualitative increase and pertains to objects as varied as property (Deut 8:13), sin (Prov 29:16), and food (Ezek 36:29). The multiplication of human offspring is a common use of רָבָה, the most frequently employed term to denote the progeny blessing, whether in its Qal or Hiphil causative form. It occurs in each of the "creation blessings" of Genesis (1:22, 28; 8:17; 9:1, 7), as well as in the Abrahamic promises of progeny (e.g., Gen 17:2; 26:4; 35:11) and the covenant blessings of Sinai (e.g., Lev 26:9; Deut 6:3; 7:13; 30:5). It is often juxtaposed with other verbs of multiplication (e.g., Gen 1:28; 9:7), but frequently appears in isolation (e.g., Gen 17:2; Deut 6:3). It appears with respect to

---

that can be transferred from one person to another (see 1:200–2). Once one possesses this power, they are able to use it at will (see Pedersen, *Israel*, 1:195; Westermann, *Blessing in the Bible*, 19; Wehmeier, "ברך," 1:277; cf. Mitchell, *Meaning of BRK*, 18). Genesis 24:60, 27:27–29, 32:27–31[26–30] and Num 22–24 are among the texts identified with this earliest stage. However, even if the historical participants in these narratives understood blessing in this manner (which is far from obvious except in Num 22:6), the text indicates in each case that Yahweh is still the source of the blessing (see Brown, "ברך," 1:762; Mowvley, "Concept and Content," 75; Wehmeier, "ברך," 1:277), except perhaps in the case of Gen 24:60. Accordingly, more recent scholarship has rejected this "magical" interpretation of blessing altogether and asserted that all blessing in the OT ultimately comes from Yahweh (see Scharbert, "ברך; בְּרָכָה," 2:286; Mitchell, *Meaning of BRK*, 2, 171, 176).

Timothy G. Crawford claims that, with only one exception, deities are invoked in all inscriptions of blessing and cursing in Syro-Palestine from 1000–600 BCE (*Blessing and Curse*, 231–32).

human population growth in nearly every OT book that touches on the subject (see Appendix B). Furthermore, it cuts across Pentateuchal source divisions, surfacing in J (Gen 16:10; 26:4), E (Gen 22:17; Exod 32:13), D (Deut 1:10; 6:3), and P (Gen 1:28; 35:11; Lev 26:9).[46] רָבַב, probably a by-form of רָבָה (see *HALOT*), is less frequently attested but appears to have a similar semantic range. It occurs only in Gen 6:1, Deut 7:7, Jer 46:23, and Hos 4:7 with respect to the increase of humankind, but, interestingly, each of these texts describes complete or ongoing multiplication rather than a promised or predicted multiplication.

פָּרָה

Unlike רָבָה, פָּרָה is predominantly employed to refer to human multiplication (in twenty-two of its twenty-nine occurrences). It always means "to bear fruit" based on the "seed" contained in the subject of the verb. Occasionally it refers to the fruitfulness of plants (e.g., Isa 32:12), but even in two of these instances (Gen 49:22; Ps 128:3) plant imagery serves as a metaphor for human proliferation. Since פָּרָה always denotes the reproduction of plants, animals (Gen 1:22; 8:17; Ezek 36:11), or humans, its semantic range appears to be confined to fertility contexts. Although the semantic range of its nominal form, פְּרִי, is much broader,[47] it is used in the common collocation פְּרִי + בֶּטֶן ("fruit of the/my/your womb") as a figure of speech for human offspring.[48] The majority of the occurrences of פָּרָה with respect to humankind appear in Genesis (thirteen of twenty-two: 1:28; 9:1, 7; 17:6, 20; 26:22; 28:3; 35:11; 41:52; 47:27; 48:4; 49:22 [2x]). The verb פָּרָה does not appear in Deuteronomy, but פְּרִי־בִטְנְךָ appears in Deut 7:13, 28:4, 11, and 30:9 to denote multiplication.

---

46. Source-critical divisions here and elsewhere are based on Friedman, *Bible with Sources*.

47. It can refer not only to children and literal fruit, but also to the results of the speech, thought, or action of a human, whether good or bad (e.g., Ps 1:3; Prov 31:16).

48. See Gen 30:2; Deut 7:13; 28:4, 11, 18, 53; 30:9; Isa 13:18; Pss 127:3; 132:11; Mic 6:7; Lam 2:20. Only in Deut 7:13; 28:4, 11; 30:9; Ps 127:3 does the phrase refer to the progeny blessing. In each case (except Ps 127:3) this is the first element in a tripartite fertility formula that also promises blessing for the ground and Israel's animals. In nearly all of the other texts (Gen 30:2; Deut 28:18, 53; Isa 13:18; Mic 6:7; Lam 2:20) it is employed in the context of curse.

פְּרוּ וּרְבוּ

In seven of its occurrences (Gen 17:6; 26:22; 41:52; 49:22; Exod 23:30; Ezek 19:10; Ps 128:3), פָּרָה appears alone with reference to the progeny blessing, and once it appears alongside עָצַם (Ps 105:24). However, elsewhere it is combined with רָבָה, usually directly preceding it (Gen 1:22, 28; 8:17; 9:1, 7; 17:20; 28:3; 35:11; 47:27; 48:4; Lev 26:9; Jer 23:3)[49] in the most recognizable articulation of the progeny blessing, "be fruitful and multiply." Given the prevalence of this juxtaposition, many scholars[50] rightly see this as hendiadys, "to be exceedingly fruitful." Source-critical scholarship has identified this hendiadys as a distinguishing linguistic characteristic of the priestly writer, and thus all occurrences of פָּרָה together with רָבָה are identified as P with the exception of Jer 23:3.

פָּרַץ and מָלֵא

Whereas רָבָה and פָּרָה denote the act of human multiplication, פָּרַץ and מָלֵא express the result of population increase: expanding across the land. פָּרַץ refers to the spread of humans in Gen 28:14, Exod 1:12, Isa 54:3, Hos 4:10, and 1 Chr 4:38, appearing alongside other expressions for multiplication in the first three texts. In Gen 1:28, 9:1, and Exod 1:7, three crucial texts referring to the progeny blessing, מָלֵא appears as the final verb in a string of verbs of multiplication, referring to the intended result of population growth—the filling of the land.

עָצַם

עָצַם follows רָבָה twice (Exod 1:7, 20) and occurs alongside פָּרָה in Ps 105:24. Among its fourteen occurrences in the MT, some clearly refer to being countless or numerous (Jer 15:8; Ps 40:6[5], 13[12]) whereas others do not provide enough contextual information to suggest whether it is numbers *per se* that is in view or rather the strength that is often (but not necessarily) found in numbers (e.g., Gen 26:16; Isa 31:1; Jer 5:6; Ps 69:5). Given this limited lexical pool and contextual information, it is unclear whether עָצַם in Exod 1:7, 20 and Ps 105:24 is synonymous with רָבָה and

---

49. The two verbs are separated by שָׁרַץ in Exod 1:7 and reversed in Jer 3:16 and Ezek 36:11.

50. E.g., Andersen, *Sentence*, 117; Cohen, *Be Fertile and Increase*, 14; Hamilton, *Genesis*, 131; Gordon J. Wenham, *Genesis*, 5.

פָּרָה in denoting multiplication or whether it expresses the result of such growth in terms of might.

Other Verbs

Although יָסַף is a common verb for increase, it is rarely used to refer to the numerical growth of humankind (see Deut 1:11; Isa 26:15). שָׁרַץ occurs in Gen 9:7 and Exod 1:7 with respect to humankind in conjunction with other verbs of multiplication. Since it generally denotes locomotion ("to move" or "swarm"; e.g., Lev 11:29, 41), perhaps this term also refers to the "filling" result of multiplication. Finally, the *hapax* דָּגָה occurs in Gen 48:16 to describe desired population growth.

Similes for Human Increase

In Gen 13:16 Yahweh promises to make Abraham's seed "like the dust of the earth" (כַּעֲפַר הָאָרֶץ). Although used only twice more (Gen 28:14; 2 Chr 1:9), in both instances this idiom refers to the size of Israel, promised (in the former) and realized (in the latter).

The most common hyperbolic simile used to depict the dramatic growth of humankind is to be "like the stars of heaven" (כְּכוֹכְבֵי הַשָּׁמַיִם; Gen 15:5; 22:17; 26:4; Exod 32:13; Deut 1:10; 10:22; 28:62; Jer 33:22; Neh 9:23; 1 Chr 27:23). This occurs first in Gen 15:5 where Yahweh compares Abraham's seed (זֶרַע) to the number of the stars of heaven in his promise to make him a great nation. Thereafter, every occurrence of the "stars" simile refers to the Abrahamic promise or the people of Israel, with the exception of Jer 33:22, where it is applied to the descendants of David and the Levites.

Finally, in his climactic reiteration of his promises to Abraham following the test concerning Isaac, Yahweh promises to multiply his seed not only "as the stars of heaven" but also "as the sand on the seashore" (כַּחוֹל אֲשֶׁר עַל־שְׂפַת הַיָּם; Gen 22:17). This same image is used with respect to the Israelites in Gen 32:13[12], 2 Sam 17:11, 1 Kgs 4:20, Isa 10:22, 48:19, and Hos 2:1[1:10] and in Jer 33:22 with respect to David and the Levites. However, unlike the two previous similes, "as the sand on the seashore" is also used in the Deuteronomistic history to express the innumerability of foreign peoples in the context of preludes to battle: of the Canaanites in

Introduction

Josh 11:4, of the Midianite coalition and, specifically, their camels in Judg 7:12, and of the Philistines in 1 Sam 13:5.[51]

Approaching the Latter Prophets

The Prophetic Profile

Within Israel's story, the prophet *par excellence*, providing a paradigm for subsequent prophets, is Moses.[52] The Mosaic prophet served as covenant mediator, intercessor for the people before God, and as God's spokesman to the people, thus always speaking that which is true (Deut 18:15–22).[53] Yet the biblical portrayal of Israel's prophets from Samuel to Elisha to Ezekiel is far from monolithic. As a result, it is difficult to paint a detailed portrait that is true of all prophecy. Some have attempted to do so, defining the prophet by his ecstatic experiences, his skill as a poet, or his social setting within the cult or royal court.[54] Although these proposals fit some of the prophets, they do not encompass all. Perhaps the common thread is that all prophets served as *intermediaries*,[55] the divinely sanctioned mouthpieces of God to the people, a definition consistent with prophecy elsewhere in the ancient Near East.[56] It is clear that the writing prophets

---

51. Other images used to depict large groups of people are common as well. Foreign peoples are said to be as numerous as "locusts" (אַרְבֶּה) in Judg 6:5, 7:12, and Jer 46:23. Elsewhere, various peoples (Judg 6:5; Jer 46:23; Joel 1:6; 2 Chr 12:3) and groups (Job 21:33; Song 6:8) are hyperbolically claimed to be "without number" (אֵין מִסְפָּר). In Job 5:25 Eliphaz states that Job's offspring could potentially be "as the grass of the earth" (כְּעֵשֶׂב הָאָרֶץ). None of these expressions is used in the context of Yahweh's promises to Abraham or the creation blessings. See Watson, *Classical Hebrew Poetry*, 316–21, regarding Hebrew hyperbole.

52. Appropriately, the writing prophets are often portrayed as types of Moses. See, for example, McKeating, "Ezekiel," 97–109; O'Kane, "Isaiah," 29–51; Seitz, "Prophet Moses," 3–27.

53. See Wilson, *Prophecy and Society*, 156.

54. See Petersen, "Defining Prophecy," 33–38, for a review and critique of these suggestions.

55. See Baker, "Israelite Prophets," 277; Petersen, "Defining Prophecy," 39–44; Wilson, *Prophecy and Society*, 124. In *The Roles of Israel's Prophets* Petersen argues that the different prophetic labels (נָבִיא, חֹזֶה, אִישׁ הָאֱלֹהִים, רֹאֶה) reflect different forms of intermediation or "roles," although "there is no one-to-one correspondence between role and role label" for חֹזֶה and נָבִיא since both "are used to refer to one essential role, that of the central morality prophet" (69).

56. See Martti Nissinen, *Prophets and Prophecy*, 1–7. Most of the extant ancient Near Eastern prophecy originates in eighteenth-century Mari and seventh-century

viewed themselves this way. They repeatedly attribute their messages to God (e.g., the familiar כֹּה אָמַר יְהוָה formula) and some record personal experiences of divine commissioning to legitimize their message (e.g., Isa 6:8–13; Jer 1:4–19).

The prophets[57] whose writings contribute to the Latter Prophets condemn the people for sin, announce impending judgment, and predict hope and restoration beyond judgment. Although Israel is the primary audience for the prophets, their three-fold message applies to foreign nations as well. The prophets are preachers.[58] The communicative intent of their rhetoric is multi-faceted, as is the intended effect on the hearers. Their purpose is not merely to announce or predict, but to persuade, transform, threaten, convict, warn, and promise. Indictments and threats of judgment often aim to effect repentance (e.g., Isa 1:27–28; Jer 3:11–14; Ezek 14:6; Jonah 3:1–10). If the people refuse or if the offer is rescinded (e.g., Jer 13:23), judgment oracles may not only announce but also actively bring the audience under judgment.[59] Salvation oracles not only encourage and extend hope to future generations but also aim to reinforce trust in Yahweh and his promises. Furthermore, like all good preachers, the prophets instruct Israel concerning the character of Yahweh, his sovereignty over all nations, and his purposes in history. Clearly, the prophets' speech acts were to have powerful effects. For example, Jeremiah is called "to pluck up and to break down, to destroy and to overthrow, to build and the plant" (Jer 1:10), and Isaiah is charged to "make the heart of this people dull" (Isa 6:10).[60] The covenant is the primary basis for prophetic activity.

Prophetic Oracles of Salvation

In his study of prophetic salvation oracles, Claus Westermann observes remarkable agreement in form and content among the salvation oracles across the various prophetic books, leading him to propose that the

---

Assyria. Although similar to Israelite prophecy in its basic intermediary nature, these prophecies differ in terms of content and the means by which they are obtained (see Walton, *Ancient Near Eastern Thought*, 252–53, 268, 273).

57. Here and throughout, when referring to one of the writing prophets, I refer to him as the implied author of the entire literary work. Furthermore, I understand him as he is portrayed in that work rather than as the historical individual who may or may not have been responsible for the final shape of the literary work as we now have it.

58. See especially Smith, *Prophets as Preachers*.

59. See Houston, "What Did the Prophets," 180.

60. See Carroll, *When Prophecy Failed*, 69–75.

majority of them were late insertions deriving from a common time and tradition.⁶¹ Employing his familiar dialectic, he notes further that "[t]he proclamation can be of an act of deliverance or a state of well-being, or of the two together," expressed through different forms.⁶² However, we will not draw such a sharp distinction between deliverance and well-being since such acts of deliverance have abiding effects and many of the blessings are initially experienced in acts of deliverance. Instead, we refer to all of these as blessings as we examine the promises that accompany the progeny blessing. We summarize the message of the salvation oracles in the Latter Prophets below on a book-by-book basis rather than according to form groupings as Westermann does.

Based on the Pentateuchal texts projecting restoration beyond exile (Lev 26:40–45; Deut 4:29–31; 30:1–10), Stuart identifies ten different "restoration blessings" that recur within the prophetic salvation oracles, two of which can be identified more readily as "deliverance" (return from exile, reunification), the others better classified as well-being (renewal of Yahweh's favor, renewal of the covenant, restoration of true worship, population increase, agricultural bounty, restoration of general prosperity, power over enemies, and freedom from destruction).⁶³ In addition, we encounter the recovery of developments in Israel's history subsequent to Sinai such as the restoration of Davidic leadership (e.g., Isa 55:3–4; Jer 23:4–6; 33:14–26; Ezek 34:23–24; 37:24–25) and the centrality of Zion, most evident in Isaiah (e.g., Isa 2:2–4; 49:14—50:3; 66) and Zechariah (e.g., 8:1–23; 14:1–21).⁶⁴ As Gowan observes, "the OT has selected the best

---

61. See Westermann, *Prophetic Oracles*, 12–13.

62. Ibid., 16.

63. See Stuart, *Hosea-Jonah*, xli–xlii. To these we may add security in the land as an eleventh blessing. Stuart ably demonstrates from the first half of the Book of the Twelve that the blessings found in the Pentateuchal texts and the Latter Prophets are essentially the same.

64. The prophetic texts of Mari and Assyria exhibit consistent themes of blessing as well: victory in battle, the gift of more land, protection, long life, general prosperity, and continual lineage on the throne. The progeny blessing is absent. Most likely, this is because these oracles are concerned with the immediate future and because they are addressed to the king and pertain to his personal success rather than to the prosperity of the populace. The promise of a continual lineage occupying the throne is similar, yet the concern is not so much with the proliferation of his descendants as it is with maintenance of power. (See Nissinen, *Prophets and Prophecy*, for the full texts of these prophetic oracles. See Walton, *Ancient Near Eastern Thought*, 245–47, for a chart based on Nissinen documenting the components of these prophetic texts.)

from Israel's past and present in order to express its hope for the future."[65] In our examination of the prophetic restoration oracles, we organize our discussion around the three primary themes of the return, the material restoration of society (including the progeny blessing), and the restoration of the relationship between Yahweh and Israel.

---

65. Gowan, *Eschatology*, 3.

2

The Progeny Blessing in the Old Testament Outside the Latter Prophets

The Centrality of the Progeny Blessing in Genesis

More than any other OT book, Genesis is preoccupied with the progeny blessing from start to finish, tracing the spread of humankind as well as the particular quest for offspring in the patriarchal narratives. Many have concluded that this blessing is not merely *a* theme of Genesis, but *the* driving motif in the book that unites the book's diverse literary units.

David Clines, in his influential work, *The Theme of the Pentateuch*, attempts to examine the entire Pentateuch as a literary unity. He proposes that "[t]he theme of the Pentateuch is the partial fulfillment—which implies also the partial non-fulfillment—of the promise to or blessing of the patriarchs."[1] Based on Gen 12:2–3 and subsequent articulations of God's promises to Abraham, he delineates three primary promises: posterity, an intimate divine-human relationship, and land. The entire Pentateuch is progressively occupied with these three promises: Gen 12–50 with posterity, Exodus and Leviticus with the divine-human relationship, and Numbers and Deuteronomy with land.[2] Although this analysis is a bit simplistic since, for example, the promise of progeny to Abraham is an ongoing concern in Exodus–Deuteronomy as well (as we will see), his case for these

1. Clines, *Theme of the Pentateuch*, 30.
2. See ibid., 30.

generalizations that underscore the preoccupation with offspring in Gen 12–50 is strong. Although he does not consider progeny to be the main "theme" of Gen 1–11,[3] he does see the three-fold promise to Abraham as a rearticulation and reaffirmation of God's initial blessing to humankind in Gen 1:26–28.[4]

In *Announcements of Plot in Genesis*, Laurence Turner argues for the primacy of the blessing of human proliferation throughout the entire book of Genesis. Like Clines, he treats the final form of the text with an eye for programmatic statements that guide the plot of the narratives. He identifies Gen 1:28 as the "announcement of plot" for Gen 1–11, viewing it as a three-fold exposition of humankind's designed role on earth (multiplication, subduing the earth, and dominion over animals),[5] and argues that every episode in Gen 1–11 is related to it.[6] The next announcement of plot in Gen 12:1–3 includes five interrelated promises, but it is the promise of nationhood that "dominates" chapters 12–25,[7] a claim that Turner demonstrates by relating each episode to the search for posterity. The subsequent announcements of plot for the Jacob story (25:23; 27:27–29, 39–40) and "the story of Jacob's family" (37:5–11) are less directly related to progeny, but these accounts retain a strong interest in the Abrahamic promises, and it is ultimately only the progeny promise that enjoys any significant fulfillment by the end of the book.[8] He concludes that these "announcements" express Yahweh's intentions for humanity, but they are frequently altered by Yahweh or frustrated by human actions so that most of them remain unfulfilled.[9] However, Yahweh specifically acts to ensure the advance of the progeny blessing so that "[o]ne receives the impression that *this* element *must* succeed."[10]

The importance of the progeny motif is confirmed even by source-critical reconstructions of the text. In Walter Brueggemann's attempt to elucidate the core kerygma of the Priestly writer, he points to Gen 1:28 as programmatic, referring to it as P's "set formula which recurs in the material at crucial places . . . the central thrust of the faith of the priestly

---

3. See ibid., 66–86.
4. See ibid., 86.
5. See Turner, *Announcements of Plot*, 21.
6. See ibid., 48.
7. See ibid., 61.
8. See ibid., 140, 172–73.
9. See ibid., 182.
10. Ibid., 181 (italics original).

circle,"[11] unfolded in the P narratives. Similarly, Wolff identifies the central kerygma of the Yahwist with Gen 12:1–4a, which includes the promise of the multiplication of Abraham into a "great nation."[12] Regardless of the validity of such historical-critical reconstructions, these scholars rightly recognize the foundational place of the progeny blessing in the Pentateuch.[13]

Although the statements of Gen 1:28 and 12:2–3 and their later echoes are sufficient to establish the importance of the progeny blessing in Genesis, its centrality is reinforced by the structural framework of the book, the so-called Toledot (תּוֹלְדֹת) formulas. Although it may seem that the various genealogies in Genesis merely stitch together the narratives as (at times lengthy) segues, many have rightly noted that they also demonstrate the success of the blessing upon humankind to "be fruitful and multiply."[14] In so doing, they imply in Gen 1–11 in particular that at least this aspect of God's blessing on creation graciously continues despite the entrance of and spread of sin.[15] In Gen 12–50 the genealogies exist for a different purpose, namely, to document the progeny of Abraham as the incipient fulfillment of Yahweh's promise to him in 12:2. However, as Robinson notes, the orderly and determinate nature of the genealogies exhibits some tension with the narratives themselves in which the promise of the next heir is frequently in jeopardy.[16] Given the programmatic nature of Gen 12:2, Hopkins rightly prioritizes the genealogies, claiming that "the contingency of the narrative will not imperil the certainty of the genealogy."[17] Within the book as a whole, one can then discern "an

11. Brueggemann, "Kerygma," 400.

12. See Wolff, "Kerygma of the Yahwist," 47.

13. In his tradition-historical reconstruction of the OT materials Gerhard von Rad identifies the "Credo" in Deut 26:5–9 as the "most important" early confession of Israel's faith. Here too we find the progeny blessing in v. 5, a reference Yahweh's multiplication of Israel in Egypt (*Old Testament Theology: Historical Traditions*, 121–22).

14. For example, Claus Westermann notes that "the effect of the blessing [of Gen 1:28] is described in the genealogies" (*Genesis 1–11*, 17). According to R. B. Robinson, "[t]he genealogies document the fruitfulness of humanity and thus become the expression of the fulfillment of God's mandate" ("Literary Functions," 600–601). According to David C. Hopkins, "success or failure in carrying out these commissions [in 1:28] determines the progress and retreat of story in Genesis" ("First Stories," 31). See also Blenkinsopp, *The Pentateuch*, 109; Fokkelman, "Genesis," 41–42; Wehmeier, "ברך," 1:278; Wenham, *Genesis 1–15*, 33.

15. See Cohen, *Be Fertile and Increase*, 60, 63.

16. See Robinson, "Literary Functions," 598, 604–6.

17. Hopkins, "First Stories," 38. J. P. Fokkelman emphasizes this tension by stating that "begetting children is a matter of course" in Gen 5, 10, and 11, a pattern that is "radically undermined" in Gen 12–50 ("Genesis," 43).

alternating pattern of enlargement and constriction" of the population.[18] Since both the structure of Genesis and the thematic content of so many of the narratives are concerned with population growth, there is little doubt that, as Walton declares, "the blessing serves as a foundation for the theological message of Genesis."[19]

The Universal Blessing: Genesis 1–11

Within the universal scope of the primeval history of Gen 1–11, blessing applies to all that God has created. Unlike some later articulations of blessing, the blessings associated with creation are graciously bestowed upon all by Yahweh apart from the requirement for humans to meet specific conditions, expressing his benevolent disposition toward them (see Gen 1:22, 28; 5:2; 8:17; 9:1, 7). Nevertheless, we encounter a struggle between blessing and curse as a result of the rebellious actions of humanity.

In these early chapters, every explicit reference to blessing relates to the fertility of humans, beasts, or vegetation.[20] Although the blessing of protection from destruction can be identified in 8:21–22; 9:11, 15, it is not until the Sinai covenant that this is expressed as a blessing. Therefore, in Gen 1–11 blessing and the gift of fertility can nearly be equated such that a theology of blessing is concurrent with a theology of fertility.

---

18. Merrill, "Old Testament History," 1:78. Genesis documents enlargement from Adam, constriction to Noah at the flood, enlargement in Gen 10–11, constriction to Abraham, and enlargement of his seed by 47:27.

19. Walton, *Genesis*, 135. Cf. Schultz, "Integrating," 1:197, on this two-fold criterion for discerning the theology of a book. From a historical rather than literary perspective, Claus Westermann claims that this blessing "was understood as the basic power of 'history'" (*Genesis 1–11*, 161). Similarly, Meredith G. Kline notes that "this vital, genealogical process is the central motif of human history. Man himself is the chief end-product of human culture. Genealogy is the primary genre of human historiography" (*Kingdom Prologue*, 69).

20. The blessing and sanctification of the seventh day in Gen 2:3 is the lone exception.

The First Blessing: Genesis 1:28

וַיְבָרֶךְ אֹתָם אֱלֹהִים וַיֹּאמֶר לָהֶם אֱלֹהִים פְּרוּ וּרְבוּ וּמִלְאוּ אֶת־הָאָרֶץ וְכִבְשֻׁהָ וּרְדוּ בִּדְגַת הַיָּם וּבְעוֹף הַשָּׁמַיִם וּבְכָל־חַיָּה הָרֹמֶשֶׂת עַל־הָאָרֶץ

And God blessed them and said to them, "Be abundantly fruitful, fill the earth, subdue it, and rule over the fish of the sea, over the birds of the heavens, and over every living thing that moves on the earth."

Our study requires a careful examination of Gen 1:28, the first biblical articulation of the progeny motif. The following questions with respect to this text must be addressed:

1. How does Gen 1:28 relate to the similar blessing upon the birds and fish in 1:22?

2. Is Gen 1:28 a command, a blessing, or some combination of the two? What, then, are the implications for divine and human responsibility in procreation? What is Yahweh *doing* when he blesses humanity in 1:28? In other words, what is the illocutionary effect of his action? What is the scope of the application of this blessing?

3. Biblically-theologically, what is the function of human multiplication within the context of Yahweh's purposes for humankind?

The Blessing on the Birds and Fish in Genesis 1:22

Although Gen 1:28 constitutes the first blessing upon humanity in the canon, it is preceded in v. 22 by God's blessing (וַיְבָרֶךְ) on the fish and birds on day five of the creation account. God's spoken pronouncement, itself the content of the blessing,[21] entails three imperatives of multiplication addressed to sea creatures (פְּרוּ וּרְבוּ וּמִלְאוּ) and a jussive statement (יִרֶב) with birds as its subject. It is doubtful that the illocutionary function is to issue a command, since non-human living creatures reproduce not out of reasoned obedience but rather out of their God-ordained, natural impulses. Therefore, it is probably best to understand God's action either as a speech-act conferring the ability to multiply or as an expression of

---

21. As is common throughout the OT, לֵאמֹר functions here as an infinitive construct of specification, further explaining the preceding action of blessing (Arnold and Choi, *Syntax*, 73; cf. Westermann, *Genesis 1–11*, 140).

his desire that they multiply, based on the ability that he has already given them.[22]

Interestingly, no blessing is bestowed upon the land animals on day six. Since they clearly have been given the ability to multiply as well, this may suggest that the blessings given in vv. 22 and 28 mean something more than the ability itself. Perhaps the key is to be found in the verb "fill" (וּמִלְאוּ), implying that there is no limitation on the extent to which birds, fish, and humanity may continue to multiply. In contrast, since land animals inhabit the same space as humankind and humankind is to rule the land animals, land animals have no such privilege of limitless increase and thus do not receive God's blessing to that end.[23]

Genesis 1:28: Command or Blessing?

God's blessing upon humanity directly follows their creation as his image (נַעֲשֶׂה אָדָם בְּצַלְמֵנוּ כִּדְמוּתֵנוּ). The blessing itself, as in v. 22 the content of God's speech, runs at least through the end of v. 28, consisting of five imperative verbs: פְּרוּ, וּרְבוּ, וּמִלְאוּ, כִּבְשֻׁהָ, and רְדוּ, all linked with coordinating *waws*. The nature of this statement, namely, whether it is a command or a blessing, has spawned great debate and shapes how we understand the progeny blessing throughout the OT and in Gen 1–11 in particular. If understood as a command, it entails obligation, demands an obedient response, is not necessarily desirable,[24] and emphasizes human responsibility. If a blessing, it entails privilege, is inherently desirable, and stresses divine endowment. If v. 28 is to be construed as a series of commands, an obedient response implies "fulfillment" and a disobedient response merits judgment. If a blessing, it is doubtful that the categories of "fulfillment" or "judgment" are appropriate.

The most obvious argument in favor of Gen 1:28 as a series of commands is that all five verbs occur in the imperative mood, which most commonly denotes a command. Furthermore, it is obvious that procreation and the multiplication of the race do take human effort in the act of

---

22. See Blocher, *In the Beginning*, 75.
23. See Shapiro, "Be Fruitful," 60, citing Exod 23:29.
24. Although even God's commands are ultimately blessings and desirable, this is only perceived by those who fear Yahweh. Sinful humanity fails to recognize this, pursuing blessings such as food and security as inherently desirable while rejecting God's commands.

The Progeny Blessing in the Old Testament Outside the Latter Prophets

sexual intercourse and the care of children, indicating, at first glance, that v. 28 portrays the progeny blessing as an obligation.[25]

However, there are strong arguments for understanding Gen 1:28 as a blessing whose illocutionary effect is not command but rather permission or promise:

1. Significantly, God's pronouncement in v. 28 is described as an act of blessing (וַיְבָרֶךְ). Given what we see elsewhere in the OT concerning the nature of divine blessings as God's gifts and actions on behalf of humanity, we might expect something similar from this blessing.

2. To command a blessing is inappropriate since all blessings are inherently desirable.[26] The "inherent desirability" of bearing children may not be patently obvious in our present global situation. However, according to Walton, "granting a blessing (as in 1:28–30) must be recognized as delineating a privilege, not an obligation. In the ancient world, the ability to reproduce was seen as a gift from God. No one in that world would have considered foregoing the opportunity. It would be inappropriate, then, to consider this as a command that couples must have children." This is evident in the attitudes, desires, and practices of individuals in the OT narratives as they strive for children and grieve barrenness, particularly in Genesis (cf. Ps 127:3–5; see discussion of this text below).[27] Certainly none would choose to reject other biblical blessings such as long life, protection, and an abundance of food; it is no less the case with progeny. Likewise, subduing the earth and ruling over other living creatures are privi-

---

25. Beale, *The Temple*, 86, 86 n. 13; Calvin, *Genesis*, 98; Goldingay, *Old Testament Theology: Israel's Gospel*, 379; Heyd, "Divine Creation," 61; Kaminski, *From Noah to Israel*, 11–12; Shapiro, "Be Fruitful," 63; and Wenham, *Genesis 1–15*, 33, are among those who view Gen 1:28 as a command. The majority of post-biblical Jewish tradition construed v. 28 as an obligation as well, although it appears that social factors greatly contributed to this interpretation since for centuries Jews were preoccupied with the survival of their own race.

26. On rare occasions, blessings are stated imperatively, although it is doubtful that these function as obligatory commands. For example, Eccl 9:7–9 functions permissively and Isa 37:30 functions as a promise of blessing (see further below).

27. *Genesis*, 134. See also Block, "Marriage and Family," 80–81. David Novak argues that, at numerous points of hardship in Jewish history, Jews were faced with "strong antinatal temptations" to the degree that bearing children was "a conscious act of faith" and not necessarily desirable ("Be Fruitful," 13). He does not, however, argue that this was the perspective of the OT itself. Jeremiah 29:6 may be the one exception in the OT where procreation is commanded due to exilic despair, a historical situation analogous to those recalled by Novak (see below).

leges that even sinful humanity would pursue naturally—and *does* through the rest of the OT, even if in a perverted manner due to the complications that enter as a result of sin.

3. Among the numerous subsequent OT articulations of the progeny blessing that we will discuss below in varying detail, never again is there any question as to whether it is a command or a blessing (with the exception of Jer 29:6). It is always at least implicitly, and usually explicitly, a gift from Yahweh for which all yearn, coming from his hand alone, and is not ultimately up to humans to "fulfill" or "obey." It is often presented as a promise later in Genesis (e.g., Gen 13:16; 17:2–6; 22:17; 48:4). Significantly, in the context of the Sinai covenant, it is not one of the laws to be obeyed but rather one of the blessings that serve as a reward for obedience (e.g., Lev 26:9; Deut 28:4, 11).

Imperatives are employed not solely to indicate commands, but at times to express permission or promises as well. Permissive imperatives occur in instances in which the addressee desires to accomplish the action expressed in the imperative (e.g., Gen 50:6; Exod 4:18; Deut 33:18; 2 Sam 18:23; 2 Kgs 2:17; Isa 45:11). This certainly appears to fit Gen 1:28, not only for the progeny verbs of multiplying and filling, but for the imperatives of subduing the earth and ruling living creatures as well.[28] Since reproduction is ultimately attributed to Yahweh (e.g., Gen 15:3; 16:1–2; 20:17–18; 21:1–2; 25:21; 29:31) yet involves human action/initiative, both aspects of permission and promise are probably in view here. Thus the blessing expresses God's intentions for humanity, allowing them to pursue the propagation of the race to the point of filling the earth while promising divine enabling.[29] Furthermore, the permissive sense in particular would fit well if the Gen 1 creation account is intended in part to be a polemic

---

28. GKC §110c asserts that Gen 1:28 functions as a promise, "the fulfillment of which is altogether out of the power of the person addressed" (cf. 1 Kgs 22:12 and Isa 54:14).

29. Schmutzer states that the imperatives of 1:22, 28 convey "*divine intention or assurance*" (*Be Fruitful and Multiply*, 79). Mitchell similarly proposes that in Gen 1:28 God expresses his "approval and desire" that humankind reproduce (*Meaning of BRK*, 62). Although similar to the ideas of "permission" and "promise," this language may undervalue God's own activity in granting the fruit of the blessing. Brueggemann states that the imperatives of Gen 1:28 are "not so much commands as authorizations by which the people are empowered to believe and act toward the future" expressing God's "will for well-being and prosperity" ("Kerygma," 400–401).

against other ancient Near Eastern cosmogonies that consider the expansion of humanity to be a negative development (see below).

4. What then is the illocutionary effect of the blessing? It seems unlikely that in uttering this blessing God is granting humanity the *ability* to reproduce, including sexual intercourse and conception,[30] since texts similar to 1:28 cannot bear this meaning (see below). Rather, the speech-act of permission/promise to humanity is itself the blessing in that it expresses God's intentions for them as well as implies his enabling them to experience the blessing of fertility. In other words, in this first blessing upon humanity, the blessing is not the fruit itself but rather the guarantee and assurance of its continual experience. The blessing on the birds and fish in v. 22 should probably be understood in the same way.

5. The imperatival hendiadys "be abundantly fruitful" (פְּרוּ וּרְבוּ) also occurs in Gen 1:22, 8:17, 9:1, 7 and 35:11, at times accompanied by other verbs of multiplication in the imperative and always introduced as a blessing, with the exception of 8:17. Given the linguistic and contextual parallels between these texts, it is likely that they all carry the same illocutionary force. However, 1:22 and 35:11 in particular are difficult to understand as commands. God's blessing to Jacob in Gen 35:11 almost certainly functions as a promise since vv. 11–12 are one of the numerous re-articulations of God's promise of progeny and land to the patriarchs. Furthermore, Jacob later recounts this very event, rephrasing it as a future promise with divine agency by employing Hiphils (הִנְנִי מַפְרְךָ וְהִרְבִּיתִךָ in Gen 48:3–4). Furthermore, with respect to God's postdiluvian blessings on living creatures (8:17) and humanity (9:1, 7), it is clear that he is not bestowing on them the ability to reproduce since they already possessed this ability.[31] Therefore, it is unlikely that this is the function of the nearly identical blessings in Gen 1:22 and 28. In each of these instances, permission/promise better fits the purpose of God's speech-act.[32]

Given these grammatical, contextual, and canonical considerations, Gen 1:28 ought to be construed as a privilege and a blessing, divinely

---

30. *Contra* Brown, "ברך," 1:758; Westermann, *Genesis 1–11*, 139–40, 160.

31. See Mitchell, *Meaning of BRK*, 63.

32. Interestingly, these texts contain the only instances in the OT in which a divine pronouncement accompanies בָּרַךְ and is the content of the blessing itself. We would thus expect that they should all function similarly and that they may together exhibit a slightly different facet of blessing from that which we find elsewhere.

given and promised, inviting humanity to pursue the propagation of the race without restraint. To treat it as an obligatory command is improper.[33] Clearly, divine and human agency are both necessary for reproduction and the growth of the human population. Although the various manifestations of the progeny blessing will stress divine action in different ways and in varying degrees (sometimes only implicitly), God's agency in blessing humanity with children receives far greater prominence than humankind's responsibility throughout the OT, corroborating our judgment in favor of blessing over command. Humankind's responsibility is simply sexual intercourse within the context of marriage, a relatively easy and desirable task, whereas it is Yahweh who must grant conception.[34]

The Biblical-theological Significance of the Progeny Blessing in Genesis 1

Obviously, reproduction is necessary to sustain the human race. Yet its function within God's creational purposes is described in Gen 1 in relation to humankind's creation as the "image of God"[35] and the other elements of the blessing of vv. 28-30: filling the earth, dominion, rule, and food production.

The progeny blessing cannot itself be a specific consequence of being created as the image of God[36] since the other creatures possess this ability

---

33. Daube, *Duty of Procreation*, 3; M. Gilbert, "Soyez féconds," 741; Gordis, "Be Fruitful," 21; Lohfink, "Seid fruchtbar," 80; Van Leeuwen, "Be Fruitful," 59–60; and Walton, *Genesis*, 134, are among the many scholars who recognize Gen 1:28 as a blessing.

34. See the theological conclusions at the end of this chapter for further reflection concerning divine-human synergism in reproduction. As Goldingay (*Old Testament Theology: Israel's Gospel*, 272) notes, "[t]he ancestors were more aware than we are that we cannot control the 'achievement' of parenthood as much as we might like or think, but are dependent on whether or not God chooses to open a womb."

35. In the context of Gen 1:26–28, the related theme of the creation of humankind as God's image tends to receive greater attention in scholarship despite the fact that this concept reappears far less frequently throughout the OT than does the progeny blessing. Although the significance of this concept undoubtedly outweighs its frequency in the text, one might wonder why the accompanying blessing does not receive comparable attention.

36. Observing that צֶלֶם typically refers to physical objects in the OT, Clines argues that to construe the preposition בְּ as a *beth* of norm ("in the image") is inappropriate since the OT resists the idea that Yahweh is physical ("Humanity," 468–75). He therefore argues persuasively for the *beth essentiae* ("as the image"), addressing objections to it and concluding that humanity "is itself the image of God" (475). The image thus

The Progeny Blessing in the Old Testament Outside the Latter Prophets

as well, even though they are not created as the image of God. Although humans are never the subject of בָּרָא and thus cannot be said to create in the sense that God creates, procreation nevertheless reflects God's act of creation.[37] Furthermore, the progeny blessing perpetuates and expands the quantity of images of God in his created order.[38]

The most immediate end for which God blesses humanity with abundant fruitfulness is that they might "fill the earth." It is unlikely that this is merely a synonymous expression referring to the numerical increase of humanity; rather, it denotes a spatial filling of the earth that results from this increase.[39] This, in turn, is to the end of subduing the earth (וְכִבְשֻׁהָ),[40] suggesting that it is in some sense to be conquered or

---

functions "as representative of one who is really or spiritually present, though physically absent" (482). Blocher (*In the Beginning*, 85) and Gerhard von Rad, (*Genesis*, 56) similarly favor the *beth essentiae*.

37. See Cohen, *Be Fertile and Increase*, 217; Gilbert, "Soyez féconds" 742; David Novak, "Be Fruitful," 12; Wenham, *Genesis 1–15*, 24–25. Perhaps this is seen most clearly in Gen 5:3 where Adam fathers a son "in his own likeness according to his image" (cf. Gen 1:26) and names him (cf. Gen 5:2).

38. In the Genesis account humankind is created with dignity as the image of God and as the pinnacle of creation. In contrast, Mesopotamian creation myths do not even include humankind within the original plan for creation. Sumerian, Akkadian, and Babylonian myths all assert that humans were created to relieve the lesser gods from their labor and to supply the gods with food (Walton, *Ancient Israelite Literature*, 29; Lambert and Millard, *Atra-Hasis*, 15; see, for example, *Atrahasis* I.1–4, 189–97; *Enuma Elish* VI.23–42; *Enki and Ninmah* 10–43). To be human is to be a lowly servant, not a ruler over creation.

In these myths, humankind is created to be self-propagating, as in Genesis (e.g., *Atrahasis* I.280–305; *Enki and Ninmah* 39), but this does not prove to be a positive endowment by the gods when overpopulation soon becomes a concern. *Atrahasis* may be closest to Gen 1:28 in that it includes an accompanying blessing (I.286; *ikarab*) pertaining to childbirth (I.289–92), perhaps including the institution of marriage as well (I.299–304), but there is no celebration of human fecundity akin to Gen 1 among Mesopotamian myths.

39. Walton helpfully comments that "the filling is not part of the privilege but is the result of the lack of any limitation on the privilege" (*Genesis*, 134–35).

40. Only here is this uncommon term used with respect to the land itself. In its most common OT usage, the objects are nations or individuals that have been defeated (Num 32:22, 29; Josh 18:1; 2 Sam 8:11; 1 Chr 22:18) or subjected to slavery (Jer 34:11, 16; Neh 5:5; 2 Chr 28:10). הָאָרֶץ is the object in Num 32:22, 29; Josh 18:1, and 1 Chr 22:18 as well, but in these texts it functions as metonymy for Israel's enemies. Brueggemann plausibly argues that the Priestly writer of Gen 1:28 appropriates the language of Num 32 and Josh 18 in particular, concluding that "*creation comes to be expressed in conquest language*" ("Kerygma," 407; emphasis original). He thus assumes semantic overlap between "subduing" and "dominion" (407).

brought to order. This probably entails agricultural mastery of the earth, specifically, according to Schmutzer, "harnessing the land's potential for general habitation."[41] If הָאָרֶץ is to be understood in the broader sense of referring to the whole world, as seems to be the case in Gen 1:1; 2:1, 4, it may also include subjugation of living creatures, thus overlapping with the following clause.[42]

Rule (וְיִרְדּוּ) over the rest of creation[43] appears to provide the ultimate purpose for the creation of humanity as God's image (cf. v. 26). Clines agrees with most commentators that rule is a consequence of the image and not "definitive of the image itself," but he rightly asserts that dominion "is so immediate and necessary a consequence of the image, it loses the character of a mere derivative of the image and eventually becomes a constitutive part of the image itself."[44] The functional nature of the image is confirmed by the ancient Near Eastern background since the Genesis account may draw here upon ancient Near Eastern practices whereby physical images of kings symbolize their rule in the realm in which the image resides, thus establishing their authority.[45] In Egyptian and Mesopotamian literature, only the king is referred to as the "image" of a god.[46] Genesis, however, democratizes this role so that all of humanity attests to the rule of

---

41. Schmutzer, *Be Fruitful and Multiply*, 86. Turner argues exclusively for the agricultural sense, interpreting הָאָרֶץ as "ground" and humanity's duties in 2:15 agriculturally as "tilling" and "keeping," subsuming them under the imperative in 1:28 to subdue the earth (*Announcements of Plot*, 34–41).

42. Filling and subduing the earth probably also entail expansion of the food supply through agriculture as its consequence (Walton, *Genesis*, 186). Clearly food production and the progeny blessing are materially bound in a circular relationship since food is necessary to sustain and expand the populace.

Beale argues that humanity's mission in Gen 1 and 2 entails the expansion of Eden through filling the earth with God's images, thus expanding the sacred space that was initially coextensive with Eden and was later embodied in the temple (*The Temple*, 82–84). Although there may be some credence to this view, given Eden's biblical-theological connections to the temple and the new heavens and new earth, expansion of sacred space is not one of humankind's explicitly stated purposes in Gen 1 and 2.

43. Following von Rad (*Old Testament Theology: Historical Traditions*, 147), Clines asserts that only the land animals are mentioned explicitly since they are humanity's only real rival for dominion, occupying the same sphere ("Humanity," 493).

44. Clines, "Humanity," 490. Dumbrell, *Covenant and Creation*, 34; Kline, "Creation," 268, similarly affirm the centrality of rule for the meaning of the image. Psalm 8 and Sir 17:3 also link the image to dominion as its core implication.

45. See Hart, "Genesis 1:1—2:3," 318; von Rad, *Genesis*, 32; Waltke, *Genesis*, 65–66; Walton, *Genesis*, 130–31.

46. See Clines, "Humanity," 475–80.

the Divine King and represents him upon earth as his images.⁴⁷ However, humanity is not simply a static representation of God's rule, but an active participant in ruling the earth as God himself rules it, corporately bringing order to the world through effective kingship,⁴⁸ thus functioning as a more dynamic "image" of his universal sovereignty than any mere stone image. The description of Eden in Gen 2 illustrates what this dominion is to look like in relation to creation, animals, God, and woman.⁴⁹ For example, by naming all animals (2:19–20) Adam exercises his dominion over them in a direct fulfillment of his role as outlined in Gen 1:26 and 28 and reflects God's own naming of the components of the cosmos in Gen 1.

The blessing thus culminates in rule over all other living creatures as humanity's chief purpose. The blessing itself encompasses the divinely ordained steps necessary to realize this end: humankind is to be abundantly fruitful in order to fill the earth in order to subdue it and rule over living creatures. The proliferation of humankind is accomplished (in part) by means of the creation of humanity as male and female (v. 27c), and the final end of rule is accomplished by means of the creation of humanity as the image of God.

Since the blessing of Gen 1:28 establishes a divine-human relationship involving divine endowment and human responsibility, some have noted that it is covenantal in nature.⁵⁰ The blessing of progeny is common to Gen 1:28 and the major OT covenants, contributing to this connection. After observing such parallels, Cohen concludes,

> The recurring motif that binds all these facets of the verse's career is that of election, the guarantee of divine providence, and an enduring relationship between God and the recipients of his blessing—in a word, the motif of covenant. Granted that many have rejected Wellhausen's identification of Gen. 1:28 as a *berit* between God and Adam; in the story of creation the verse in fact does not display the formal, technical trappings of a binding, contractual arrangement. Still, the blessings of our verse do take on a formulaic role in the divine covenants with

---

47. See, e.g., Waltke, *Genesis*, 66.

48. See Walton, *Genesis*, 136.

49. See Dumbrell, *Covenant and Creation*, 35–36. Norbert Lohfink appropriately views this rule as referring to governance over, domestication of, and care for the animal world (*Theology of the Pentateuch*, 12–13), "something like a paradisiacal peace among all species which, however, is no longer possible after the Flood" (13).

50. See e.g., Cohen, *Be Fertile and Increase*, 33; Dumbrell, *Covenant and Creation*, 33–43; Kline, *Kingdom Prologue*, 18.

Noah, the patriarchs, and the Hebrew nation. . . . What begins as a general description of the human condition in the order of God's creation eventually serves as a metaphor for the peculiar station of Israel among the other nations of the world.[51]

Indeed, it is tempting to see Gen 1:28 as the first covenant since it defines humanity's relationship to God and the world. However, it may be best not to label it as such since the text refers to it as a blessing rather than as a covenant and since its reiteration in Gen 9:1–7 is not referred to as a covenant either, even though the Noahic covenant directly follows in the text. It is more accurate to say that Gen 1:28 is the fundamental relationship that God establishes with his created images and that he then initiates subsequent arrangements with his creatures within the context of this universal established relationship that the OT refers to as "covenants."[52]

The multiplication of humankind in Gen 1 is a means to an end rather than an end in itself. However, it is foundational to God's purposes for the world and essential for humanity's spread and survival.[53] Taken as a whole, these purposes in Gen 1:26–28 constitute the establishment of civilization,[54] the ultimate end of which is to glorify humankind's creator. The progeny blessing, viewed holistically as the entire process from conception to the growth and sustenance of a child, as well as the survival and expansion of the human race, is perhaps the most basic expression of God's common grace toward humankind. Even as we trace the spread of sin throughout Gen 1–11, God's grace is continually extended to humanity through their consistent ability to procreate and thereby experience and promulgate God's blessing.

Excursus: The Jewish and Christian History of Interpretation of Genesis 1:28 and Its Realization

Since the first century CE, both Jewish and Christian interpreters have reflected extensively on the progeny blessing, particularly as it appears in Gen 1:28 as one of God's purposes for creation. Both interpretive traditions

---

51. Cohen, *Be Fertile and Increase*, 65–66.

52. See Williamson, *Sealed*, 52–58, who argues persuasively that Gen 1:28 should not be understood as a "covenant."

53. For this reason Jewish interpretation has often construed the multiplication of their people as an end in itself. See the following excursus.

54. See Kline, *Kingdom Prologue*, 69; Köhler, *Old Testament Theology*, 133; Walton, *Genesis*, 136.

have examined this text with an eye to its abiding relevance, but they have often diverged in terms of how it is to be understood and applied.

The multiplication clause of Gen 1:28 plays a more prominent role within Jewish rabbinic interpretation than in Christian interpretation.[55] As we will see in the course of our study, the entire OT witness views procreation as a blessing. In contrast, subsequent oral tradition consistently treats it as an obligation.[56] Since even marriage itself is subordinated to the command to reproduce, a man may justly divorce a barren wife in order to fulfill his duty to procreate.[57] Both Shammai and Hillel define the minimum number of children in order to "fulfill" the mandate as two,[58] but later rabbinic thought encourages procreation to the fullest extent possible in the interests of Jewish population growth.[59]

According to the Talmud, the command to procreate applies to Jews alone, on the somewhat counter-intuitive grounds that "a commandment that was given to the sons of Noah and was not repeated at Sinai is intended only for the sons of Israel and not for the sons of Noah."[60] In support of the Talmudic understanding, Shapiro suggests that "[i]t may, moreover, be possible that once the earth was replenished with human beings, the

---

55. For a summary of this history, see Cohen, *Be Fertile and Increase*, chs. 2–4; Gordis, "Be Fruitful," 21–29; Heyd, "Divine Creation," 57–70; Harry M. Jacobi, "Peru U'revu," 83–95; Novak, "Be Fruitful," 12–31; and Shapiro, "Be Fruitful," 59–79.
Schmutzer observes that "sexual reproduction (Gen 1:28a) completely overwhelms the parallel injunction for 'ruling' in the same verse (Gen 1:28b)" in rabbinic interpretation (*Be Fruitful and Multiply*, 223) and surmises that this is because after loss of the land "sexual reproduction itself became a quantifiable *means* of expressing 'dominion'; progeny became the basis for land-claim" (223).

56. See *b. Yebam.* 61b–66a; *b. Sanh.* 62ab; *t. Yebam.* 8:4. See Cohen, *Be Fertile and Increase*, 68; Novak, "Be Fruitful," 12; Shapiro, "Be Fruitful," 63. Maimonides thus lists "be fruitful and multiply" as the first command in the Hebrew Bible both logically and chronologically (see Heyd, "Divine Creation," 61).

57. See Cohen, *Be Fertile and Increase*, 138–40; *m. Yebam.* 6:6; *b. Yebam.* 64a; *t. Yebam.* 8:5.

58. See *m. Yebam.* 6:6; *t. Yebam.* 8:4; *b. Yebam.* 61b–62a. They differ, however, on the required genders of the offspring.

59. Gordis observes a direct correlation between the emphasis upon Gen 1:28 as a command and the threatened existence (and small population) of the Jewish people ("Be Fruitful," 23–25).

60. *b. Sanh.* 59ab. Cf. *b. Yebam.* 62a; and Cohen, *Be Fertile and Increase*, 113–15, 144–54. According to *Even Ha-ezer* 1.5 (cited in Jacobi, "Peru U'revu," 87–88), the *command* applies directly to Jews alone, but all of humanity experiences "the *blessing* of God" to the end of worldwide proliferation, expressing somewhat of a mediating position.

commandment was removed from the Noachides and transferred to the children of Israel, who were few in number [cf. Deut 7:7], to ensure their physical survival, so that their covenant with God will be continued throughout the generations."[61] However, Cohen rightly notes that

> [t]he progression of the Genesis cosmogony and primeval history militated against an understanding of "be fertile and increase" as a commandment to the Jews [alone]. The enunciation of a similar blessing to the fish and the birds, the nexus between the primordial blessing and creation in God's image, the juxtaposition of the call to fill the earth with the conferral of dominion, both on the sixth day of creation and in the aftermath of the flood, the recurrence of the *prh/rbh* hendiadys five times in the first eleven chapters of Scripture, and the universal focus of the primeval history—all these placed greater demands on the exegete and the enumerator of the commandments intent on defending the Talmudic understanding of our verse.[62]

Rabbinic literature attributes a multifaceted significance to the duty of procreation:

1. Based in part on the juxtaposition of Gen 9:6 and 9:7, the failure to procreate is tantamount to murder since, like murder, it prevents life.[63]

2. Since a human is the image of God, to neglect procreation is "as though he has diminished the divine image."[64]

3. Some thus believed that "when the commandment of fruitfulness is neglected, the Divine Presence departs from Israel."[65]

---

61. Shapiro, "Be Fruitful," 70.

62. Cohen, *Be Fertile and Increase*, 219.

63. See *t. Yebam.* 8:7; *b. Yebam.* 63b; Heyd, "Divine Creation," 65–66. See Novak, "Be Fruitful," 72, for the first four points.

64. *b. Yebam.* 63b: "It was taught: R. Eliezer stated, He who does not engage in propagation of the race is as though he sheds blood; for it is said, *Whoso sheddeth man's blood by man shall his blood be shed,* and this is immediately followed by the text, *And you, be ye fruitful and multiply.* R. Jacob said: As though he has diminished the Divine Image; since it is said, *For in the image of God made he man,* and this is immediately followed by, *And you, be ye fruitful* etc. Ben 'Azzai said: As though he sheds blood *and* diminishes the Divine Image; since it is said, *And you, be ye fruitful and multiply.*" Cf. *t. Yebam.* 8:7; *Even Ha-ezer* 1.1 of the *Shulchan Aruch*, as cited in Jacobi, "Peru U'revu," 83.

65. Novak, "Be Fruitful," 75. Cf. *b. Yebam.* 64a; *Even Ha-ezer* 1.1 of the *Shulchan Aruch*, as cited in Jacobi, "Peru U'revu," 83.

The Progeny Blessing in the Old Testament Outside the Latter Prophets

4. It directly contributes to God's purpose for the world according to Isa 45:18. Aside from Gen 1:28, Isa 45:18 is easily the most frequently cited text pertaining to the progeny blessing in rabbinic literature.[66] It is often quoted to demonstrate that procreation is not merely a means to an end, but is the very end itself for which God created the world.[67]

5. Fulfillment of this command is considered to be a prerequisite for the coming of the messianic age.[68]

In contrast to the Jewish view in which few callings are higher than that of procreation, Christians have often downplayed Gen 1:28, giving more attention to the related theme of the *imago Dei*.[69] A literal understanding of Gen 1:28a posed a theological problem for those who sought to live in light of the impending parousia, which created an urgency that "detracted from the urgency of creating succeeding generations."[70] Spurred on by Paul's teaching in 1 Cor 7 concerning the goodness of singleness for the sake of the kingdom, much of the history of Christian interpretation of Gen 1:28[71] maintains that this is a command, but that it is no longer obligatory. This is not only because celibacy is a higher calling but also because it has already been fulfilled through the expansion of humankind across the earth.[72]

Augustine made "the single most extensive and influential contribution" to the Christian interpretation of Gen 1:28a.[73] In his early writings, he understood it allegorically, as did most in his day, but he later became

---

66. E.g., *b. Pesaḥ.* 88b; *Meg.* 27a; *Ḥag.* 2b; *Yebam.* 62ab; *B. Bat.* 13a; *m. Giṭ.* 4:5; *'Ed.* 1:13.

67. See Cohen, *Be Fertile and Increase*, 77; Heyd, "Divine Creation," 59; Shapiro, "Be Fruitful," 65–66. See our treatment of Isa 45:18 below.

68. According to *Gen. Rab.* 24:14, "The messianic king will never come until all those souls intended for creation have been created." Cf. Cohen, *Be Fertile and Increase*, 115–20.

69. See Cohen, *Be Fertile and Increase*, 221, for the reasons for this.

70. Ibid., 224. In other words, they questioned, "[h]ow ought one to reconcile this terrestrial orientation of the biblical cosmogony with the otherworldly kerygma of the church?" (222)

71. For a summary of this history, see ibid., ch. 5; Yegerlehner, "Be Fruitful and Multiply."

72. See Cohen, *Be Fertile and Increase*, 231, 259. Cohen states that this was the "overwhelming consensus" of the fathers (231). According to Gilbert, Tertullian and Cyprian were among those who held this position ("Soyez féconds," 738–39).

73. Cohen, *Be Fertile and Increase*, 246.

a proponent of the literal interpretation, viewing procreation as a blessing and a gift of marriage to be enjoyed by all humanity, Christians included.[74] He argued that sexual union was the God-ordained means of reproduction even before the Fall,[75] combating the common interpretation that sexual intercourse was inherently evil and that alternative means of reproduction existed before the Fall.[76] However, according to some, since the literal sense of Gen 1:28a has been fulfilled, it is now to be realized in the spiritual growth of the church.[77] As Cohen notes, "The assertion that the primordial blessings of fertility, increase, and dominion specifically prefigured the triumph of the church and the contemporary experience of Christians and Christianity presupposed the recognition that our verse bespoke divine election and favor. . . . Christians like Augustine who construed 'be fertile and increase' strictly in its literal, historical sense forfeited an exclusive claim to the election that it bespoke."[78] Aquinas believed that the progeny blessing must still be fulfilled collectively by humanity, but that virginity is to be preferred for Christians.[79] Luther, followed by Melanchthon, understood the progeny blessing as natural law, still applicable for all of humanity.[80] Calvin similarly understood the blessing literally as the privilege of all humanity.[81]

Unfortunately, generally speaking, the history of the interpretation of Gen 1:28a, whether Jewish or Christian, has not been based upon a rigorous exegetical examination of the text. Rather, it appears that sociological or theological concerns have shaped these communities' understanding of God's proclamation of blessing, "be fruitful and multiply." On the one hand, Jewish interpretations seem to be the product of a concern with the

---

74. See DCD 14.22; CCSL 48:444 (cited in Cohen, 251). See Cohen, *Be Fertile and Increase*, 247–52.

75. *On the Literal Interpretation of Genesis* 9.3.5–6, cited in Louth, *Genesis 1–11*, 39.

76. See Louth, *Genesis 1–11*, 37. See, e.g., John of Damascus, *On the Orthodox Faith* 4.24 (cited in Louth, 41).

77. E.g., Eusebius of Caesarea, *Demonstratio evangelica* 9.3.8, GCS 23:410 (cited in Cohen, *Be Fertile and Increase*, 234); cf. Thomas Aquinas, *Summa contra gentiles* 3.136, *Opera omnia* 14:412–14 (cited in Cohen, *Be Fertile and Increase*, 263).

78. Cohen, *Be Fertile and Increase*, 266–67.

79. See ibid., 262.

80. See ibid., 307–8. According to Luther, *Vom ehelichen Leben*, *Werke*, 10, 2:276, "Just as God does not command anyone to be a man or a woman but creates them the way they have to be, so he does not command them to multiply but creates them so they have to multiply" (cited in Cohen, *Be Fertile and Increase*, 307).

81. See Calvin, *Genesis*, 97–98.

preservation of their often-threatened people group, as well as an abiding conviction of the importance of their existence within God's created order as his elect people. On the other hand, the in-breaking of the new age and the hope of Christ's impending return have shaped many Christian interpretations of Gen 1:28a so that "be fruitful and multiply" has been spiritualized, deemed obsolete and outdated given the population of the earth, or discarded as a second-tier blessing in favor of celibacy. Our interpretation, however, does share common ground with the interpretations of Augustine, Luther, and Calvin.

The Effect of the Genesis 3 Curses on the Blessing

Due to the disobedience of Adam and Eve in the garden, the fullness of God's blessing on humanity as delineated in Gen 1:28–30 is short-lived. The penalty of death (2:17; 3:3) is accompanied by a series of curses (3:14–19) that modify the original blessings and serve as programmatic statements for the experience of humanity thereafter, and in the book of Genesis in particular.[82] Friction and struggle will be the new norm among the divinely ordained relationships between humanity and living creatures (v. 15), man and woman (v. 16b), and humanity and the ground (vv. 17–19).[83] Furthermore, each element of the blessing of Gen 1:28–30 is affected in this frustration of relationships: dominion over living creatures becomes a struggle as a result of humanity's capitulation to the animal kingdom by succumbing to the serpent's temptation (v. 15);[84] procreation is affected in the address to the woman (v. 16); and the blessing of food is attained only through toil due to resistance from the cursed ground (vv. 17–19).

אֶל־הָאִשָּׁה אָמַר	To the woman he said,
הַרְבָּה אַרְבֶּה עִצְּבוֹנֵךְ וְהֵרֹנֵךְ	"I will greatly increase your anxiety in conception;
בְּעֶצֶב תֵּלְדִי בָנִים	in pain you will bear children.
וְאֶל־אִישֵׁךְ תְּשׁוּקָתֵךְ	Your desire will be for your husband,
וְהוּא יִמְשָׁל־בָּךְ	And he will rule over you." (Gen 3:16)

---

82. See Turner, *Announcements of Plot*, 47–48.

83. See Waltke, *Genesis*, 94; Wenham describes the effect of the curses as "disruption of their appointed roles" (*Genesis 1–15*, 81).

84. See Turner, *Announcements of Plot*, 44–45.

I Will Surely Multiply Your Offspring

The address to the woman relates to her two roles as mother (cf. Gen 1:27–28) and as wife (cf. Gen 2:18–25).[85] Ironically, as she multiplies (רָבָה; cf. Gen 1:28) in her role as mother, God will "surely multiply" (הַרְבָּה אַרְבֶּה)[86] her pain (עִצְּבוֹנֵךְ). But it is not immediately obvious how the progeny blessing is altered in v. 16. Typically, עִצְּבוֹנֵךְ is considered to be synonymous with עֶצֶב in the following clause, both denoting physical pain.[87] The imposed penalty is thus not the frustration of the blessing of procreation itself but rather the curtailment of any "blessedness" that may have accompanied the birth process.

However, for lexical and contextual reasons, there is good reason to believe that עִצְּבוֹנֵךְ refers to mental anxiety rather than physical pain:

1. With the exception of Eccl 10:9, every occurrence of the cognate verb (עָצַב) refers to "mental or emotional distress"[88] and most occurrences of the nominal forms do as well.

2. הֵרוֹן, though a unique form in the MT, clearly derives from the lexical field of הרה, which always denotes conception or pregnancy, not the process of childbirth itself (cf. also הֵרָיוֹן in Hos 9:11 and Ruth 4:13 with respect to conception). Physical pain would be inappropriate to the hendiadys "pain in conception" but mental anxiety would be.[89]

3. If we grant that the next clause (בְּעֶצֶב תֵּלְדִי בָנִים) *does* refer to physical pain in childbirth so that the clauses are related synthetically rather than synonymously, the clauses together describe how the entire reproductive process is now altered negatively. Walton paraphrases v. 16a, "I will greatly increase the anguish you will experience in the birth process, from the anxiety surrounding conception to the strenuous work of giving birth."[90]

4. This accords better with the effect of the curse on dominion and food acquisition, both of which are now not simply painful, but more difficult to enact.

---

85. See Blocher, *In the Beginning*, 180; Westermann, *Genesis 1–11*, 261.

86. This same construction (finite Hiphil form of רָבָה preceded by the infinitive absolute) occurs elsewhere in the OT only in Gen 16:10 and 22:17, both with respect to the progeny blessing.

87. Furthermore, the other two uses of עִצָּבוֹן (Gen 3:17 and 5:29) likely refer to physical pain in light of the phrase (וּמֵעִצְּבוֹן יָדֵינוּ; 5:29).

88. See Meyers, "עָצַב," 279.

89. See ibid., 280; Walton, *Genesis*, 227.

90. Walton, *Genesis*, 227.

The Progeny Blessing in the Old Testament Outside the Latter Prophets

5. In the context of the book of Genesis, barrenness and the emotional anxiety associated with the difficulties of procreation are recurring themes in the patriarchal narratives. The physical pain surrounding the birth process is never mentioned.

This latter interpretation (i.e., "mental anxiety") would then entail an alteration of the progeny blessing itself, since procreation would no longer take place at the behest of the human will, but would be frustrated by high infant mortality rates or barrenness.[91] Thus Walton rightly concludes that the blessing of Gen 1:28–30 "is transformed from a bounteous privilege that came easily in God's precious provision to a grim taskmaster that yields its fruits haphazardly to its beneficiaries only under great duress."[92]

The progeny blessing continues to play a role in the remainder of the primeval history. Throughout, a tension exists between God's gracious provision for the progress of the progeny blessing and its regress as a result of the curse, further sin, or judgment on sin.[93] On the one hand, humankind successfully procreates and multiplies, but on the other hand, conditions outside the garden threaten both the ability to procreate and the ongoing existence of humans. Thus the exponential growth of humanity that we assume would have taken place in the garden is restrained. Every major literary unit in the primeval history reflects or develops this dynamic in some fashion:

1. As a result of expulsion from the garden, access to the tree of life and the eternal physical life associated with it is permanently blocked (3:22). The entrance of death into the human experience remains the greatest impediment to the corporate proliferation of humankind.

2. Immediately following expulsion from the garden, Genesis records the first successful reproductions and explicitly cites Yahweh's intervention in the birth of Cain (4:1–2; cf. v. 25).[94] However, this is fol-

---

91. If the enigmatic phrase וְאֶל־אִישֵׁךְ תְּשׁוּקָתֵךְ in v. 16b refers to "sexual desire," its (partial) purpose may be to indicate that the natural inclination to reproduce will go on despite the difficulties now related to the process (see Turner, *Announcements of Plot*, 24; Walton, *Genesis*, 228).

92. Walton, *Genesis*, 239. In the words of Blocher, "the blessing becomes a burden" (*In the Beginning*, 181).

93. Following von Rad (*Genesis*, 152f), Clines describes this as "spread of sin— spread of grace" (*Theme of the Pentateuch*, 83).

94. Although the syntax is awkward here, it is more feasible that אֵת "expresses accompaniment for the purpose of providing help" than that it identifies the direct object (Arnold and Choi, *Syntax*, 101, citing Gen 4:1).

lowed by Cain's murder of Abel, the first death and the first manifestation of sin's negative effects on population growth (cf. Gen 4:23). The subsequent history of humankind has demonstrated that similar acts of murder—and war—are one of the major impediments to the proliferation of humankind. It is clear, however, that Cain's judgment is not infertility since vv. 17–24 record the fruitful line of Cain.[95]

3. The linear genealogy of Gen 5 that traces the line of humanity from Adam to Noah documents the spread of humanity under the blessing,[96] as do the other *Toledot* formulas.[97] Nevertheless, curse lingers in the background since the constant refrain of death has (literally) the final word in the record of each man in the genealogy.[98]

4. As a transition between the genealogy and the flood account,[99] Gen 6:1 confirms that the process of human multiplication is well under way (כִּי־הֵחֵל הָאָדָם לָרֹב). However, as a result, the earth was not merely filled with people but with violence (וַתִּמָּלֵא הָאָרֶץ חָמָס; vv. 11, 13).[100] In response, Yahweh brings a flood to bring about nearly total population decimation (6:7, 13, 17; 7:4, 21–23). This creation reversal allows him to begin anew based on the "creation starter package" that Noah takes with him on the ark.

5. Following Noah's emergence from the ark, God reaffirms his commitment to humanity by issuing postdiluvian blessings (9:1–7) that

---

95. God does judge at times through imposing infertility, however (see Gen 20:17–18; 2 Sam 6:23).

96. Note v. 2, with vv. 3–32 as the result of the blessing.

97. See Kaminski, *From Noah to Israel*, 76; Turner, *Announcements of Plot*, 25; Westermann, *Genesis 1–11*, 17. In this genealogy in particular, the recurring phrase, "and he had other sons and daughters" (וַיּוֹלֶד בָּנִים וּבָנוֹת) may serve to highlight the fertility granted to the earliest humans as well as God's grace in ensuring the birth of both males and females necessary for procreation.

98. See Clines, *Theme of the Pentateuch*, 72; Turner, *Announcements of Plot*, 26. See vv. 5, 8, 11, 14, 17, 20, 27, 31.

99. Although 6:1–8 (specifically vv. 5–8) clearly introduce the flood narrative, the *Toledot* structural break in 6:9 suggests that, from a literary perspective, 6:1–8 belongs to the preceding genealogy.

100. Prior to these verses, מָלֵא occurs only twice, in the creational blessings upon birds and fish (1:22) and humans (1:28) to fill the earth with their own species. Given that the increase of humankind has just been stressed (5:1—6:1), these verses likely allude to the blessings of Gen 1, suggesting that the unintended, post-Fall, result of the good blessing of multiplication was a corresponding spread of violence. Westermann rightly notes that 6:1ff demonstrates that multiplication, though a blessing, can have negative effects regarding humanity's relationship to God (*Genesis 1–11*, 370).

mirror those of Gen 1 as part of God's "new creation." He then pledges in an unconditional covenant with all of humanity and all living creatures (9:8–17) that he will never again decimate the population comprehensively (cf. 8:21–22). The blessing itself unmistakably parallels Gen 1:26–30 since it expresses God's intentions for humankind with respect to multiplication (9:1, 7), dominion (9:2, 5–6?), and food (9:3–4), even alluding to humanity's creation as the image of God (9:6). The nature of dominion and the source of food are modified from Gen 1:26–30, given the new postlapsarian condition (cf. 8:21) within which this "new creation" is inaugurated. However, the progeny blessing remains unchanged in its expression[101] and is even brought to greater prominence through its restatement in v. 7, serving as an inclusio around the entire blessing.[102] Certainly the progeny blessing has been affected by the Fall (cf. 3:16), but the basic manner in which it is to be realized is unaltered. This abiding universal blessing demonstrates God's refusal to allow his purposes to be frustrated despite the failure of those through whom they will be realized.[103] The aftermath of the Flood account affirms that the progeny blessing *will* now be realized on a grand scale, guaranteed by the covenant out of pure grace since nothing has changed in the heart of humanity (8:21).

Excursus: The Impetus for and Purpose of the Flood in Ancient Near Eastern Literature

The Genesis flood account's hope for future human proliferation is not shared by other ancient accounts. Flood stories abound in the ancient Near East, but there is not agreement concerning the impetus for the flood and its ultimate purpose. The Babylonian *Epic of Gilgamesh*, dating back to at least the Old Babylonian period (2000–1600 BCE), claims that the purpose of the flood was "To impose punishment of the sinner for his sin/

---

101. Genesis 9:1 repeats 1:28 verbatim (פְּרוּ וּרְבוּ וּמִלְאוּ אֶת־הָאָרֶץ) whereas 9:7 introduces a new verb of increase previously used only with respect to other living creatures (שִׁרְצוּ) and repeats וּרְבוּ (see Porten and Rappaport, "Poetic Structure," 363–69, for a cogent argument in favor of retention of the MT).

102. This emphasis on the future success of the progeny blessing is probably due to the fact that the judgment of the Flood eliminated the progress made thus far with respect to this blessing.

103. See Dumbrell, *Covenant and Creation*, 33.

on the transgressor for his transgression" (XI.21), not unlike the negative moral evaluation of humanity that provided the grounds for the flood in Gen 6:5, 11–13.

The seventeenth-century Babylonian account of *Atrahasis* provides a different impetus for the flood. Following the creation of humanity for the purpose of serving the gods, they reproduce: "Twelve hundred years [had not yet passed]/[When the land extended] and the people multiplied (*mtd*)" (I.352–53). We immediately learn that Enlil, the god of earth, is deprived of sleep by their "noise/uproar" (*rigmu*) (I.354–59), and plans a plague in order to alleviate the disturbance (I.360). With help from Enki, god of the underworld, Atrahasis averts the plague (I.364–416). Again we read that "Twelve hundred years [had not yet passed]/[When the land extended] and the people multiplied (*mtd*)" (II.i.1–2), and again Enlil loses sleep due to the noise (*rigmu*) (II.i.3–8). In the remainder of tablet II, Enlil imposes a famine and then intensifies it, each time thwarted by Enki and Atrahasis. Finally, with the approval of the other gods, a flood is imposed that successfully destroys humanity (III.iii.11–16), with the exception of Atrahasis who has, again, received help from Enki. Realizing their need for humanity, the gods regret destroying them so completely. The epic ends with the introduction of three provisions whereby the spread of humankind will be prevented by natural means rather than decimated: some women will be barren, infant mortality rates will be high, and certain cultic roles will entail celibacy (III.vii.1–8).[104] As far as the gods are concerned, this resolution must be deemed successful and a "blessing" for those who, like Enlil, cannot tolerate "noise."

Since the discovery of this text, a lively debate has ensued regarding the meaning of the "noise/uproar" (*rigmu*), which Enlil deems to be intolerable to the point of wiping out humankind. Some understand this to be literal "noise," the real problem therefore being overpopulation, while others see it as a figurative expression for evil-doing and/or rebellion against the gods so that the flood has punitive goals.[105] In support of the

---

104. Tikva Frymer-Kensky argues that, just as *Atrahasis* presents three new ordinances that are designed to solve the problem that brought about the need for the flood, so Genesis presents three new ordinances enclosed within the blessing of 9:1–7 ("Atrahasis Epic," 150–54). A comparison of these ordinances highlights tremendous differences. The three impositions in *Atrahasis* of barrenness, infant mortality, and celibacy are usually *curses* upon man in the OT (e.g., Exod 23:26; Deut 7:14; 28:53–57). In Gen 9:1–7, Yahweh issues blessings designed to graciously preserve humanity despite their evil.

105. Albertz, "Motiv für die Sintflut," 3–16; Frymer-Kensky, "Atrahasis Epic," 147–55; Kikawada and Quinn, *Before Abraham Was*, 42; Kilmer, "Mesopotamian Concept,"

latter interpretation, it has been noted that 1) a similar idiom for wicked behavior is employed in Gen 18:20–21 and 19:13 with respect to Sodom and Gomorrah;[106] 2) we would expect that Gilgamesh, which apparently depends on Atrahasis, would share the same perspective as Atrahasis concerning the impetus for the flood;[107] 3) previously in the epic, *rigmu* refers to the war-cry and rebellious complaints of the igigi gods;[108] and 4) Enlil's explicit complaint concerns "noise," not the number of humans.[109]

In favor of overpopulation, the following arguments have been adduced: 1) Enlil's plans and actions are directly aimed at population decimation;[110] 2) the numerical expansion of humanity is noted just prior to Enlil's complaint of noise and his attempts to bring plague and famine, so it is likely that this is the very problem that occasions Enlil's actions, and (in the case of II.i.1–2) that his initial plague had failed in its purpose;[111] 3) the three ordinances that conclude Atrahasis speak directly to the matter of overpopulation but would have little or no bearing on the wickedness or rebelliousness of humanity; 4) the most likely explanation for Enlil's lack of sleep is literal, audible, noise;[112] 5) the semantic range of *rigmu* is different from צְעָקָה in Gen 18:20–21 and 19:13, and the two terms cannot be equated.[113] Since the overpopulation view accounts much better for the structure of the entire narrative, it is to be preferred. Regardless, the resolution to Atrahasis has negative implications for the future fertility of humanity.[114]

160–77; Lambert and Millard, *Atra-Hasis*, 9; and Moran, "Some Considerations," 245–55, argue for the former position while Finkelstein, "Bible and Babel," 431–44; and Oden, Jr., "Divine Aspirations," 197–216, opt for the latter.

106. See Finkelstein, "Bible and Babel," 437.

107. See Moran, "Some Considerations," 252; Oden, "Divine Aspirations," 208.

108. See Moran, "Some Considerations," 252; Oden, "Divine Aspirations," 208–9.

109. See Moran, "Some Considerations," 252; Oden, "Divine Aspirations," 207.

110. See Kilmer, "Mesopotamian Concept," 168.

111. See ibid., 169; Moran, "Some Considerations," 254.

112. See Moran, "Some Considerations," 253.

113. See ibid., 255. See 253–55 for additional arguments against the interpretation of *rigmu* as rebelliousness.

114. Although overpopulation does not appear to be a problem in other Mesopotamian flood accounts, this is not without parallel in the ancient world. In the Old Iranian/Avestan account of Yima, the gods curb an overbearing population explosion through a harsh winter (see Kikawada and Quinn, *Before Abraham Was*, 49–50; Kilmer, "Mesopotamian Concept," 175). Later, *The Iliad* and *The Cypria* are concerned with overpopulation as well (see Kikawada and Quinn, *Before Abraham Was*, 37).

As Frymer-Kensky notes, the flood account in Genesis "is emphatically not about overpopulation."[115] As Noah leaves the ark, God instructs him to "be fruitful and multiply and fill the earth" (Gen 9:1; cf. 8:17 and 9:7), leaving no question regarding the desirableness of human proliferation in the eyes of Yahweh. With the possible exception of a few wisdom texts, human fertility is always considered to be a blessing from Yahweh in the OT, and never is there a trace of concern with "overpopulation." Kikawada and Quinn thus rightly highlight the polemical nature of the blessing of fecundity in Gen 9:1, 7 when they note that "this command, so long familiar to us, is in its cultural context utterly startling."[116] If the author was familiar with the flood tradition contained in Atrahasis, perhaps this statement even intentionally subverts the negative anthropology contained in the Babylonian depiction of humankind.[117]

6. The juxtaposition of the Table of Nations in Gen 10 and the account of Babel in Gen 11:1–9 presents us with a problem regarding the progress of progeny blessing. Most commentators view Gen 10 as the "fulfillment" of the blessing reissued in 9:1, 7.[118] The confusion of languages and the scattering at Babel, however, must be understood as judgment. The difficulty lies in the fact that these two texts are clearly linked,[119] the latter episode explaining the worldwide dispersion of nations presented in the former. Assuming that these accounts are not in conflict and can be reconciled, one possibility is that the sin of those at Babel was a refusal to obey Yahweh's command to "fill the earth" (1:28; 9:1, 7) and that he therefore forces them to obey it through confusion of languages and scattering.[120] However, it is unlikely that these prior texts are to be construed as commands (see above). Alternatively, if we understand "fill the earth" as a blessing it seems odd and contradictory that what is clearly construed and intended as judgment at Babel (11:6–9) is in fact blessing.

115. Frymer-Kensky, "Atrahasis Epic," 150. Cf. Kilmer, "Mesopotamian Concept," 174.

116. Kikawada and Quinn, *Before Abraham Was*, 38.

117. See Blenkinsopp, *The Pentateuch*, 57.

118. See, e.g., ibid., 88; Clines, *Theme of the Pentateuch*, 74; Hamilton, *Genesis*, 330; Kikawada and Quinn, *Before Abraham Was*, 69; Turner, *Announcements of Plot*, 29; von Rad, *Genesis*, 144; and Westermann, *Genesis 1–11*, 528–29.

119. Compare 10:5, 20, 31 and 11:1, 6, 9 with respect to the number of languages; 10:5, 18, 25, 32 and 11:4, 9 with respect to the division/scattering of the peoples.

120. See Turner, *Announcements of Plot*, 31–32; Waltke, *Genesis*, 161.

Carol Kaminski has proposed a more satisfying solution. She demonstrates that פּוּץ (11:4, 8, 9), commonly translated "to scatter" or "to disperse," is never a blessing but often a curse elsewhere in the OT.[121] In fact, it is correlated with population *decrease* in the context of the exile (cf. Deut 4:27; 28:64).[122] Similarly, the terms used for the spread of humankind in 9:19 (נָפַץ), 10:18 (פּוּץ) and 10:5, 32 (פָּרַד) do not have the same positive connotations as multiplication terms like שָׁרַץ and מָלֵא used thus far in Genesis.[123] Moreover, since those at Babel are afraid of being scattered (11:4), it is probably a legitimate fear. Also, God's purpose in scattering them is not to fill the earth, but to punish and prevent pride. Therefore, although it is undeniable that the Table of Nations demonstrates that the progeny blessing is being realized under God's common grace, the language used in Gen 10–11 for this spread, the negative connotations it is given in Gen 11, and the absence of the verbs used to denote the progeny blessing argue against seeing this as the "fulfillment" or ideal enjoyment of the blessing of 9:1, 7.[124]

7. The genealogy of Shem following the Babel account (11:10–26) *does*, however, point to the full realization of the progeny blessing. Although the genealogical formulae differ slightly, this linear *Toledot* seems to function like that of Gen 5. Whereas Gen 5 traced the line from Adam to Noah and appeared to be a realization of the original creational blessing, Gen 11:10–26 traces the line from Noah to Abram, the one through whom God's intentions to bless all creation will be realized.[125] Thus the final spread of sin at Babel is immediately followed by the identification of the individual through whom blessing will come to all nations, and Gen 1–11 ends on a note of hope. However, just prior to Yahweh's programmatic promise to Abram in Gen 12:2–3, we are informed emphatically that the blessing of progeny has been withheld from the matriarch of Yahweh's covenant people: "Sarai was barren; she had no child" (11:30).

---

121. פּוּץ clearly has negative connotations in the remainder of its uses in the Pentateuch: Gen 49:7; Exod 5:12; Num 10:35; Deut 4:27; 28:64; 30:3.

122. See Kaminski, *From Noah to Israel*, 31–40.

123. See ibid., 44, 58.

124. See ibid., 43, 59. See chs. 1–4 for the complete argument.

125. See ibid., 76.

Conclusion: Genesis 1–11

In the primeval history the blessing of progeny is not simply one blessing among many (as it is elsewhere in the OT), but one of the most fundamental purposes for humanity created as God's image. Furthermore, unlike later occurrences of blessing, the blessings associated with creation in Gen 1–11 (1:22, 28; 5:2; 8:17; 9:1, 7) are graciously bestowed upon *all* by God apart from any requirement for humans to meet specific conditions, expressing his benevolent disposition toward them. Nearly every literary unit in Gen 1–11 is concerned to some extent with tracing the advance of the different elements of the blessing of Gen 1:28–30, with the progeny blessing rising to greatest prominence in this early history of humanity. God's original intention to bless humankind in the context of perfect fellowship with himself was forfeited in the Fall, resulting not merely in physical pain in childbearing but in new hindrances to the full realization of the progeny blessing, some of which we see in the following chapters: banishment from the garden (ch. 3), murder (ch. 4), death (ch. 5), large-scale judgment for sin (chs. 6–9), and infertility (ch. 11). Nevertheless, by God's common grace expressed in the covenant with Noah and creation, humanity *as a whole* will continue to experience God's blessing of children and population growth, although individual people and nations have no such guarantee. Although it is not until Gen 12 that this blessing is bestowed upon a particular individual, Gen 1–11 prepares us for this particularization by not connecting Gen 10:1—11:9 to the blessing of 1:28 and 9:1, 7 and by tracing Abram's lineage (11:10–32).

THE PATRIARCHAL BLESSINGS: GENESIS 12–50

With Abraham we encounter a decisive turn in the contours of blessing in the OT. Although it is obvious that surrounding nations continue to experience blessings such as agricultural abundance, progeny, and military prosperity, beginning in Gen 12 the OT record is predominantly concerned with the blessings that Yahweh bestows upon Abraham and his descendants. The book of Genesis continues to focus on blessing, particularly the progeny blessing. However, the rapid pace of Gen 1–11 that documents dozens of generations, affirming Yahweh's blessing of progeny with little comment, slows to trace merely a few generations in Gen 12–50 to whom blessing was promised yet realized only in part and with difficulty.

The Progeny Blessing in the Old Testament Outside the Latter Prophets

The question of the preservation and multiplication of Abraham's lineage lingers over the entirety of the patriarchal narratives.[126]

Genesis 12:1–3

As many have argued, God's initial charge and pronouncement of blessing upon Abraham in 12:1–3 serve as Yahweh's gracious response to the judgment of Babel, the climactic intervention of Yahweh in the pattern of sin and grace evident in Gen 1–11.[127] Contingent upon his obedience to the call to leave his home and family, Abraham will be the recipient of blessing (v. 2a), resulting in blessing for others (vv. 2b–3). Noth, von Rad, and Wolff draw attention to the programmatic nature of these three verses for the theology of the Yahwist and the whole of the Pentateuch, emphasizing the final clause as the goal of Yahweh's redemptive plan, namely, blessing for the nations through Israel.[128] Although this may be the intended goal of the Abrahamic blessing in the context of the entire OT narrative, the immediate focus is not upon the nations but upon the extent to which Yahweh will bless Abraham himself, blessing so great that all nations are affected by it.[129]

---

126. As Clines summarizes, "in thematic terms, Genesis 12–50 is primarily concerned with the fulfilment (or, perhaps, the non-fulfilment) of the posterity-element in the divine promises to the patriarchs. . . . [A]n intricate pattern of selections, threats, separations, and contentions forms the bulk of the Genesis material, preventing the rapid growth of the Abrahamic family, but never negating the fulfilment of the promise" (*Theme of the Pentateuch*, 48). See also Turner, *Announcements of Plot*, 61, 140, 172–73.

127. See Brueggemann, *Theology of the Old Testament*, 498; Clines, *Theme of the Pentateuch*, 85–86; Dumbrell, *Covenant and Creation*, 59; Turner, *Announcements of Plot*, 52. Hamilton ("Seed of the Woman," 253–73) demonstrates that the blessings of Gen 12:1–3 correspond to and address the curses introduced in 3:14–19.

128. Wolff views Gen 12:1–4b as the core kerygma of the Yahwist with v. 3b as the true center ("Kerygma of the Yahwist," 47), namely, that "it is Yahweh's purpose to bless all the nations of the earth in Israel" (63). Dumbrell refers to 12:1–3 as "a theological blueprint for the redemptive history of the world" (*Covenant and Creation*, 66). See also Noth, *Pentateuchal Traditions*, 237–38; von Rad, "Form-Critical Problem," 67.

129. See Grüneberg, *Abraham*, 243–44. Abraham's role in conveying blessing to the nations as expressed in the Niphal נִבְרְכוּ (v. 3b) is probably best understood in the middle voice ("acquire blessing"). This is preferable to the passive or reflexive voice on account of grammatical considerations and the structure of Gen 12:1–3 (see the detailed arguments of Mitchell, *Meaning of BRK*, 31–33 n. 3; Wenham, *Genesis 1–15*, 277–78). Furthermore, the patriarchal narratives of Gen 12–50 (and subsequent uses of בָּרַךְ in the Niphal in 18:18 and 28:14 and in the Hithpael in 22:18 and 26:4)

I Will Surely Multiply Your Offspring

The first stated consequence[130] of Abraham's positive response to Yahweh's call looks far beyond his own lifetime: "I will make you into a great nation" (וְאֶעֶשְׂךָ לְגוֹי גָּדוֹל).[131] Grüneberg asserts that "a significant part" of being a great nation is "numerical strength" since this is "a natural part of a nation's greatness."[132] However, to be a "great nation" often encompasses far more, including possession of land, political stability, and military strength. One or more of these facets may rise to prominence depending on the context,[133] but Gen 46:3 and Deut 26:5 suggest that the size of the people is primarily in view in this phrase in Gen 12:2 since these other aspects were not yet a reality while Israel was in Egypt.

Subsequent References to the Promised Blessing

Later references to the Abrahamic blessing *explicitly* promise numerous offspring, employing a wide array of images to express the grand scope of this promise:

1. "I will make your descendants as the dust of the earth" (13:16; cf. 28:14)

2. "I will greatly multiply (וְהַרְבָּה אַרְבֶּה) your seed as the stars of the heavens and as the sand on the seashore" (22:17; cf. 15:5; 16:10; 26:4; 32:13[12])

3. "I will make you exceedingly fruitful (וְהִפְרֵתִי אֹתְךָ בִּמְאֹד מְאֹד)" (17:6)

4. "I will make him fruitful (הִפְרֵיתִי) and multiply him exceedingly (הִרְבֵּיתִי אֹתוֹ בִּמְאֹד מְאֹד)" (17:20; cf. 28:3; 35:11; 47:27; 48:4);[134]

---

demonstrate that Abraham and his seed are both "mediator and paradigm" of blessing (Grüneberg, *Abraham*, 245; see also Carroll R., "Blessing the Nations," 23–24). The middle voice encompasses both of these senses.

130. A volitional verb followed by *waw* + imperfect commonly denotes purpose or result (see Joüon, *Grammar*, §116b; Wenham, *Genesis 1–15*, 266; Westermann, *Genesis 12–36*, 144).

131. Although it is unusual to refer to Israel in a positive light as a גּוֹי rather than as an עַם, she is also referred to as a גּוֹי גָּדוֹל in positive contexts in Gen 18:18, 46:3, and Deut 26:5. The use of גּוֹי here likely suggests that Israel will be a political entity, a nuance not necessarily present in עַם (see Dumbrell, *Covenant and Creation*, 65–66; Grüneberg, *Abraham*, 163).

132. Grüneberg, *Abraham*, 162–63. See also Dumbrell, *Covenant and Creation*, 68; Waltke, *Genesis*, 205; Wenham, *Genesis 1–15*, 275.

133. See Ronald E. Clements, "גּוֹי," 428–29.

134. All five of these texts are attributed to the Priestly writer since "to be fruitful

5. "You will spread out (פָּרַצְתָּ) to the west, east, north, and south" (28:14).

The promise to Abraham is reiterated and expanded on numerous occasions (12:7; 13:14–17; 15:1–7, 18–21; 17:1–8; 22:17–18). The meaning of being blessed as a great nation with a great name is further delineated primarily in terms of the material blessings of land and progeny within the context of a covenant relationship with Yahweh. Although not all of these texts lay clear obligations on Abraham, it is clear from 12:1, 17:1, 10, 18:19, 22:16–18, and 26:5 that God's promises are contingent upon Abraham's response, which is, in the final evaluation of 22:18, acceptable to Yahweh.[135] Yahweh has already blessed Abraham with wealth and possessions (12:16; 13:2, 6), military victory (14:15), and protection (20:1–18). However, the Abraham story is primarily concerned from start to finish with the quest for the son required for the eventual fulfillment of the national promises.[136] Yahweh promises Abraham a son (15:4; 17:15–21; 18:10, 14), eventually specified to be from Sarah (17:15–21).[137] Although the promise is long delayed due to her barrenness (16:1–2), Isaac is finally born (21:1–2). The realization of the promise is threatened one final time (Gen 22), resulting in Yahweh's climactic declaration of 22:12, 16–18. Throughout, Yahweh is in full control of Abraham's acquisition of progeny (15:3; 16:1–2; 21:1–2).

---

and multiply" is considered to be one of his distinguishing phrases in both previous (Gen 1:22, 28; 8:17; 9:1, 7) and later (Exod 1:7; Lev 26:9) texts. Other recurring expressions are not believed to be unique to any given source, but cut across sources. For example, the stars simile is present in both J (15:5; 26:4) and E (22:17; cf. Exod 32:13). Similarly, the sand simile is present in both J (32:13[12]) and E (22:17). Furthermore, there is a variety of language used to express the Abrahamic progeny promise even within sources. Overall, the numerous texts related to this promise in Gen 12–50 are evenly dispersed among J, E, and P. Therefore, if these sources are accepted this promise has always been central to Israel's self-identity as a people descended from Abraham. It is also important to note that the phrase "be fruitful and multiply" links the blessings of Gen 1–11 to the Abrahamic blessings, a relationship we will explore below.

135. See Kline, *Kingdom Prologue*, 309–11; Turner, *Announcements of Plot*, 58, 92–93. Youngblood identifies fifteen texts that demonstrate the obligatory nature of the covenant for Abraham, including 12:1, 7; 14:22–23; 15:9–10; 17:1, 9–14; 18:19; 22:2, 16–18; and 26:4–5 ("Abrahamic Covenant," 31–46). See also Wright, *Mission of God*, 205–8, with respect to the interplay between conditionality and unconditionality in the Abrahamic covenant.

136. See Turner, *Announcements of Plot*, 61–95.

137. Ishmael will be a great nation as well (16:10; 17:20; 21:13, 18, demonstrated in 25:12–18 where twelve princes are named), the initial realization of the expanded promise that Abraham will father "a *multitude* of nations (הֲמוֹן גּוֹיִם)" (17:4, 5).

Toward the end of Abraham's life, the narrator concludes that "Yahweh had blessed [him] in every way" (24:1; cf. 24:35).

Yahweh then makes the same promises to Isaac that he had made to Abraham (26:3–5, 24), and Isaac too sees blessing in his own lifetime (25:11; 26:12–14, 28–29). In 26:3–5, 24, Yahweh emphasizes that the fulfillment of the promises depends not on Isaac but upon God's commitment to Abraham based on his obedience. Again the progeny promise is initially in jeopardy due to barrenness, but Yahweh grants conception (25:21).

Finally, the same promises are passed on to Jacob (28:13–15; 35:11–12), and Jacob receives God's blessing in his lifetime as well (30:43; 32:11[10]; 33:11). This time God grants progeny in greater abundance: his twelve sons become a household of seventy prior to his death (46:27).[138] Famine is the final great threat to the promise of progeny in Genesis, but this too is overcome, once again through Yahweh's preservation, this time by means of Joseph's exile to Egypt (50:20). By the end of Genesis, we see very little progress in terms of the land promise, but Yahweh has repeatedly acted to advance the progeny promise.[139]

The Universal Blessing and the Particular Abrahamic Blessing

Clearly, there is a connection between the blessing on all of humanity to "be fruitful and multiply" and the promise that God will make Abraham into a "great nation" with innumerable descendants. But what is the nature of this relationship exegetically, theologically, and logically? Both are explicitly designated as blessings from Yahweh: the early history of blessing

---

138. As with Ishmael, with Esau we see that even the rejected son is blessed with nationhood and abundant progeny (25:23; 35:11; 36:1–43), advancing the promise of 17:6 (see Turner, *Announcements of Plot*, 135, 137).

139. The ultimate goal of blessing for the nations is not forgotten in the course of the patriarchal narratives, either in the periodic restatements of the promises (e.g., 18:18; 22:18; 26:4; 27:29; 28:14) or in the concerns of the narratives themselves. At times foreigners receive blessing as a result of their contact with Abraham and his descendants (e.g., 30:27–30; 39:2–5; 41:57). Furthermore, Biddle, "Endangered Ancestress," 599–611, argues that the three stories of the "endangered ancestress" (12:10–20; 20:1–18; and 26:1–11) demonstrate both that the patriarchs are the *means* of blessing for the nations and that curse or blessing for the nations depends on their relationship to the patriarchs as stated in Gen 12:1–3 (610–11). However, the patriarchal narratives are primarily concerned with the promised blessings for Abraham and his descendants.

The Progeny Blessing in the Old Testament Outside the Latter Prophets

in Gen 1–11 that is expressed largely in terms of fertility carries over into the patriarchal narratives where blessing pertains primarily to human proliferation.[140] In addition, the Abrahamic progeny promise frequently employs the same terms as in Gen 1–11 (namely, פָּרָה and רָבָה), suggesting that there is no fundamental difference between the universal progeny blessing of Gen 1:28; 9:1, 7 and that given to Abraham (although פָּרָה and רָבָה now usually occur as Hiphils, emphasizing Yahweh's direct agency). As Westermann notes, the Abrahamic promises continue to have universal ramifications and they continue the theme of blessing as distinct from deliverance/salvation.[141]

Accordingly, it is commonly claimed that the progeny blessing is "reaffirmed or reapplied"[142] to Abraham. But how does this affect the universal blessing? Does Genesis suggest a transfer of the creational blessing to Abraham, so that it no longer applies to the whole of humanity but solely to Abraham? Or is the blessing particularized or intensified for him, implying that the universal blessing continues and remains unchanged? In favor of the former, never again in the whole of the OT do we encounter statements akin to those in Gen 1–11 that extend the blessing of progeny to all nations. Hereafter promises of progeny, whether conditional or unconditional, appear only with respect to Israel.

However, there is good reason to believe that the blessing remains upon all humanity: 1) Since it is a creation blessing, reiterated in the postlapsarian creation blessings of Gen 9:1–7, it is assumed that this blessing graciously persists. As with the creation blessing of the provision of food and the creation of humanity as the image of God, there is no need to reaffirm periodically its validity in the text. 2) Obviously, the nations continue to multiply following Gen 12. Throughout Israel's history, she encountered nations "greater and mightier" (Deut 4:38; 9:1; 11:23) and more populous than herself. Furthermore, the OT writers acknowledge the immense size of other peoples on occasion, employing language similar to that applied to Israel.[143] History attests to the fact that humanity as a whole has, with

---

140. Our previous judgment that Gen 1:28 and 9:1, 7 are to be construed as blessings rather than commands provides further continuity between these two manifestations of the progeny blessing in that both emphasize divine action rather than human obligation.

141. See Westermann, *Genesis 12–36*, 158.

142. Kaminski, *From Noah to Israel*, 94. See also Clines, *Theme of the Pentateuch*, 85–86; John Sailhamer, *Pentateuch as Narrative*, 139; Wenham, *Genesis 1–15*, 275.

143. Josh 11:4, Judg 7:12, and 1 Sam 13:5 liken the Canaanites, the Midianite confederation and their camels, and the Philistines, respectively, to "the sand that is on the seashore" in number. See also Judg 6:5, Jer 46:23, and 2 Chr 12:3.

periodic setbacks, continued to grow over the centuries. Although it may not be stated as such, God has in his common grace continued to enable other peoples to flourish, blessing them with numerous descendants (e.g., Josh 11:4; 1 Sam 13:5) as well as with other blessings such as food and military might. Thus, on the basis of the covenant God made with Noah, his sons, and all creatures (9:8–17), the survival and proliferation of humankind as a whole is assured.[144]

But if the progeny blessing endures for all of humanity, in what sense is the Abrahamic blessing distinct and meaningful? The primary difference appears to lie precisely in the fact that the Abrahamic blessing is guaranteed for a particular people. In contrast, the guarantee that God will bless all of humanity with progeny provides no assurance that any individual nation or people group will survive or expand. Although life may flourish outside of Yahweh's covenant with Israel, it is precarious since sin and its effects impede and frustrate the progress of the progeny blessing. Through murder and war humans take life from each other. Yahweh himself, through war, barrenness, famine, and pestilence, takes life from individuals and at times decimates entire cities (e.g., Sodom and Gomorrah, Jericho) or nations (e.g., the oracles against the nations in the Latter Prophets) on account of their sin (cf. Deut 28).

Only Israel is guaranteed that she will receive protection from these human and divine threats to the blessing and will become a "great nation." Yahweh sovereignly protects Abraham (in war, in hostile nations, and from barrenness) and Israel (e.g., preservation through Joseph in Egypt, provision in the wilderness) and causes them to grow. Although Yahweh is responsible for all conception and birth (see 1 Sam 2:5; Pss 107:38, 41; 113:9; 127:3), by repeatedly noting his agency the patriarchal narratives appear to suggest that Yahweh acts specially on the patriarchs' behalf to grant progeny. Furthermore, by demanding adherence to his commands, Yahweh encourages Abraham and his descendants to rid themselves of some of the sinful causes of decimation, such as murder and instigation of wars.[145]

How then does the election of Abraham and his offspring relate to blessing for the nations and the progeny blessing in particular? Some have noted that the pronouncement that Abraham is now to be the channel of

---

144. See Goldingay, *Old Testament Theology: Israel's Gospel*, 101; *contra* Kaminski, *From Noah to Israel*, 101, 104; see her discussion on 96–101.

145. The connection between obedience and the preservation of life, leading to population expansion, is more evident in the Sinai covenant (see below).

The Progeny Blessing in the Old Testament Outside the Latter Prophets

blessing for the nations (Gen 12:3; 18:18; 22:18; 26:4; 27:29; 28:14) is in tension with the creational blessing for all humankind.[146] The nature and content of the blessing mediated through Abraham is not defined here. If the "blessing" that comes through Abraham is entirely different from the creational blessings, this conflict is easily resolved. However, blessing thus far pertains primarily to fertility in the book of Genesis, so the blessing in view here may as well. Furthermore, Gen 20:17–18, where God closes the wombs of the women in the house of Abimelech and later opens them based on Abimelech's dealings with Abraham and Sarah, suggests that the progeny blessing may be included in the blessing the nations experience through Abraham. Still, the aforementioned tension is not a contradiction. Perhaps the extent of the experience of God's universal blessing (including that of progeny) for different peoples depends upon their response to Abraham/Israel if or when they encounter him/her. In the midst of conflict with other nations, Israel's progeny blessing "trumps" the universal progeny blessing under which the nations reside (e.g., Judg 7:19—8:12; 2 Kgs 19:32–35) since their blessing depends on their response to Israel (Gen 12:3).[147]

The Abrahamic progeny blessing is also distinct from the universal blessing in its purpose. Whereas the purpose of the blessing in 1:28 is to rule in reflection of the rule of the Divine King, Abraham is promised that his descendants will be a "great nation" to the ultimate end of extending blessing to the nations. Yahweh's original intention was that all of humanity was to live under his Kingship. By calling Abraham and his descendants in the context of a covenant, he again creates and multiplies a special people (Exod 19:5–6) that lives under his Kingship, mirroring his creation intent, yet now this people serves a redemptive purpose on behalf of the nations.[148] Therefore, although Yahweh's act of making Abraham into a "great nation" is a blessing in itself and contributes to the multiplication of humankind as a whole, it does not appear that the intent of his promises to Abraham

---

146. For example, Terence Fretheim states, "[B]lessing belongs primarily to the sphere of creation; it is a gift of God. . . . As such, all the families of the earth are *not* dependent upon their relationship to Abraham for blessing; it rains on the just and the unjust, and families continue to thrive" (*Pentateuch*, 48).

147. The progeny blessing as we have been discussing it here with regard to other nations pertains not to the rate of birth or conception but to the population flux of the whole people, thus including the death of existing persons.

148. Logically speaking, it seems necessary for God to create a whole nation for himself in order for their influence to be felt throughout the inhabited world. See Wright, *Mission of God*, 329–33, on the missional function of this text.

is to "fulfill" the progeny blessing of 1:28 or 9:1, 7.[149] Yahweh's purpose in multiplying Abraham recaptures his purpose at creation that has been all but lost among the nations who continue to multiply, yet do not know the God by and for whom they were created. The Abrahamic covenant is thus the "redemptive version" of the creation blessings since eventually the curse will be lifted and replaced by the blessing through Abraham.[150]

INITIAL FULFILLMENT IN EGYPT

In Gen 46:3 Yahweh appears to Jacob in a dream and assures him that in Egypt he will make him into a גּוֹי גָּדוֹל. Such a declaration is surprising, since it implies a lengthy stay for the sons of Israel and reveals that the location for the birth of this great nation will not be the promised land of Canaan but rather Egypt. It is further significant in that the promise entails the same formulation (גּוֹי גָּדוֹל) as the first promise to Abraham in 12:2. This not only anticipates the imminent realization of the first of the Abrahamic promises but also underscores the progeny element in the meaning of גּוֹי גָּדוֹל. The early chapters of Exodus emphasize the great expansion of the people (Exod 1:7–12, 20–21; 5:5), but at the time of the exodus it is difficult to define the "greatness" of this new nation in terms of political strength, military might, or the possession of much land (although they do acquire much material wealth upon their departure).

A tally of the descendants of Jacob who went to Egypt follows, seventy in all (46:8–27).[151] At the conclusion of Gen 47, which contrasts

---

149. *Contra* Kaminski, *From Noah to Israel*, 109, who argues that the patriarchal promises are the means by which the blessing of 9:1 is realized.

150. See Kline, *Kingdom Prologue*, 329. In discerning the relationship between the creational and Abrahamic manifestations of the progeny blessing, Gen 35:11 may be especially significant. In 35:11–12 Yahweh blesses Jacob with what is unmistakably a rearticulation of the Abrahamic promises, entailing multiple nations, kings, and land. However, the imperatives "be fruitful and multiply" (פְּרֵה וּרְבֵה) are undoubtedly "intended to recall the primaeval blessing" since this hendiadys in the imperative occurs elsewhere in Genesis (and in fact in the entire OT) only in Gen 1–11 (Kaminski, *From Noah to Israel*, 117. Cf. von Rad, *Genesis*, 339; Westermann, *Genesis 12–36*, 553). Although the significance of this link is not immediately obvious, perhaps it depicts Jacob (newly renamed "Israel," introducing the nation) and his offspring as a "new creation," a microcosm of the original creation, underscoring Israel's redemptive significance on behalf of all nations.

151. In the context of the book of Genesis, this number is significant as a parallel to the seventy nations in Gen 10, again portraying the nation of Israel as a microcosm of all the nations on earth. See Ackerman, "Literary Context," 78; Cassuto, *Exodus*, 8.

the good fortunes of Israel (vv. 1–12, 27) with the subjugation of all of Egypt to the Pharaoh as a result of the famine (vv. 13–26), the narrator states that in Goshen Israel "was fruitful and multiplied greatly" (וַיִּפְרוּ וַיִּרְבּוּ מְאֹד; v. 27). This significant clause anticipates Exod 1:7–12, which describes the same growth.[152] Furthermore, this is the first time in Genesis that we encounter the progeny verbs as converted imperfects, indicating a completed act. Prior to Gen 47 this blessing has been a promise and a desire but not a reality, neither for humanity in Gen 1–11 nor for Abraham's descendants in Gen 12–50.

Exodus 1

In no other passage in the entire OT do the theme and terminology of human proliferation dominate as they do in the narrative of Exod 1. The first six verses of the book provide a summary of the move of the descendants of Jacob to Egypt as recounted in Gen 46–50. The passing of that generation (v. 6) provides a transition between the account of the patriarchs and the immediate "sons of Israel" (בְּנֵי יִשְׂרָאֵל, v. 1) and the nation of the "children of Israel" (בְּנֵי יִשְׂרָאֵל, v. 7) and the exodus some 400 years later (see Exod 12:40).[153]

Exodus 1:7 provides the only information concerning the Israelites during this time period, a remarkably brief account for so long a time since the remaining four books of the Pentateuch following the exodus cover only about forty years. This creates the impression that Yahweh was altogether absent from his people during these centuries. Although God's great act of deliverance in the exodus provided the basis for the official creation of the people of Israel and the Sinai covenant, he was quietly but powerfully present and at work on behalf of his people during their stay in Egypt,[154] blessing his people mightily, particularly in multiplying their progeny.[155] Exodus 1:7 describes the extent of the blessing as strongly and

---

152. See Waltke, *Genesis*, 591; Westermann, *Genesis 37–50*, 172.

153. G. F. Davies describes the movement from v. 1 to v. 7: "With the people transformed from the countable (70) to the innumerable, and with the list of proper names being matched by a list of verbs of increase, the passage shifts from the static to the dynamic" (*Israel in Egypt*, 34).

154. See Fretheim, *Exodus*, 25.

155. Jeffrey M. Cohen seeks a natural explanation for this outrageous growth, turning to prosperous conditions in Goshen as described in Gen 47:6, 11 and the sociological observation that repressed people compensate through high birth rates ("Fertility," 195–98). Indeed, these may have been two of the means by which Yahweh

comprehensively as could be imagined, employing all five verbal expressions for human proliferation encountered previously in Genesis:

וּבְנֵי יִשְׂרָאֵל פָּרוּ וַיִּשְׁרְצוּ וַיִּרְבּוּ וַיַּעַצְמוּ בִּמְאֹד מְאֹד וַתִּמָּלֵא הָאָרֶץ אֹתָם[156]

God's bestowal of the blessing of progeny upon his covenant people provides the backdrop for the following events in Exod 1 and, ultimately, the entire exodus event. Prior to his showdown with Pharaoh, leading to the exodus deliverance, God duels with Pharaoh in Exod 1:8–22. Giving unconscious testimony to the extent of Yahweh's blessing, the "new king" of Egypt (v. 8) acknowledges that the Israelites are "more and mightier" than the Egyptians (רַב וְעָצוּם מִמֶּנּוּ, v. 9). He sees this as a threat and thus subjects them to forced labor "lest they multiply" (פֶּן־יִרְבֶּה, v. 10) all the more. However, Sailhamer observes that "the more the king tries to thwart God's blessing the more that blessing increases"[157] (see v. 12). The failure of this indirect effort at population control is followed by a more overt effort through the slaughter of newborn boys (vv. 15–21). In response, God (who finally makes an overt appearance in the text himself on behalf of the midwives)[158] continues to bless the people: "and the people multiplied and became very mighty" (וַיִּרֶב הָעָם וַיַּעַצְמוּ מְאֹד, v. 20), exacerbating the

---

increased his people (see Exod 1:12). Ackerman, however, claims that slavery normally leads to population reduction ("Literary Context," 83). Regardless, Cornelius Houtman rightly notes that "the question 'how' [the population explosion] could have happened does not seem to have concerned [the author]" (*Exodus*, 232).

156. The two most common verbs of human increase, פָּרָה and רָבָה, appear together again, but are separated in Exod 1:7 by שָׁרַץ, the only case in the OT in which these verbs are not immediately juxtaposed as hendiadys. As previously noted, this phrase is employed in the context of both the creation blessings (Gen 1:22, 28; 8:17; 9:1, 7) and the Abrahamic promises (Gen 17:20; 28:3; 35:11; 47:27; 48:4). שָׁרַץ (cf. Gen 8:17 and 9:7) and מָלֵא (cf. Gen 1:22, 28; 9:1) are used previously with respect to multiplication only in the context of the creation blessings. As discussed above, עָצַם may denote the strength that commonly results from large numbers rather than multiplication itself. The verbal form occurs previously only in Gen 26:16; more significant may be Gen 18:18, in which the nominal form is used to reiterate the promise that Abraham will become "a great and mighty nation" (גּוֹי גָּדוֹל וְעָצוּם) (see Siebert-Hommes, *Let the Daughters Live!*, 62). Although an adverbial expression and thus not an expression of multiplication itself, it is noteworthy that the intensifier "בִּמְאֹד מְאֹד" occurs only three times previously (Gen 17:2, 6, 20), all in the context of the promise to Abraham of numerous progeny. See below concerning the implications of these observations.

157. Sailhamer, *Pentateuch As Narrative*, 242.

158. It may be significant that none of the statements concerning multiplication in Exod 1 explicitly name Yahweh as the agent of this blessing. Perhaps this is intentional literary crafting, emphasizing God's absence from his people with respect to their current need for deliverance from bondage. God enters the scene to that end in 2:24–25.

"problem" of v. 9 (רַב וְעָצוּם). It is clear that the Egyptian king, the anti-creation agent of death, cannot succeed in his quest to subvert the divine King's life-giving blessing of progeny.[159] However, Pharaoh's efforts continue (v. 22) and Israel remains enslaved, leaving them in a state of despair prior to Yahweh's intervention in the exodus.

Fulfillment of the Abrahamic Progeny Promise

There is little doubt that Exod 1 (as well as Gen 47:27) is intended to document the realization of the Abrahamic promise of numerous progeny. Some scholars understand this as a partial fulfillment of the promise.[160] However, most see Exod 1:7 as a complete fulfillment.[161] The evidence supports this latter assessment:

1. The terminology employed in Exod 1:7, denoting completed action, echoes much of the terminology used to articulate Yahweh's promise of many descendants to Abraham in Genesis.

2. Yahweh promises Jacob that it will be in Egypt that he will make him into a "great nation" (גּוֹי גָּדוֹל, Gen 46:3). This prevents any differentiation between the terminology of "great nation" and verbs of multiplication in terms of their meaning and time of fulfillment, and suggests that the initial promise of Gen 12:2a finds its realization in Exod 1:7.

3. Although the expectation of further proliferation of the Israelites does not disappear from the Pentateuch, there is comparatively little emphasis on this following Exod 1. Nor is there another text in the OT that emphasizes the realization of the blessing so heavily.

4. Some later texts identify this time as the fulfillment of this promise (see Deut 1:10; 10:22; 26:5; Ps 105:24).

---

159. See Fretheim, *Exodus*, 27, 32. Cf. Ackerman, "Literary Context," 88.

160. Clines claims, "certainly Israel has not yet become a 'great nation'; the promise of progeny awaits a fuller realization" (*Theme of the Pentateuch*, 56). However, he offers no exegetical evidence for this judgment, and it is doubtful whether a future "fuller realization" necessitates denying fulfillment of the promise in Exod 1 (see below). Similarly, Ackerman asserts that the progeny promise is only "in the process" of fulfillment ("Literary Context," 78).

161. See, e.g., Beale, *The Temple*, 106; Cassuto, *Exodus*, 9; Childs, *Exodus*, 2; Davies, *Israel in Egypt*, 30; Durham, *Exodus*, 5; Fretheim, *Exodus*, 24–25; Gilbert, "Soyez féconds," 731; Houtman, *Exodus*, 1:221; Kaminski, *From Noah to Israel*, 132, 134; Shapiro, "Be Fruitful," 61.

5. It is, at the least, suggestive that following Yahweh's remembrance of the covenant he made with Abraham (Exod 2:24–25) he mentions only the promise of land in speaking to Moses (3:6–8, 16–17; cf. 6:1–8). One plausible explanation for this is that the land is the sole focus since it is the primary promise still outstanding.

Not only do the historical circumstances surrounding the fulfillment of the multiplication promise prompt the exodus from Egypt, but theologically the fulfillment of the promise to make of Abraham a "great nation" creates anticipation for the fulfillment of the other primary material covenant promise, that of land.[162] The failure of Pharaoh to thwart the realization of the progeny promise and Yahweh's continual blessing in vv. 8–21 provide hope and confidence that Yahweh will just as certainly be with his people as they take possession of the promised land.

Exodus 1:7 and the Universal Progeny Blessing

Although some resist seeing any direct connection between Exod 1:7 and the universal blessing of Gen 1:28 and 9:1, 7, maintaining that Exod 1 relates to the Abrahamic promise alone,[163] there is good reason to believe that this text alludes to these creation texts:[164] 1) Four of the five verbs in Exod 1:7 are used to denote the universal progeny blessing in Gen 1:28 and 9:1, 7 and two of them (שָׁרַץ and מָלֵא) are employed exclusively in these texts and not in references to the Abrahamic promise. 2) The intended result of the multiplication of humankind in Gen 1:28 and 9:1, "filling the earth" (וּמִלְאוּ אֶת־הָאָרֶץ) is echoed in Exod 1:7 (וַתִּמָּלֵא הָאָרֶץ אֹתָם). It is significant that the text does not state that they filled Goshen (as in Gen 47:27) or Egypt, but rather that they filled הָאָרֶץ, most likely an allusion to Gen 1:28 and 9:1.[165] 3) Thematically, the creation

---

162. See Ackerman, "Literary Context," 78; Davies, *Israel in Egypt*, 30; Durham, *Exodus*, 5; Houtman, *Exodus*, 221. Remarkably, the fulfillment of the "great nation" promise is recorded in just a few verses whereas the narrative documenting the fulfillment of the land promise extends from Exodus to Joshua. Perhaps this is partially due to the fact that Yahweh makes himself more clearly known in acts of deliverance than in blessing.

163. See, e.g., Houtman, *Exodus*, 232–33.

164. See Ackerman, "Literary Context," 77; Brueggemann, "Kerygma," 406; Childs, *Exodus*, 2; Fretheim, *Exodus*, 25–26.

165. See Fretheim, *Exodus*, 25.

of the nation of Israel at the beginning of Exodus parallels the creation of humanity at the beginning of Genesis.

However, the significance of this allusion is harder to discern. At the very least, these parallels portray the events of Exod 1:7 as the creation of a new people. Some assert that Exod 1:7 indicates that not only the Abrahamic blessing but also the blessing of Gen 1:28 is "completely fulfilled."[166] However, this is by no means clear from the evidence and claims too much, implying that Yahweh no longer has any interest in the proliferation of humankind apart from ethnic Israel. Nor does this fit well with our judgment that Gen 1:28 is a blessing rather than a command to be fulfilled. Fretheim offers a more cautious understanding that better accounts for Israel's redemptive purpose: "God's intentions in creation are being realized in this family . . . a microcosmic fulfillment of God's macrocosmic design for the world."[167] Exodus 1:7 is a crucial realization of the universal progeny blessing, but Yahweh's gracious intention to bless the nations with progeny remains and is hence not "fulfilled" in Israel alone.

Israel's Population in Flux: Exodus 2—Numbers

Unlike Gen 1 through Exod 1, Exod 2 through Numbers has relatively little to say about the progeny blessing, either in terms of historical growth or in terms of the expectation of growth. Doubtless this is because 1) the focus in this material is almost entirely upon the nation of Israel, 2) the Abrahamic promise of numerous progeny has been realized and the fulfillment hopes now revolve around land,[168] and 3) it covers a relatively brief time-span (about forty years), leaving little time for further growth. Nevertheless, this material does record the preservation and growth of the people of Israel, population reductions as punishment for sin, and fresh

---

166. Cassuto, *Exodus*, 9. See also Beale, *The Temple*, 106.

167. Fretheim, *Exodus*, 25. Similarly, Ackerman: "The narrator is clearly saying that the destiny of man, as announced at the Creation and after the Flood, is in the process of being fulfilled by the descendants of Israel" ("Literary Context," 77). See also Kaminski, *From Noah to Israel*, 134. In general, Israel is called to be a microcosm of all of humanity by *modeling* the relationship with Yahweh that all peoples ideally ought to have. Thus she enjoys a special role in Yahweh's redemptive plans for the world. Israel enjoys blessings of progeny and land to this end. Specially in covenant with Yahweh, Israel does not reflect the *actual* relationship of Yahweh to the nations.

168. See von Rad, "The Promised Land," 84.

possibilities for future growth within the context of the covenant blessings of the Sinai covenant.

The Growth and Preservation of Israel in the Wilderness

In contrast to the simple statement of Exod 1:7, the population flux of the people of Israel is *described* in Exodus through Numbers through Yahweh's acts toward Israel for good or for ill. In the exodus, many of the plagues result in the decimation of Egypt and her population, culminating in the Passover (Exod 12:12–13) and the military defeat at the יַם־סוּף (Exod 14). Yahweh preserves Israel throughout these plagues and in the יַם־סוּף encounter (Exod 14:30) on the basis of the Abrahamic covenant and for the purpose of cultivating fear of and trust in Yahweh (Exod 14:31). In the wilderness, Yahweh continues to sustain Israel through his blessings that often take the form of small-scale deliverances from death. Yahweh blesses them with his guiding presence in the cloud and fire (Exod 13:21–22; Num 9:15–23), protects them, granting victory over enemies (Exod 17:8–13; Num 21:1–3; 21:21–35; 31:7–12), provides water (Exod 15:22–25; 17:6), and provides food (Exod 16:4, 13–14, 35). All these blessings serve not only to instruct the people in the knowledge of Yahweh but also to preserve the nation physically.

Decimation Due to Covenant Unfaithfulness

Prior to ratification of the Sinai covenant, Israel repeatedly exhibits a lack of faith in Yahweh to protect her (Exod 14:11–12) and provide for her in the wilderness (Exod 15:24; 16:2–3; 17:2–3), but Yahweh does not punish his people. A major shift occurs following Israel's pledge to abide by the "book of the covenant" (סֵפֶר הַבְּרִית; Exod 24:7) in Exod 24:1–8.[169] Now Yahweh's blessing is no longer unconditional but is contingent upon the people's promised adherence to Yahweh and his law.

Accordingly, the unfaithfulness of the people in the "Golden Calf" incident results in judgment. Interestingly, Yahweh's initial threat is to revoke the progeny blessing to Abraham and transfer it to Moses (Exod 32:10; cf. Num 14:12; Deut 9:14). In his defense of the people, Moses appeals, in part, to Yahweh's unconditional promise to multiply the patriarchs (v. 13), prompting Yahweh to relent (וַיִּנָּחֶם יְהוָה עַל־הָרָעָה, v. 14).

---

169. See Goldingay, *Old Testament Theology: Israel's Gospel*, 377.

However, Yahweh still punishes them for their sin by the hand of the Levites (v. 28) and directly (vv. 33–35; וַיִּגֹּף יְהוָה אֶת־הָעָם). Yahweh's exchanges with Moses (vv. 7–14, 31–35) provide a paradigm for Yahweh's covenantal treatment of Israel's sin. On the one hand, Yahweh will never completely wipe out Israel on account of the Abrahamic covenant (i.e., Moses "wins" the first discussion); on the other hand, Israel will still be punished for her unfaithfulness under the Sinai covenant (i.e., Moses "loses" the second discussion). Clearly, this dynamic has ramifications for the size of the population.

During the subsequent wilderness wanderings Yahweh repeatedly imposes the death penalty on Israel on account of her sin: the Amalekites and Canaanites strike (וַיַּכּוּם) Israel (Num 14:44–45) when they proceed without Yahweh (Num 14:43); fourteen אֶלֶף and 700 are killed in a plague (Num 17:14[16:49]) because of grumbling (וַיִּלֹּנוּ; 17:6[16:41]); Yahweh sends serpents against the people as judgment for grumbling (Num 21:6–9); and twenty-four אֶלֶף die in a plague as a result of an idolatrous alliance with Baal of Peor (Num 25:1–9).[170]

The Military Registrations of Numbers 1 and 26

Moses is instructed to register all males twenty and over by tribe both at the point of their departure from Sinai (Num 1:1) and following the forty years of wilderness wanderings (Num 26:1–4, 63–65). Although the first is taken specifically for military purposes (Num 1:3, 20, 22, etc.) and the second for the sake of land allotments (Num 26:52–56), we are surely meant to compare these registrations. Excluding Levites, the MT lists totals of 603 אֶלֶף and 550 in Num 1:46 (cf. 2:32) and 601 אֶלֶף and 730 in Num 26:51.[171] Despite wars, plagues, and judgments, Yahweh has sustained the original population of his people as they left Egypt, underscoring his covenant faithfulness. He has not, however, caused them to increase. Given the perpetual covenant-breaking of Israel, this maintenance of the population is certainly an act of grace and compassion while still punishing the guilty, reflecting Yahweh's character as described in Exod 34:6–7.[172] This is

---

170. See also Num 11:1, 33; 16:31–35. The punishment of forty years of wilderness wanderings (Num 14:26–38) could itself be viewed as decimation of the entire generation as punishment, although the overall population size is preserved in the succeeding generation.

171. See Excursus below regarding the best understanding of אֶלֶף here and elsewhere.

172. Dennis T. Olson notes well the theological function of this new registration:

the "net result" of the tension between judgment and preservation during the wilderness wanderings.

Just prior to the second registration, in Num 22–24 the foreign prophet Balaam proclaims "accolades and promises that are unsurpassed in the rest of the Pentateuch."[173] The vast population of Israel serves as the impetus for Moab's fear (22:3; cf. vv. 5, 11) and Balak's commissioning of Balaam. Balaam's first blessing (23:7–10) culminates in a recognition[174] of the great size of Israel: "Who can count the dust of Jacob/Or number the fourth part of Israel?" (v. 10).[175]

Prospects for Future Proliferation

Although God has already made of Abraham a great nation, he intends to continue to bless Israel. The Sinai covenant offers new opportunities for blessing, building on the Abrahamic promises, but they now operate within the context of conditional covenant blessings. These future blessings find their fullest expression in Exod 23:20–33, Lev 26:3–13, and Deut 28:1–14,[176] all of which contain the blessing of progeny.[177]

The "Covenant Code" (Exod 20:22—23:33), the first formal articulation of Yahweh's covenant laws according to the biblical narrative, concludes with Yahweh's future acts on behalf of Israel (23:20–33; cf. the introduction to the code in 20:22–24). Since the focus throughout these verses is on entry into Canaan and its conquest, Yahweh portrays himself predominantly as the warrior who will defeat the Canaanites (vv. 22–23, 27–29, 31). However, vv. 25–26 anticipate the blessings Yahweh will grant

---

"The second census list is both a sign of completed judgment on the first generation and a sign of God's promise for a new generation" (*Numbers*, 163).

173. Ibid., 151. Since these four oracles of blessing are "put into the mouth" of Balaam (Num 23:5, 12), the source is divine rather than human and thus they should be construed as certainties rather than mere wishes.

174. In the first oracle it appears that Balaam is "acknowledging them as a blessed nation" (Levine, *Numbers 21–36*, 140) at the present rather than anticipating their future blessedness.

175. The meaning of this line is clear regardless of the textual difficulties.

176. From a source-critical perspective, Exod 23 is regarded as the Elohistic articulation of the blessings and curses, Lev 26 that of the Priestly writer(s), and Deut 28 that of the Deuteronomist. Although there are distinguishing features of each and differences in emphasis, the function of the blessings in each appears to be the same.

177. The Decalogue consists primarily of stipulations rather than covenant blessings and curses. However, the reward of long life in the land is tied to honoring one's parents in both versions (Exod 20:12; Deut 5:16).

The Progeny Blessing in the Old Testament Outside the Latter Prophets

once Israel is settled in the land: food and water (v. 25), health (v. 25), progeny, (v. 26), and long life (v. 26). "None will miscarry[178] nor be barren in the land" (לֹא תִהְיֶה מְשַׁכֵּלָה וַעֲקָרָה בְּאַרְצֶךָ) clearly implies the birth of more children since all who desire children will bear them. Furthermore, the promise of long life (אֶת־מִסְפַּר יָמֶיךָ אֲמַלֵּא) will result in the multiplication of the population as a whole. These blessings are contingent upon their worship of Yahweh alone once in the land (vv. 24–25a; cf. vv. 22, 32–33), with the threat of curse in the event of failure (vv. 21b, 33b).

Verses 27–31 return to the conquest itself, explaining that it will be gradual "until you are fruitful and take possession of the land" (עַד אֲשֶׁר תִּפְרֶה וְנָחַלְתָּ אֶת־הָאָרֶץ, v. 30). Thus the proliferation of the people is not only a conditional blessing once the land is settled but a guarantee for the period between the exodus and the completed conquest, since becoming more numerous is a precondition for complete settlement.

Leviticus 26 consists of a more comprehensive and structured list of blessings (vv. 4–13) that accompany obedience to Yahweh's laws (v. 3), followed by a long list of corresponding curses (vv. 16–39)[179] that result from disobedience (vv. 14–15, 21, 23, 27). Unlike Exod 23, Lev 26 focuses entirely on the blessings that Israel will enjoy once she has settled in the land. Toward the end of the list, the progeny blessing appears in its "Priestly" articulation: "I will make you fruitful and multiply you" (וְהִפְרֵיתִי אֶתְכֶם וְהִרְבֵּיתִי אֶתְכֶם, v. 9).

Interestingly, the progeny blessing is immediately followed by a reference to "my covenant" (וַהֲקִימֹתִי אֶת־בְּרִיתִי אִתְּכֶם). Is this a reference to the Abrahamic covenant? If it is, the covenant is being maintained/upheld[180] specifically by means of Yahweh's continual multiplication of the people but by the other blessings as well. Or is it a reference solely to the Sinai covenant? If so, the progeny blessing no longer enjoys a special role, but is simply one desirable blessing among many for the enjoyment of life within the land. When initiated by Yahweh, the word בְּרִית occurs only in ch. 26

---

178. The Piel of שָׁכַל can convey either miscarriage (e.g., Gen 31:38; Job 21:10) or bereavement of existing children (e.g., Gen 42:36; Lev 26:22). Whether the child is lost before or after birth, the effect is the same.

179. Not surprisingly, the aim of many of the curses is population *decimation*: death by the sword of enemies (vv. 17, 25), bereavement (וְשִׁכְּלָה; cf. Exod 23:26) of children by beasts (v. 22), reduction in numbers (וְהִמְעִיטָה, the antonym of וְהִרְבֵּיתִי in v. 9; v. 22), eating one's own children (v. 29), and "rotting away" (יִמָּקּוּ) in exile (v. 39).

180. וַהֲקִימֹתִי אֶת־בְּרִיתִי typically denotes the maintenance of a previously enacted covenant rather than the creation of a new one (e.g., Gen 17:7, 9, 19, 21; Exod 6:4; see Hartley, *Leviticus*, 463; Milgrom, *Leviticus 23–27*, 2343–46). This is true regardless of whether this is a reference to the Abrahamic or Sinai covenant.

in Leviticus. Among the other occurrences, those in vv. 15 and 25 clearly refer to the Sinai covenant and vv. 44 and 45 likely do.[181] However, the Abrahamic covenant is in view in the three occurrences of בְּרִית in v. 42. The possibility of future restoration from exile appears to be grounded in Yahweh's faithfulness to both covenants (vv. 40–45), suggesting that the two are not to be seen as separate but complementary, the Sinai covenant serving as a "renewed and expanded" version of the covenant with the patriarchs.[182] The context of v. 9, the offer of blessing or curse depending on Israel's obedience to Yahweh's laws, is clearly that of the Sinai covenant. However, it seems likely that the Abrahamic covenant is in view here as well since the juxtaposition of "my covenant" and the progeny blessing recalls the connection between these concepts in the Abrahamic covenant (cf. Gen 17:2, 6–7; note וַהֲקִמֹתִי אֶת־בְּרִיתִי in v. 7).

Therefore, Lev 26:9 appears to treat the Abrahamic and Sinai covenants as complementary, establishing continuity not only between these two covenants but also between the role of the progeny blessing in both as well. The blessing, central to Yahweh's covenant with Abraham, remains active despite fulfillment in Exod 1:7. It now functions within the contingencies of the Sinai covenant and is supplemented by other material and spiritual blessings, but it remains an Abrahamic blessing.[183] Since all the blessings of vv. 3–13 contribute to the retention of the land and the proliferation of the people, the blessings of the Sinai covenant underscore and elaborate upon the promises of the Abrahamic covenant.

In summary, following realization of the Abrahamic progeny blessing, Yahweh will continue to multiply Israel prior to entry into the land (Exod 23:30). Further multiplication in the land remains a possibility, given covenant obedience (Exod 23:26; Lev 26:9). However, even if curse rather than blessing is incurred, Lev 26:40–45 promises that, should they confess their sin, Yahweh will "remember" (וְזָכַרְתִּי, vv. 42, 45) his covenant, implying a future for the progeny blessing beyond covenant breach and exile.[184]

---

181. See Milgrom, *Leviticus 23–27*, 2337, 2339.

182. Ibid., 2344.

183. Hartley, *Leviticus*, 463 and Wenham, *Leviticus*, 329, see the progeny blessing in v. 9 as a reference to the further "fulfillment" of the Abrahamic blessings.

184. The biblical portrayal of the progeny blessing continues to cut across the traditional source-critical divisions of the Pentateuch: E (Exod 1:8–12, 20–21), P (Exod 1:7), and D (Deut 26:5) all attest to fulfillment in Egypt, and E (Exod 23:26), P (Lev 26:9), and D (Deut 28:4, 11) all foresee a future for the blessing contingent upon covenant faithfulness, listing the progeny blessing among their respective catalogues of covenant blessings.

The Progeny Blessing in the Old Testament Outside the Latter Prophets

DEUTERONOMY

In three major addresses (1:5—4:40; 5:1—28:69[29:1]; 29:1[29:2]—30:20), Moses recounts in Deuteronomy what Yahweh has graciously done for Israel in the past, describes how she is now to respond to such grace as she enters the land, and looks well into the future that entails eventual exile, but promises restoration beyond it. Thus it comes as no surprise that no other book within the OT exhibits as many facets of the progeny blessing as does Deuteronomy so that every major strand of the progeny blessing pertaining to Israel is present. Indeed, one could derive a mini-OT theology of the progeny blessing almost entirely from Deuteronomy. Deuteronomy acknowledges Yahweh's past multiplication of Israel, explicates the conditions for further multiplication, and predicts population decimation and subsequent proliferation in the distant future.

The Covenant Blessings of Deuteronomy

Given Israel's imminent entry into the land of Canaan, it is not surprising that the land is a central focus throughout the book.[185] The land is graciously given to Israel on the basis of the promise to "your fathers" (אֲבֹתֶיךָ; e.g., 1:8; 6:10; 11:9; 19:8; 27:3). Even though land retention is the result of obedience (e.g., 5:33), the land itself is not referred to as a blessing—although the agricultural benefits of the land are. Rather, the land is the setting in which the covenant blessings will be enjoyed (e.g., 15:4; 23:20; 28:8, 11; 30:5, 16) as well as the geographical context for Torah observance.[186] The fulfillment of the progeny promise to Abraham took place in Egypt, outside the promised land. From now on, further multiplication of Israel will be tied to possession of the land. Moreover, population decimation will be strongly associated with loss of land.

When Deuteronomy is subdivided into a covenant structure on the basis of parallels to other ancient Near Eastern treaty documents,[187]

---

185. In Deuteronomy, Moses "defines the shape and character of new Israel, of Israel in the land and for the land and over the land" (Brueggemann, *The Land*, 44).

186. Note particularly the introduction to the laws of Deut 12–26 in 12:1. As Wehmeier summarizes, "For Deuteronomy the blessing does not consist in the gift of the land itself—this idea is always related to God's oath—but in the maintenance and furthering of Israel's life within the promised land" ("Deliverance and Blessing," 38).

187. After surveying the formal ANE treaty evidence, Kitchen concludes that the OT covenant-like documents in Exodus, Deuteronomy, and Josh 24 are closest to the Hittite treaties, and would fit best in the period of 1400–1200 BCE (Kitchen, *On the*

67

28:1–14 alone is typically identified as "covenant blessings." This is certainly the climactic and most comprehensive presentation of the blessings since it is only here that both blessing and curse are unfolded as the opposing results of Israel's response to the covenant. However, conditional promises of blessings are present throughout the book, primarily in Deut 4–11 (see 7:12–16 as the most comprehensive). At times blessing is simply summarized as life (תִּֽחְיוּ; 4:1; 5:33; 6:24; 8:1; 16:20; 30:16, 19), well-being (יִיטַב לְךָ; 4:40; 5:16, 29, 33; 6:3, 18, 24; 12:25, 28; 22:7; 28:63; 30:5), longevity in the land (תַּאֲרִיךְ יָמִים עַל־הָאֲדָמָה; 4:40; 5:16, 33; 6:2; 11:9; 17:20; 22:7; 25:15; 30:20; 32:47), or "blessing" itself (הַבְּרָכָה; 7:13; 11:26–27; 14:29; 15:4, 6, 10, 18; 23:20; 24:19; 30:16, 19).[188] When specified, blessing consists of especially fertility of the land (6:3, 10–11; 7:13; 8:7–10; 11:9–15; 16:15; 27:3; 28:4–5, 8, 11–12; 30:9), of people (6:3; 7:13–14; 8:1; 13:17; 28:4, 11; 30:5, 9, 16), and of animals (7:13–14; 8:13; 28:4, 11; 30:9). In addition, blessing entails supremacy over enemy peoples (7:1–2, 16, 22–24; 11:23–25; 15:6; 28:7, 10, 12), health (7:15), and the special favor of Yahweh (7:12–13; 28:1, 9; 29:12[13]).

As in the ancient Near Eastern treaties, the blessings and curses play a vital role in Deuteronomy, encouraging covenant faithfulness and enforcing the relationship with the suzerain[189]—the blessings as motivation for

---

Reliability, 286–88; cf. Kline, *Treaty*, 42–43). The seventh-century dating of Deuteronomy that has been widely accepted since de Wette and Wellhausen is not compelling, and it is quite plausible that the book could have been written in the second millennium BCE, accurately preserving the speeches of Moses (See Block, "Recovering," 403; Kitchen, *On the Reliability*, 299–307). Based on his evaluation of common arguments in favor of the seventh-century date (see *Grace in the End*, 45–64), J. G. McConville rightly concludes that "the tendency to date Deuteronomy in the seventh century owes much to habit; the data themselves are capable of quite other constructions" (*Grace in the End*, 56–57). However, this question is of secondary importance for our purposes since we are tracing the development of the progeny blessing based on Israel's understanding of her own faith and history in the context of the final form of the text and the completion of the canon.

188. Note Deut 5:33 as an example of the first three expressions: "You are to walk in all the way which Yahweh your God has commanded you in order that you may live and that it may go well with you and that your days may be long in the land you are about to possess." Nearly all of these expressions of blessing directly follow the condition of obedience.

189. See, e.g., Miller, *Deuteronomy*, 194; Olson, *Deuteronomy*, 120; Tigay, *Deuteronomy*, 497. Steymans offers three options for the illocutionary function of Deut 28 from a speech-act perspective: 1) Moses is commanding a ritual; 2) Moses appeals for obedience based on predictions of blessing and curse contingent upon Israel's response to the commands; 3) Moses invokes blessing and curse upon the people contingent upon their response to the commands (*Deuteronomium 28*, 202–7). The second option

The Progeny Blessing in the Old Testament Outside the Latter Prophets

obedience and the curses as a deterrent against disobedience. Such sanctions were carried out by Yahweh himself, undergirded by the belief that he is ultimately responsible for all historical processes of cause and effect, i.e., "the interdependence of divine, human, and natural worlds."[190] Thus, the aim of the promise of blessing is perfect harmony between Yahweh, Israel, and the land, and blessing itself is the fruit and visible demonstration of such harmony, ultimately so that Israel and her God will acquire fame among the nations (26:18–19; 28:10).

Yahweh's Past Blessing of Progeny

In his recollection of Yahweh's actions on behalf of Israel in the past, Moses primarily emphasizes Yahweh's care for the people in the wilderness and their recent military victories. However, Deut 1:10, 10:22, and 26:5 recount his past multiplication of the people.

Moses begins his review of the history of Israel's relationship with Yahweh by recalling the command at Horeb to set out for the land "sworn" (נִשְׁבַּע) to "your fathers, to Abraham, to Isaac, and to Jacob" (1:8). This is immediately followed by an account of leadership delegation (1:9–18; cf. Exod 18:13–23; Num 11:14–17). However, the very point in recounting this episode may lie in the cause for delegation, namely, the multiplication of the people. Moses' claim that Yahweh has "multiplied" (הִרְבָּה) them so that they are "today like the stars of heaven in number" (הַיּוֹם כְּכוֹכְבֵי הַשָּׁמַיִם לָרֹב) uses the language of the promise to Abraham (Gen 15:5; 22:17; 26:4; Exod 32:13), clearly alluding to it in light of vv. 8 and 11. Moses thus affirms with other texts (Gen 46:3; 47:27; Exod 1:7) that the promise was fulfilled in Egypt.[191]

In the context of an appeal to his audience for covenant fidelity (10:12—11:32), Moses again refers to the fulfilled progeny blessing using the same "stars" metaphor (10:22). This time, previous "great and awesome

---

appears to fit best given other statements of blessing throughout the book and since most of Deut 28 consists of predictions of Yahweh's actions. However, the formulae of Deut 28:3–6, 16–19 may function as invocations (as in the third option).

190. Olson, *Deuteronomy*, 120.

191. See Block, *Deuteronomy*, 64; McConville, *Deuteronomy*, 65; Miller, *Deuteronomy*, 28. Juxtaposed with v. 8, this account may function theologically to instill in Israel confidence that Yahweh will indeed fulfill the land promise on the basis of his completed fulfillment of the progeny promise. Furthermore, as McConville (*Deuteronomy*, 159–60) notes, "[s]uch an expansion was a necessary practical condition of filling, and thus holding, the promised land."

deeds" (אֶת־הַגְּדֻלֹּת וְאֶת־הַנּוֹרָאֹת; 10:21), of which the multiplication of Israel from only seventy people appears to be one, form the basis for Israel's obligation to fear and serve (10:20) as well as love and obey Yahweh (11:1; cf. 10:12–13).[192]

The procedure for the annual offering of first fruits in 26:1–11 (cf. Exod 23:16, 19; 34:22, 26; Lev 23:10; Num 28:26; Deut 16:9–12) is especially significant. This includes the recitation of a succinct confession (vv. 5b–10a)[193] encapsulating Yahweh's gracious work: proliferation in Egypt (v. 5b), deliverance from Egyptian bondage (vv. 6–8), and the gift of the land (v. 9). Here Israel confesses that she "became a great nation, mighty and populous" (לְגוֹי גָּדוֹל עָצוּם וָרָב; v. 5), employing three adjectives for emphasis and echoing the Abrahamic promise yet again (see Gen 12:2; 46:3). In this summary, God's great act of deliverance in the exodus is juxtaposed with two blessings, that of progeny and land, the very two material blessings promised to Abraham. Multiplication here is not one blessing among many but elevated in importance, since it appears alongside the most prominent act (the exodus) and gift (the land) of Yahweh.

However, these three texts using hyperbolic language to describe Israel's growth are tempered by other texts in Deuteronomy that acknowledge that Israel is still smaller than the peoples whom she is about to displace. Moses reminds Israel periodically that these seven nations are "more populous and stronger than you" (גּוֹיִם רַבִּים וַעֲצוּמִים מִמֶּךָ; 7:1), but Israel will defeat them despite this (cf. also 7:17; 9:1; 11:23; 20:1). In fact, Yahweh's election is not due to Israel's size but despite it, "for you were the fewest of all peoples" (כִּי־אַתֶּם הַמְעַט מִכָּל־הָעַמִּים; 7:7). Such statements do not contradict Deut 1:10, 10:22, and 26:5,[194] but they do place them in proper historical and theological perspective, underscoring Yahweh's gracious election without negating his gracious blessing of progeny.

---

192. It is not altogether clear whether 10:22 refers to the present conquest generation as the fulfillment of the progeny promise or to God's blessing in Egypt. Perhaps the latter is more likely since the exodus generation is in view in 1:10 where the same metaphor is used. However, there may be no need to choose between these options since the population of the conquest generation remained approximately the same as that of the exodus generation according to Num 1 and 26.

193. Von Rad has isolated vv. 5b–9 from its present context as possibly Israel's most ancient "historical credo" containing "the principle facts of God's redemptive activity" ("Form-Critical Problem," 4; see 3–5).

194. *Contra* Tigay, *Deuteronomy*, 87; Weinfeld, *Deuteronomy 1–11*, 369.

The Progeny Blessing in the Old Testament Outside the Latter Prophets

The Conditional Progeny Blessing in the Land

As is the case in Exod 23:26, 30 and Lev 26:9, fulfillment of the initial promise to Abraham does not imply that further multiplication is no longer in Yahweh's intentions for Israel. This is first evident in Deut 1:10–11 where, immediately following his declaration that the blessing has been realized, Moses proclaims, "May Yahweh, the God of your fathers, cause you to increase (יֹסֵף) a thousand times more than you are and bless you, just as he has promised you!" Although this is a wish/prayer (jussive) rather than a prediction, it appears that Yahweh's promise of multiplication ideally will entail further multiplication, reflecting the "already and not yet" experience of Yahweh's blessings that typifies Deuteronomy.[195]

The progeny blessing figures prominently in promises of blessing that recur throughout the book. At the end of a series of imperatives to obey Yahweh's commands and promises of resulting well-being (5:23—6:3), a final charge in v. 3a is followed by its goal: "so that it may go well with you and so that you may multiply greatly (תִּרְבּוּן מְאֹד), just as Yahweh, the God of your fathers, has promised you, in[196] a land flowing with milk and honey" (v. 3b). Similarly, the people are exhorted to respond in obedience in 8:1a "in order that you may live and multiply (וּרְבִיתֶם) and enter and possess the land that Yahweh swore to your fathers" (v. 1b). In the context of instructions concerning spoil (13:17–18[16–17]), one result of obedience is "that [Yahweh] may multiply you (וְהִרְבֶּךָ), just as he swore to your fathers" (13:18[17]; cf. also 1:10–11).

None of these three texts lists material covenant blessings such as agricultural prosperity or sovereignty over enemy peoples. Rather, these statements employ general terms for well-being, suggesting that progeny is not considered to be just one of many potential material blessings, but perhaps a fundamental or particularly important one. Its significance here seems to lie in the fact that each text cites the promise or oath God made with the fathers, linked specifically to multiplication in 6:3 and 13:18[17] and to the land in 8:1, probably references to the Abrahamic promises (see below). Thus, God promises prosperity (e.g., "life," "it will go well") in the land and the proliferation of the people as the benefits of covenant fidelity within the Sinai covenant in order to maintain and further these same benefits promised to Abraham.

195. See McConville, *Deuteronomy*, 65. Moses' desire to see Israel expand is further reflected in his blessings on the tribes (33:6, 17, 20).

196. Although the preposition is lacking in the Hebrew, this phrase appears to function as a locative adverbial phrase.

I Will Surely Multiply Your Offspring

The progeny blessing is contingent upon obedience in 7:12–16 as well. In this case, the charge is followed by a fuller description of blessing (vv. 13–16). This list is prefaced by a general statement of blessing: "[Yahweh] will love you, bless you, and multiply you" (וַאֲהֵבְךָ וּבֵרַכְךָ וְהִרְבֶּךָ; v. 13a),[197] verifying again that multiplication is not simply one blessing among many, but plays a pivotal role for Israel since it is one of the Abrahamic promises.[198] Verses 13b–16 then provide details. Blessing in general (as we have seen previously) primarily consists of fertility in the land: of humans (פְּרִי־בִטְנְךָ),[199] of the ground (פְּרִי־אַדְמָתֶךָ), and of domestic animals (v. 13b). Multiplication is not the primary focus in this case, but rather a component of the comprehensive fertility blessing. However, the progeny blessing is again in focus in v. 14b, where it is expressed negatively as the lack of barrenness (and supported in v. 15 by lack of disease), likely in verbal dependence upon Exod 23:26.[200] Thus it appears that the exposition of blessing in the land in Deut 7:13–16 treats the progeny blessing both as a foundational blessing (v. 13a) and as simply one blessing among others (vv. 13b, 14b).

In the climactic catalogue of covenant blessings and curses in Deut 28, the blessings and curses are presented with parallel structures: 1) an opening condition of obedience (vv. 1–2) or disobedience (v. 15); 2) concise formulas conveying the comprehensiveness of blessing (vv. 3–6) and curse (vv. 16–19); and 3) detailed blessings (vv. 7–14) and curses (vv. 20–68) that emphasize divine agency, interspersed with reiterations of the basic condition (see vv. 9, 13–14 within the blessings). Fertility is at the heart of the introductory blessing formulas (vv. 4–5), enclosed by statements invoking blessing at all places (v. 3) and at all times (v. 6). In v. 4a the same three aspects of fertility are mentioned as in 7:13b (בָּרוּךְ פְּרִי־בִטְנְךָ וּפְרִי אַדְמָתְךָ וּפְרִי בְהֶמְתֶּךָ), expanding on animal fertility in v. 4b and land fertility in v. 5. Within the detailed blessings, which deal

197. See Block, *Deuteronomy*, 212. It appears that the Masoretes understood this as a summary as well, dividing the verse with the *athnach* unusually early at וְהִרְבֶּךָ.

198. Tigay sees this as a clear reference to the Abrahamic covenant since two out of the three elements of the promises are mentioned, namely, blessing and progeny (*Deuteronomy*, 88). The third, land, is cited at the end of v. 13 in connection with the promise to the fathers.

199. This expression is a common Deuteronomic articulation of the progeny blessing (7:13; 28:4, 11; 30:9) and always occurs alongside fertility of land and animals. Only in Ps 127:3 does this expression denote the progeny blessing outside Deuteronomy.

200. Weinfeld demonstrates the literary relationship between the covenant blessings of Exod 23:20–33 and Deut 7:12–26, asserting that the latter is dependent upon and expands the former (*Deuteronomy 1–11*, 377–82).

The Progeny Blessing in the Old Testament Outside the Latter Prophets

primarily with fertility of the land (vv. 8, 11–12), Israel's relationship to her enemies (vv. 7, 10, 12–13), and her special relationship with Yahweh (vv. 9–10), v. 11 reiterates the three-fold fertility formula. Within the blessings of 28:1–14, fertility plays a prominent role, but (as in 7:13b) there is nothing conspicuous about the multiplication of humanity in particular.

Moses presents Israel with the final, climactic, choice between "life and death, blessing and curse" (v. 19) in 30:15–20, echoing earlier texts (e.g., 11:26–28; 27:12–13; 28:1, 15). In this summation of many of the themes of the book, the intent and result of love of God and obedience to his commands (v. 16a) are that "you will live and multiply (וְרָבִיתָ) and Yahweh your God will bless you in the land which you are entering to possess" (v. 16b). This coalescence of the themes of multiplication, blessing, and land is unmistakably Abrahamic, a thesis verified by v. 20b, which mentions the three patriarchs by name in connection with the land promise. Thus the final choice regarding covenant faithfulness in Deuteronomy is framed in part using Abrahamic terms, demonstrating the continuity of the covenants made with Abraham and the nation of Israel.

These texts may appear to be contradictory since the language of conditionality ("if you obey") is at times juxtaposed with the language of unconditionality ("you will receive the promised blessings"). However, this tension may be more apparent than real, since the promise itself presupposes contingency, even in the Abrahamic covenant. Divine grace and human obligation within the covenant relationship remain intertwined both in the Abrahamic and Sinai covenants to the extent that it may not be fully possible to separate conditional from unconditional aspects of the relationship. Israel knows that Yahweh is inclined to bless graciously and that she must obey to receive blessing, but the way in which this dynamic unfolds in a given context or situation cannot be fully anticipated.[201] Deuteronomy's emphasis on Israel's obligation to respond to God's grace with loyalty suggests that the blessings are primarily conditional for any given generation,[202] although the book is filled with grace as well.

201. According to Walter Brueggemann, *Theology of the Old Testament*, 419, "[t]he attempt to factor out conditional and unconditional aspects of the covenant is an attempt to dissect and analyze the inscrutable mystery of an intimate, intense relation that, by definition, defies all such disclosure. Yahweh is all for Israel, and that includes both Yahweh's self-giving and Yahweh's intense self-regard." See Wright, *Mission of God*, 205–8.

202. The same might be said for the individual, since Deuteronomy smoothly oscillates between addressing the nation and addressing the individual. Generally speaking, Deuteronomy appears to address the nation, yet the nation obviously is made up of individuals who bear personal responsibility contributing to the whole.

Corresponding Curses of Decimation

Whereas the potential for blessing is emphasized throughout Deuteronomy, perhaps to stress Yahweh's intent for Israel, curses occur almost solely in 28:15–68. As in Lev 26, population decimation, the negation of the progeny blessing, is a prominent theme. If Israel fails to fulfill her covenantal obligation to conform her life to the ethical standards dictated by Yahweh, she will be cursed (אָרוּר) in the same realms of fertility in which she was to be blessed (vv. 17–18). The aim of the curses is destruction and death (עַד הִשָּׁמֶדְךָ וְעַד־אֲבָדְךָ; v. 20; cf. v. 45), and many of the specific curses, such as disease and sword (vv. 21–22) and eating one's own children in the midst of siege (vv. 52–57), accomplish this directly.

The clearest reversal of the progeny blessing occurs in a climactic description of the reversal of the exodus and all blessings enjoyed since Egypt (vv. 58–68), "a divine liquidation of the whole history of salvation."[203] If disobedient, Israel's proliferation will be reversed, emphasized first in v. 62a by comparing the end result of curse to the end result of former blessing: "you will be left few in number (מְתֵי מְעָט) whereas you were as the stars of heaven in number (כְּכוֹכְבֵי הַשָּׁמַיִם לָרֹב)." The first clause alludes to Deut 26:5 (מְתֵי מְעָט, referring to the seventy who went to Egypt; cf. 4:27)[204] while the second alludes to Deut 1:10 and 10:22, employing the favorite metaphor of Deuteronomy for the Abrahamic progeny blessing. Yahweh's delight underscores this complete reversal: "as Yahweh rejoiced (שָׂשׂ) in doing you good (לְהֵיטִיב אֶתְכֶם) and multiplying you (וּלְהַרְבּוֹת אֶתְכֶם), so he will rejoice (יָשִׂישׂ) in causing you to perish and destroying you" (v. 63). The reversal of the progeny blessing is followed by the reversal of the gift of the land, namely, exile (vv. 63b–68), even depicted as a return to Egypt (v. 68). Therefore, this final description of covenant curse (vv. 58–68) portrays Yahweh's judgment in the Sinai covenant as a revocation of the patriarchal blessings.[205] Although curse and exile are only a possibility in Deut 28, they are portrayed elsewhere as a future certainty (4:25–28; 29:21–28[22–29]; 31:16–21, 29), based in part on Israel's poor track-record (e.g., 9:12, 16, 23–24; 29:3[4]).

---

203. Von Rad, *Deuteronomy*, 176. See Head, "Curse," 218–26; Tigay, *Deuteronomy*, 271.

204. See Head, "Curse," 221.

205. See ibid., 222, 225.

The Progeny Blessing in the Old Testament Outside the Latter Prophets

The Progeny Blessing beyond Exile

Unlike extant ancient Near Eastern treaties,[206] curse and exile are not to be the last word. Restoration of blessing is graciously promised in 30:1–10 (cf. also 4:29–31). Although it continues to use common Deuteronomic language, this text is radical and surprising in that Yahweh appears to do for Israel everything that previously was expected of them in response to Yahweh.[207] Moses predicts that they will repent/return to Yahweh (v. 2).[208] Obedience is now a *gift* (vv. 2, 8, 10).[209] Whereas Yahweh once demanded that they circumcise their hearts (10:16), he will now do it himself (v. 6).

As a result, Israel will experience blessing in even greater measure. Addressing the future generation of exiled Israelites, Moses promises, "Yahweh your God will bring you into the land which your fathers possessed that you might possess it; and he will do good to you (וְהֵיטִבְךָ) and multiply you (וְהִרְבְּךָ) more than your fathers" (v. 5). The renewed promises of blessing conclude, "for Yahweh will again rejoice (יָשׁוּב לָשׂוּשׂ) over you for good (לְטוֹב) just as he rejoiced (שָׂשׂ) over your fathers" (v. 9b). These two verses allude unmistakably to 28:63,[210] depicting a reversal of the reversal of the Abrahamic promises so that the blessings of progeny, land, and טוֹב are reinstated and intensified. Indeed, vv. 4–7 depict the

---

206. See McConville, *Deuteronomy*, 425.

207. As von Rad aptly states, "our text can no longer be called an exhortation; it contains no admonitions, but, with regard to Israel's future, simple affirmative propositions, that is, it is clothed altogether in the style of prophetic predictions" (*Deuteronomy*, 183).

208. Verses 1–2 are often understood as the protasis and vv. 3f. as the apodosis, stressing Israel's initiative in repentance. However, the beginning of the apodosis is ambiguous, and it is quite likely that it begins in v. 1b with וַהֲשֵׁבֹתָ, placing the initiative even for repentance in Yahweh's hands (see Brettler, "Predestination," 175–77; see also Craigie, *Deuteronomy*, 361). Although this would create some tension between v. 2 and the "free will" thought of the rest of Deuteronomy, it coincides well with Yahweh's new action in v. 6. Furthermore, the כִּי clauses of vv. 1 and 10 are ambiguous. Verse 1a is best translated temporally since Yahweh's work throughout suggests certainty rather than mere possibility (cf. 4:29–31). In v. 10, the two כִּי clauses are probably best understood causally (see McConville, *Deuteronomy*, 428) or perhaps as asseveratives (Brettler, "Predestination," 177), again denoting certainty. Brettler ("Predestination," 185–87) concludes that since this deterministic thought is unique to Deuteronomy it must be a late addition influenced by Jeremiah. However, it is not at odds with the rest of the book to assert that Yahweh has determined from the beginning that he will deal with Israel in a new way following exile in order to preserve his promises (cf. 4:31).

209. See Olson, *Deuteronomy*, 128.

210. See Head, "Curse," 221; McConville, *Deuteronomy*, 408.

restoration of Israel's relationships to the land (vv. 4–5), to Yahweh (v. 6), and to the outside world (v. 7). The three-fold fertility formula, which is central to the two primary blessings lists of Deut in 7:13 and 28:4, 11 then reappears between predictions of future obedience (vv. 8, 10) in v. 9: וְהוֹתִירְךָ יְהוָה אֱלֹהֶיךָ בְּכֹל מַעֲשֵׂה יָדֶךָ בִּפְרִי בִטְנְךָ וּבִפְרִי בְהֶמְתְּךָ וּבִפְרִי אַדְמָתְךָ לְטוֹבָה. As in 7:12–16 and 28:1–14, the progeny blessing is stated twice in 30:1–10, underscoring its importance for the distant future as well as for the present. As in 7:12, the topical content of 30:5 indicates that this blessing is important due to God's prior promises to the patriarchs. Moreover, it is because of the patriarchal promises that the hope of Deut 30:1–10 exists at all.

Within the Pentateuch Deut 30:1–10 is not the only text that predicts a future for Israel beyond inevitable exile. Deuteronomy 4:29–31 simply predicts future repentance. Leviticus 26:40–45 promises that Yahweh will remember the covenant and the land (vv. 24, 45) conditioned upon confession of iniquity (vv. 40–41). However, only Deut 30:1–10 describes a return to the land and future blessing. These three texts bear a salvation-historical correspondence to the message of the Latter Prophets concerning repentance, blessing and restoration beyond exile. Deuteronomy 30:1–10 is of particular importance for our purposes in that this is the only text apart from the Latter Prophets that promises multiplication for Israel even following covenant breach and curse.

Continuity between the Abrahamic and Sinai Covenants

The projection of the multiplication blessing into the future presents an interesting question: since Deuteronomy attests that the blessing has already been realized (1:10; 10:22; 26:5), in what sense must the promise still be fulfilled? In other words, how does the Abrahamic promise relate to the further promise in the Sinai covenant? We cannot answer this question adequately without examining the relationship between these two covenants.

Deuteronomy frequently refers to that which Yahweh "swore to your fathers" (אָבוֹת appears as the indirect object of נִשְׁבַּע twenty-four times), linking the present generation to the past commitments of Yahweh to his people. In these formulations, "the land" is the most frequent direct object (הָאָרֶץ in 1:8, 35; 6:10, 18, 23; 8:1; 10:11; 19:8; 26:3, 15; 31:7; הָאֲדָמָה in 7:13; 11:9, 21; 28:11; 30:20; 31:20; 34:4). Other objects include הַבְּרִית (4:31; 7:12;

8:18), הַשְּׁבֻעָה (7:8), הַדָּבָר (9:5), and the progeny blessing (13:18[17]).²¹¹ Five additional texts refer to what Yahweh has "promised" (דִּבֶּר) to the fathers. In these, הָאָרֶץ (19:8; 27:3), the progeny blessing (1:11; 6:3) and peoplehood (29:12[13]) occur as the objects of the promise.

It is hard to overlook the fact that that which is predominantly promised or sworn to "the fathers" in Deuteronomy—namely, land and progeny—is the basic content of the covenant sworn to the patriarchs as recorded in Genesis. Deuteronomy 1:8–11 erases any doubt about the identity of the fathers at the outset of the book by equating them with Abraham, Isaac, and Jacob (v. 8). Verse eight refers to the land "sworn" to the patriarchs followed in v. 11 by progeny "promised" to Israel, the two material blessings of the Abrahamic covenant. Thereafter, the three patriarchs are named in five additional texts citing the promises to the fathers (6:10; 9:5; 29:12[13]; 30:20; 34:4), thus reminding Israel of the ancient nature of the promises of land and progeny. Therefore, "the fathers" in Deuteronomy generally refer to the patriarchs, although there are a few exceptions in which they appear to refer to the exodus generation (5:3) or to the present and future generations (30:5).²¹²

In light of these texts, we see a close interdependence between the Abrahamic and Sinai covenants throughout Deuteronomy.²¹³ Texts concerning the fulfillment of the promises to the patriarchs operate within the contingencies of Sinai (e.g., 7:12; 8:1; 11:8–9; 13:18–19[17–18]), providing a new context for the further realization of the promises. Perhaps none is more significant (or clearer) than the final choice presented in 30:15–20. Obedience, resulting in life and blessing, is opposed to disobedience, re-

---

211. The progeny blessing is also present in three of the texts (7:13; 8:1; 28:11) in which the land is the direct object.

212. Thomas Römer argues that the fathers throughout the book refer not to the patriarchs but to the exodus generation ("Deuteronomy," 112–38) and that the covenant refers to the covenant made at Horeb (122, 125–26). Based on a source and redaction-critical model, Römer asserts that Israel's history began in the exodus for the original text of Deuteronomy (122) and that the names of the patriarchs in Deuteronomy were late additions "to separate Deuteronomy from the Deuteronomistic History and reinforce the cohesiveness of the Pentateuch" (137; see his argument at length in his published dissertation, *Israels Väter*). See Norbert Lohfink's rebuttal of Römer, *Die Väter Israels*. Diachronic analysis aside, it is clear that in the final form of the text "the fathers" are usually the patriarchs.

213. Dumbrell rightly claims that a "basic theological aim [of Deuteronomy] is to unite the Sinai and Abrahamic covenants, to marry nation and land" (*Covenant and Creation*, 117). Similarly, von Rad: "Deuteronomy has fused together in a most intimate way the promise of the land made to the patriarchs and the tradition of the commandments given at Mt. Sinai" ("The Promised Land," 91).

sulting in death and curse, the contingencies of Sinai familiar throughout Deuteronomy. However, the summarized blessing employs Abrahamic categories rather than the language of Deut 28 (v. 16b), and the passage concludes by mentioning the land promise "to your fathers, to Abraham, Isaac, and Jacob" (v. 20b), conditional upon obedience (v. 20a).

The blessings in Deuteronomy suggest agreement among the two covenants as well, with the blessings of Sinai serving as an expansion of the Abrahamic promises. Although the summaries of blessing in the book are often expressed in Abrahamic terms, the most comprehensive lists of blessings (7:12–16; 28:1–14; 30:1–10) go beyond the basic categories of blessing, land, and progeny. However, even these texts are closely tied to Abraham (see 7:12; 30:5; and the allusion to 28:1–14 in 30:19). Furthermore, it appears that the individual blessings in these lists merely facilitate the retention and expansion of the blessings of land and progeny so that these remain the "core" blessings even in the context of the Sinai covenant. Fertility of land and domestic animals (7:13–14; 28:4–5, 8, 11–12; 30:9) guarantees the blessed quality of the land and preserves life. Power over enemy peoples (7:16; 28:7, 10, 12; 30:7) enables retention of the land and prevents decimation of the population.[214] Likewise, health (7:15) preserves life and enables Israel to continue to grow. All these blessings are expressions of the overarching blessing of Yahweh's favor (7:12–13; 28:1, 9). Similarly, all the curses result in decimation of the population, loss of enjoyment of the land, or loss of the land altogether, seen most clearly in 28:58–68.

Therefore, as with the covenants as a whole, with respect to the blessings and curses Deuteronomy holds Abraham and Sinai together without conflict. Sinai confirms the Abrahamic covenant, expanding its simpler promises and contextualizing them for a people about to take possession of the land. Even Sinai's demand of loyalty to Yahweh is analogous to the obedience required of Abraham (Gen 12:1; 18:19; 22:16–17; 26:5).[215]

---

214. In addition, one might argue that the position of Deuteronomy regarding enemy peoples corresponds to Abraham's relationship to the nations first stated in Gen 12:3, namely, that those who curse Israel will be cursed by Yahweh.

215. See Kline, *Treaty*, 23; *contra* Weinfeld, who accentuates the differences between the Abrahamic and Sinai covenants by arguing that the former is an unconditional grant (see Weinfeld, "Covenant of Grant," 184–203). Thus, it becomes difficult to view them as complementary. Youngblood criticizes Weinfeld's distinction and lists a number of texts that suggest that the exodus deliverance and the Sinai covenant are based on the Abrahamic covenant (Exod 2:24; 3:6; 6:4–5, 8; 32:13; Lev 26:42; Deut 1:8; 7:7–8), underscoring their unity ("Abrahamic Covenant," 42–44).

How, then, are these two progeny traditions related? Although it may be tempting to posit two separate promises and appeal to a distinction between the covenants in answer to this question, this seems impossible since even the future expectation of multiplication is grounded in the fulfillment of the promise to the patriarchs (1:11; 6:3; 13:18[17]). The answer may lie in an already-and-not-yet dynamic inherent in God's promises and in the nature of blessing. The promise of progeny has been realized. However, greater realizations of the promise remain possible because, unlike one-time deliverances or events, blessing usually can be not only maintained but also enjoyed in greater ways. These new possibilities for numerical growth that Yahweh intends for his people are based on the Abrahamic promise, but are now mediated through the Sinai covenant. Thus we should not refer to the previous realization of the blessing while in Egypt as the one and only fulfillment that rules out greater blessing. Perhaps the nature of the Abrahamic promise is better understood as an instance of OT "inaugurated eschatology" from the perspective of the conquest generation whereby they have received blessing, but will enjoy it even more if obedient. From the standpoint of Deuteronomy, the blessing beyond exile in Deut 30:1–10 is the ultimate manifestation of the progeny blessing for Israel.

Concerning the land promise, von Rad observes that "promises which have been fulfilled in history are not thereby exhausted of their content, but remain as promises on a different level, although they are to some extent metamorphosed in the process."[216] This is the case for the progeny blessing as well. The key metamorphoses from the fulfilled Abrahamic expectation are an increased emphasis upon Israel's covenant obligations as a condition for further blessing as well as a more complex manner of fulfillment that will entail decimation prior to greater multiplication.

Israel's History in the Land: From the Conquest to the Return from Exile

In the historical narratives that treat the period from the conquest to the return from exile, the Sinai covenant, and particularly its Deuteronomic expression, dictates the experience of Israel. Israel's covenant faithfulness is rewarded and her apostasy is punished, although not apart from much

---

216. Gerhard von Rad, "The Promised Land," 93. Similarly, Clines asserts that although the promise has been fulfilled, "it has not yet been completely fulfilled. . . . [I]ts scope is understood as continually broadening" (*Theme of the Pentateuch*, 63).

patience and mercy from Yahweh. Little is said in these books regarding the promise to Israel of numerous progeny or its realization, perhaps for several reasons: 1) The authors of the historical narratives seldom cite these earlier promises or explicitly note their fulfillment. Instead, they *describe* and *demonstrate* blessing or curse rather than simply state, for example, the enjoyment of blessing, as Deuteronomy frequently does. 2) This paucity of references to multiplication also may be due to the fact that Israel's history is largely one of failure and curse rather than of success and blessing. 3) Furthermore, the final author/editor may have regarded the Abrahamic promise of progeny to have been realized, in confirmation of Deut 1:10; 10:22; 26:5.[217] Nevertheless, these books contribute to a fuller understanding of the progress of the progeny blessing, primarily through tracing the growth of Israel.

Joshua

The book of Joshua is concerned almost solely with obtaining the land promised to the fathers (1:6; 21:43), documenting the conquest of the land in Josh 1–12 and its division among the tribes in Josh 13–21. Although some of the territory of Canaan remains unconquered (13:1–7, 13; 16:10; 17:12–13; 23:5), in Josh 21:43–45, "a theological conclusion" to the book thus far,[218] the narrator nevertheless affirms that Yahweh has given them "all the land" (v. 43), rest in the land (v. 44a), and dominion over all their enemies (v. 44b) to the extent that "not one promise among all the good promises that Yahweh promised to the house of Israel failed; everything came about" (v. 45; cf. Josh 11:16–23; 23:14). Although this statement pertains primarily to the corporate and individual[219] land promises, it likely encompasses the previously-fulfilled progeny promise as well. Interestingly, as with the progeny blessing, fulfillment of the Abrahamic land promise does not preclude future greater realizations (cf. 1 Kgs 5:1[4:21], 4[4:24]).

---

217. Regardless of whether or not one accepts Martin Noth's theory regarding the creation of the Deuteronomistic History encompassing Deuteronomy–Kings (see Noth, *Deuteronomistic History*), these books bear the mark of a common theology, and thus it is preferable to read Joshua–Kings together with Deuteronomy. As Wolff notes, Joshua–Kings "dialogue between the Deuteronomic tradition and the contemporary situation" ("Kerygma of the Yahwist," 91).

218. Butler, *Joshua*, 234. See also Howard, Jr., *Joshua*, 397.

219. Namely, the promises to Caleb (Josh 14:6–15; 15:13–19) and the daughters of Zelophehad (Josh 17:3–6).

The Progeny Blessing in the Old Testament Outside the Latter Prophets

According to the book of Joshua, this era was characterized not only by military success but also by obedience and covenant faithfulness to Yahweh (Josh 24:31; cf. 22; 24:14–28). Accordingly, with the exception of Josh 7, God repeatedly grants Israel victory in battle (2:24; 6:21; 8:24–26; 10:10–11, 28–43; 11:8–14), which paves the way for further multiplication by conquering enemy peoples who could be an obstacle to future growth. At this point, with the exception of Rahab, there is little indication that the inclusion of these foreign peoples into the Israelite community will contribute to the multiplication of Israel.

Overt references to the progeny blessing occur in Josh 17:14–18 and 24:3-4. In 17:14–18 the tribes of Joseph complain about the size of their land allotment since they are "numerous" (עַם־רָב) on account of having been "blessed" (בֵּרְכַנִי) by God (v. 14), a claim that Joshua verifies (v. 17; cf. Deut 33:17).

Joshua 24 records a covenant renewal ceremony in light of possession of the land, and contains the typical elements of covenant documents. The introductory "historical prologue" documenting the history of the relationship (vv. 2b–13) begins with the patriarchs, recalling that Yahweh "multiplied [Abraham's] seed" (אֶת־זַרְעוֹ [Qere] וָאַרְבֶּה) upon arrival in Canaan. The initial generations of the patriarchs appears to be in mind, prior to migration to Egypt (vv. 3b–4). This is a unique expression for the progeny blessing in two respects: 1) Thus far, statements affirming that Yahweh has multiplied his people in the past have always focused on the proliferation of Israel while in Egypt, as in the historical summary in Deut 26:5b–9 (although Deut 10:22 may refer to the conquest generation). Joshua 24 cites the progeny blessing in conjunction with Abraham himself and not with reference to the sojourn in Egypt. 2) Although the pursuit of offspring is a driving concern in the patriarchal narratives and the initial patriarchal generations are the beginning of the fulfillment of the progeny promise to Abraham, these generations are never said elsewhere to constitute the "multiplication" (רָבָה) of Abraham's seed. This verb usually denotes multiplication on a grander scale. Joshua 24:3 thus focuses on God's supernatural action to fulfill the immediate promise of a son to Abraham rather than on his grander blessing of multiplying the people in Egypt. Perhaps Joshua emphasizes this stage in God's past provision of progeny in light of the occasion, namely, (re)possession of the land of Canaan. The patriarchal period was the only time in which God had provided progeny for his people while in the promised land, and drawing attention to this may give hope to the people that he will continue to do so now that they have returned to it.

Judges

The introductory chapters of Judges relate a sharp downward turn in the covenant faithfulness of Israel following the days of Joshua (Judg 2:7–10), initiating a cycle of syncretism and idolatry, divine anger, Israel's subjugation by her enemies, Yahweh's raising up of a deliverer, and worse idolatry (2:11–19). It does not appear that Judges is interested in tracing the population of Israel since casualty figures for Israel are rare and the narrator does not comment on her expansion as a people. However, the progeny motif is related to the larger theological point of the book. Yahweh will punish Israel, but he will remain faithful to his covenant commitment (cf. 2:1) despite Israel's apostasy, delivering her repeatedly, and thus preserving her. Judges never mentions Israel's decimation as a result of her subjugation to other peoples,[220] perhaps because the narratives focus on the deliverances rather than on oppression. The book does, however, note casualties resulting from in-fighting among the tribes of Israel (9:42–49; 12:6; 20:21, 25; 21:8–12), including the near-eradication of Benjamin (20:35, 46), demonstrating that decimation is not the work of Yahweh or enemy peoples alone, but is sometimes inflicted by Israel on herself.

Samuel

Similarly, the book of Samuel shows little interest in the progeny promise to Israel. As in Judges, the Samuel narratives record reductions of the population, whether in battle (1 Sam 4:10; 2 Sam 18:7) or as direct acts of God's judgment (1 Sam 6:19; 2 Sam 24:15). Nevertheless, the prophet Samuel confirms that "Yahweh will not abandon his people" (1 Sam 12:22). In 2 Sam 24, David's military census may well demonstrate the degree to which Israel has grown (see below). However, David's deed is not construed as a celebration of God's blessing on the people, but rather as a sinful act (vv. 1, 10) resulting in the curse of pestilence (v. 15).

The introduction of kingship, including the questions of whether and how it should be established, constitutes a major theme of the book of Samuel. Although there is no direct relationship established between the multiplication of the people and kingship, it is evident that good kingship benefits the people (see 2 Sam 5:12). The good king will model and encourage covenant faithfulness, so that a correlation will exist between the

---

220. However, the Philistines and Ammonites "crushed and oppressed" (וַיִּרְעֲצוּ וַיְרֹצְצוּ; Judg 10:8) Israel, which may imply decimation.

blessing of progeny on Israel and good kingship. Though unexpressed in Samuel, this correlation will be evident in Kings and will become explicit in the Prophets.

Furthermore, the Davidic covenant involves a personal "progeny promise" to David, namely that Yahweh will grant him an eternal "house," kingdom, and throne (2 Sam 7:16).[221] Although this refers to an enduring line rather than to a "great nation" as promised to Abraham, it is nevertheless noteworthy that each of the OT covenants (Noahic, Abrahamic, Sinai, Davidic, New) includes a promise or blessing of future progeny as a key element. Logically, the promise of progeny is necessary for a covenant to endure beyond the immediate recipient(s). At the same time, this underscores that God's OT covenants primarily endure through the offspring of the recipient(s) rather than through extending their benefits to other peoples or families. From this we may also infer that the blessing of life is the most fundamental gift from Yahweh to his people. The promise of descendants is not mundane. The consistency of this promise suggests that it is universally desirable and a precious gift not to be taken for granted.

Kings

At the beginning of the book of Kings we encounter a tacit acknowledgement of God's blessing of progeny. Prior to his request for wisdom, Solomon expresses that he is overwhelmed by his responsibilities as king, in part because the people are "too many to be counted or numbered" (לֹא־יִמָּנֶה וְלֹא יִסָּפֵר מֵרֹב ;3:8).

Kings depicts Solomon's reign as the time of the fulfillment of Yahweh's promises. Solomon himself declares on the occasion of the dedication of the temple that the Davidic (1 Kgs 8:20, 24) and Pentateuchal (1 Kgs 8:56) promises have been realized in his kingship.[222] In 1 Kgs 4:20—5:8[4:20–28], his reign is characterized as the pinnacle of Israel's enjoyment of blessing in the land. This summary of his reign begins, "Israel and Judah were as numerous as the sand on the sea (רַבִּים כַּחוֹל אֲשֶׁר־עַל־הַיָּם לָרֹב); they were eating and drinking and joyful"

---

221. Hamilton observes that the formulation "who will come from your body" (אֲשֶׁר יֵצֵא מִמֵּעֶיךָ) with respect to the promised offspring occurs only in Gen 15:4 and 2 Sam 7:12, suggesting that 2 Sam 7:12 may intentionally allude to the Abrahamic covenant, linking the covenants ("Seed of the Woman," 268).

222. See VanGemeren, *Progress of Redemption*, 233.

(v. 20; cf. 3:8).²²³ This depiction of abundant progeny and prosperity is then followed by a description of sovereignty over neighboring kingdoms, rule over a vast amount of land, agricultural abundance, security, and peace, corresponding precisely to the various facets of blessing found in the covenant blessings of Sinai.²²⁴ However, the progeny blessing itself uses the vocabulary of the Abrahamic promise (Gen 22:17; 32:13[12]). Furthermore, the extent of the land surely refers back to that which was promised to Abraham in Gen 15:18–21 (cf. also Deut 1:7). This interweaving of Abrahamic and Sinai blessings again suggests that there is ultimately no dichotomy between the covenants with Abraham and at Sinai with respect to the promised blessings.

But how does the realization of the progeny blessing here relate to previous fulfillments? The "sand" metaphor indicates that the progeny promise to the patriarchs has been and is still fulfilled. Yet its inclusion among the expanded blessings of the Sinai covenant in 1 Kgs 4:20—5:8[4:20–28] suggests that the greater realization of the progeny blessing promised at Sinai is now being enjoyed as well. Thus, scholars are right to point out that the extent of progeny and land in 1 Kgs 4:20—5:1[4:20–21] constitutes a fulfillment of the Abrahamic promises,²²⁵ but the fulfillment of the progeny element is not new. What is new is the fuller enjoyment of the Abrahamic progeny blessing as anticipated at Sinai. First Kings 4:20—5:8[4:20–28] may not intend to depict Solomon's reign as the perfect and ideal realization of the progeny blessing upon Israel, since Deut 30:5 predicts an even greater proliferation of the nation beyond exile and since the people presumably would have continued to expand had they and their kings remained faithful to Yahweh. However, this text does appear to identify Solomon's time as the zenith of Israel's historical experience of the covenant blessings, including that of progeny.

---

223. The Old Greek text does not include this verse, but it is present in all other Versions and Hebrew MSS. External evidence thus favors its inclusion.

224. See House, *1, 2 Kings*, 118. A comparison of 1 Kgs 4:20–5:8[4:20–28] with Deut 28:1–14 yields the following parallels:

Progeny: 4:20a and 28:4a, 11a
Agricultural abundance: 4:20b, 5:2[4:22], 8[4:28] and 28:4a, 5, 8, 11, 12
Subjection of other peoples: 5:1[4:21], 4[4:24] and 28:7, 10, 13
Abundant livestock: 5:3[4:23], 6[4:26], 8[4:28] and 28:4b, 11
Peace and security: 5:4b–5[4:24b–25]; not explicit in Deut 28, but present in Sinai blessings elsewhere (cf. Lev 26:6 for peace, Lev 26:5 and Deut 12:10 for security).

225. See Fretheim, *First and Second Kings*, 36–37; Nelson, *First and Second Kings*, 40; Provan, *1 and 2 Kings*, 56; VanGemeren, *Progress of Redemption*, 233.

Following Solomon's reign, as God had forewarned (1 Kgs 9:3–9), the blessed state of Israel slowly dissipates as king after king is unfaithful to Yahweh, ultimately leading to exile (2 Kgs 17:6–23; 25:21; cf. Deut 29:21–27[22–28]). Occasionally we detect a correlation between kingship and the progeny blessing: the reign of a disobedient king corresponds to population decimation, both of that king's own household (1 Kgs 14:7–20; 2 Kgs 9:7–10) and of the nation as a whole (2 Kgs 13:7).

Chronicles

Although Chronicles follows Samuel/Kings closely in many respects, it differs from these books in some key areas regarding the progeny blessing. Chronicles is more concerned with genealogies, lists of individuals and groups, and the sizes of these groups, citing more census numbers and battle figures than do Samuel/Kings.[226] Thus Chronicles may be more helpful when attempting to estimate population sizes throughout the monarchy (see below). Furthermore, Chronicles exhibits a retribution theology so that blessings reflect divine favor toward the king. One such manifestation of this favor is numerous progeny for the king (1 Chr 3:1–9; 14:2–7; 2 Chr 11:18–22; 13:21; 21:1–3). However, an untimely death is a result of disobedience (2 Chr 21:18–19; 24:25; 25:27–28; 33:24–25).[227]

In the midst of a list of prominent men involved in David's army and government (1 Chr 27), a brief aside (vv. 23–24) provides a new interpretation of David's census, previously recorded in 1 Chr 21. Although there is no clear allusion to the progeny blessing in this prior account, the Chronicler now writes that David limited his counting "because (כִּי) Yahweh had said he would multiply (לְהַרְבּוֹת) Israel as the stars of heaven" (v. 23). Whether the text implies that David,[228] or Joab (cf. 1 Chr 21:6), or God himself[229] is responsible for halting the census, the logic appears to be that to carry out a complete census would be tantamount to doubting God's progeny promise.[230]

---

226. Samuel/Kings include census figures in 2 Sam 24:9 and battle figures in 1 Kgs 12:21; 20:15; 2 Kgs 13:7; 24:16. Chronicles lists census figures in 1 Chr 5:17–18; 7:5; 12:23–40; 21:5–6; 23:3; 27:1–15; 2 Chr 17:14–19; 25:5; 26:13 and battle figures in 2 Chr 11:1; 13:3; 14:8; 28:6.

227. See Dillard, *2 Chronicles*, 78–79.

228. So Japhet, *1 & 2 Chronicles*, 474.

229. So Selman, *1 Chronicles*, 247.

230. So Knoppers, *1 Chronicles 10–29*, 898; Williamson, *1 and 2 Chronicles*, 177.

I Will Surely Multiply Your Offspring

As in 1 Kgs 3:8, Solomon cites the vast population of the people in his prayer for wisdom (2 Chr 1:9). But whereas in 1 Kgs 3 he mentions the size of Israel in order to explain why he is overwhelmed by his role as king, in 2 Chr 1:9 he cites Israel's size to acknowledge the greatness of the kingship Yahweh has granted him. Furthermore, whereas in 1 Kgs 3:8 Solomon simply states that the people are innumerable, here they are said to be "numerous as the dust of the earth" (רַב כַּעֲפַר הָאָרֶץ), one of the patriarchal metaphors (cf. Gen 13:16 and 28:14). Unlike 1 Kgs 3:8, then, this account stresses that the progeny promise to Abraham has been realized, couching the fulfillment of this promise in the context of Solomon's desire to see the fulfillment of Yahweh's promise to David. Solomon may thus express faith in Yahweh's ability to fulfill the Davidic promise on the basis of his fulfillment of the prior promise to Abraham.

Interestingly, Chronicles does not include a description of Solomon's reign similar to 1 Kgs 4:20—5:8[4:20–28], perhaps because the Chronicler is primarily interested in Solomon's kingship as it pertains to the temple and worship. Although elements of this description are present elsewhere (e.g., 2 Chr 9:25–26), there is no statement resembling 1 Kgs 4:20 regarding the progeny blessing. Given the differences between Kings and Chronicles in the episode concerning Solomon's prayer for wisdom, 2 Chr 1:9 may function in Chronicles similarly to 1 Kgs 4:20 in Kings, namely, to portray Solomon's reign as the zenith of enjoyment of the progeny blessing during the monarchy. However, there is no hint that such fulfillment in 2 Chr 1:9 may also entail the realization of the further promises of numerous progeny under the blessings of the Sinai covenant. This verse is probably best understood as a reaffirmation that God has fulfilled his promise to Abraham, even though Israel experiences it in an even greater way now than previously in Egypt or during the conquest.[231]

Nehemiah

In the context of confession of sin and recommitment to Yahweh, the post-exilic Israelite community recalls Yahweh's compassion (cf. vv. 17, 19, 27, 31) toward them from creation to the exile (Neh 9:5b–31). Given the emphatic fulfillment statement in Exod 1:7, it might be expected that the multiplication of the people would be included prior to the exodus

---

231. In addition, absent from Samuel/Kings, Chronicles notes that the family of Shimei did not "multiply" (הִרְבּוּ) like the sons of Judah" (1 Chr 4:27) and that the half-tribe of Manasseh in trans-Jordan "was numerous" or "multiplied" (רָבוּ; 1 Chr 5:23).

deliverance (perhaps between verses 8 and 9). Instead, it appears in the midst of the description of the conquest (vv. 22–25). The people confess that Yahweh "multiplied (הִרְבִּיתָ) their sons as the stars of heaven" (v. 23a). Throughout vv. 16–22, "they" refers to the exodus generation. The following verses then provide a transition to the next generation, noting that "their sons" (בְּנֵיהֶם) multiplied (v. 23a) and entered the land (v. 24a).[232] This need not imply that this was the first occasion on which the progeny promise was realized, but it may be included here rather than earlier in the text for two reasons: 1) The "stars" metaphor may be intended to echo the pronouncements of Moses in Deut 1:10 and 10:22 that address the conquest generation. 2) Since vv. 23b–25 recall the fulfillment of the land promise, and it is therefore at this point that the Abrahamic promises *as a whole* are realized, it is noted here that the progeny promise has been fulfilled as well, even if Yahweh had already made them a great nation while in Egypt.

The historical books are silent concerning a future, greater proliferation of the people of Israel beyond exile as in Deut 30:5, 9. That will be left to the Latter Prophets.

Excursus: The Interpretation of אֶלֶף and the Population of Israel

The focus of our study is the promises, realizations, and hindrances to God's blessing of progeny, not numbers. However, we cannot neglect to examine actual figures recorded at key points along the way in Israel's historical narratives since they ought to reflect the progress of the progeny blessing as described in the text. Unfortunately, our conclusions here must be tentative since determining Israel's actual population at *any* point in her history is fraught with difficulties.

In the exodus and conquest accounts, it is doubtful that אֶלֶף means "thousand" given archaeological evidence concerning population sizes in the second millennium BCE and intertextual difficulties this would create. For example, if we take the statements of Deut 7:1, 7 seriously, a population of nearly 3,000,000 for Israel would imply that there were at least seven times the inhabitants in the promised land at the time of the conquest, a figure that is preposterous archaeologically and beyond what

---

232. Clines (*Ezra, Nehemiah, Esther*, 196) and Williamson (*Ezra, Nehemiah*, 316) thus rightly note that the referent is the Num 26 census.

I Will Surely Multiply Your Offspring

the land has ever sustained in its history.[233] Furthermore, Exod 1:15 cites only two midwives for the entire population.

Numerous proposals have arisen to account for these seemingly large numbers.[234] Most satisfying is the recent explanation of C. J. Humphreys,[235] a modified form of G. E. Mendenhall's earlier theory regarding the meaning of אֶלֶף.[236] Based on the widely recognized fact that אֶלֶף can at times refer not to "a thousand" but rather to a family or military unit, he interprets Num 1:21 (שִׁשָּׁה וְאַרְבָּעִים אֶלֶף וַחֲמֵשׁ מֵאוֹת), for example, to mean, "46 troops and 500 men" rather than "46,500 men." As a result, the total census figure in Num 1:46 (שֵׁשׁ־מֵאוֹת אֶלֶף וּשְׁלֹשֶׁת אֲלָפִים וַחֲמֵשׁ מֵאוֹת וַחֲמִשִּׁים) originally read, "598 אֶלֶף (troops) and 5 אֶלֶף (thousand) and 550 men," a number later conflated when the former use of אֶלֶף was misunderstood. The total census of Num 1 would thus be 5,550 and that of Num 26 5,730, suggesting that the total population of Israel prior to the wilderness wanderings would have been around 20,000.[237] This proposal is enticing since it explains the text as we have it and since it yields numbers that are historically plausible without downplaying the extraordinary growth reported in Exod 1:7.[238] Since these revised figures still suggest that the population was approximately the same pre- and post-wanderings, this adjustment has limited relevance for the present work.

The historical books from the conquest to the return from exile contain many more large numbers documenting either battle participants or the size of a king's army tabulated through a census. Unfortunately, these numbers present us with some thorny interpretive issues as well: 1) numbers have been "peculiarly susceptible to [textual] corruption;"[239] 2) numbers often disagree in parallel texts between Samuel/Kings and

---

233. Cf. Fouts, "Defense," 377–78, 383 n. 31.

234. See helpful summaries in Allen, "Numbers," 680–88; E. W. Davies, "Mathematical Conundrum," 449–65.

235. Humphreys, "Number of People," 196–213; Humphreys, "Numbers in the Exodus," 323–28.

236. Mendenhall, "Census Lists," 52–66.

237. See Humphreys, "Number of People," 211.

238. Kitchen, *On the Reliability*, 265; Provan et al., *Biblical History*, 130–31; and Rendsburg, "An Additional Note," 392–95, are among those who have found Humphreys' arguments to be convincing (although Longman only expresses an "openness" to them in *Biblical History*).

239. Wenham, "Large Numbers," 20.

The Progeny Blessing in the Old Testament Outside the Latter Prophets

Chronicles;[240] and 3) many of the figures appear to be unrealistically large when אלף is translated as "thousand."

Regarding this last difficulty, on the basis of texts such as Judg 6:15 and Mic 5:1[2], Mendenhall has suggested that "*'Elef* originally referred to a subsection of a tribe; the term was then carried over to designate the contingent of troops under its own leader which the subsection contributed to the army of the Federation."[241] Alternatively, Wenham has proposed that in many instances אֶלֶף has been pointed incorrectly, and ought to be rendered as אַלּוּף, referring to a "commander" or the "professional, fully-armed soldier."[242] The latter translation makes particularly good sense of the narratives of the battles of Gibeah (Judg 20) and Ai (Josh 7–8).[243] Furthermore, this makes better sense of accounts such as 2 Chr 13:3 in which 400 אלף in Judah are pitted against 800 אלף in Israel resulting in 500 אלף Israelite casualties or 2 Chr 28:6 in which there were 120 אלף casualties from Judah in only one day of fighting.[244] The historical books would thus record only the involvement of the elite warriors in battles, representative of the larger fighting contingents involved.[245] If אלף is here understood as "thousands," the figures seem implausible.[246] These proposals are not without their problems[247] and do not easily make sense of all texts. At times one

---

240. J. Barton Payne ("Validity," 109–28) counts nineteen such disagreements and seeks to reconcile them. See also Wenham, "Large Numbers," 21–24.

241. Mendenhall, "Census Lists," 66.

242. Wenham, "Large Numbers," 25. Typically, this term denotes a tribal chief (e.g., Gen 36:10–30, 40–43; Zech 12:5–6). "Professional soldier" is an extension of this meaning that is not clearly attested elsewhere in the OT apart from this group of texts. However, the very fact that it fits well with many texts validates its consideration as a lost sense within the semantic domain of אַלּוּף.

243. See ibid., 25–26.

244. See ibid., 50–51.

245. See ibid., 42.

246. Even Payne, who conservatively attempts to translate אֶלֶף as "thousand" wherever possible, admits that this is not feasible in some cases, opting for Wenham's "trained warrior" interpretation for texts such as 1 Chr 21:5, 2 Chr 13:3, and 14:9 ("Validity," 214–17).

247. E.g., Dillard rejects both suggestions since they cannot make sense of the booty tally of 50 אלף camels, 250 אלף sheep, 2 אלף donkeys, and 100 אלף men in 1 Chr 5:21 (*2 Chronicles*, 222). He represents another common view, namely, that the figures are typological, hyperbolic, and serve theological purposes: "it is clear that large armies are an index of royal piety for the author (13:3; 14:8; 25:5; 26:11–15). The figure assigned to Jehoshaphat is roughly triple that assigned to Abijah, Asa, Amaziah, and Uzziah. . . . The Chronicler is seeking to show the degree to which divine favor rested on Jehoshaphat" (135; cf. also Japhet, *1 & 2 Chronicles*, 689). Fouts ("Defense," 383–87)

must simply make a judgment or suggest an emendation. However, they certainly merit our consideration, and nearly all scholars who attempt to accept the text apart from attributing these numbers to hyperbolic fabrication have adopted "military units"[248] or "trained warrior" as the meaning of אֶלֶף in order to make sense of it.

There is perhaps little that can be said regarding the progress of the progeny blessing on the basis of these figures since they serve military purposes and there is no indication that any of them are included in order to document the extent of this blessing. Moreover, given the uncertain meaning of אלף and the fact that these figures always represent only a portion of the population, attempts to calculate the population of Israel on the basis of the OT text remain highly speculative. Nevertheless, these figures may still reflect the general fluidity of the population of Israel.[249] Perhaps the safest way to trace this growth is through a comparison of the Num 26 census, David's census, and the largest battle figures from the divided monarchy. However, even this approach is not without difficulty, even if we assume the consistency of the use of אלף.[250]

---

draws a similar conclusion, arguing that inflated numbers were a common ANE "rhetorical device," citing several ANE texts where battle figures are far too big. Although it is possible that the OT writers are using hyperbolic figures intentionally, this interpretation is less likely than others that reinterpret אלף since the numbers often seem to be far too exact to be completely invented (as in Num 1 and 26). Furthermore, the proper interpretation of the ANE parallels may be just as nebulous as the OT numbers. Nor should we simply assume that the OT writers adopt common ANE practice in this regard.

248. See, e.g., Anderson, *2 Samuel*, 285; Kitchen, *On the Reliability*, 264–65; McCarter, Jr., *II Samuel*, 510; Selman, *2 Chronicles*, 407.

249. If one were to adopt the hyperbolic interpretation, it would be difficult to say anything at all concerning the growth or reduction of the population since there is no guarantee that any of the numbers reflect historical realities.

250. For example, we cannot simply assume that the size of military units remained constant or that the proportion of trained warriors to the population as a whole remained constant.

The Progeny Blessing in the Old Testament Outside the Latter Prophets

The conquest generation (Num 26:51)	601 אלף
David's census (2 Sam 24:9)	800 אלף in Israel; 500 אלף in Judah
David's census (1 Chr 21:5–6)	1,100 אלף in Israel; 470 אלף in Judah[251]
Civil war (2 Chr 13:3)	800 אלף in Israel; 400 אלף in Judah
Jehoshaphat's army (2 Chr 17:14–19)	780 אלף in Judah; 380 אלף in Benjamin
Amaziah's census (2 Chr 25:5)	300 אלף in Judah and Benjamin

Based on textual and archaeological evidence, scholars agree that the population of Israel in David's time was greater than in Moses'. For example, Wenham proposes that the exodus generation consisted of 70,000 people and that 500,000 Israelites lived during the United Monarchy.[252] Purely based on archaeological evidence, Finkelstein estimates that 21,000 Israelites were present in Canaan around 1150 BCE, and 51,000 by 1000 BCE.[253] William Dever estimates that "[B]y the 12th century, [the population of the hill country] had grown to ca. 50 thousand, by the 11th century to ca. 80 thousand, and in all likelihood to ca. 100 thousand by the mid-late 10th century."[254] Kitchen agrees that the population of Israel doubled from 1150–1000 BCE.[255] One might speculate that the population continued to grow during the divided kingdom, but it is difficult to say so with much confidence given the complications with numbers. This evidence appears to corroborate the outlook of Kings (and perhaps of Chronicles as well) that Israel experienced the progeny blessing in greater measure during Solomon's reign than at any previous time. First and Second Kings record no figures after Solomon's reign that can compete with David's census in size, leaving us with the impression that the blessing was never enjoyed in greater measure after Solomon's reign. Chronicles, however, records army sizes for subsequent kings that surpass David's census, perhaps suggesting that Israel continued to grow. Whether Chronicles intends to convey this, and whether this was historically the case, given the many complications we have cited, is difficult to say.

---

251. The figure of 1,100 אלף excludes Levi and Benjamin. In addition, it is not clear whether the 470 אלף from Judah are included in the 1,100 אלף. See Williamson for an explanation regarding the changes in Chronicles from Samuel (*1 and 2 Chronicles*, 145; see also Japhet, *1 & 2 Chronicles*, 377–78; Knoppers, *1 Chronicles 10–29*, 753).

252. See Wenham, "Large Numbers," 52.

253. See Finkelstein, *Archaeology*, 332–34. See also the archaeological studies cited by Fouts, "Defense," 383 n. 31.

254. Dever, *Biblical Writers*, 127.

255. See Kitchen, *On the Reliability*, 239.

It is a relatively small group that returns to the land when Cyrus issues his edict, recorded as 42,360 individuals in Ezra 2:64 and Neh 7:66.[256] An even smaller contingent arrives with Ezra (Ezra 8:1–20). However, the population of Yehud during this period remains contested as well. On the basis of archaeological evidence, Finkelstein estimates that approximately 30,000 people inhabited the province during the fifth and fourth centuries.[257] Carter estimates even fewer, proposing that the population ranged from 13,000 to 21,000 between 538 and 332 BCE.[258]

The Universal Blessing

Interestingly, the "sand on the sea(shore)" metaphor is employed not only to depict the pinnacle of Israel's experience of the progeny blessing (1 Kgs 4:20) in Joshua—Kings, but also to refer to the size of *foreign* peoples: a Canaanite coalition (Josh 11:4), the Midianite coalition and their camels (Judg 7:12; cf. 6:5), and the Philistines (1 Sam 13:5). The situation is similar in each of these instances: a comparatively small Israelite army confronts an enemy people and God grants Israel victory. The metaphor thus serves to accentuate the odds against Israel by hyperbolically exalting the numerical immensity of the enemy, magnifying the greatness of the victory granted by Yahweh. It is thus unlikely that these texts intend to demonstrate the universal progress of the progeny blessing. Nevertheless, they do confirm that Yahweh continues to bless other peoples with offspring.[259]

PSALMS AND WISDOM LITERATURE

The Pentateuch and historical books are chiefly concerned with the *progress* of the progeny blessing, both universally in Gen 1–11 and in its

---

256. In these censuses it appears that אלף refers to "thousand" and that the numbers are meant to reflect historical reality, enumerated down to the last individual. Perhaps a semantic shift in the meaning of אלף occurred around the time of the exile so that by this time אלף was understood almost exclusively to refer to "thousand," resulting in misunderstandings of the term in earlier texts.

257. Finkelstein and Silberman, *The Bible Unearthed*, 308.

258. Carter, "Opening Windows," 440.

259. Second Chronicles 12:3 claims that the invading Egyptian army of Shishak was "without number" (אֵין מִסְפָּר). In this case, this description underscores the coming judgment on the people of Judah.

The Progeny Blessing in the Old Testament Outside the Latter Prophets

covenantal context addressed to *corporate* Israel. In contrast, with the exception of Ps 105:24, the Psalms and Wisdom Literature leave the progress of the blessing to the side, instead *explaining* and *qualifying* the nature of the progeny blessing for the *individual*. Therefore, this corpus makes a crucial contribution to an OT theology of the progeny blessing, in some cases introducing complexity and adding nuance to a simplistic perspective that one might derive from the rest of the OT.[260]

Psalms

Psalm 105:24 contains the only mention in the Psalms of a historical promise or fulfillment of the progeny blessing. Psalm 105 is a hymn of praise to God for his covenant faithfulness, recounting his key blessings and deliverances on Israel's behalf from Abraham to the conquest. The land promise is the focal point of the summary of the Abrahamic covenant (v. 11). The progeny promise is lacking, although v. 12 states that they began "few in number" (מְתֵי מִסְפָּר כִּמְעָט). Following the summary of Joseph and the move to Egypt (vv. 16–23) and prior to Egypt's oppression of Israel and the plagues (vv. 25–36), at precisely the placement of Exod 1, the Psalmist recalls, "Then he made his people very fruitful (וַיֶּפֶר), and made them mightier (וַיַּעֲצִמֵהוּ) than their enemies" (v. 24). The inclusion of this verse underscores the importance of the multiplication of the nation, while slightly reinterpreting Exod 1:7. Whereas Exod 1:7 simply states the fact of Israel's expansion, employing Qal verbs, leading some to assert that God may be uninvolved in this growth,[261] Ps 105:24 uses two of the same verbs, yet in their Hiphil form, clearly indicating that this was Yahweh's doing.[262] Whereas the similar historical review of Yahweh's relationship with Israel in Neh 9 appears to combine the fulfillment of the progeny and land blessings on the occasion of the entry into the land, Ps 105 keeps these realizations separate.

Psalm 107 is a "thanksgiving liturgy"[263] consisting of four theoretical instances of Yahweh's deliverance (vv. 1–32) followed by "a hymnic

---

260. See Mitchell, *Meaning of BRK*, 44–52, for a helpful overview of blessing in the Wisdom Literature.

261. See e.g., Goldingay, *Old Testament Theology: Israel's Gospel*, 255.

262. There is likely little significance in the choice of these two verbs, and the inclusion of only two is probably simply due to the poetic sensibilities of the psalmist in devoting two parallel lines to the progeny theme.

263. Kraus, *Psalms 60–150*, 325.

I Will Surely Multiply Your Offspring

recitation of ways in which the Lord reverses the conditions of human beings"[264] in vv. 33–43. Regarding the hungry (רְעֵבִים), God "blesses them so that they multiply greatly" (וַיְבָרֲכֵם וַיִּרְבּוּ מְאֹד; v. 38a), and grants them the other fertility blessings of agriculture (v. 37) and cattle (v. 38b) as well. Furthermore, he makes the families of the needy (אֶבְיוֹן) "like the flock" (כַּצֹּאן; v. 41), almost certainly a reference to numerical expansion (cf. Ezek 36:37–38).[265] Although exiled Israelites doubtless claimed this hope offered to the "hungry" and "needy,"[266] explicit covenant language is lacking, implying that this is how God relates to the hungry and needy in general and that it is in his nature to bless those who lack blessing. Thus, the recipients and conditions for the enjoyment of the progeny blessing are different here from what we encounter in Israel's narratives. The promised blessing is not necessarily for sons of Abraham or for those who fulfill the condition of keeping God's commands. Rather, it is addressed to the disadvantaged and oppressed. The conditions are neither ethnic nor ethical, but socioeconomic.

Similarly, Ps 113 exalts God for his gracious action on behalf of the helpless, the lowest classes of society (vv. 7–9). The last praiseworthy act celebrated in the psalm is that he makes the barren woman (עֲקֶרֶת) "a joyful mother of sons" (אֵם־הַבָּנִים שְׂמֵחָה; v. 9). As in Ps 107, God blesses a particular type of needy person, but in this case the blessing addresses the need directly. Similarly, in 1 Sam 2:1–10 Hannah declares that it is in God's nature to provide children for barren women, generally speaking (v. 5b).[267] This claim is corroborated by specific instances in the OT narratives in which God provides offspring for women languishing in barrenness (cf. Gen 11:30; 17:15–19; 25:21; 29:31; Judg 13:2–3; 1 Sam 1–2), a condition that jeopardized one's value as a woman and carried a severe social stigma. Although Pss 107 and 113 identify the types of people whom God blesses with offspring universally, these are also the subgroups within

---

264. Mays, *Psalms*, 344.

265. This is more commonly a negative comparison, denoting moral waywardness (Isa 53:6), lack of good leadership (Num 27:17; 1 Kgs 22:17; 2 Chr 18:16; Zech 10:2), and imminent destruction (Jer 12:3; Ps 44:12, 23[11, 22]; 49:15[14]).

266. Psalm 107 is probably addressed to the exilic generation. Verses 33–35 contain language similar to language employed in Isaiah concerning return from exile and it is likely that the deliverances of vv. 1–32 are a paradigm for Israel's return. See Kraus, *Psalms 60–150*, 330; Mays, *Psalms*, 346.

267. The thematic and linguistic content of these two hymns is so similar that a literary relationship between the two is likely. Most notably, 1 Sam 2:8 and Ps 113:7 are identical. However, whereas Ps 113 exalts God only for lifting the needy, 1 Sam 2:1–10 also praises him for debasing the proud and wicked.

The Progeny Blessing in the Old Testament Outside the Latter Prophets

the nation of Israel who are encouraged to anticipate individual blessings of progeny within the context of the corporate blessing upon the nation.

Whereas these psalms address the who of the progeny blessing, Ps 127 addresses why offspring are a blessing, a fact that has been assumed and implied throughout the Pentateuch and historical books, but seldom treated directly. Genesis 1:28 suggests that multiplication is a blessing insofar as it enables humanity as a whole to rule over the rest of creation. Psalm 127 now indicates how children are a blessing to the individual and the family, clarifying that the proliferation of people is not a blessing to all humanity at the expense of the family unit, but is a blessing at both levels. The first stanza affirms that Yahweh is the source of blessing in work (vv. 1–2) and the second that Yahweh is the source of the blessing of sons (vv. 3–5), thus treating the two primary spheres of ordinary life, work and family, and attributing success in both realms to God.

Verse 3 first refers to sons (בָּנִים) as a נַחֲלָה from Yahweh. Just as the land of Canaan was a freely given inheritance (נַחֲלָה; e.g., Num 34:2) to Israel, sons are graciously given as a possession. Furthermore they are a reward (שָׂכָר; unmerited as in Gen 15:1; Isa 40:10; 62:11) so that the man with many is blessed or "happy" (אַשְׁרֵי; v. 5). Verse 4 then compares sons[268] to "arrows in the hand of a warrior." Estes offers three possible referents for this simile in the context of vv. 3–5: 1) the general protection provided by sons; 2) the production of manpower for warfare; and 3) the positive impact that sons can make on society.[269] The second option best fits the image, although it may include the first option as well, and perhaps even the third. A related benefit of having many sons is that "[the father] shall not be put to shame when he speaks with his enemies in the gate" (ESV; v. 5). The phrase כִּי־יְדַבְּרוּ אֶת־אוֹיְבִים בַּשָּׁעַר could be either a legal image ("to speak with the enemies at the gate") or a military image ("to drive away the enemies[270] at the gate"). Historically speaking, the gate, as the "cultural center of the city," would have been the appropriate setting for dealing with legal matters with ones "enemies."[271] On the other hand, the gate

---

268. Due to the simile in v. 4 and on account of the continuation of the military image in v. 5 where these בָּנִים are confronting "enemies," vv. 3–5 probably pertain to sons in particular rather than to both sons and daughters.

269. See Estes, "Like Arrows," 306, 310.

270. This interpretation interprets אֶת as the definite direct object marker and adopts a rare דבר root, meaning "to drive away" (cf. Song 5:6; Ps 18:48[47]; 2 Chr 22:10).

271. Estes, "Like Arrows," 309.

would also have been the battleground for repelling the enemy.²⁷² Therefore, it appears that either one could be a possible contextual reading, both explicating the value of sons. This leads Estes to believe that the language here is intentionally ambiguous so as to encompass both possibilities.²⁷³ It is indeed difficult to favor one interpretation strongly over the other. Whereas the military interpretation best fits the literary context, the legal interpretation entails a more natural reading of יְדַבְּרוּ. Yet even the latter may imply strength when facing one's enemies. Therefore, Ps 127 highlights one particular benefit of having sons that was more germane to the ancient Near East than to our own day, namely, the protection, security, and military strength that they provide.²⁷⁴ Here the progeny blessing is not addressed to any particular individuals or groups; nor are conditions introduced.²⁷⁵

However, Ps 128 does introduce qualifications. The two psalms are so similar linguistically and in thematic content (namely, work and family)²⁷⁶ that they are doubtless meant to be interpreted together given their juxtaposition, together presenting a holisitic outlook on work and family.²⁷⁷ In this psalm blessedness is attributed to the one who "fears Yahweh" in v. 1 (אַשְׁרֵי) and v. 4 (יְבֹרַךְ), forming an inclusio around a description of the resulting enjoyment of work and family (vv. 2–3). In light of the reference in Ps 127:3 to progeny as the "fruit of the womb" (פְּרִי הַבָּטֶן), it is likely that the comparison of the wife to a "fruitful vine" (כְּגֶפֶן פֹּרִיָּה) in Ps 128:3a primarily denotes a large family,²⁷⁸ although it may also encompass every-

---

272. See Fleming, "Psalm 127," 442.

273. See Estes, "Like Arrows," 309.

274. See Kraus, *Psalms 60–150*, 455.

275. Although this is the only OT text that directly addresses the value of children to the family or society at any length, other benefits are evident where the OT reflects the concerns of ancient Near Eastern familial society: 1) They assist with the family work; 2) they care for their parents in old age (e.g., Gen 47:12; Ruth 4:14–15); 3) they bury their parents (e.g., Gen 50:1–14); 4) they bring joy and gladness to parents (e.g., Ps 127:3; Eccl 6:3); 5) they serve the larger community through war (e.g., Num 1) or accomplishing special tasks (e.g., Judg 13:2–5); 6) they maintain the family name (e.g., 1 Sam 24:22[21]; 2 Sam 4:7; Job 18:17–19) and inheritance (e.g., Deut 25:5–10; Ruth 4:10). Given the many benefits of children and the shame and grief in producing none, a man could resort to polygamy, concubinage, and levirate marriage (Gen 38:8; Deut 25:5–10)—all evident in the OT—in order to bear offspring. See Gordis, "Be Fruitful," 21; Scalise, "God as Provider," 579–81; Yegerlehner, "Be Fruitful and Multiply," 39–41.

276. Miller identifies nine internal parallels ("Psalm 127," 129).

277. See Mays, *Psalms,* 401.

278. See Kraus, *Psalms 60–150*, 459.

thing else she contributes to the family. Therefore, whereas Ps 127 treats the source and blessed nature of progeny, Ps 128 provides the context for the blessing, asserting that such blessing is conditional upon fearing Yahweh. This corroborates the Pentateuchal covenant blessings that are conditional upon covenant faithfulness, at times expressed as "fearing Yahweh" (e.g., Deut 4:10; 5:29; 6:2; 8:6; 28:58).

Job

At the end of his first speech (4:1—5:27), Eliphaz describes the blessings and deliverances (5:18-27) that Job can expect to experience if only he will accept God's rebuke (5:17). Among these are "many descendants (רַב זַרְעֶךָ) ... as the grass of the earth (כְּעֵשֶׂב הָאָרֶץ)" (v. 25) and long and healthy life (v. 26; cf. 18:17-19). Since he has just lost his seven sons and three daughters (1:2, 18-19), this is "cruel irony,"[279] and Job will not acknowledge his sin and that his suffering is a rebuke from God, thus repudiating Eliphaz's retribution theology. However, in the end, Job's blamelessness is vindicated when his former life is restored, including seven sons and three daughters (42:13),[280] in addition to their descendants (42:16).

The retribution theology of Job's friends, including the belief that the righteous will experience the progeny blessing, corresponds well to the thought of Deuteronomy—Kings and the generalizations of Proverbs (e.g., 2:21-22). However, they not only assert that sin inevitably leads to suffering but also make the further claim that suffering must necessarily have been caused by sin. The book of Job provides a corrective to this naïve view, demonstrating that life is more complex than this and that personal sin is not the only explanation for suffering. With respect to Job and his progeny, his personal experience of the curse of "decimation" occurred despite his blamelessness. However, he did ultimately enjoy this blessing beyond suffering, suggesting that those who fear Yahweh will be blessed in the end (cf. Ps 128:1-4). This is so even if this is not always recognized or the case throughout the entire course of one's life. In the context of the OT canon, the book of Job offers a nuanced understanding of the covenant blessings and curses, whose focus is primarily corporate, teaching

---

279. Clines, *Job 1-20*, 153.

280. Whereas the number of his sons and daughters is simply restored, Job's other possessions are doubled. However, even progeny could be said to have been granted in greater measure if his children's children are included.

that individual cases often defy a simplistic one-to-one correspondence between one's righteousness and one's experience of personal blessing.

Proverbs

Along with the covenant blessings and curses, the wisdom tradition in the book of Proverbs affirms that God blesses the righteous and curses the wicked (2:21–22; 3:33; 8:32–36). The proverbs are greatly concerned with the type of conduct that leads to blessing or curse in order to define and encourage wisdom. As a result, the content of blessing is seldom mentioned, although the long life that results from acquiring wisdom is a frequent theme (3:2; 4:10; 9:11; 10:27; 19:23). Accordingly, the blessing of children is never mentioned as a result of righteous or wise living, even though 17:6 affirms the goodness of grandchildren and 14:28 acknowledges a king's advantage in reigning over a numerous people for the sake of his glory.[281]

However, the proverbs themselves, which begin in Prov 10, qualify and challenge the blessedness of progeny that is stated or assumed elsewhere in the OT. The very first verse, which Waltke views as an "introductory educational proverb" for all of 10:1—22:16,[282] states that "a wise (חָכָם) son gladdens a father, but a foolish (כְּסִיל) son is a grief to his mother" (10:1). Throughout the rest of the book, the blessing and joy that a wise son brings to his parents is contrasted with the grief (תּוּגַת; 10:1; 17:21), vexation (כַּעַס; 17:25), ruin (הֹוּת; 19:13), and shame (מֵבִישׁ; 19:26; 29:15) that a foolish son brings upon them (cf. 10:1; 15:20; 17:21, 25; 19:13, 26; 23:15–16, 24–25; 27:11; 28:7; 29:3, 15, 17).[283] Beyond the family unit, Proverbs portrays the righteous as a blessing to the city and to society, in contrast to the wicked who have a detrimental effect on others and on the city as a whole (cf. 11:10–11; 12:26; 16:13, 27–29; 28:12, 28; 29:2). In fact, the city rejoices when the wicked perish (בַּאֲבֹד; cf. 11:10).

Therefore, according to Proverbs, sons are a blessing to their parents only if they are wise. People are a blessing to others and to society only if they are righteous. The foolish and wicked must be deemed a curse rather

---

281. It is possible, however, that this refers not to the quantity of subjects under his rule but rather to the extent of his popular support (see Waltke, *Proverbs: Chapters 1–15*, 605).

282. See ibid., 450.

283. Even the one apparently unqualified statement concerning the goodness of sons in 17:6 is tempered by two entirely negative statements concerning the sorrow of having foolish sons just verses later (vv. 21, 25).

than a blessing.[284] The wise and righteous not only experience blessing, but also yield blessing for others.

Ecclesiastes

The cynical perspective of life lived apart from God in Ecclesiastes further tempers the blessed nature of children. After describing the futility in hoarding or possessing wealth that is never enjoyed (5:12–16[13–17]; 6:1–2), in 6:3–6 Qohelet hyperbolically addresses the futility in failing to enjoy abundant progeny and long life: "If a man fathers one hundred and lives many years so the days of his years are many, but his soul is not satisfied (תִשְׂבַּע) with good things and he does not even have a burial, I say better the miscarriage than him" (v. 3). It is clearly assumed that progeny and long life are indeed great blessings meant to enhance one's enjoyment of and quality of life. But they are not experienced automatically as blessings. Rather, they function as blessings only when they are actively enjoyed. If God does not enable (יַשְׁלִיטֶנּוּ) a man to enjoy the gifts he has given him (v. 2), life is not worth living.

Conclusion

The Psalms specify the *recipients*, the kinds of people whom Yahweh delights to bless with children: the hungry (107:38), the needy (107:41), the barren (113:9), and the one who fears Yahweh (128:3). These categories may be complementary since there is often a correlation between the

---

284. A similar perspective is present in deutero-canonical wisdom literature. Sirach 16:1–3 states the preference for quality over quantity in the starkest possible terms:

> Do not desire a multitude of worthless children,
>   and do not rejoice in ungodly offspring.
> If they multiply, do not rejoice in them,
>   unless the fear of the Lord is in them.
> Do not trust in their survival,
>   or rely on their numbers;
> for one can be better than a thousand,
>   and to die childless is better than to have ungodly children. (NRSV)

The Wisdom of Solomon deems the offspring of the "ungodly" "accursed" and the undefiled barren woman and the eunuch blessed in comparison (3:10–14). Furthermore, "childlessness with virtue" (4:1) is preferable to the illegitimate "prolific brood of the ungodly [that] will be of no use" (4:3; NRSV).

helpless and fearers of Yahweh. Psalm 127 describes *why* sons are a blessing, namely, because they defend and protect the family. The book of Job challenges the mechanical *operation* or *bestowal* of the blessing. It qualifies a strict retribution theology, teaching that the enjoyment of the progeny blessing at any given time in one's life does not always correspond neatly or directly to one's righteousness. Although Proverbs and Ecclesiastes both affirm that children are a blessing, generally speaking, both books moderate this perspective, teaching that children are *not necessarily* a blessing, providing a counterbalance to Psalm 127. Whereas Proverbs qualifies the blessed nature of children based on the conduct of the child, Ecclesiastes tempers the blessing on the basis of the father's experience of blessing (6:3–6). Based on careful observation of the realities of life, prudential wisdom attests that children are a blessing to a father only when he enjoys his children and only when the children follow in the paths of wisdom summarized by "the fear of Yahweh."

Although the OT narratives often verify that the righteous are blessed with children, Job and Ps 113:9 better explain the situation of individuals such as the matriarchs or Hannah who suffered through long periods of barrenness and apparent inexplicable curse prior to Yahweh's intervention on their behalf, finally addressing their affliction with the blessing of offspring. Furthermore, Proverbs and Ecclesiastes corroborate some OT narratives that demonstrate that sons are not necessarily a blessing (e.g., the sons of Eli, Samuel, and David). Difficulties regarding the ability to have children or the ability to consider them a blessing are no doubt the result of sin in the world and the curse of Gen 3:16, a curse that affects the righteous and the wicked alike.

Conclusions

Having treated the progeny blessing throughout the OT apart from the Latter Prophets, we are now in a position to summarize the basic contours of the blessing, including its prominence, its purpose, its scope, its history of promise and realization, its contribution to continuity between the covenants, the dynamic between the individual and national experience of it, and its theological contribution.

The Progeny Blessing in the Old Testament Outside the Latter Prophets

Prominence

The progeny blessing bursts onto the scene at the start of the biblical account of history, driving and permeating the book of Genesis. From the first blessing upon humanity (1:28) to the curses (3:16) to the postdiluvian blessing (9:1, 7), to the Abrahamic promises, to the initial realization of the promises in the patriarchal narratives, the progeny blessing is an abiding concern for God and for humanity. Together with land, numerous progeny is the promised material blessing of the Abrahamic covenant, arguably just as important as land in the life of Israel, despite the comparative lack of "press" it receives in the text. It appears in the three major blessing lists of the Sinai covenant in Exod 23, Lev 26, and Deut 28, and surfaces in a number of blessing summaries in Deuteronomy (e.g., 7:13–14; 8:1; 30:16). Furthermore, God's past blessing of Israel with offspring merits inclusion in extended summaries of Yahweh's historical acts on Israel's behalf (Deut 26:5; Josh 24:3; Ps 105:24; Neh 9:23). It appears less frequently outside of the Pentateuch, but certainly does not fade from view. Its frequency in the writings of the classical prophets will further underscore its importance.

Purpose

The function of the progeny blessing in God's design for humanity is best understood from the first time it occurs. Genesis 1:28 reveals the divinely ordained steps necessary to realize the purpose of humankind first introduced in v. 26: humankind is to be abundantly fruitful *in order to* fill the earth *in order to* subdue it, culminating in rule over living creatures. Thus, Yahweh's gift of progeny plays an essential role in the anthropology of the OT, namely, to sustain the human race, perpetuating and expanding the quantity of images of God that reflect him and rule as his representatives over his created order. The Psalms and Wisdom Literature note additional benefits of children for the family unit or individual: protection or security (Ps 127) and enjoyment in life (Eccl 6:3–6).

In its basic purpose the progeny promise for Israel is simply a specific manifestation of the universal blessing. However, for Israel it takes on added significance. The progeny blessing enables Israel to serve her redemptive purpose of extending blessing to all nations since it is doubtful that Israel could have influenced the nations as a holy nation and a kingdom of priests on behalf of Yahweh as he intended had he not made her a relatively large nation and placed her at such a pivotal crossroads in the land of Canaan. As was the case universally in Gen 1:28, multiplication was not an end in itself, as if God's interest was simply in the quantity of people. Rather, it was a means to the end of having many of a certain kind of people, namely, a large people belonging to and devoted to Yahweh (Exod 19:3–6).[285] Given the parallels between God's purposes for creation as delineated in Gen 1:28 and Israel's mission, the multiplication of the nation of Israel (as one of these parallel aspects) points to the ultimate realization of God's purposes in and through Israel. Thus the function of the progeny blessing for Israel more accurately reflects its intended creational function (i.e., as a means of ruling in imitation of God's rule) than does its operation among the nations who have no such aims. The Sinai covenant adds a dimension to the function of the progeny blessing without losing its other function(s). Since the initial promise has been realized, it is now employed to maintain the covenant relationship, functioning (along with other blessings) as motivation and reward for covenant faithfulness.

Scope

In Gen 1–11 the blessing of progeny is God's gift to all of humanity, although human sinfulness impedes its worldwide effect. In the OT historical accounts all blessing runs through Abraham following Gen 12 and the blessing of offspring is thereafter only promised to him and his descendants. One might conclude from this that the scope of the blessing has been narrowed to a particular people. However, it appears that the blessing is still universal, since there were always larger surrounding nations throughout Israel's history and Israel was undoubtedly never the largest nation on earth at any given time. Rather, Israel is unique in having a specific *guarantee* from Yahweh that she would experience this blessing whereas this was not the case for other nations. Wisdom Literature and the Psalms do not reflect further on this Israel-nations distinction but rather identify the types of individuals more likely to experience God's blessing of offspring: the helpless (Ps 107:38, 41, 113:9), those who fear Yahweh (Pss 127–128), and the righteous (Job 5:25).

---

285. Moreover, as Mitchell states, "God's blessing is a visible sign of his favor that attracts the attention of others and makes them desire God's blessing too" (*Meaning of BRK*, 166).

The Progeny Blessing in the Old Testament Outside the Latter Prophets

Promise and Realization

From Gen 1:28 we might assume that, in accordance with Yahweh's enabling and intention, humanity would flourish easily and without restraint. However, the futility curses in response to sin greatly complicate the realization of the blessing. Throughout the OT, sin will impede the progress of the expansion of humankind (e.g., the Flood account; the covenant curses of Lev 26 and Deut 28; judgments on the nations). However, the reiteration of the creation blessing in Gen 9:1–7 and the Noahic covenant in 9:8–17 ensure that the universal progeny blessing has not and will not be revoked. God will continue to grant offspring in order to sustain and expand the human race.

The history of the promise and realization of the progeny blessing concerning Israel is of much greater interest to the OT writers. The promise to make of Abraham a "great nation" (Gen 12:2) first entailed the promise to provide for him a son, fulfilled only after many years.[286] The national promise is realized in Egypt as described in Exod 1:7 and corroborated by Deut 1:10, 26:5, and Ps 105:24.[287] However, although it shares language with Gen 1:28 and 9:1, it is unlikely that Exod 1:7 constitutes a complete "fulfillment" of the creation blessing. The realization of the Abrahamic progeny promise does not preclude enjoyment of the blessing in even greater measure. Deuteronomy in particular anticipates new possibilities for national growth, based on the Abrahamic promise, though now mediated through the Sinai covenant and its contingencies. First Kings 4:20 (cf. 2 Chr 1:9) depicts the reign of Solomon as the pinnacle of Israel's historical enjoyment of Yahweh's gift of offspring. However, in light of the decline of the fortunes of the nation due to covenant unfaithfulness, this certainly fell short of the extent to which Israel could have been blessed with offspring. According to Deut 30:1–10, the proliferation of the nation at the time of the restoration of the people to the land following exile will transcend previous growth, an incredible assertion of faith echoed in the Latter Prophets.

---

286. The promise of a son to Abraham is the most prominent among other OT instances in which progeny is promised to an individual and later granted (e.g., Hannah; the mother of Samson), a type scene that reappears in the NT in the case of Elizabeth.

287. Note that Josh 24:3 and Neh 9:23 identify different times for the fulfillment of the blessing for reasons suggested above.

I Will Surely Multiply Your Offspring

Covenant Continuity

Scholars often emphasize discontinuity between the covenants in the OT. Although we have not comprehensively argued for continuity between the covenants, we have suggested that the role of the progeny blessing vis-à-vis the covenants is one argument that can be marshaled in favor of continuity. First, the blessing is a significant element in each of the major OT covenants: the creation blessing of Gen 1:28 (should it be regarded as a covenant), the Noahic covenant, the Abrahamic covenant, the Sinai covenant, the Davidic covenant, and the "New" covenant.

Second, we see continuity in the way that the progeny elements in these covenants relate to each other. The progeny blessing does not function identically in each covenant, but the ways in which they do relate appear to be complementary. In the Noahic covenant Yahweh's desire to bless humanity with progeny is upheld and the future of humanity is guaranteed. The content and aims of the Abrahamic covenant mirror the content and aims of the blessing of Gen 1:28, portraying Israel as a microcosm of all humanity. Furthermore, the language of the fulfillment of the Abrahamic promise in Exod 1:7 alludes to Gen 1:28. Deuteronomy presents future possibilities for growth in the context of the Sinai arrangement as a further realization of the Abrahamic promise (see above). God's promise to David to establish for him a perpetual throne and thus a continuous line of descendants functions within the parameters of the Sinai covenant. Given David's covenant-keeping conduct,[288] perhaps the Davidic covenant should be regarded as an individual manifestation of the corporate promise that covenant faithfulness will result in blessing for "the fruit of the womb." Finally, we will see in the Latter Prophets that the progeny element in the "New" covenant is related to these prior covenantal expressions. Although the contours of these covenants vary, Yahweh's commitment to endow all of humanity—and specifically his covenant people—with progeny remains constant.

---

288. Cf. 1 Kgs 3:6, 14; 9:4; 11:4, 6, 33–34, 38; 14:8; 15:3, 5, 11; 2 Kgs 16:2; 22:2; 1 Chr 7:17; 2 Chr 17:3; 29:2; 34:2.

The Progeny Blessing in the Old Testament Outside the Latter Prophets

National and Individual Experiences of the Blessing

Our predominant focus has been on the blessing of progeny at the national and universal level. Although we have noted its impact upon specific individuals along the way, a brief consideration of the dynamic between its corporate and individual expressions is now appropriate.

At the national level, the covenant blessings and curses imply that a direct correlation exists between Israel's covenant faithfulness and her multiplication as a people. However, the OT resists such a strict correlation at the individual level, borne out both in narrative material and in the wisdom literature (which is more concerned with individual righteousness and blessing than elsewhere in the OT).[289] Although some of the most exemplary figures in the OT have many sons and daughters (e.g., David), other righteous individuals have few children or may wait for decades before enjoying children at all. For Abraham and Isaac tension exists between the national promise and their present individual (non-)experience of Yahweh's blessing of offspring. In our consideration of Job we have seen that righteousness does not always correlate to blessing. Furthermore, it appears that the lack of blessing is felt more acutely within the family unit. Barrenness is the key problem in a number of OT narratives, whereas the inability of a nation or people group to expand does not seem to be addressed with comparable grief.

On the whole, however, one should be cautious about dichotomizing how the blessing affects nations and individuals. The realization of the Abrahamic promise certainly entails the blessing of progeny for individuals within the nation, although it may not encompass all, as seen, for example, in 1 Sam 1–2. The language used to describe the covenant blessings and curses in Deuteronomy suggests fluidity between the corporate nation and the individual, as we would expect. Often the size of the whole nation is in view (e.g., 1:10–11; 28:62–63; 30:5), but statements concerning blessing "in the fruit of your womb" (7:13; 28:4, 11; 30:9) and lack of barrenness (7:14) seem to specifically address individuals—even as the wider book addresses the entire nation in its demand for faithfulness. Furthermore, the benefits of numerous progeny are conceived of similarly.

---

289. Brueggemann expresses this tension in his dialectical structure for OT theology between "structure legitimation" (i.e., a strict retribution theology akin to Deuteronomy) and "embrace of pain" (protests that the common theology does not always work, as in the case of righteous barren individuals, that spur God to action). See Brueggemann, "Shape for Old Testament Theology, I: Structure Legitimation," 28–46; "Shape for Old Testament Theology, II: Embrace of Pain," 395–415.

The national benefits relate to strength (e.g., Exod 1:7, 20; Deut 9:14) and influence, to the end of extending blessing and knowledge of Yahweh to the nations, as noted above (cf. Gen 12:2–3; Exod 19:3–6). The benefits for the family entail protection and strength (Ps 127:3–5) as well as maintaining and strengthening the family name (e.g., 1 Sam 24:22[21]; Job 18:17–19; Deut 25:5–10), although the benefits are not exhausted in these texts. With respect to the covenant curses of decimation, even though the nation is primarily in view, it is clear that they affect both the corporate and the individual spheres. Threats concerning war, destruction or disease (Deut 28:20–22, 45, 59–61) seem more corporate, but the loss of "sons and daughters" (Deut 28:32, 41) and the graphic description of eating one's children (Deut 28:53–57) certainly strike its hearers personally even as such curses decimate the nation. In sum, the nation is obviously made up of individuals who in general will experience the blessing (or curse) in accordance with the ebb and flow of the nation. Nevertheless, some individuals will experience blessing (or curse) contrary to the experience of the nation as a whole.

Theology

During the course of our inquiry into the function and progress of the progeny blessing in the OT, we must never lose sight of some fundamental affirmations that such texts make concerning the character of Yahweh. First, Yahweh is a life-giving God, the Creator of all living things and the source of all human life. Second, he is a sustaining God, promising in the Noahic covenant to preserve the human race despite their disposition to sin, meriting death. Third, he is a God whose *own* disposition is to bless, not curse. These beliefs concerning the nature of Yahweh undergird the testimony of the OT concerning progeny that we have encountered thus far. Although they may be the most obvious conclusions that can be drawn from texts concerning the progeny blessing, they are probably also (and perhaps for that very reason) the most crucial. In the face of competing claims from foreign fertility deities and the temptation to doubt Yahweh's power and character, the OT affirms as early as Gen 1:28 that Yahweh is a God who provides all offspring, who desires humanity to expand, and who desires to continue to bless his people.

However, it is just as clear that the multiplication of the human race involves both divine action and human responsibility. The majority of

The Progeny Blessing in the Old Testament Outside the Latter Prophets

the statements concerning national future proliferation as well as most of those that record its accomplishment explicitly attribute these acts to Yahweh (e.g., Gen 13:16; Lev 26:9; Deut 30:5; Ps 105:24; 113:9), to the extent that those that do not cite his agency almost certainly assume it (e.g., Exod 1:7). Yahweh's intervention is explicit in some individual cases as well (Gen 21:1–2; 25:21; 29:31; 30:22; Ruth 4:13). And even though births are commonly reported apart from explicit reference to Yahweh's participation, Scalise rightly notes that "[m]arriage blessings, such as Genesis 24:60 and Ruth 4:11–12, as well as personal names which testify to divine aid in conception and childbirth, suggest that the LORD was recognized as the source of fertility in a general way, not just in the case of special individuals."[290] Furthermore, when human efforts to reproduce fail, even this failure is at times attributed to Yahweh (see Gen 30:2; 1 Sam 1:5–6).

Nevertheless, multiplication entails human responsibility as well. Many of these same texts reflect the obvious reality that men and women must make a joint effort to procreate within the confines of marriage and family, "the context in which blessing and curse became effective."[291] Despite our judgment that Gen 1:28 and 9:1, 7 are not commands but rather express God's intentions and desires for which he has provided the enablement, this still entails human initiative and cooperation. On a larger scale, humanity's moral responsibilities are tied to their proliferation since sin (e.g., war, murder) is the true threat to expansion. This is clearly the case for Israel under the Sinai covenant as well. Following the ratification of the Sinai covenant and demonstrated throughout the historical books, a tension exists between Yahweh's preservation of his people due to his covenant commitment to the patriarchs and their judgment and decimation as a result of their persistent rebellion and apostasy. In sum, human and divine participation are held together in synergy throughout the OT, the one never fading from view even when the other aspect is stressed in any given passage.[292]

---

290. Scalise, "God As Provider," 582.

291. Goldingay, *Old Testament Theology: Israel's Gospel*, 268.

292. Goldingay describes this dynamic as it pertains to the progeny promise in the patriarchal narratives as follows: "So this promise too is imperiled by circumstances, by human action and also by Yahweh's action. It comes true through Yahweh's action and through human action, though human action complicates the way that happens" (ibid., 237).

3

The Progeny Blessing in the Book of Isaiah

Introduction to the Book of Isaiah

Isaiah's Use of Prior Traditions

IN THE FOLLOWING ANALYSIS of texts in Isaiah that refer to the blessing of progeny we will attempt to relate each text to prior progeny traditions. Thus, we begin by summarizing Isaiah's use of prior traditions in general.

Nowhere in the Latter Prophets do we see such consistent use of Zion traditions as in the book of Isaiah. The Zion tradition, most prominent in the Psalms, entails the belief that Zion is the center of the world by virtue of God's enthronement there as King (Isa 2:2–4; 6:5; 8:18; 24:23; 33:17, 22; 52:7; 60:14), the cosmic mountain to which all nations will gather one day (Isa 2:2–4; 49:22; 60–62), and the source of blessing (Isa 4:2–6; 11:6–9; 25:6–9; 30:19–26; 33:17–24; 49:19–21; 51:3; 54; 60–62) and the law of Yahweh (Isa 2:3; 51:4).[1] Moreover, this tradition is closely tied to the election tradition concerning David as king (Isa 9:5–6[6–7]; 11:1–5, 10; 16:5; 32:1; 55:3–5), implicitly ruling from Zion. Isaiah employs many other historical traditions as well, including references to creation (40:26; 42:5; 45:7, 12, 18; 51:3; 57:16), Noah (54:9–10), the patriarchal blessings (10:22; 29:22; 41:8–10; 43:27–28; 48:18–19; 51:1–2; 61:7–9), the Sinai covenant (2:3; 4:5–6; 42:24–25; 56:1–8), the wilderness wanderings (4:5–6; 41:17–20; 43:19–21; 48:21; 49:9–11), and especially the exodus (11:16; 40:3–5;

---

1. See Roberts, "Zion," 93–108, for a full description of the common elements of the Zion tradition. See also Gowan, *Prophetic Books*, 65–68.

42:16; 43:1-6, 14-21; 48:20-21; 49:8-12; 51:9-11; 52:11-12; 55:12-13; 63:9-13).[2] These allusions, concentrated within Isa 40-55 in particular, are typically employed to describe the future restoration of the nation within the categories of Yahweh's past acts and covenantal promises. The progeny blessing is a key aspect of the creation, patriarchal, exodus, and Sinai traditions. Although the proliferation of Israel does not appear to be a dimension of the Zion tradition, it would not be at odds with it since God's presence at Zion is clearly associated with blessing. In our examination below, we will attempt to locate each text (and the Isaianic progeny portrayal as a whole) within one or more of these traditions.

Future Hope in Isaiah

For Isaiah, judgment on Judah and Zion is not final, but is rather administered for the purpose of restoring a holy people (4:3) to a renewed Zion (e.g., 1:26-27) following judgment, and thus has a purifying effect (1:25; 4:4; 48:10). Perhaps more than any other book in the Latter Prophets, Isaiah holds judgment and salvation together, never lingering on judgment without also proclaiming hope beyond it.[3] As Oswalt states, "Deliverance is to be found *through* judgment, not in spite of it, and the election-love of God is not called into question by judgment but, rather, *demonstrated* by it."[4]

Given the pervasive scope of salvation in Isaiah, its diverse expressions, and the poetic nature of most such texts, it is difficult to summarize adequately the content and development of future hope in the book, a task more manageable for the other writing prophets. We will attempt to do so only in broad strokes in order to provide a general context for the Isaianic progeny texts. Due to this diversity, one must not necessarily assume that all texts of future deliverance and prosperity refer to the same time period and the same events.[5] Nevertheless, a number of common themes unite them.

2. See especially Anderson, "Exodus Typology," 177-95; Schultz, "Isaiah," 204-5.

3. Although most salvation oracles occur in Isa 40-66, they occur with nearly the same frequency in Isa 1-39 as well. See 1:26-27; 2:2-4; 4:2-6; 8:23-9:6[9:1-7]; 10:20-22; 11:1-16; 14:1-3, 32; 16:5; 19:17-25; 25:6-9; 26:1-19; 27:2-6, 9, 12-13; 29:17-24; 30:18-26; 31:5, 7; 32:1-5, 15-18; 33:19-24; 35:1-10.

4. Oswalt, "God's Determination," 153.

5. However, when the literary context of the entire book becomes determinative in interpretation rather than a reconstructed (and often speculative) historical setting for each text, these texts are pulled together into a tighter unity to depict a time beyond exile.

The return from exile plays a prominent role in Isaiah (10:21; 11:11–12, 16; 14:1–2; 27:12–13; 35:8–10; 40:3–5; 43:1–6, 14–21; 48:20–21; 49:12, 22–23; 51:9–11; 52:11–12; 60:4–9; 62:10; and possibly 42:16; 45:13; 55:12; 57:14; 66:22) and is logically prior to other restoration blessings. Unlike other prophets, Isaiah also emphasizes the journey itself in which Yahweh will supernaturally clear the way as in the first exodus (35:8–10; 40:3–4; 43:19–20; 48:21; 62:10).

The political and social restoration of Israel revolves around the redemption of Zion (1:26–27; 2:2–4; 14:32; 18:7; 24:23; 52:1–10; 59:20; 60–62; 65:17–25).[6] Zion will be rebuilt (44:26–28; 45:13; 60:10) and protected (4:5–6; 31:5; 33:20) and a Davidic king will again rule from Jerusalem in justice and righteousness (9:5–6[6–7]; 11:1–5; 16:5; 32:1–2). God's blessing upon the people will be expressed in numerous other ways, usually—but not always—tied to Zion's restoration: the nation will multiply (9:2[3]; 44:3–4; 49:19–21; 51:2–3; 54:1–3; 60:22; 65:20, 23; 66:7–9), they will be more powerful than their enemies (11:14; 14:1–2; 19:17; 41:11–12; 45:14; 49:23; 54:14–17; 60:12–14; 62:8), and they will experience peace (9:6[7]; 33:19–20; 52:7; 54:14–17; 60:17–18) and security (26:1; 32:18; 33:20). Yahweh will heal the people (30:26; 33:23–24), including the physical maladies of the impaired (29:18; 35:5–6). Both the return and the new life of prosperity in the land will evoke joy in the people (9:2[3]; 29:19; 35:1–2, 10; 41:16; 44:23; 51:11; 52:7–9; 55:12; 60:5; 61:3, 7, 10; 65:13–14, 18–19).[7]

Furthermore, Isaiah emphasizes peace in the animal kingdom (11:6–9; 65:25) and the holistic renovation of the natural order into a lush, fertile land (29:17; 30:23–25; 32:15; 35:1–2, 6–7; 41:18–20; 43:19–20; 55:13). However, only in 30:23–25 is there any indication that this rehabilitation is for agricultural purposes. This blessing of arable land yielding abundant food as found in the covenant blessings (Lev 26:4–5, 10; Deut 28:4–5, 8, 11–12) and other prophets (e.g., Jer 31:5, 12; Ezek 34:26–27; 36:29–30)

---

6. Although Zion is the focal point of restoration, texts such as 44:26 and 61:4 that anticipate the rebuilding of the cities of Judah imply that Zion is not Isaiah's sole concern but rather representative of (and the theological center of) the whole land.

7. In general, comparable texts of hope beyond exile in Jeremiah simply list a number of restoration blessings in prose. Similarly, Ezek 34–37 clearly identifies different future material benefits, yet develops them more fully. In contrast, in Isaiah it is sometimes difficult to identify specific blessings as found in the covenant blessings of Deut 28 and Lev 26 since nearly all of these Isaianic texts employ poetry and make frequent use of metaphor and imagery. Furthermore, Isaiah tends to use more general images of prosperity or speaks simply of future salvation rather than painting a detailed picture of what the future will look like.

is not emphasized by Isaiah as an aspect of renewed blessing in the land. Rather, the transformation of nature in Isaiah is for the sake of the comfort and joy of the returning exiles as they make their journey home, as well as a manifestation of Isaiah's concern with the restoration of the entire created order.[8] Given the lofty and other-worldly language used in many of these restoration texts, it is difficult to imagine that this merely envisions a return to former prosperity. Rather, this will be prosperity that transcends anything previously experienced in Israel's history.

Isaiah's vision of the future goes beyond the rehabilitation of the land and Israelite society to the rehabilitation of the ruptured relationship between Yahweh and Israel. Yahweh's renewed favor toward his people (12:1; 14:1; 27:2-5; 30:18-19; 33:21-22; 35:4; 41:8-9, 17; 43:1-7, 20; 44:1-5; 44:21-22; 46:4, 13; 51:16; 65:24), often expressed as his "compassion" (רחם; 14:1; 30:18; 49:10, 13, 15; 54:8, 10; 55:7; 60:10) toward them, is the basis for all of his activity on their behalf. On the basis of the work of the servant figure of 52:13—53:12, he will forgive the sins of Israel (27:9; 33:24; 40:2; 43:25; 44:22; 53:4-6, 11-12), so that Israel, chosen to be Yahweh's servant (41:8-9; 43:10; 44:1-2; 45:4; cf. 42:18-25; 44:21; 48:20), may once again function properly in its servant capacity. Furthermore, Yahweh will pour out his Spirit on them (44:3-4; cf. 59:21) and make (כרת) an "everlasting covenant" (ברית עולם; 55:3; 61:8; cf. 54:10; 59:21) with them. In that day, the people will be regarded as holy (4:3-4; 62:12) and serve him as priests and ministers (61:6; 66:21). They will again rely on Yahweh (10:20), worship him (27:13; 29:23; 30:22; 31:7; 66:23), and be glorified as a result (55:5; 60:9). God will undertake all of this ultimately for the sake of his own name and glory (48:9-11; cf. 37:35; 40:5; 42:10-12; 43:7, 20-21, 25), yet this entails their salvation.

However, it appears that not all of ethnic Israel will return to Yahweh and experience these benefits. At key points in the book, particularly at the beginning (1:27-28; cf. also 3:10-11) and the end (65:8-16; 66:3-24), there is a clear distinction between the righteous who are faithful to Yahweh and wicked sinners who will be punished. The former are sometimes referred to as the "remnant" (שאר; 4:3; 10:20-22) or the "servants" (עבדים; 54:17; 56:6; 63:17; 65:8-9, 13-15; 66:14) who benefit from the work of the individual servant. At times this remnant concept in Isaiah pertains to his immediate eighth-century audience, namely, those who will

---

8. See Gowan, *Eschatology*, 114. Since moral conduct affects the land (Isa 24:5-6), it makes sense that removal of sin and obedience to Yahweh would be correlated with rejuvenation of the land.

be spared in the coming destruction (e.g., 1:9; 7:22; 30:17; 37:31–32), often to make a pessimistic point concerning the totality of the judgment.⁹ The exilic community then claims this remnant concept in Isa 40–55, explicitly in 46:3. Finally, in Isa 56–66 "the remnant idea is both contracted and expanded."¹⁰ On the one hand, the righteous (true remnant) are separated from the wicked among the returned exiles (e.g., 57:13, 20–21; 59:20); on the other hand, righteous foreigners are included among the former (56:6–8; 60:6; 66:18–23). Overall, the trajectory of the book moves toward the remnant as the post-exilic purified community (cf. also 4:2–3).¹¹ We must consider whether the blessing of progeny upon Israel pertains to this righteous remnant alone when the nation is restored from exile.

Future salvation for the nations, while barely present in Jeremiah and Ezekiel, plays a prominent role in Isaiah. However, this is a complex topic since the book at times relegates foreign peoples to a subservient role vis-à-vis Israel (e.g., 14:1–2; 18:7; 45:14; 49:22–23; 60:6, 11, 13–14), while in other places elevating them to equal standing with the righteous remnant within ethnic Israel (e.g., 19:16–25; 25:7–9; 45:22–26; 56:1–8; 66:18–24). In light of these latter texts, we must question whether the future proliferation of the people of Israel transcends the usual ethnic boundaries and entails the inclusion of foreigners as well, so that corporate multiplication of the nation is not solely the result of physical reproduction within Israel but the result of conversion as well. We will explore this below following our discussion of texts that explicitly pertain to the progeny blessing.

THE PROGENY BLESSING IN ISAIAH

As we have seen thus far, it is usually easy to identify the progeny blessing since consistent vocabulary (e.g., פָּרָה, רָבָה) and stock phrases are employed in its articulation. This is not the case in Isaiah. Isaiah does use some of the typical language (see 9:2[3]; 10:22; 48:19). However, due to the book's proclivity for poetic imagery and metaphor that is inherently more ambiguous, at times we remain uncertain regarding the presence of the blessing and must conclude that it is probable or possible, or that a description of prosperity *may include* the blessing of progeny (27:6;

---

9. See Hasel, *The Remnant*, who argues that both the positive and negative aspect of the remnant motif (and both the historical and eschatological meaning) was present in the prophet Isaiah's teaching from the beginning of his ministry.

10. Webb, "Zion," 79.

11. See ibid., 72–81.

44:3–4; 49:19–21; 51:2–3). As a result of this additional complication in the book of Isaiah, when a reference to the blessing is uncertain, we will first examine the likelihood of its presence and treat it only briefly if this likelihood is low.

Population Decimation in Isaiah

In order to understand the role of the progeny blessing in Isaiah fully, we must examine it within the context of the frustration and negation of the blessing through judgment. In accordance with the covenant curses of Lev 26 and Deut 28, the nation of Israel will experience the reversal of the patriarchal blessings as a result of their rebellion against Yahweh by means of decimation and removal from the land. Decimation is the climactic and final note of the programmatic introductory chapter (1:28–31; cf. also 1:19–20). The complete destruction of the rebels concludes the other "bookend" as well, providing the final image in the book (66:24). In between, death pervades the judgment oracles of Isaiah.

In the personification of Zion as a mother in the Zion songs of 49:14—50:3 and 54:1–17, her past and present condition are described using the language of barrenness (49:21; 54:1), infertility, and loss of children (49:20, 21). In both contexts, these metaphors evoke grief over the decimation of Zion, but then introduce the reversal of this condition through the recovery of her children.[12] Thus Isaiah employs the full range of language depicting the reduction of Israel's population, both through the loss of existing persons (death, destruction, desolation, bereavement) and the prevention of new life (barrenness).[13]

This comprehensive judgment applies to the nations as well. Those who remain in Moab will be "very few" (מְעַט מִזְעָר; 16:14) and, due to her pride, Babylon will be subject to loss of children (שְׁכוֹל) and widowhood (אַלְמֹן; 47:8–9). In the context of a sweeping statement of judgment and de-creation (24:1–23), "the inhabitants of the earth burn so that few men are left" (v. 6) on account of their disobedience (v. 5). Moreover, God will wield his sword against all nations in his wrath (34:1–17). Since Yahweh is sovereign over and judges all nations, decimation is not the fate of Israel

---

12. This need not entail the actual barrenness of the women of Israel, but is rather a powerful image of the diminution of the nation. See below for a more detailed discussion of these texts.

13. In addition, in light of Isa 59:6–7, the wicked within the post-exilic community may themselves contribute to the nation's decimation through their violence.

alone. However, for Israel, Yahweh pledges that population reduction is not the end of the story and will, in fact, be reversed. Other nations receive no such promise.

Isaiah 9:2[3]

Chapters 6–12 function as a literary unit in Isaiah, unified by the historical setting, namely, impending judgment at the hands of the Assyrians. One of Isaiah's primary concerns here is to contrast the present failed Davidic kingship under faithless Ahaz with a future king who will succeed in the same office when Yahweh intervenes on Israel's behalf. Furthermore, recurring themes such as the remnant and the role of children in both signifying and accomplishing God's purposes bind these chapters together. As a result of the people's failure to fear and trust in God (8:11–15, 19–20), they will be plunged into darkness and gloom (8:21–22).

However, this is not the end. Isaiah 8:23—9:6[9:1–7] provides present motivation for trusting Yahweh[14] by predicting the reversal of the Assyrian judgment outlined in 7:17—8:22. Light (8:23—9:1[9:1–2]) will replace darkness and gloom (8:22). Distress and dismay (8:21–22) will become joy and gladness (9:2[3]). Whereas their spoil (שָׁלָל) was carried away (8:1, 3–4), they will now rejoice as if dividing it (שָׁלָל; 9:2[3]). Assyrian oppression will be broken (9:3–4[4–5]) and the tumultuous reign of Ahaz will be replaced with the peaceful reign of a new king (9:5–6[6–7]). In light of the reversals within the immediate literary context, the multiplication of the nation (9:2[3]) may function as a reversal of the decimation suggested in 7:20–25 (and possibly 8:21–22).[15] This vision of political and social restoration will be accomplished by the "zeal of Yahweh" (קִנְאַת יְהוָה; v. 6[7]). The central blessing of joy and gladness (v. 2[3]) is caused by three acts of God introduced by כִּי-clauses: the end of oppression, the elimination of war, and, climactically, the birth of a king.[16]

The proliferation of the people immediately precedes the promise of joy:

---

14. See Oswalt, *Isaiah: Chapters 1–39*, 238.
15. See ibid., 243.
16. It is unclear whether each of these three acts are independent causes for joy or whether the former two are grounded in the third, elevating the importance of the birth of the king. Perhaps this ambiguity is intentional.

הִרְבִּיתָ הַגּוֹי	You have multiplied[17] the nation;
לֹא [לוֹ] הִגְדַּלְתָּ הַשִּׂמְחָה	For them you have magnified joy;
שָׂמְחוּ לְפָנֶיךָ	They rejoice before you
כְּשִׂמְחַת בַּקָּצִיר	As with joy during the harvest,
כַּאֲשֶׁר יָגִילוּ	As they are glad
בְּחַלְּקָם שָׁלָל	When they divide the spoil.

We must first treat a textual problem in the initial line of the verse since the presence of the progeny blessing in v. 2[3] depends on which reading we favor. Three primary readings are possible: 1) The MT (Kethiv), followed by Symmachus, the Vulgate, and the KJV, reads, לֹא הִגְדַּלְתָּ הַשִּׂמְחָה ("you have not magnified joy"). 2) The Masoretic correction (Qere), followed by the Targum, Syriac, and most modern translations, reads, לוֹ הִגְדַּלְתָּ הַשִּׂמְחָה ("for them[18] you have magnified joy").[19] 3) Many commentators[20] have emended the text and fused the particle to the previous word, creating the reading, הִרְבִּיתָ הַגִּילָה ("you have multiplied the gladness"). This latter reading would fit the context extraordinarily well. Rather than the brief insertion of the progeny blessing between the themes of light and joy, both of which receive more extended treatment, we simply have light transitioning to joy. Furthermore, this would create synonymous parallelism between the multiplication of gladness and the increase of joy in the next line. In addition, the verbal form of הַגִּילָה occurs later in the same verse (cf. הַשִּׂמְחָה and שָׂמְחוּ in v. 2[3] as well). But despite its appeal, this option must be rejected: 1) No external manuscript evidence exists for such a reading. 2) The corruption of הגילה into a more difficult reading of הגוי לא or הגוי לו seems unlikely since it entails the alteration of ה to א or ו.[21] The first option (i.e., the Kethiv) is also unlikely

---

17 Most of the verbs throughout vv. 1–6 are perfects. In general, these should be understood as "prophetic perfects" (i.e., "rhetorical futures") whereby the author is so certain of the future realization of his statements that he views them as completed acts (see GKC §106n). Whether the verbs in vv. 5–6 are prophetic perfects depends on one's view regarding the identity of the child.

18. This reading is to be understood as preposition לְ of advantage plus the third masculine singular pronoun referring to הַגּוֹי, frontloaded for emphasis.

19. It is difficult to reconstruct the *Vorlage* of the LXX, but it is most likely based on this reading since it mentions the nation (τοῦ λαοῦ) and nothing is negated.

20. This conjecture was first proposed by William Selwyn, *Horae Hebraicae*, 15–36, and has been adopted, for example, by Blenkinsopp, *Isaiah 1–39*, 246; Clements, *Isaiah 1–39*, 106; Gray, *Isaiah: I–XXXIX*, 169; Kaiser, *Isaiah 1–12*, 203; Watts, *Isaiah 1–33*, 131; Wegner, *Kingship and Messianic Expectation*, 140; Wildberger, *Isaiah 1–12*, 386; Wolff, *Frieden ohne Ende*, 53–56.

21. Although by the second century BCE ה and ו look somewhat similar in some

since it contradicts the following line. Therefore, the second option is best since it fits contextually and has manuscript support.[22] The Kethiv likely arose either from the confusion of homophones in the copying process or as a result of the ambiguous spelling לוא (found in 1QIsaa) which could be understood as either of the first two variants.[23]

As we have seen, רָבָה is the most common term used to denote the progeny blessing, and there is little doubt that it refers here to the numerical expansion of the people.[24] Although גּוֹי typically refers to foreign peoples, in the present context it functions as a parallel word pair with הָעָם (9:1[2]) with respect to Israel.[25] The primary focus is on the northern tribes (8:23[9:1]), but since the passage culminates in the rule of a Davidic king, probably all twelve tribes are in view as the object of רָבָה. Although the purpose or goal of the expansion of the population is not entirely evident, perhaps it is an additional means by which Yahweh will "magnify joy" beyond those mentioned in vv. 3–6[4–7]. Proliferation of people results in proliferation of rejoicing, both because it is a blessed thing to expand as a people and because more people are able to experience the benefits of freedom from oppression and the just reign of the Davidic king.[26]

The time period to which 9:1–6[2–7] refers depends on the historical and literary setting of the oracle as well as the identity of the child in vv. 5–6[6–7].[27] Many have interpreted 9:1–6[2–7] as a birth announcement

---

texts written in proto-semitic script, in general these letters are not confused easily in proto-semitic epigraphy.

22. See Barthélemy, *Isaïe, Jérémie, Lamentations*, 60–63; de Waard, *Isaiah*, 42–43; Childs, *Isaiah*, 77; Motyer, *Isaiah*, 100–101; Oswalt, *Isaiah: Chapters 1–39*, 240.

23. See Barthélemy, *Isaïe, Jérémie, Lamentations*, 61. According to the Masoretic note in the Mp, this is one of seventeen instances in the MT in which לֹא is to be read as לוֹ (see Mm 1795), so evidently this was a common error.

24. Although רָבָה occurs seven times elsewhere in the book (1:15; 23:16; 30:33; 40:29; 51:2; 55:7; 57:9), only in 51:2 where it refers to the Abrahamic promise does it refer to the multiplication of people.

25. גּוֹי (72x) is clearly the preferred term to refer to foreign nations in the book of Isaiah. However, גּוֹי refers to Israel at least seven times, six of which occur in Isa 1–26. Two of these texts portray Israel as a wicked nation deserving of judgment (1:4; 10:6) while the others anticipate future salvation for Israel (9:2[3]; 26:2, 15, 49:7). When Israel is referred to as a גּוֹי in Isa 1–39, it is always in parallelism with עַם (1:4; 9:1–2[2–3]; 10:6) except in 26:2, 15.

26. We will see this correlation between just Davidic kingship and the multiplication of the people in the land elsewhere (see Jer 3:16; 23:3; 30:19; 33:22).

27. Although some have assigned an exilic or post-exilic date to the oracle (e.g., Vollmer, "Jesaja 9:1–6," 343–50), this is unlikely since there is no indication that Davidic kingship has ceased and is in need of reinstatement. Moreover, given the

or accession oracle referring to Hezekiah.²⁸ Christopher Seitz argues for this position from the literary context, positing that Isa 9 is the fulfillment of the son predicted in 7:14 and that the promised results of Hezekiah's reign in vv. 1–6[2–7] are confirmed by the deliverance of Jerusalem in 701 BCE as recorded in Isa 36–39. Hezekiah then serves as the model for ideal kingship in Isa 11, a truly messianic text.²⁹ However, without downplaying the significance of Hezekiah's kingship and the events of 701, these referents do not appear to satisfy the lofty language of 9:1–6[2–7]. In the case of the progeny blessing, it is difficult to see how the Assyrian conquest of Judah (Isa 36–37) can be reconciled with the multiplication of the nation. Furthermore, it is highly unlikely that the titles of v. 5[6] would be ascribed to a mere human king.³⁰ It is more likely that this is a messianic figure anticipated in the indeterminate future, and thus associated more closely with Isa 11 than with 7:14.³¹ Accordingly, God will multiply the nation at some point in the future following Assyrian oppression. In the final form of the book, this expectation is deferred to a time beyond the Babylonian exile, associated with the rise of the king of vv. 5–6[6–7]. Although the immediate literary context mentions neither a "remnant" nor a "return," it seems reasonable to infer from the wider context (in particular from the similar text in Isa 11) that it is the returned remnant (שְׁאָר; see 4:3; 7:3; 11:11, 16) that will experience this growth. Although Israel's numbers have shrunk through purifying judgment, hope remains that she will again be numerous.

There are no overt textual indicators that help us to identify this occurrence of the progeny blessing with any of the primary strands of the tradition within the OT. However, the parallels between 9:1–6[2–7] and 1 Kgs 4:20—5:14[4:20–34] are striking. During Solomon's prosperous reign, "Judah and Israel were as numerous as the sand by the sea" and "joyful" (שְׂמֵחִים; 1 Kgs 4:20), the same elements juxtaposed in Isa 9:2[3]. In the

---

northern regions cited in 8:23[9:1], the oracle was most likely delivered between 733 and 722 (see Motyer, *Isaiah*, 99; cf. Childs, *Isaiah*, 79; Clements, *Isaiah 1–39*, 104).

28. See, for example, Blenkinsopp, *Isaiah 1–39*, 249; Clements, *Isaiah 1–39*, 105. This view was popularized by Albrecht Alt, "Jesaja 8,23—9,6," 206–25.

29. See Seitz, *Isaiah 1–39*, 71–75, 86–87.

30. The parallels between this text and Egyptian coronation hymns are weak, particularly in light of the fact that, whereas the Pharaoh was considered to be divine, this was far from the case in Israel. See especially Paul D. Wegner, who concludes that 9:1–6 does not exhibit the form of an accession oracle ("Isaiah IX 1–6," 103–7).

31. See Childs, *Isaiah*, 80–81; Motyer, *Isaiah*, 102–3; Oswalt, *Isaiah: Chapters 1–39*, 245.

same text, Solomon's Davidic reign over a united kingdom is described as peaceful (5:4[4:24]; שָׁלוֹם) and free of subservience to foreign peoples (5:1, 4–5[4:21, 24–25]), similar to the description in Isa 9:1–6[2–7]. Elsewhere, the queen of Sheba observes that he rules with "justice and righteousness" (1 Kgs 10:9; מִשְׁפָּט וּצְדָקָה; cf. the description of Isa 11:1–5). Although it would be difficult to argue for literary priority or dependence, it is possible that Isaiah was familiar with these Solomonic traditions and employed them in his depiction of the future ruler, presenting Solomon as a paradigm. Thus, 1 Kgs 4:20 may serve as the primary intertext for the progeny blessing in Isa 9:2[3].[32] Primarily, this indicates a return to the height of Israel's prosperity, but secondarily points to the realization of the Abrahamic promises of land and progeny.[33]

Isaiah 10:22

Between the two oracles of hope associated with a coming Davidic king in 9:1–6[2–7] and 11:1–16, we encounter judgment oracles against Israel (9:7[8]—10:4) and Assyria (10:6–34) on account of their pride. In the midst of the latter oracle, two brief prose notes (vv. 20–23, 24–27) treat Yahweh's salvific action on behalf of Israel, a consequence of his wrath toward Assyria. These verses share many expressions with surrounding texts, particularly with Isa 9 and 11.[34] Thus vv. 20–27 are very much at home in the broader literary context and may even function to connect these two larger oracles of hope.

The first section (vv. 20–23) pertains to the remnant motif, introduced in v. 19 with respect to the coming decimation of Assyria. In the future ("in that day," v. 20) a remnant will "depend on" (וְנִשְׁעַן; v. 20) and return[35] to "the mighty God" (אֵל גִּבּוֹר; v. 21; used elsewhere only in Isaiah in 9:5[6]), primarily a reference to repentance rather than to physical return

---

32. See Motyer, *Isaiah*, 100.

33. Note from our discussion above that 1 Kgs 4:20—5:1[4:20–21] itself appears to allude to the realization of the Abrahamic promises. Furthermore, Isa 51:2, which explicitly refers to the Abrahamic promise, is the only other occurrence of רָבָה with respect to people in Isaiah.

34. One of the clearest correspondences is between 9:3[4] and 10:26–27, which share the following vocabulary: עֹל, סָבְלוֹ, מַטֵּה, שֶׁכֶם, מִדְיָן.

35. The repeated statement, "a remnant will return" (שְׁאָר יָשׁוּב; vv. 21, 22), clearly alludes to Isaiah's son in 7:3 while anticipating expansion of the theme in 11:11–16. Apart from the uses of שְׁאָר in these texts (7:3; 10:19, 20, 21, 21, 22; 11:11, 16), it occurs only five more times in Isaiah (14:22; 16:14; 17:3; 21:17; 28:5).

(see v. 20). However, the enthusiasm triggered by vv. 20–21 is then tempered by vv. 22–23: the return of a remnant is a negative concept as well that indicates the extent of Yahweh's judgment on his people. An allusion to God's blessing of progeny introduces v. 22:

כִּי אִם־יִהְיֶה עַמְּךָ יִשְׂרָאֵל כְּחוֹל הַיָּם
שְׁאָר יָשׁוּב בּוֹ

Unfortunately, the logic of the passage as well as the historical referent for the statement regarding Israel's size are unclear because of the flexibility of 1) the conjunctions כִּי אִם and 2) the imperfect aspect of יִהְיֶה. Although כִּי and אִם often function together as a strong adversative, to introduce oath clauses, or to denote limitation, none of these options works well here. The two particles thus function separately. Many commentators ascribe a causal function to כִּי,[36] but it is difficult to see what v. 22 would then be supporting, so an adversative sense may be more appropriate. אִם almost certainly functions concessively. Regarding the timing of this clause, some commentators assert that this is a past reality (i.e., "although your people were . . ."),[37] but it is unlikely that the imperfect verb יִהְיֶה would refer to the past since iterative and inceptive senses do not fit. Childs renders יִהְיֶה as a finite future (i.e., "although your people will be . . .").[38] It is unlikely that God's renewed blessing of the people after punishment is in mind since this would undercut the emphasis on judgment in vv. 22–23, but it could refer to Israel's future size just prior to judgment. Or perhaps it functions as a present stative (i.e., "although your people are . . .")[39] and thus refers to the current size of the nation.[40] Alternatively, it could be a contingent use (i.e., "even if your people are . . ."), expressing a possible, but not necessarily present, situation.[41] Although there is no consensus on this matter, perhaps the present sense is best, since 1 Kgs 4:20 claims that

---

36. See for example, Gibson, *Hebrew Grammar*, 156b; Blenkinsopp, *Isaiah 1–39*, 256; Wildberger, *Isaiah 1–12*, 434.

37. See Hasel, *The Remnant*, 318; Kaiser, *Isaiah 1–12*, 240; Wildberger, *Isaiah 1–12*, 434.

38. Childs, *Isaiah*, 89.

39. See *IBHS* §31.3c.

40. There may not be a significant difference between the present and future renderings as long as they refer to Israel's pre-judgment population.

41. See GKC §160a; Blenkinsopp, *Isaiah 1–39*, 256; Oswalt, *Isaiah: Chapters 1–39*, 268; Watts, *Isaiah 1–33*, 152.

Israel was legitimately as numerous as the "sand by the sea" in Solomon's day.[42] The basic logic of the text then appears to be:

> A remnant will return!
> But . . . although/even if the people are as numerous as the sand by the sea,
> Only a remnant will return.

Therefore, the same statement, "a remnant will return," is both a beacon of hope (v. 21) and a word of judgment (v. 22).[43]

Since vv. 20–27 occur in the literary context of the present and coming Assyrian oppression, "the one who struck them" (מַכֵּהוּ; v. 20) should be understood as Assyria (cf. v. 24),[44] and the "remnant" probably has the northern kingdom primarily in view, particularly in light of 11:11–16, which expands upon vv. 20–23 and indicates that the return is physical as well as spiritual. Therefore, if v. 22a is a statement regarding Israel's present or future size, it probably refers to her size in Isaiah's own day or in the near future prior to the Assyrian decimation of the northern kingdom.[45] With respect to the remnant's return, little more can be said other than that it will accompany or follow Assyria's demise as described in Isa 10, and in the final form of the book may be pushed beyond the Babylonian exile as well.[46]

In all likelihood, v. 22a refers to God's promise of progeny to Abraham.[47] Although Joshua–Kings employ the sand metaphor to denote the vast size of other peoples (Josh 11:4; Judg 7:12; 1 Sam 13:5), with respect to the people of Israel it is only used with reference to the Abrahamic blessing (Gen 22:17; 32:13[12]). Furthermore, other occurrences of this metaphor (see 1 Kgs 4:20; Isa 48:19; Jer 33:22; Hos 2:1[1:10]) appear to

---

42. Isaiah may not have had this text at his disposal, but the tradition may have been known to him. This is all the more plausible given the parallels between Isa 9:1–6[2–7] and 1 Kgs 4–5.

43. Paul quotes Isa 10:22–23 in Rom 9:27–28 to make the same point that we are arguing here, namely, that the remnant concept within Israel pertains to those who will return spiritually to Yahweh and that this concept expresses both hope and judgment. See Moo, *Romans*, 614–16.

44. See Clements, *Isaiah 1–39*, 115; Seitz, *Isaiah 1–39*, 94.

45. While all twelve tribes are in view in this statement, the focus is on the ten northern tribes.

46. See Blenkinsopp, *Isaiah 1–39*, 172.

47. See Childs, *Isaiah*, 95; Kaiser, *Isaiah 1–12*, 241; Motyer, *Isaiah*, 117; Oswalt, *Isaiah: Chapters 1–39*, 271.

allude to Abraham as well.[48] Specifically, this may be another allusion to 1 Kgs 4:20. This is more likely to be the case if 1 Kgs 4:20 is the primary intertext for 9:2[3] and if 10:22 refers to the present size of the people. Isaiah 10:22 would then allude to the fact that the Abrahamic promise of increase has already been realized.

However, the text does not necessarily aim to assert the present, possible, or future realization of the Abrahamic promises. Rather, it claims that those who return will be but a remnant despite the present, possible, or future realization of the promise. In other words, the Abrahamic covenant does not protect them from God's wrath. John Oswalt summarizes, "They were evidently arguing that God's promises to multiply them would be kept to the extent that they would always be a numerous people. Isaiah responds that it does not matter how numerous they might be or become; righteousness cannot be abrogated because of position. The one who is Sovereign has decreed their destruction because of their sin, and the number of their population will have nothing to do with the outcome."[49]

Read alongside 9:1–6[2–7], a fuller picture emerges. The people are left as a mere remnant in 10:20–27, but 9:2[3] has already announced that this will not be the end of the Abrahamic promise—God will indeed multiply them again! Therefore, the prophetic pattern of past blessing—judgment—restored blessing is evident from these two texts citing Yahweh's life-giving work of expanding his people. Moreover, this reflects the character of God in the prophets: he is not to be mocked and will judge his own people for sin (10:23), but he is also merciful and remains committed to his people (9:6[7]).

Isaiah 26:15

Following the oracles against the nations (Isa 13–23), Isa 24–27 deals with Yahweh's comprehensive judgment of the earth and deliverance for those who trust in him.[50] Judah's song of trust in God (26:1–6) introduces their

---

48. See below on Isa 48:19, the only other Isaianic text that uses the sand metaphor.

49. Oswalt, *Isaiah: Chapters 1–39*, 271. See also Hasel, *The Remnant*, 329–30.

50. Although in the past Isa 24–27 often has been designated as apocalyptic literature, several commentators no longer find this to be convincing (e.g., Blenkinsopp, *Isaiah 1–39*, 346; Oswalt, *Isaiah: Chapters 1–39*, 440–41). Regardless, 26:11–19 does not bear the marks of the apocalyptic genre and is situated within the present world order. Due to the absence of concrete historical markers, it is difficult to date this passage with any certainty.

prayer of dependence and hope that Yahweh will ultimately save them even though they are presently suffering (vv. 7–21).

Changing pronouns, temporal shifts, and the lack of clear historical referents create difficulties in tracing the logic of this text. Nevertheless, in vv. 12–15 it appears that the people's expectation (or possibly prayer) that God will establish peace for them (v. 12a) is grounded in his past work on their behalf (v. 12b), grammatically indicated by the shift from imperfect to perfect verbs in vv. 12b–15. First, this past work entailed his destruction of foreign "lords" (אֲדֹנִים) who had ruled over them (vv. 13–14). In addition (v. 15):

יָסַפְתָּ לַגּוֹי יְהוָה	You have added to the nation,[51] O Lord,
יָסַפְתָּ לַגּוֹי נִכְבָּדְתָּ	You have added to the nation,[52] you are glorified;
רִחַקְתָּ כָּל־קַצְוֵי־אָרֶץ	You have extended all the borders of the land.

It is not immediately evident that יָסַפְתָּ לַגּוֹי denotes the multiplication of the people, a difficulty masked by English translations that render the phrase "you have increased/enlarged the nation." Although יָסַף is a common verb, only in Deut 1:11 does it denote the numerical growth of Israel. Furthermore, it is grammatically unlikely that the preposition לְ denotes the direct object of increase since there is no precedent for this when paired with יָסַף. Rather, לְ marks גּוֹי as the indirect object (see Gen 30:24; Lev 19:25; 2 Sam 12:8; Prov 3:2; 9:11) or object of advantage (see Deut 19:9), in this case with an implied or unspecified direct object. This ambiguity may account for the LXX reading: "Increase evils on them, O Lord; increase evils on all the glorious ones of the earth" (πρόσθες αὐτοῖς κακά, κύριε, πρόσθες κακὰ πᾶσιν τοῖς ἐνδόξοις τῆς γῆς).[53] Nevertheless, it is highly probable that v. 15 does indeed refer to the progeny blessing:[54] 1) Although the formulation of Deut 1:11 is somewhat different (יֹסֵף עֲלֵיכֶם;

---

51. In light of the present context, the reference to the land in v. 15b, and its use in 26:2, גּוֹי refers to Israel here, and perhaps to Judah in particular (cf. 26:1). Although it is interesting that two of the four clear uses of גּוֹי to denote Israel in salvific contexts in Isaiah (9:2[3]; 26:2, 15; 49:7) occur in the context of the progeny blessing, there do not appear to be sufficient contextual or linguistic parallels to posit a relationship of literary dependence between 9:2[3] and 26:15.

52. Although one Ms does not repeat this phrase, it is present in all other Mss and Versions. Repetition may be characteristic of the style (cf. 27:5; see Wildberger, *Isaiah 13–27*, 554) and may serve to emphasize the point.

53. Although it is possible that the translator possessed a different *Vorlage*, it is more likely that he chose in his loose translation to specify a negative direct object since גּוֹי typically denotes foreign peoples.

54. See Hill, "יסף," 478. Contra Kaiser, *Isaiah 13–39*, 209.

The Progeny Blessing in the Book of Isaiah

Hiphil + עַל rather than Qal + לְ), it appears that both prepositions typically specify the indirect object in both stems (see 1 Chr 21:3; Ps 115:14; Deut 4:2; Num 36:3-4; 1 Kgs 12:14; Isa 38:5) so that Deut 1:11, where the progeny blessing is more clearly in view, is a legitimate parallel. In many of these cases where the direct object is implied, it is identical with the indirect object, as we are arguing here. Although clear cases in which לְ is used in the same way are lacking, it is also unusual for the direct object to be unspecified with לְ as here. 2) The literary context favors "people" as the implied direct object. The expansion of God's people would be a fitting contrast to the decimation of their enemies in the previous verse. In addition, the expansion of the land in the following clause[55] would be an appropriate necessary result. One would think that any other direct object that would not be as readily discernable from the surrounding context (e.g., wealth, knowledge, produce) would be specified.

The temporal realization of v. 15 is also in question. The perfect verbs could be rendered either as complete perfects (i.e., past fulfillment)[56] or as prophetic perfects (i.e., future fulfillment).[57] Harmonization with progeny texts elsewhere in the book is of little help since Isaiah attests to both the past (10:22; 51:2) and future (e.g., 9:2[3]; 54:1-3) proliferation of Israel. Literary context may not be decisive either since both interpretations contrast with v. 14. However, throughout vv. 11-19 imperfect verbs consistently refer to the present or future and perfect verbs appear to consistently refer to the present or past without any clear uses of the prophetic perfect. Therefore, the use of prophetic perfects in only one verse in the middle of this purposeful alternation between aspects is quite unlikely.

If, as we have argued, v. 15 refers to Yahweh's past multiplication of the people, it then provides an additional example of his past faithfulness toward his people. Not only has he destroyed their enemies (vv. 13-14), but he has also multiplied Israel (v. 15).

Although 26:1 mentions only Judah, גּוֹי probably has the entire nation of Israel in mind since Israel's traditions never attest to such growth for Judah alone. God's purpose in multiplying the people is summarized

---

55. To "remove" or "make far" (רִחַקְתָּ; cf. Isa 6:12; 29:13) the "ends" (קַצְוֵי; cf. Ps 48:11[10]; 65:6[5]) of the land is an unusual way to speak of expanding territory, but it is difficult to see that it could have any other meaning.

56. See Blenkinsopp, *Isaiah 1-39*, 366, 368; Motyer, *Isaiah*, 216-17; Snoek, "(Dis)continuity," 212-13; Wildberger, *Isaiah 13-27*, 558, 565.

57. See Childs, *Isaiah*, 191; Clements, *Isaiah 1-39*, 215; Johnson, *From Chaos to Restoration*, 78; Kaiser, *Isaiah 13-39*, 209, 212; Oswalt, *Isaiah: Chapters 1-39*, 482.

in the one word, נִכְבַּדְתְּ, "you are (or have been) glorified/honored."[58] It is unspecified whether Israel herself or the nations glorify God, but it is clear that Yahweh's expansion of the people has resulted in both blessing for Israel and glory for himself (cf. 48:9–11). Perhaps Yahweh's own motivation buttresses the hope of the people that God will again bring blessing (vv. 12a, 19) as he has in the past (vv. 12b–15).

Although there are no overt references either to the Abrahamic promises or to the united monarchy, v. 15 may allude to both progeny traditions. It is no coincidence that the blessings of progeny and land, the two material blessings of the Abrahamic covenant, are juxtaposed in v. 15. However, since v. 15 recalls not the promise but the realization of the promise, it corresponds most closely to Solomon's day when the Abrahamic promises of both progeny and land (unlike Exod 1:7) were realized as indicated in 1 Kgs 4:20—5:1[4:20–21].[59] Furthermore, peace and the defeat of enemies are common to both texts (see 1 Kgs 5:4[4:24]). Therefore, it appears that the people recall Yahweh's past covenantal faithfulness as realized during the reign of Solomon to give them confidence that a similar time of שָׁלוֹם is forthcoming.

Although their stated desire is for well-being (שָׁלוֹם; v. 12) and not the blessing of progeny, we might infer that their recollection of God's blessing in the past (v. 15) leads them to expect its renewal in the future, an inference that may be further justified by 27:6.

Isaiah 27:6

Judgment of the earth concludes Isa 26 (vv. 20–21), followed by the defeat of Leviathan in 27:1. The restoration of Israel is the climactic goal of this activity (vv. 2–6).[60] The nation is depicted as a vineyard cared for by Yahweh (vv. 2–5), followed by a brief interpretation of this metaphor in v. 6 that continues to employ agricultural imagery:

---

58. The Niphal of כָּבֵד appears six times in Isaiah (3:5; 23:8, 9; 26:15; 43:4; 49:5), each time with a stative or passive meaning, but Yahweh is the subject only here.

59. Blenkinsopp, *Isaiah 1–39*, 370; and Wildberger, *Isaiah 13–27*, 565, both suggest this dual reference.

60. See Marvin A. Sweeney, "New Gleanings," 65.

The Progeny Blessing in the Book of Isaiah

⁶¹ הַבָּאִים יַשְׁרֵשׁ יַעֲקֹב   In coming days Jacob will take root,
יָצִיץ וּפָרַח יִשְׂרָאֵל   Israel will blossom and sprout
וּמָלְאוּ פְנֵי־תֵבֵל תְּנוּבָה   And they will fill the whole world with fruit/produce.

Since the progeny blessing is sometimes denoted through imagery of "fruitfulness" (e.g., פָּרָה; Deut 7:14; 28:4, 11), it is possible that v. 6 depicts the numerical "blossoming" of the people of Israel. The Isaiah Targum flattens the imagery and interprets v. 6 as a reference to return from exile and subsequent expansion: "They will be gathered from among their exiles and they will return to their land; there those of the house of Jacob will beget (יתילדון) children, those of the house of Israel will become numerous (יפשון) and multiply (יסגון), and sons' sons will fill the face of the world" (my translation). Clements and Kaiser similarly identify this imagery with the proliferation of the people.[62]

However, this interpretation is questionable. First of all, the parable of the vineyard in 5:1–7 may point us in a different direction. Given multiple parallels between these two texts, it is evident that 27:2–6 functions as a reversal of 5:1–7, primarily with respect to God's disposition toward his vineyard, Israel: 1) Yahweh had formerly laid his vineyard waste and let briars and thorns come up (5:5–6), but now he will guard it, care for it, and eradicate all briars and thorns (27:3–4); 2) before he had withheld rain (5:6), but now he will water it (27:3); 3) in the past he had judged his vineyard because of its yield of "wild" or "nasty" grapes (בְּאֻשִׁים; 5:2, 4), but now Yahweh will guarantee that the vineyard will be fruitful (27:6). In 5:7 the bad grapes in the parable are "nasty" because of the lack of justice (מִשְׁפָּט) and righteousness (צְדָקָה) in Israel. Therefore, the "fruit" (תְּנוּבָה)[63] in 27:6 probably should be defined in similar ethical categories rather than as the physical reproduction of the people.[64] In other words, the primary point of comparison is not between few good grapes and many good grapes, but between bad grapes and good grapes, quality rather than quantity. However, since v. 6 is concerned with quantity as well, it remains

---

61. Although some construe הַבָּאִים as a substantival participle referring to the returning Israelites, it is probably an adverbial accusative of time, shorthand for "coming days" (Watts, *Isaiah 1–33*, 347; Wildberger, *Isaiah 13–27*, 588; Joüon, *Grammar*, §126i). See Wildberger, *Isaiah 13–27*, 588, for a review of options.

62. Clements, *Isaiah 1–39*, 220; Kaiser, *Isaiah 13–39*, 226.

63. תְּנוּבָה occurs only five times in the OT. It occurs three times in construct with שָׂדַי/שָׂדֶה (Deut 32:13; Ezek 36:30; Lam 4:9), suggesting that תְּנוּבָה may be better rendered "produce." Only here is it employed metaphorically.

64. Cf. Motyer, *Isaiah*, 220.

possible that the numerical expansion of the people is an implicit means by which the fruit of justice and righteousness fills the world.

Furthermore, Israel's "flourishing" in v. 6 is general and ambiguous, perhaps intentionally so. Although floral imagery is employed elsewhere with reference to Israel (see Ps 72:16; 90:6; 92:8[7]; 103:15 for ציץ; Ps 92:8[7], 13–14[12–13]; Prov 11:28; Isa 66:14; Hos 14:6[5], 8[7] for פרח), in none of these contexts is it clear that such images refer specifically to the progeny blessing (although Ps 92:8[7] is a possibility). Rather, they appear to denote general prosperity or restoration. This may include the progeny blessing (along with, for example, spiritual well-being, agricultural fecundity, peace, health, and security), but it is not the primary referent. Finally, it is unclear whether "filling the world with fruit" refers to the expansion of Israelites across the earth or whether it pertains to the spread of Yahwism and righteousness and justice to the nations,[65] which may not entail physical proliferation.

Therefore, it is unlikely that the primary referent of v. 6 is the expansion of Israel's population, although it may be implicit as an aspect of general prosperity and a means of "filling the world." We tentatively suggest that, insofar as the multiplication of the people is included within v. 6, it functions as a response to the hopeful cry of the people in 26:15: just as Yahweh has increased the nation in the past, so he will do it again.

Isaiah 44:3–4

Although it is unclear when Isa 40–55 was written, it is fairly clear that it addresses the exilic situation. Isaiah declares that the time of Israel's punishment is now over (40:1–2; 41:8–10; 54:7–8) and tries "to convince the exiles that Yahweh is God, Yahweh *can* do something about their predicament, and Yahweh *intends* to do it in the immediate future."[66] One prominent facet of this salvific message is that Yahweh *can* restore the numerical greatness of his people once again and *intends* to do so.

The first indication of this occurs in the so-called "fear not" oracle of 44:1–5. In 43:22–28 Yahweh reminds the people that their punishment at the hands of Babylon is deserved on account of their sins. However, he will graciously wipe out their sins "for his own sake" (למעני; v. 25), and show them renewed favor (44:1–5). As many have recognized, 44:1–5 is similar

---

65. So Oswalt, *Isaiah: Chapters 1–39*, 495.

66. Gowan, *Prophetic Books*, 147. See 148–59 for an excellent summary of the theological message of Isa 40–55 in a six-step logical progression.

The Progeny Blessing in the Book of Isaiah

to the "fear not" oracle of 43:1–7 in language and function.[67] Together they present a holistic vision of Israel's future: 43:1–7 depicts Yahweh's deliverance of his people and the return to the land while 44:1–5 portrays the ensuing blessing he will pour out on them. Deliverance and blessing work in conjunction to restore a numerous people to the land. The basic logic of 44:1–5 is fairly straightforward: 1) In light of Israel's elect status as his "servant" (v. 1), 2) they are not to fear (v. 2) 3) because Yahweh will pour out his רוּחַ, in other words, his blessing (בְּרָכָה),[68] on Israel's descendants (v. 3); 4) as a result, they will thrive (v. 4) 5) and identify themselves with Yahweh once again (v. 5; see below on the interpretive possibilities for v. 5). As in 27:6, Isaiah uses floral imagery to describe the renewal of the future generation of Israel in v. 4:

וְצָמְחוּ בְּבֵין חָצִיר   They will sprout/flourish among the grass
כַּעֲרָבִים עַל־יִבְלֵי־מָיִם   Like willow trees along streams of water.

To comprehend this metaphor, we must first examine a text-critical issue that affects its meaning as well as the likelihood that the progeny blessing is present. Some MT manuscripts (as well as Theodotian, Symmachus, the Vulgate, and the Syriac) read a compound preposition בְּ plus בֵּין, "in between" or "among." Thus, the comparison is presented in the second line while בְּבֵין חָצִיר offers circumstantial spatial information. However, a few MT manuscripts (as well as 1QIsa, LXX, and the Targum) read preposition כְּ rather than בְּ, creating an additional comparison in the first line, perhaps parallel to the comparison in the second. Neither בְּבֵין nor כְּבֵין is attested elsewhere in the OT, although אֶל־בֵּין (Ezek 31:10, 14) and עַל־בֵּין (Ezek 19:11) occur with a spatial meaning. All things considered, we favor בְּבֵין[69] because כְּבֵין is somewhat awkward since there is no object to which Israel's descendants are being compared as a parallel to כַּעֲרָבִים in the next line. The LXX makes better sense of the line, reading, "they will spring up like grass" (καὶ ἀνατελοῦσιν ὡσεὶ χόρτος).[70] Although this may be a satisfying comparison and would refer to the quantitative expansion

---

67. Goldingay sees these two texts as parallel oracles that constitute the second part of two four-part cycles in 42:18—45:8 (*Message of Isaiah 40–55*, 217–18).

68. Given the tight semantic and syntactical parallelism between vv. 3aα and 3aβ and between 3bα and 3bβ, it appears that רוּחַ and בְּרָכָה here function as a synonymous word pair. Furthermore, v. 3b may explicate the imagery of v. 3a.

69. See Barthélemy, *Critique textuelle*, 322–24; Oswalt, *Isaiah: Chapters 40–66*, 163 n. 4.

70. This reading is adopted by Blenkinsopp, *Isaiah 40–55*, 229; Childs, *Isaiah*, 338; Westermann, *Isaiah 40–66*, 134; and the NIV.

of Israel, it disregards בֵּין. We conclude, then, that v. 4 compares the future generation of Israelites only to willows among grass, not to both willows and grass.

It is not entirely clear, then, whether this image makes a quantitative comparison, referring to the growth of the population, a qualitative comparison, referring more generally to the future renewal and well-being of the people, or both. On the one hand, the language in v. 3 of "blessing" (בְּרָכָה) and "descendants" (זֶרַע) is reminiscent of the Abrahamic blessing. Although בְּרָכָה is used sparingly in Isaiah (19:24; 36:16; 65:8), and only here of God's blessing on his people, Isa 51:2[71] may provide us a warrant for seeing v. 3 as an allusion to the Abrahamic promise and thus the fertility imagery of v. 4 as the renewed expansion of Abraham's offspring (see also 65:23). Moreover, population growth is a dominant concern in this part of the book addressing the exilic generation (see below on 49:19–21; 54:1–3).[72] On the other hand, however, the image in v. 4 appears to be more qualitative in nature. Previously in the book, particularly in Isa 40, humanity was compared to grass (חָצִיר) to describe his transience and weakness (vv. 6, 7, 7, 8; cf. also 37:27; 51:12). To say that Israel's descendants will grow as willows[73] among grass draws a contrast between weakness/poverty and strength/prosperity so that the primary point of the metaphor is that Israel's offspring will thrive unlike the previous generation.[74] Furthermore, the outpouring of Yahweh's רוּחַ on his people in 32:15–20 results in justice, righteousness, peace, and security. Since the imagery in 44:3–4 appears to be more qualitative in nature, the sense here may be nearer to that of 32:15–20. We would conclude, then, with Goldingay that "[t]he promised refreshment of the desert points to a renewal of the community at all levels, in numbers, status, morale, faith and social life."[75] In other words, the metaphor concerns renewal and prosperity broadly speaking. However, this certainly entails the expansion of the people, especially in light of the possible reference to the Abrahamic blessing.

71. "Look to Abraham, your father . . . I called him so that I might bless him (וַאֲבָרְכֵהוּ) and multiply him (וְאַרְבֵּהוּ)."

72. Blenkinsopp, *Isaiah 40–55*, 233; Oswalt, *Isaiah: Chapters 40–66*, 164, 166; Van Winkle, "Proselytes," 353–55; Wright, *The Mission of God*, 496–97, interpret v. 4 as a reference to the progeny blessing.

73. עֲרָבָה may refer to the Euphrates poplar or willow. Its five OT occurrences (Lev 23:40; Isa 15:7; Ps 137:2; Job 40:22) describe it as a tree that grows by the water, thus well-watered.

74. See Goldingay, *Message of Isaiah 40–55*, 231.

75. Ibid., 229. See also Baltzer, *Deutero-Isaiah*, 186; Hanson, *Isaiah 40–66*, 82–83.

If vv. 3–4 allude to the Abrahamic blessing,[76] they restore hope to the people that the Abrahamic promises are not void. They must have feared that exile would be their final end, that they would remain cursed and homeless. Yahweh assures them here and (more clearly) in later texts (e.g., 49:19–21; 54:1–3; 66:7–9) that the Abrahamic promises concerning progeny and land will again be realized. Yahweh remains the primary actor, bringing renewal by means of his רוּחַ / בְּרָכָה and rooted in his election of Israel (vv. 1–2).

The flourishing of Israel's descendants will coincide with unspecified individuals identifying themselves with Yahweh and Israel (v. 5). Given Isaiah's emphasis on the future inclusion of Gentiles within the people of God, this may refer to or include Gentile proselytes.[77] If so, v. 5 supplements the expansion of the nation through physical means with the further expansion of the nation through conversions to Yahwism.[78] However, given the focus on Israel throughout vv. 1–4, it is better to view these individuals as nominal or syncretistic Israelites[79] who return to Yahweh, depicting the spiritual renewal of the nation that will accompany societal and political restoration.[80] We will explore the question of Gentile inclusion in the progeny blessing in more depth below.

Isaiah 45:18

After Yahweh introduces his plan to deliver Israel through Cyrus (45:1–13), he anticipates the effect this will have on the nations, namely, their acknowledgement of Yahweh (vv. 14–25). Throughout the chapter, God's

---

76. Blenkinsopp, *Isaiah 40–55*, 233; Goldingay, *Message of Isaiah 40–55*, 230; Oswalt, *Isaiah: Chapters 40–66*, 164–67, assert that these are allusions to Abraham.

77. So Baltzer, *Deutero-Isaiah*, 187; Begg, "Peoples and Worship," 46; Blenkinsopp, *Isaiah 40–55*, 233; Gelston, "Universalism," 386; Westermann, *Isaiah 40–66*, 136–38; Wright, *Mission of God*, 496–97.

78. See Westermann, *Isaiah 40–66*, 136.

79. Evidently, apostasy was a widespread problem in the exilic period (see Isa 48:5; Jer 16:13; 44:15–19; Ezek 20:39). As a result, there would have been a need for ethnic Israelites to reassert their identification with Yahweh and with Israel as a Yahwistic nation.

80. So Grisanti, "Relationship of Israel and the Nations," 78–90; Kaminsky and Stewart, "God of All the World," 150–51; Motyer, *Isaiah*, 343; Wilson, *Nations in Deutero-Isaiah*, 83. See especially Van Winkle, "Proselytes," 341–59. Goldingay, *Message of Isaiah 40–55*; and Oswalt, *Isaiah: Chapters 40–66*, 168, see the merits of both perspectives and prefer ambiguity.

sovereignty and exclusivity are at the fore, punctuated by the frequent refrain (with some variations), "I am Yahweh, there is no other" (vv. 4, 5, 14, 18, 21, 22). Verses 14–19 contrast Yahweh with idols and those who confess Yahweh with those who cling to idols. Israel will not suffer shame for her adherence to Yahweh because he alone is God (v. 18). This refrain is introduced in v. 18 by means of an extended messenger formula that draws attention to Yahweh's role as Creator through multiple substantival participles:

כִּי כֹה אָמַר־יְהוָה	For thus says Yahweh,
בּוֹרֵא הַשָּׁמַיִם	The one who created the heavens
הוּא הָאֱלֹהִים	(He is God),
יֹצֵר הָאָרֶץ	The one who formed the earth
וְעֹשָׂהּ	And the one who made it
הוּא כוֹנְנָהּ	(He established it;
לֹא־תֹהוּ בְרָאָהּ	He did not create it to be empty,[81]
לָשֶׁבֶת יְצָרָהּ	He formed it to be inhabited):
אֲנִי יְהוָה וְאֵין עוֹד	"I am Yahweh and there is none else."

Unlike most other prophetic texts that contain the progeny blessing, v. 18 does not occur in the context of a restoration oracle delineating the future blessings that Israel will enjoy. Nor does it trace the progress of God's gift of offspring through history, either by promise or realization. Rather, v. 18 includes a foundational proposition that explains and logically precedes his disposition to bless humanity with progeny throughout human history. It is a statement of intent rather than of action or promise.

Verse 18 draws on Israel's creation narrative as found in Gen 1–2:[82] 1) בָּרָא (cf. Gen 1:1, 21, 27; 2:3, 4) and יָצַר (cf. Gen 2:7, 8, 19), the two primary verbs of creation in Gen 1–2, each occur twice in v. 18, first as parallel participles, then as parallel perfects, creating an inclusio around the introduction of Yahweh. 2) The focus of God's creating work is הַשָּׁמַיִם and הָאָרֶץ (cf. Gen 1:1; 2:1, 4). 3) Given the creational context, תֹהוּ is almost certainly a reference to the initial state of the land as תֹהוּ וָבֹהוּ (Gen 1:2). 4) That God created the earth "to be inhabited" (לָשֶׁבֶת) is thus probably a reference to God's initial blessing upon humanity to "be fruitful and mul-

---

81. תֹהוּ is likely an adverbial accusative of purpose. Given the usage of this word in Gen 1:2, Isa 24:10, and 34:11, תֹהוּ appears to convey the sense of "empty," "deserted," or the absence of life. Derivatively, in context, it suggests purposelessness.

82. At the very least, Isa 45:18 draws on the creation *tradition* as recorded in Gen 1–2. Given the common concepts and terminology, v. 18 may even be textually dependent on Gen 1–2.

tiply and fill the earth" in Gen 1:28. Therefore, the prophet here exhibits awareness of the universal progeny blessing and alludes to it in the context of Yahweh's claim to universal sovereignty. This is hardly surprising given the emphasis in this section of Isaiah on Yahweh's role as Creator in order to assert his control over all so-called gods and world affairs.

Specifically, this clause is probably included in order to correct an errant belief or confront a pagan view, thus heightening the contrast between Yahweh and the false gods of the nations. Not only is Yahweh the sole Creator, but he also created the world with purpose. What is more, humanity is central to this purpose, contrary to pagan belief that assigned no meaningful purpose to them apart from serving the gods.[83] In v. 19 Yahweh addresses the people's concern in v. 15 by claiming that not only does he have purposes for humanity, but he also has made these purposes known.[84] Secondarily, the reminder of God's creational purposes may give hope to Israel. Interestingly, תֹהוּ is employed in 24:10 to refer to empty cities (קִרְיַת־תֹּהוּ), the result of judgment. Since תֹהוּ is contrary to Yahweh's fundamental purpose, the exiles may have concluded that it is within his purposes to bring his people back to their אֶרֶץ in order to again inhabit the cities.[85]

This brief comment that Yahweh "created the earth to be inhabited" reaffirms the importance of the progeny blessing in Yahweh's purposes for creation that form the bedrock for the OT's salvation-historical narrative.[86] Although humanity itself exists for a greater end (cf. vv. 22–23), v. 18 implies that humans are the end for which God created the world. It reaffirms humanity as the "very good" climax of his creating work and reminds us that death, war, famine, and infant mortality are contrary to Yahweh's ultimate purposes for the world.

---

83. See Oswalt, *Isaiah: Chapters 40–66*, 218; Walton, *Ancient Near Eastern Thought*, 214–15.

84. See Hanson, *Isaiah 40–66*, 110; Oswalt, *Isaiah: Chapters 40–66*, 214.

85. Baltzer, *Deutero-Isaiah*, 246; Goldingay, *Message of Isaiah 40–55*, 290–91.

86. Aside from Gen 1:28, Isa 45:18 is the most frequently cited text in rabbinic literature in support of the obligatory nature of reproduction (e.g., *b. Pesah.* 88b; *Meg.* 27a; *Hag.* 2b; *b. Yebam.* 62ab; *B. Bat.* 13a; *m. Git.* 4.5; *'Ed.* 1.13; see our earlier excursus). This text may have been deemed important due to its universal scope or creational basis. However, given the rabbinic concern with the imperative to reproduce, it may have been deemed important because reproduction is here described not just as *a* purpose of creation, but as *the* purpose of creation. In addition, a statement of purpose may entail human obligation, assuming that humanity's purposes should be aligned with those of God.

I Will Surely Multiply Your Offspring

Isaiah 48:19

Isaiah 48 confronts Israel's rebellion against Yahweh (vv. 1, 4–5, 8) and exhorts the nation to "listen" (vv. 1, 12, 14, 16; cf. 18) and respond in obedience. The chapter culminates in a brief reflection concerning what might have been, had they listened to Yahweh in the first place (vv. 17–19), followed by the announcement of return from Babylon (vv. 20–21; cf. 40:3; 43:5-7, 16–19), rooted in Yahweh's concern for his own name (vv. 9–11). With deuteronomic echoes (cf. Deut 5:1, 6), Yahweh introduces himself in v. 17 not only as Redeemer (גֹּאֲלֶךָ) and the Holy One of Israel (קְדוֹשׁ יִשְׂרָאֵל), but also as their instructor (מְלַמֶּדְךָ). Verses 18–19 then express divine regret concerning the path that Israel has chosen by ignoring Yahweh's instruction:

לוּא הִקְשַׁבְתָּ לְמִצְוֹתָי	18	If only you had paid attention to my commandments!
וַיְהִי כַנָּהָר שְׁלוֹמֶךָ		Then your well-being would have been like a river,
וְצִדְקָתְךָ כְּגַלֵּי הַיָּם		And your vindication[87] like the waves of the sea;
וַיְהִי כַחוֹל זַרְעֶךָ	19	Your offspring would have been like the sand,
וְצֶאֱצָאֵי מֵעֶיךָ כִּמְעֹתָיו		And the issue[88] of your womb like its grains;
לֹא־יִכָּרֵת וְלֹא־יִשָּׁמֵד שְׁמוֹ מִלְּפָנָי		Their name would never be cut off or destroyed from me.

Since the wider context looks to the future, some understand these verses to refer to present and future possibilities contingent upon obedience rather than to the past.[89] However, לוּא/לוּ + perfect consistently refers to complete past time,[90] sometimes to express a wish (Num 14:2; 20:3; Deut 32:29; Josh 7:7; Isa 63:19[64:1]) and sometimes to introduce the protasis of an unreal condition as here (Judg 8:19; 13:23).[91] Had they obeyed, they would have been blessed with numerous progeny, but they did not

---

87. The precise meaning of צְדָקָה here is unclear. Given the semantic and syntactical parallelism in vv. 18–19, it most likely denotes some benefit that could be enjoyed by Israel. Thus, it may denote God's justice exercised on their behalf, i.e., "salvation" (cf. Isa 46:13; 51:6; 56:1 where צְדָקָה and יְשׁוּעָה/תְּשׁוּעָה are parallel terms). See Blenkinsopp, *Isaiah 40–55*, 291.

88. צֶאֱצָאִים, employed only in Isaiah (7x) and Job (4x), is often a word pair with זֶרַע (see Isa 44:3; 48:19; 61:9; 65:23; Job 5:25; 21:8). Note as well the parallel syntactical structures in both v. 18b and 19a: וַיְהִי + כְּ[noun] + [subject]ךָ; [subject]ךָ + כְּ[noun].

89. See Westermann, *Isaiah 40–66*, 203.

90. See Arnold and Choi, *Syntax*, 55.

91. See GKC §151e. See also Huehnergard, "Asseverative *la*," 569–93, for a complete survey of the use of לוּא/לוּ in Semitic languages.

The Progeny Blessing in the Book of Isaiah

obey, so they experienced curse rather than blessing.[92] God will graciously restore Israel (vv. 20–21) despite past disobedience, but deliverance never would have been necessary if they had obeyed in the first place.

Does this interpretation of vv. 18–19 imply that Israel had never experienced the blessing of progeny to the extent that it could be said that they were as numerous as the sand? If so, this would contradict 1 Kgs 4:20 which states that Israel was as numerous as the sand in Solomon's day (יְהוּדָה וְיִשְׂרָאֵל רַבִּים כַּחוֹל אֲשֶׁר־עַל־הַיָּם לָרֹב). It would conflict with Isa 10:22 as well, if 10:22 alludes to the size of the population in Isaiah's day (כִּי אִם־יִהְיֶה עַמְּךָ יִשְׂרָאֵל כְּחוֹל הַיָּם). Perhaps authors disagreed regarding whether or not Israel had become this numerous. But there may be a better explanation. In previous generations Israel had indeed enjoyed the fullness of the progeny blessing. However, because of the decimation that occurred in the Assyrian and Babylonian judgments, the immediate exilic audience of vv. 17–19 could no longer claim to be "as the sand." It is doubtful that v. 18 suggests that Israel had never in her history experienced שָׁלוֹם (cf. 1 Kgs 5:4[4:24]) or צְדָקָה, so the same is probably the case regarding their size in v. 19. Therefore, we suggest that vv. 17–19 addresses the exilic generation in particular and thus declare that, if they had heeded Yahweh, they would have continued to experience Yahweh's blessing. It is not that the blessing was never realized but rather that it was lost and currently void as a result of their covenant breach. Isaiah 10:22 addresses a pre-exilic audience looking ahead to judgment while 48:19 addresses an exilic audience that has suffered the curse of decimation.

It is likely that זַרְעֶךָ becoming as חוֹל alludes to the Abrahamic promises[93] since these two terms occur together elsewhere only in the context of the Abrahamic promise (Gen 22:17; 32:13[12]; cf. 1 Kgs 4:20; Isa 10:22;

---

92. Nearly all commentators understand these verses as past regret. See, for example, Baltzer, *Deutero-Isaiah*, 298; Blenkinsopp, *Isaiah 40–55*, 291; Childs, *Isaiah*, 369; Goldingay, *Message of Isaiah 40–55*, 356–59; Motyer, *Isaiah*, 382; Oswalt, *Isaiah: Chapters 40–66*, 281–82. Psalm 81:14[13] is the only other place in the OT where Yahweh says, "if only" (לוּא/לוּ), which suggests that spoken divine regret is rare. As Westermann has shown, there are a number of formal parallels between Ps 81 and the present text (*Isaiah 40–66*, 203–4).

93. חוֹל occurs only in 10:22 and 48:19 in Isaiah, strengthening the link between these two texts. Typically, the simile reads, "as the sand *of the sea*" (כְּחוֹל הַיָּם). Perhaps הַיָּם is left out here for the sake of rhythm or poetic parallelism (see Oswalt, *Isaiah: Chapters 40–66*, 279 n. 75) or because הַיָּם was mentioned in the previous line. Regardless, the use of the shortened form is of little consequence since this is such a common simile.

Jer 33:22;[94] Hos 2:1[1:10]) and since clear references to these promises occur in the wider literary context (cf. 51:2). Furthermore, the final clause of v. 19 reflects a concern for their "name" (שֵׁם) as in Gen 12:2.[95] Although there is no direct reference to retention of the land in vv. 18–19, it is assumed that שָׁלוֹם was to be enjoyed in the land.

Once again we suggest that Isaiah alludes to the Abrahamic promise via its fulfillment in Solomon's time. Intriguingly, the only two Isaianic progeny texts that employ the sand simile are also the only two that refer to Israel's pre-exilic size. Perhaps this is mere coincidence, but it seems plausible that for Isaiah (and perhaps for pre-exilic Israel) this was the standard expression for denoting Israel's pre-exilic size, rooted in the realization of the Abrahamic blessing in Solomon's day. The condition of שָׁלוֹם common to both texts (cf. 1 Kgs 5:4[4:24]) strengthens this possible allusion, reminding the people of the era of prosperity that they had lost.

Grammatically, vv. 17–19 refer to the past, but Goldingay rightly notes that, rhetorically, "'if only' expresses a wish that something still hoped for in the future might already have happened."[96] Accordingly, vv. 17–19 encourage the people to learn from past mistakes and obey Yahweh.[97] Yahweh quickly erases lingering doubt concerning the relevance of the Abrahamic promises by announcing Israel's return to the land in vv. 20–21 and the expansion of the people once again in 49:19–21, already promised in 9:2[3] and 44:3–4.

Isaiah 49:19–21

Although not the sole focus of Isa 40–66, these chapters contain two stories, the story of the servant and the story of Zion. The servant figure, at times equated with Israel and at times ministering to Israel, is prominent

---

94. This text directly applies the progeny blessing to the lines of David and Levi and may be a specific application or adaptation of the Abrahamic promise.

95. Commentators are widely agreed that 48:19 refers specifically to the patriarchal promises. See, for example, Baltzer, *Deutero-Isaiah*, 299; Blenkinsopp, *Isaiah 40–55*, 295; Goldingay, *Message of Isaiah 40–55*, 358; Motyer, *Isaiah*, 382; Oswalt, *Isaiah: Chapters 40–66*, 282.

96. Goldingay, *Message of Isaiah 40–55*, 357. See also GKC §151e. Both also note that the rhetorical effect is the same in 63:19[64:1], the only other Isaianic text to employ לוּא/לִי.

97. Baltzer, *Deutero-Isaiah*, 298; Childs, *Isaiah*, 372–73; Oswalt, *Isaiah: Chapters 40–66*, 280. As Oswalt notes, v. 22 underscores this ethical imperative to keep Yahweh's commands and prevents the people from taking their election (and the deliverance of vv. 20–21) for granted (284).

in Isa 40–55 and described with masculine language.[98] The story of Zion, depicted as both the mother of the people of Israel and the wife of Yahweh, is told in Isa 49–66, using feminine language. These two figures overlap in Isa 49–55, where the text alternates between the servant and Zion. Interestingly, "[t]he two groups of metaphors run parallel and never cross each other's lines."[99] Nevertheless, it is not difficult to observe parallels between the two figures in terms of their emotions, their treatment, and their relationship to Yahweh.[100] Furthermore, both Zion and the servant are portrayed in a positive light since guilt is placed on the "children," the people of Israel.[101] Despite the lack of a direct connection, the interlacing of servant and Zion texts along with these parallels invites their comparison.[102] Generally speaking, the people of Israel are restored by means of the work of the servant, a restoration experienced by mother Zion as well.[103]

Zion's personification as a woman is not novel. Cities were typically personified as women in other Semitic cultures (although usually because they were represented by goddesses),[104] and the OT prophets often apply this imagery to Jerusalem.[105] This personification radically shapes Isaiah's treatment of the desolate city in Isa 49–66. There is a clear progression in this story "from desolate loneliness and rejection to happiness, marriage, and the birth of her children."[106] Zion is described as a barren woman (49:21; 54:1), drawing on the type-scene of the barren matriarch as found

---

98. The isolation of four distinct "Servant Songs," first proposed by Bernard Duhm, is unwarranted and obscures this larger story and the interplay between Israel as servant and an individual servant sent to minister to Israel. See Mettinger, *Farewell*.

99. Jeppesen, "Mother Zion," 124.

100. See Sawyer, "Daughter of Zion," 99–100.

101. See Jeppesen, "Mother Zion," 125.

102. However, Marjo C. A. Korpel, following L. E. Wilshire ("Servant-City," 356–67), goes too far by equating Zion and the servant and arguing that these metaphors are interchangeable ("Female Servant," 153–54).

103. See especially Jeppesen, "Mother Zion," 109–25; Sawyer, "Daughter of Zion," 89–107.

104. See Schmitt, "Motherhood of God," 569.

105. See Isa 1:21–26; 3:16–17; 4:4; 37:22; Jer 2:2; 4:31; 31; Ezek 16; 23; Mic 4:9–10. In Isa 40–66, Zion is introduced as female in 40:1–2. Daughter Zion is contrasted in Isa 49–66 with daughter Babylon (46–47) who is to be deprived of her children and widowed (47:8–9), the reverse of Zion's future.

106. Sawyer, "Daughter of Zion," 102. As Sawyer notes, Zion sometimes appears to represent the people themselves and their plight, even as Zion as "mother" and the people as "children" remain distinct in the metaphor (101). See also Koole, *Isaiah III: Isaiah 56–66*, 49.

in the stories of Sarah, Rachel, Rebecca, Samson's mother, and Hannah.[107] This devastating condition is addressed three times (49:19–21; 51:1–3; 54:1–3) in slightly different, yet complementary, descriptions of the recovery of her children. It is difficult to determine whether the exilic longing for a restored population in the land shapes the use of the maternal metaphor or whether the metaphor itself prompts this emphasis on the proliferation of children since childbearing was a woman's chief concern and source of joy. Regardless, the hope for the expansion of the nation in the land is the focal point of the reversal of the fate of Zion. Thus it is in these chapters in Isaiah that the progeny blessing plays a particularly prominent role, perhaps more so than in any other place in the prophetic books.

Isaiah 49:1–13 continues the story of the servant by specifying his two-fold task to both restore Israel and serve as a "light for the nations" (vv. 5–6). The work of the servant in this text culminates in the return of the people to the land, facilitated by God's care for them on the journey (vv. 8–13), grounded in his "compassion" (רָחַם; vv. 10, 13). Isaiah 49 thus furthers the argument of Isaiah beyond that of Isa 40–48. In Isa 40–48 Israel's hope is to be based on the belief that Yahweh, as the sole sovereign God, can deliver them. Isaiah 49 begins to address a different concern by declaring that God not only can deliver them but also wants to.[108]

However, Zion, who speaks only here in the entire book, disputes Yahweh's claim that he will show compassion by lamenting that Yahweh has "abandoned" (עֲזָבָנִי) and "forgotten" (שְׁכֵחָנִי) her (v. 14). Yahweh's reply (49:15—50:3) corrects her misperception. Yahweh's compassion for Zion exceeds even that of a mother for her child (v. 15). The miraculous appearance of a multitude of her children (vv. 17–21) will serve as the expression of his love and as irrefutable evidence of his pledge, "I will not forget you" (וְאָנֹכִי לֹא אֶשְׁכָּחֵךְ; v. 15). This extravagant repopulation will be accomplished by means of the return, aided by the nations (vv. 22–23), and accompanied by the destruction of their enemies (vv. 24–26), both actions resulting in knowledge of Yahweh (vv. 23, 26). In light of this bright future, Yahweh implies in 50:1–3 that he had only left his "wife" for a time on account of her iniquities, not divorced her as she thought.

Verses 17–18a foresee the return of the people to the land, accompanied by the departure of their enemies.[109] With evocative poetry, Yahweh

---

107. See Callaway, *Sing, O Barren One*, 59–72.

108. See Oswalt, *Isaiah: Chapters 40–66*, 303–4.

109. It is difficult to determine whether v. 17 refers to the "hastening" of "your builders" or of "your children" given the ambiguity of the consonantal text בניך. External evidence is divided, with 1QIsaa, LXX, and the Vulgate favoring בָּנַיִךְ and the

The Progeny Blessing in the Book of Isaiah

then describes the result of the return from the perspective of Zion and her children:

חַי־אָנִי נְאֻם־יְהוָה	18	"As I live," declares Yahweh,
כִּי כֻלָּם כָּעֲדִי תִלְבָּשִׁי		"Surely you will put them all on as an ornament;
וּתְקַשְּׁרִים כַּכַּלָּה		and bind them on like a bride.
כִּי חָרְבֹתַיִךְ וְשֹׁמְמֹתַיִךְ [110]	19	As for your waste and desolate places
וְאֶרֶץ הֲרִסֻתֵיךְ		and destroyed land:
כִּי עַתָּה תֵּצְרִי מִיּוֹשֵׁב		surely now you will be too cramped[113] for your inhabitants,
וְרָחֲקוּ מְבַלְּעָיִךְ		and those who swallowed you up will be far away.
	20	
עוֹד יֹאמְרוּ בְאָזְנַיִךְ בְּנֵי שִׁכֻּלָיִךְ		The children of your bereavement will yet say in your ears,
צַר־לִי הַמָּקוֹם		'The place is cramped for me;
גְּשָׁה־לִּי וְאֵשֵׁבָה		make room for me that I may dwell there.'
וְאָמַרְתְּ בִּלְבָבֵךְ	21	Then you will say in your heart,
מִי יָלַד־לִי אֶת־אֵלֶּה		'Who has borne these for me?
וַאֲנִי שְׁכוּלָה וְגַלְמוּדָה [111]		for I am bereaved and barren,
גֹּלָה וְסוּרָה [112]		exiled and put away;
וְאֵלֶּה מִי גִדֵּל		who has brought these up?
הֵן אֲנִי נִשְׁאַרְתִּי לְבַדִּי		look, I was left alone;
אֵלֶּה אֵיפֹה הֵם		where did these come from?'"

MT and Syriac favoring בָּנָיִךְ. "Builders" works well in the immediate context given the reference to Zion's walls in the previous clause, but "sons" works better in the wider context that describes the return in vv. 18–21. There is some appeal in siding with commentators who entertain the possibility of intentional ambiguity and accept both options (for example, Baltzer, *Deutero-Isaiah*, 321; Childs, *Isaiah*, 392), but this may simply be an admission that a decision between the two is nearly impossible. We would note, however, that if "builders" is correct, v. 17 depicts a rebuilding effort in preparation for those who arrive in the land, explicit in other places (cf. 44:26–28; 45:13; 58:12; 60:10; 61:4). This juxtaposition of rebuilding and repopulation appears elsewhere in the prophets, particularly in Ezek 36:10–14, 33–38.

110. The two כִּי clauses in v. 19 most likely continue the oath statement of v. 18b. See ESV; NRSV; Koole, *Isaiah III: Isaiah 49–55*, 62; Oswalt, *Isaiah: Chapters 40–66*, 308.

111. גַּלְמוּד is used elsewhere only in Job 3:7, 15:34, and 30:3 and appears to denote a barrenness or emptiness in all of its uses. Thus Zion both has lost her children (שְׁכוּלָה) and is unable to have more (גַּלְמוּדָה).

112. These two words are missing in the LXX and often thought to be an interpolation.

113. The Qal form of צרר can be either transitive or intransitive, as here, denoting restriction in either a physical or figurative sense (cf. Isa 28:20). The intransitive verb + מִן is to be rendered "too much" or "too little" (GKC §133c; see 2 Kgs 6:1).

137

Here the return is not simply a promise but an accomplished reality: there they are standing in front of her, not of her own doing, but due to Yahweh's compassionate intervention.[114] Accordingly, mother Zion's three questions in v. 21 express amazement and shock that she still has any children at all—much less so many!

Although the final result of many children is clearly the main thrust of this vivid text, we may inquire further into when, where, and who Yahweh has blessed with progeny. In most prophetic texts, multiplication follows the return to the land. Although it is difficult to know how much the imagery ought to be pressed for details, in 49:19–21 it appears that the crowded state is the result of a sudden return, not the return of a few who then multiply. Moreover, since their oppressors will be removed from the land (vv. 17–19), yet there is still insufficient room for all those who return, those who return must outnumber those who were exiled.[115] Overcrowding is all the more striking since many had perished in the exilic judgment. We may infer then that Yahweh has multiplied the people even while they were in exile, in preparation for the return. Regarding the identity of the "children of bereavement" (בְּנֵי שִׁכֻּלָיִךְ),[116] they could possibly be the very children of which she was bereaved when they were carried off into exile. More likely, they are simply a new generation of Israelites who were born in exile during the time of her bereavement,[117] still clearly recognizable as "her children."[118] Although vv. 19–21 are consistent with Deut 30:1–10 in

---

114. This appears to be a reversal of the prophet Isaiah's original commission in 6:11–12: he was instructed to preach until cities were "without inhabitant" (מֵאֵין יוֹשֵׁב; v. 11), the land was a "desolation" (שְׁמָמָה; v. 11) and the people were "far away" (רִחַק; v. 12). Now the "desolate places" (וְשֹׁמְמֹתַיִךְ) will be too crowded "for inhabitants" (מִיּוֹשֵׁב) and it is their enemies who will be "far away" (וְרָחֲקוּ) (v. 19).

115. See Motyer, *Isaiah*, 394. Although the focus here is on the city of Zion, it is unlikely that v. 19a refers to Zion alone, and thus the people face overcrowding even after filling all of the cities previously laid waste and destroyed (contra Baltzer, *Deutero-Isaiah*, 326).

116. The abstract plural שִׁכֻּלִים occurs only here (see Joüon, *Grammar*, §136h). Although the שכל root at times denotes miscarriage (i.e., loss of children not yet born; see Exod 23:26), it more often refers to the loss of existing children through violent or natural means (cf. Isa 47:8–9).

117. See Blenkinsopp, *Isaiah 40–55*, 312; Goldingay and Payne, *Isaiah 40–55*, 191; Oswalt, *Isaiah: Chapters 40–66*, 308.

118. In light of the NT, some entertain the possibility that this great returning throng is the result not of physical multiplication but of the expansion of the nation by means of Gentile proselytes (e.g., Koole, *Isaiah III: Isaiah 49–55*, 50, 64; Motyer, *Isaiah*, 95). In the present passage the nations appear to be either subservient to Israel (vv. 22–23) or punished by Yahweh (vv. 24–26) and nothing is said regarding their

predicting an expansion of the people of Israel that will exceed that of pre-exilic times, this text is surprising in that it suggests that this will occur prior to the return.

Yahweh's gracious restoration of Zion's many children to the land and the mending of the relationship between Zion and Yahweh constitute a recovery of the blessings of the Abrahamic covenant. However, the circumstances surrounding the proliferation of Israel in vv. 19–21 may correspond typologically to the initial realization of the Abrahamic progeny promise as recorded in Exod 1:7. This possibility is strengthened by the portrayal of the return as a second exodus elsewhere in Isa 40–55 (40:3–5; 42:16; 43:1–6, 14–21; 48:20–21; 49:8–12; 51:9–11; 52:11–12; 55:12–13). Just as God had multiplied the people outside of the land in preparation for their initial entry into the land, so he will once again multiply them outside of the land of promise prior to bringing them back in a second exodus. Nevertheless, this must remain a tentative conclusion since the multiplication of the people outside of the land must be inferred from 49:14–21 and nothing is said regarding when and how this came about.[119]

In this initial scene in the Zion story, we witness the reversal of her destitute state, from abandoned to loved, from bereaved and barren to filled with children, from desolate to inhabited. Familial relationships between Yahweh, Zion, and Israel are restored. From the perspective of mother Zion, the proliferation and return of Israel is for the purpose of her happiness and an expression of Yahweh's compassion toward her. For the exilic audience, represented both by the children and by mother Zion, this is a message that flies in the face of their current reality, a message of hope that Yahweh will restore them and will continue to bless them in preparation for the return even while in exile.

---

inclusion within Israel. Therefore, this interpretation is unlikely unless we incorporate broader contextual considerations based on other Isaianic texts that relate the nations to Israel in this manner (see below).

119. However, the fact that this has taken place "behind the scenes" may give even greater weight to a correspondence to Exod 1:7 since there the fact of multiplication is noted, yet Yahweh's agency is not explicit.

See below on Jer 29:6 where the people are instructed to multiply while in Babylon. A stronger case can be made there in favor of a typological correspondence between the proliferation of the people in Egypt and their expansion in Babylon.

I Will Surely Multiply Your Offspring

Isaiah 51:2–3

Following the story of Zion in 49:14—50:3, the servant speaks in 50:4–9. Despite (or because of) his obedience to Yahweh (vv. 4–5), he is persecuted (v. 6), yet ultimately vindicated by Yahweh (vv. 7–9). The elect (v. 10) are then distinguished from the rebels (v. 11), the former identified as those who both fear Yahweh and obey the servant. Isaiah 51 returns to the story of Zion (51:1—52:12), but it is those who listen to the servant (50:10) who are addressed first in 51:1–8 rather than personified Zion (although Zion is present in v. 3). Each stanza (vv. 1–3, 4–6, 7–8) begins with an exhortation to "listen" to Yahweh, pertains to coming salvation, and culminates in joy or the realization of deliverance.

The first stanza, like 49:14–21, primarily addresses the exilic concern that the people are few in number and that Zion is desolate. Its aim is to comfort and encourage:

שִׁמְעוּ אֵלַי רֹדְפֵי צֶדֶק	1	Listen to me, pursuers of righteousness,[120]
מְבַקְשֵׁי יְהוָה		Those who seek Yahweh:
הַבִּיטוּ אֶל־צוּר חֻצַּבְתֶּם		Look to the rock from which you were hewn,
וְאֶל־מַקֶּבֶת בּוֹר נֻקַּרְתֶּם		And to the quarry/cistern from which you were dug.
הַבִּיטוּ אֶל־אַבְרָהָם אֲבִיכֶם	2	Look to Abraham, your father
וְאֶל־שָׂרָה תְּחוֹלֶלְכֶם		And to Sarah who bore you in pain;
כִּי־אֶחָד קְרָאתִיו		For when he was one man I called him,
וַאֲבָרְכֵהוּ וְאַרְבֵּהוּ		So that I might bless him[121] and multiply him.[122]
כִּי־נִחַם יְהוָה צִיּוֹן	3	For Yahweh will comfort Zion;
נִחַם כָּל־חָרְבֹתֶיהָ		He will comfort all her waste places,
וַיָּשֶׂם מִדְבָּרָהּ כְּעֵדֶן		He will make her wilderness like Eden,
וְעַרְבָתָהּ כְּגַן־יְהוָה		And her desert like the garden of Yahweh;
שָׂשׂוֹן וְשִׂמְחָה יִמָּצֵא בָהּ		Joy and gladness will be found in her,
תּוֹדָה וְקוֹל זִמְרָה		Thanksgiving and the sound of song.

---

120. It is unclear whether the synonymous word pair, "pursuers of צֶדֶק" and "seekers of Yahweh," refers to salvation/vindication or to right conduct. Both senses are possible for both phrases, but the latter is more likely in this context given 50:10–11 and the similar address in 51:7. See Motyer, *Isaiah*, 403; Oswalt, *Isaiah: Chapters 40–66*, 334. Baltzer, *Deutero-Isaiah*, 345; and Koole, *Isaiah III: Isaiah 49–55*, 138–39, entertain the possibility of a double referent.

121. 1QIsaa reads ואפרהו rather than וַאֲבָרְכֵהוּ, probably either due to assimilation to the common hendiadys found in Genesis or the substitution of a roughly synonymous verb. The LXX adds "and loved him" (καὶ ἠγάπησα αὐτὸν) prior to וְאַרְבֵּהוּ, underscoring Yahweh's favorable disposition toward Abraham (and analogously toward the people).

122. וַאֲבָרְכֵהוּ וְאַרְבֵּהוּ are probably waw conjunctive + imperfect rather than waw

The rock imagery, the recollection of Abraham and Sarah, and the comforting of Zion are intimately related. Therefore, we must examine the significance of each, particularly with respect to the blessing of progeny.

Although it is typically Yahweh who is portrayed as a "rock" in the OT, vv. 1–2 compare Israel's ancestral parents, Abraham and Sarah, to a rock or quarry.[123] The significance of the metaphor is multi-faceted. First, it points to the origin of the people and identifies them with Abraham and Sarah,[124] implying that this distant past has present relevance for them. Furthermore, some find here an allusion to the wilderness traditions in which Yahweh brought water from the rock for the people, life from inanimate lifelessness.[125] Therefore, in light of v. 2, the "rock" may refer to the infertile couple from which Yahweh eventually brought forth life.[126]

Indeed, the people are to look to Abraham precisely because he began as only one man,[127] without an heir, a situation analogous to their own diminished numerical status in exile. Given their solidarity with Abraham, God's fulfilled intention to bless and multiply Abraham remains relevant for their own situation in indicating how they can expect him to work in the future on their behalf.[128] Only blessing and progeny[129] are mentioned

---

consecutive constructions, denoting purpose and future fulfillment from Abraham's frame of reference (see GKC §107b). This need not imply that, from the exilic standpoint, the promise to Abraham has yet to be realized.

123. Note the repetition of הַבִּיטוּ.

124. Childs, *Isaiah*, 402; Koole, *Isaiah III: Isaiah 49–55*, 141–42; Kuntz, "Contribution," 148, 153; Oswalt, *Isaiah: Chapters 40–66*, 334.

125. See Baltzer, *Deutero-Isaiah*, 345–46; Goldingay, *Message of Isaiah 40–55*, 420.

126. Koole, *Isaiah III: Isaiah 49–55*, 141–42.

127. אֶחָד functions here as an adverbial accusative of state with respect to Abraham.

128. Only here does Isaiah cite Abraham with an appeal to Abrahamic traditions (although he is mentioned in 29:22; 41:8; and 63:16) and this is the only mention of Sarah outside Genesis. Only in 9:2[3] does he employ רָבָה elsewhere with respect to human increase, despite the fact that this is the most common term for the blessing in the OT. Both terms, בָּרַךְ and רָבָה, are common in the Abrahamic blessing as recorded in Genesis, occurring together in Gen 17:20, 22:17, 26:4, 24, and 28:3. (In addition, they appear together in Gen 1:22, 28, and 9:1 with respect to the universal blessing and also in Deut 7:13, 30:16, and Ps 107:38 with respect to the progeny blessing.) Most likely, the tradition of the Abrahamic promises underlies this text rather than any specific text in Genesis, although Gen 12:2–3 (given קְרָאתִיו) or 22:17 provide the closest linguistic parallels.

129. Goldingay observes that the only two uses of the ברד root in Isa 40–55 relate blessing to the multiplication of the people and thus infers that for Deutero-Isaiah the progeny blessing is the key element in the Abrahamic blessing (*Message of Isaiah 40–55*, 421).

in vv. 1-2, but v. 3 treats the restoration of the land, the other material Abrahamic blessing.[130]

Verse three then shifts from the past to the future.[131] Ultimately, the exiles are to look to Abraham, their father, because (כִּי) Yahweh is about to comfort Zion, resulting in joy and gladness. The faithfulness of Yahweh to his promises in the past strengthens their faith in his promises for the future. Yahweh's comforting (נִחַם) of Zion and her waste places (חָרְבֹתֶיהָ) is a frequent (cf. 40:1; 49:13; 51:12; 52:9; 66:13), yet general, concept. Perhaps this is accomplished by means of the renewed fertility of the land, as depicted in the following parallel lines. In addition, it may entail rebuilding. However, there is good reason to believe that Yahweh's "comforting" acts consist primarily in the multiplication of his people in Zion: 1) The juxtaposition of the comforting of his people in 49:13 with the replenishment of mother Zion with children in 49:14-21 suggests that the comforting of Zion consists in filling her with people. 2) In 49:19 Zion's "waste places" (חָרְבֹתַיִךְ) are "cured" through this replenishment. 3) It is possible that the analogy between Abraham and the audience is loose and simply indicates that Yahweh will give them a positive future as he granted their father a positive future. However, Yahweh may recall the promise of progeny to Abraham precisely because it is this same blessing that Yahweh is about to grant once again.[132]

Because v. 3 is ambiguous, it is also unclear whether the multiplication of the people at Zion will be accomplished by means of the return from exile, the physical proliferation of the people, or both. On the one hand, appeal to the Abrahamic tradition might suggest that the blessing functions as it does in Genesis, namely, as physical reproduction. On the other hand, the return is emphasized in the immediately following context (vv. 9-11), and 49:15-23 equates restoration of children with the return. Therefore, the best understanding of v. 3a is that it entails both the return

---

130. Abraham also may serve as a model of faith. Just as he "feared" Yahweh (יָרֵא; Gen 22:12) and "obeyed" him (שָׁמַעְתָּ; Gen 22:18; cf. Gen 26:4-5), so the people are to fear (יְרֵא; 50:10) and listen (שִׁמְעוּ; 51:1) to Yahweh (see Goldingay, *Message of Isaiah 40-55*, 421; Koole, *Isaiah III: Isaiah 49-55*, 136, 141).

131. The perfect verbs are rhetorical futures (i.e., prophetic perfects).

132. Goldingay concludes, "It makes sense to infer that here the renewal of joyful gladness issues from the fulfillment of the promise of blessing in the multiplying of the people (vv. 1-2), which constitutes the comforting of Zion and the blossoming of her desolation" (*Message of Isaiah 40-55*, 424). See also Janzen, "Rivers in the Desert," 140; Oswalt, *Isaiah: Chapters 40-66*, 335. Both Janzen and Goldingay (424) suggest that the rejuvenation of the wilderness in v. 3b consists in its reinhabitation, furthering this motif.

The Progeny Blessing in the Book of Isaiah

and the proliferation of the people. It is unclear in vv. 1–3 whether the expansion of the people would take place in exile or following the return. Nor is it clear whether v. 3 pertains solely to Zion and her immediate surroundings,[133] or to the wider promised land.[134]

In sum, the focus throughout vv. 1–3 is on the progeny promise as realized in the past and anticipated in the future. Just as Abraham began childless, yet became a great nation, so the current exilic community, though small, will experience similar growth. Or, employing the feminine imagery of the Zion story, just as God "blessed" barren Sarah with a great nation, so he will "comfort" barren Zion with many children.

Isaiah 51:2 offers the most overt reference to a prior progeny tradition in the book of Isaiah, increasing the likelihood that other references to the progeny blessing allude to the Abrahamic blessing as well. Isaiah 40–55 in particular is preoccupied with the question of the continuing validity of the Abrahamic covenant, since the exilic community had lost both land and people.[135] The progeny question is answered primarily in the Zion texts, first in 49:14–21, now in 51:1–3, and then in the third major Zion text in Isa 54.

Isaiah 54:1–3

As Isaiah recalls the outpouring of Yahweh's wrath against Zion (51:17–23), we again encounter her children. Her children are no longer present and able to help her (v. 18) since they have themselves been punished (v. 20). Indeed, as we learned in 49:19–21, she has been entirely bereaved of those whom she bore (יָלְדָה) and brought up (גִּדְלָה; v. 18). However, this Zion text concludes with her coming redemption and the announcement of her salvation (52:1–12). In the final "servant" text (52:13—53:12), the servant suffers for the sins of "many" (רַבִּים; vv. 11, 12), and as a result "he will see his offspring (זֶרַע)" (v. 10). Mother Zion will benefit from the work of the servant as well, since his offspring are also hers (see below).

As in Isa 49, Isa 54 is rich with feminine imagery, portraying Zion as mother (vv. 1–3), wife (vv. 4–10), and finally as physical city (vv. 11–17). Verses 1–10 contain three imperatives addressed to Zion as well as to the people of Israel whom she represents[136] (vv. 1a, 2, 4a), followed by justifica-

---

133. See Goldingay, *Message of Isaiah 40–55*, 422.
134. See Koole, *Isaiah III: Isaiah 49–55*, 146.
135. See See Goldingay, *Message of Isaiah 40–55*, 421.
136. Although there is a distinction between Zion and her children in this familial

tions for these commands based on what Yahweh will do, introduced by כִּי (vv. 1b, 3, 4b–10). Logically prior to vv. 1–3, in vv. 4–10 Yahweh instructs her not to fear (v. 4a) since she will never again be ashamed: Yahweh will never again forsake his wife (v. 7) but instead will show tender compassion toward her forever (vv. 7, 8, 10). Because of this love, Zion once again has a future as a mother:

רָנִּי עֲקָרָה לֹא יָלָדָה	1	"Rejoice, barren one who has not given birth!
פִּצְחִי רִנָּה וְצַהֲלִי		Break forth into rejoicing and cry out,
לֹא־חָלָה		you who have not been in labor!
כִּי־רַבִּים בְּנֵי־שׁוֹמֵמָה		For the children of the desolate one are more numerous
מִבְּנֵי בְעוּלָה אָמַר יְהוָה		than the children of the married one," says Yahweh.
הַרְחִיבִי מְקוֹם אָהֳלֵךְ	2	"Enlarge the place of your tent,
וִירִיעוֹת מִשְׁכְּנוֹתַיִךְ יַטּוּ		And let them stretch out the curtains of your dwellings;
אַל־תַּחְשֹׂכִי		Do not hold back;
הַאֲרִיכִי מֵיתָרַיִךְ וִיתֵדֹתַיִךְ חַזֵּקִי		Lengthen your tent ropes and strengthen your pegs.
כִּי־יָמִין וּשְׂמֹאול תִּפְרֹצִי	3	For you will spread out right and left,[137]
וְזַרְעֵךְ גּוֹיִם יִירָשׁ		That your offspring might possess nations
וְעָרִים נְשַׁמּוֹת יוֹשִׁיבוּ		And inhabit desolate cities."

Although Zion is not named in vv. 1–3, there is little doubt that she is the one now characterized as barren.[138] Significantly, although rarely used in the OT (12x) and only here in Isaiah, עָקָר is employed to describe the barren condition of the matriarchs Sarah (Gen 11:20), Rebekah (Gen 25:21), and Rachel (Gen 29:31). Furthermore, since 51:2 has implicitly compared Zion to barren Sarah, 54:1 is likely an allusion to Sarah.[139] Despite her hopeless condition, she is to rejoice since her children[140] will be

imagery, they are not entirely distinguishable since Zion represents the people and the people themselves are to "rejoice" (v. 1) and "fear not" (v. 4). See Abma, *Bonds of Love*, 104; Beuken, "Isaiah LIV," 64.

137. This is probably a merism, denoting spreading out in all directions.

138. Zion was previously described not as barren but as bereaved (49:19–21; cf. also 51:18–20). Apparent inconsistency between these two descriptions should not trouble us given the nature of metaphor (and since barrenness is cited in 49:21 as well). Furthermore, Zion's barrenness pertains to her present childlessness and inability to bear rather than to her past.

139. See Baltzer, *Deutero-Isaiah*, 434; Goldingay, *Message of Isaiah 40–55*, 525; Motyer, *Isaiah*, 445 (cf. Gal 4:21–31). Beuken, "Isaiah LIV," 37–43, goes too far in arguing that vv. 1–3 are not about Zion but exclusively about Sarah as the representative of the people.

140. The "desolate one" (שׁוֹמֵמָה) is clearly a reference to Zion (cf. 49:19), made explicit in the Targum. This is a fitting double reference, appropriate terminology for a forsaken woman (2 Sam 13:20) as well as for a waste city (cf. 49:8, 19; 54:3; 61:4; 62:4).

more numerous that those of a fruitful, married woman (cf. v. 5).[141] Like Sarah, Zion will be fruitful because of the favor of Yahweh, who delights to bless the barren (Judg 13:3; 1 Sam 2:5; Ps 113:9). The extent of her fruitfulness remains ambiguous thus far, but the allusion to Sarah who bore a "great nation" is suggestive.

Regarding the identity of her children, the reference to "many" (רַבִּים) in v. 1 may indicate that her children are identical with those who have benefited from the servant's work in the previous verses (53:11–12), especially since, with the exception of 42:20, רַבִּים in the plural occurs elsewhere in Isa 40–66 only in the preceding servant text (52:14, 15; 53:11, 12). This identification is strengthened when the people are referred to as "servants" at the end of Isa 54 (v. 17), finally merging the servant and Zion stories. Their sins are forgiven and they are taught by Yahweh (54:13). They are defined more by their relationship to Yahweh than by ethnicity, and thus may include Gentile proselytes as well.[142] Nothing is said of their origin, but given the prior emphasis on the return in Zion texts, we may assume that this refers to those in exile.

Because of her many children, Yahweh instructs Zion to enlarge her tent, using three different verbs for expansion, and summarized in the command, "do not hold back!" (אַל־תַּחְשֹׂכִי). Commentators largely agree that this tent imagery is a "deliberate archaism"[143] that recalls the patriarchal period and builds on the previous allusion to Sarah. Here we begin to sense that Zion's new "spreading" (תִּפְרֹצִי, v.3) population will dwarf her former population. The verb פָּרַץ occasionally denotes the multiplication of people since spreading implies growth (see Exod 1:12). This too may allude to the patriarchal period since Jacob is promised that his offspring (זַרְעֶךָ)[144] will spread (וּפָרַצְתָּ) in all directions (Gen 28:14).

See Abma, *Bonds of Love*, 86; Darr, *Isaiah's Vision*, 178.

141. Given the patriarchal allusions, it is more likely that this is a reference to the fruitful rivals of the matriarchs (so Callaway, *Sing, O Barren One*, 67–68) or to fruitful women in general (so Childs, *Isaiah*, 428; Koole, *Isaiah III: Isaiah 49–55*, 352–53; Motyer, *Isaiah*, 445) than a metaphorical reference to Babylon or Rome (so Targum). If the "married one" refers to pre-exilic Israel, this would indicate a greater scope for future proliferation, but this seems equally unlikely.

142. Baltzer asserts that these children include proselytes (*Deutero-Isaiah*, 435) and Goldingay entertains this possibility as well (*The Message of Isaiah 40–55*, 524). Evidently, Paul read 54:1–3 inclusively as well, since he cites v. 1 in Gal 4:27 with respect to Gentile Christians.

143. Baltzer, *Deutero-Isaiah*, 436.

144. Note that this term is used in 53:10 as well, again identifying Zion's offspring with the servant's offspring.

The intended result is that "your offspring will possess nations" (וְזַרְעֲךָ גּוֹיִם יִירָשׁ) and "inhabit desolate cities" (וְעָרִים נְשַׁמּוֹת יוֹשִׁיבוּ). The theme of forcibly "(dis)possessing the nations" (i.e., the Canaanites) is prevalent in Deuteronomy (Deut 4:38; 9:1; 11:23). However, this may be yet another allusion to the patriarchal promises (see Gen 22:17; 24:60; 28:4, all of which include זֶרַע and יָרַשׁ regarding possessing the nations).[145] Although the nature of this "possession" remains somewhat vague, the relationship between Israel and the nations in 49:22–26 and in the Genesis texts entails subjugation, so this is likely the case here as well. As in 49:19, we see that the remedy for "desolate cities" in Israel and beyond[146] is filling them with people, a reversal of the judgment sentence upon the nation in Isa 6:11–12.

While v. 1 does not specify the number of Zion's children and v. 2 does not indicate the extent of expansion, v. 3 leaves no doubt about the magnitude of the growth that has taken place. Zion and her children have spread out beyond Israel to the nations, suggesting a larger population than that of the pre-exilic period. The means by which this is accomplished remains unspecified, but given the allusions to the patriarchs and the patriarchal blessings throughout vv. 1–3 and in 51:2, the physical reproduction of God's people probably plays a large role.

Because of these allusions, Abma appropriately concludes that "one could thus argue that Zion in Isa 54:1–3 is addressed as a patriarch or as a matriarch in disguise."[147] Both of the material promises of the Abrahamic covenant are included here since v. 3 concerns filling the land. Thus Yahweh declares his intention to uphold the Abrahamic promises[148] that were jeopardized by Israel's disobedience and appeared to have been lost through exile. The present exilic era is like the patriarchal period: they are small now and presently despairing, but he has promised to make them into a great nation. Patriarchal and Zion traditions thus merge to encourage trust in Yahweh and hope for the future. This will all take place because of Yahweh's powerful familial commitment to Zion, ultimately for the joy of the people (i.e., Zion).

---

145. See Abma, *Bonds of Love*, 96; Korpel, "Female Servant," 156 n. 15.

146. Although the שׁמם root typically refers only to the cities of Israel in Isaiah (1:7; 6:11; 49:8, 19; 61:4; 62:4; 64:9[10]), parallelism with the previous line suggests that this may include the desolate cities of the nations as well (see 17:9). The scope of growth expands throughout vv. 1–3, so it would be anticlimactic if the last clause reverted back to focus on the land of Israel alone.

147. Abma, *Bonds of Love*, 97.

148. See Hanson, *Isaiah 40–66*, 171; Oswalt, *Isaiah: Chapters 40–66*, 417.

The literary development of the relationship between the servant and Zion has now reached its climax. Nowhere is it clearer than in Isa 53–54 that the two figures are related. Generally speaking, both are exalted by Yahweh from a position of suffering to a position of prosperity with a positive future.[149] For our purposes, the most crucial parallel is that they both yield offspring who are to be equated (particularly in light of 54:17). Thus, the stories intersect in that both Zion and the servant are related to the people, the servant in an active role and Zion in a passive role. It appears that mother Zion has children only because of the work of the servant who is Yahweh's agent for bringing her back to himself. Therefore, this new realization of the progeny blessing can be attributed indirectly to the servant.[150]

The story regarding the recovery of Zion's children also continues to build. Interestingly, each time the text shifts to Zion following treatment of the servant theme in Isa 49–54, the initial theme is the same: grief regarding lack of children and of hope for the future. The diminished population was clearly a concern for the exilic audience, one that Isaiah deals with decisively. Zion's story is not complete. The themes of 49:14–21 and 54:1–3 again coincide in 62:4–5 where it is said that Zion will no more be called "forsaken" (עֲזוּבָה; cf. 49:14) or "desolate" (שְׁמָמָה; cf. 54:1) but rather "married" (בְּעוּלָה; cf. 54:1, 5), both to Yahweh and to her children. Zion and her children will resurface for the last time at the conclusion of the book in 66:7–9 (see below).

Isaiah 60:22

In Isa 60–62 we encounter the book's climactic exposition of the future glorified Zion.[151] The introductory chapter highlights the relationship

---

149. See Abma, *Bonds of Love*, 105–7; Korpel, "Female Servant," 163–66; Sawyer, "Daughter of Zion," 100; Willey, *Remember*, 232–33, for a detailed exposition of these correspondences.

150. See Koole, *Isaiah III: Isaiah 49–55*, 352.

151. See Tate, "Isaiah in Recent Study," 38–43, for a summary of source- and redaction-critical theories regarding the development of Isa 56–66. It is generally agreed that Isa 60–62 form the core of this material, given its affinities to Isa 40–55. Some scholars attribute the other texts pertaining to the progeny blessing (65:20, 23; 66:7–9) to this early stage as well, due in part to similarities to Isa 40–55. Others assign Isa 65–66 to the final stage in the development of the book. These diachronic analyses draw attention to similarities in content and formulation between some of the texts we are treating in Deutero- and Trito-Isaiah and thus contribute to our synchronic analysis, regardless of how the text developed.

between Zion and the nations: they will be attracted to Zion, bring her tribute, and serve her (vv. 3–14). Verses 15–22 then contrast her former state of destitution with her future eternal state of glory, concluding with a brief description of the condition and experience of the people of the city (vv. 21–22). In this new Zion, all of the inhabitants will be צַדִּיקִים. Since the צדק root often denotes "salvation" or "vindication" in Isa 40–66 (e.g., 56:1; 58:8; 59:16, 17; 61:10; 62:1 in Isa 56–66), some see this as a reference to the whole community of Israel who have been delivered from exile.[152] However, the ethical sense of צדק is also prominent in Isa 56–66, which emphasize the responsibility to live a just and righteous life before Yahweh (e.g., 56:1; 57:1, 12; 58:2; 59:4; 64:5[6]), thus dividing the community, not along ethnic but along ethical lines.[153] This latter sense is more likely since here צַדִּיקִים characterizes the people. Therefore, the inhabitants of the city are the righteous remnant, to be identified with the "servants," namely, the offspring of Mother Zion and the servant (53:10–11; 54:13, 17).[154] On the basis of 56:1–8, this may include foreigners as well (see below).

The righteous will possess the land forever, resulting in God's glory (v. 21). Furthermore, they will multiply and be great (v. 22):

| הַקָּטֹן יִהְיֶה לָאֶלֶף | The smallest[155] will become a thousand,[156] |
| וְהַצָּעִיר לְגוֹי עָצוּם | And the least a mighty nation. |

The referent of the "smallest" and "least" is ambiguous. It may refer to insignificant or weak individuals (cf. Deut 1:17; 1 Sam 15:17; Isa 36:9 for קָטֹן; Judg 6:15 for צָעִיר). Alternatively, it may refer to families or groups[157] who are numerically small, unimportant, or both (cf. 1 Sam 9:21). A less

---

152. See Volz, *Jesaia II*, 248–49; Westermann, *Isaiah 40–66*, 363.

153. According to Oswalt, *Isaiah: Chapters 1–39*, "if chs. 40–55 speak of hope to a people who fear themselves cast off, chs. 56–66 call for a realized righteousness from a people who have lapsed into a careless dependence upon position."

154. See Beuken, "Main Theme," 70–71; Childs, *Isaiah*, 499; Koole, *Isaiah III: Isaiah 56–66*, 258; Oswalt, *Isaiah: Chapters 40–66*, 558–59.

155. Since they possess the article, הַקָּטֹן and הַצָּעִיר are superlatives, not simply substantival adjectives (GKC §133g).

156. Many render אֶלֶף here as "clan" on account of the word pair with גּוֹי עָצוּם and since it appears to have this meaning elsewhere (e.g., Num 10:4; Josh 22:21, 30; Judg 6:15; 1 Sam 10:19), but this meaning appears nowhere else in Isaiah (or in the Latter Prophets), and is thus less likely. "Clan" may stress influence more than numerical expansion, but the difference between these two understandings is slight. The LXX amplifies this line further with a plural rendering (χιλιάδας).

157. See Brueggemann, *Isaiah 40–66*, 210.

The Progeny Blessing in the Book of Isaiah

likely possibility is that the diminished numerical status of the nation is in mind (cf. Amos 7:2, 5) since it would not be a fitting hope for them to become merely a אֶלֶף. Clearly, the point is partly a quantitative one, regardless of the rendering of אֶלֶף. Individuals or small groups will become numerous in the new Zion, underscored in the second colon, which goes beyond the first in scope. This, however, is inseparable from a rise to prominence and influence, so the transformation is both quantitative and qualitative. Since vv. 15–22 contain multiple contrasts between the former condition of Zion and her future condition, the small or insignificant state of certain individuals or groups probably pertains to their current state prior to the glorification of Zion, forming one final contrast.

It is doubtful that the juxtaposition of land and the multiplication of the righteous is mere coincidence. Once again, the realization of the Abrahamic promises underlies expectations for the ideal future.[158] Not only is "possessing the land" (יִירְשׁוּ אָרֶץ; v. 21) a patriarchal echo (see above), but also becoming a "mighty nation" (גּוֹי עָצוּם) is reminiscent of the same promise made to Abraham (see Gen 18:18; Deut 26:5).[159] Just as Yahweh made Abraham and Sarah into a great nation (cf. 51:2), so he will do for multiple insignificant individuals or groups in the future. The Abrahamic promise of progeny is thus replicated on a grand scale, perhaps its ultimate fulfillment, which transcends even the original promise.

The proliferation of the children of mother Zion in 49:19–21 and 54:1–3 seems to revolve around the return from exile. In contrast, given cosmic elements such as the removal of the sun and moon (vv. 19–20), the setting of Isa 60 looks further into the future to a time when Zion's glorification is final and the people will possess the land לְעוֹלָם (v. 21). This may not mean that the multiplication of the righteous servants of Yahweh will take place within this eternal state, but it does mean that by that time they will have become more numerous than Israel had previously experienced, consistent with Deut 30:5.

---

158. See Blenkinsopp, *Isaiah 56–66*, 217; Brueggemann, *Isaiah 40–66*, 210; Koole, *Isaiah III: Isaiah 56–66*, 261; Motyer, *Isaiah*, 499; Schultz, "Nationalism and Universalism," 141.

159. Although this designation is not used solely of Israel in the OT (see Joel 1:6; Mic 4:3; Zech 8:22), it is only applied elsewhere to Israel in these two texts and in Num 14:12 where God offers to make Moses into a replacement "mighty nation" (cf. Deut 9:14).

I Will Surely Multiply Your Offspring

Isaiah 65:9, 20, 23

Isaiah 65–66 appears to function as a concluding "bookend" for the book of Isaiah since it recapitulates many of the themes introduced in Isa 1, including indictment, judgment on the wicked, and vindication for the righteous, the major themes of the book as a whole. The enduring offspring of Yahweh is a significant theme in Isa 65–66. Not only will Yahweh sustain them (65:9; cf. 60:22), but they will also experience fullness of life (65:20, 23) and become more numerous (66:7–9).

Yahweh first emphasizes that he will still punish the rebellious and idolatrous among his people (65:1–7). However, he will preserve a righteous remnant (vv. 8–9a) with whom he will deal favorably, in contrast to the wicked (vv. 9b–16). Yahweh resolves, "I will bring forth (וְהוֹצֵאתִי) offspring (זֶרַע) from Jacob" (v. 9a). Since יָצָא is never used to denote the expansion of the people elsewhere in the OT and since the point is not the extent of the people but rather the survival of the righteous remnant, it is unclear whether this statement refers to the physical proliferation of the righteous. It does, however, refer to Yahweh's active work in creating and preserving children in the ethical or spiritual sense in order to ensure that he will always have worshippers. Once again, the theme of the perpetuation of Yahweh's true offspring is juxtaposed with "possessing" (וִירֵשׁוּהָ, יוֹרֵשׁ) the land (v. 9b; cf. 57:13), likely another allusion to the Abrahamic blessings.[160]

In vv. 9–16, this same group is called "my chosen ones," "my servants," and "my people who seek me" (v. 10). "My chosen ones" (בְּחִירַי; vv. 9, 15) has previously referred to the servant (42:1) and to Israel (45:4) in the singular, and to the returning exiles in the plural (43:20). Similarly, "my servants" (עֲבָדַי), the dominant designation for the righteous remnant in the present passage (vv. 8 [2x], 13 [3x], 14, 15), identifies this group with the "servants" in 54:17, the offspring of the servant and mother Zion (cf. also 56:6; 63:17; 66:14).[161] In prior texts, there was little indication that these terms were to be defined more narrowly than the entire exilic community. But in light of the further definition provided by vv. 8–16, it is clear that those who will enjoy the Abrahamic promises will not be de-

---

160. See Blenkinsopp, *Isaiah 56–66*, 277; Brueggemann, *Isaiah 40–66*, 241; Motyer, *Isaiah*, 526; Watts, *Isaiah 34–66*, 344.

161. See Beuken, "Main Theme," 77. Beuken argues that "servants" constitutes the central theme of Isa 56–66, reaching its climax in 65:8–16. Although this is not the only designation for the group, these chapters do indeed focus heavily on the identity and future of the true people of Yahweh.

fined simply ethnically, as we might have assumed, but rather with respect to their obedient relationship to Yahweh.¹⁶²

This extended contrast between blessing for Yahweh's servants and curse for the rebels culminates in a description of the destiny of the "chosen ones" (v. 22) in the "new heavens and new earth" (vv. 17–25). Verses 20 and 23 pertain to life itself with clear implications for the extent of population growth, v. 20 to longevity and v. 23 to preservation from curse. Verse 20 presents the first reason for the shared joy between Yahweh and his people (vv. 18–19):

לֹא־יִהְיֶה מִשָּׁם עוֹד עוּל יָמִים	There will no longer be there an infant of only a few days,¹⁶³
וְזָקֵן אֲשֶׁר לֹא־יְמַלֵּא אֶת־יָמָיו	Or an old man who does not fill out his days,
כִּי הַנַּעַר בֶּן־מֵאָה שָׁנָה יָמוּת	For the youth will die at one hundred years old,
וְהַחוֹטֶא בֶּן־מֵאָה שָׁנָה	And the one who fails to reach one hundred years old
יְקֻלָּל	will be considered¹⁶⁴ to be cursed

Although some of these phrases pose interpretive difficulties, the overall impression is clear. Infant mortality will be eliminated and the old man will live out a full life (v. 20a), a merism that indicates the abolition of premature death of any sort. Verse 20b then redefines the standards of normal life expectancy. Grammatically, the first line could indicate that the person currently a נַעַר from the perspective of the vision will eventually die at one hundred, but the choice of נַעַר would then be unhelpful as a point of reference. More likely, the idea is that a person who dies at one hundred will still be considered a נַעַר. Thus, one hundred is not the new life expectancy but well below it. The parallel line may likewise indicate that one hundred will be a brief life. Since חָטָא commonly means "sinner," many render this line, "the sinner one hundred years old will be (considered) accursed."¹⁶⁵ However, חָטָא occasionally means "to miss" (Judg 20:16; Prov 8:36; 19:2; Job 5:24). This fits the context better¹⁶⁶ since the intrusion of "sinners" in this idyllic picture seems odd. Therefore, according to v. 20, there will be no premature death. Instead, all will live a full life to

---

162. See Blenkinsopp, *Isaiah 56-66*, 275; Oswalt, *Isaiah: Chapters 40-66*, 646.

163. This appears to be an adverbial accusative of time where the plural יָמִים designates "some" or "a few" (see GKC §139h; cf. Gen 24:55; 40:4; Dan 8:27; Neh 1:4).

164. Probably an estimative Pual (see IBHS 419).

165. See LXX; ESV; Koole, *Isaiah III: Isaiah 56-66*, 458; Motyer, *Isaiah*, 530; Oswalt, *Isaiah: Chapters 40-66*, 659.

166. See Blenkinsopp, *Isaiah 56-66*, 283; Watts, *Isaiah 34-66*, 349; Westermann, *Isaiah 40-66*, 407.

the extent that one hundred years will be considered a short life, possibly alluding to the lifespan of the patriarchs (or even the antediluvian generations) as the norm.[167] This does not have a direct impact on proliferation through reproduction, but it implies that the people will expand greatly at the corporate level.[168]

Verses 21–22 affirm that the people will not only live long, but they also will enjoy the work of their hands throughout life. Verse 23 then returns to the theme of the eradication of premature death in the new heavens and new earth:

לֹא יִיגְעוּ לָרִיק	They will not labor in vain
וְלֹא יֵלְדוּ לַבֶּהָלָה	Or bear children for calamity,
כִּי זֶרַע בְּרוּכֵי יְהוָה הֵמָּה	For they are the offspring blessed by Yahweh,
וְצֶאֱצָאֵיהֶם אִתָּם	And their descendants with them.

Since יָגַע is not used elsewhere with reference to childbirth, "laboring in vain" is probably a reference to work in general, continuing the thought of vv. 21–22. However, the next line complements this assertion and hints at the reversal of the curse of Gen 3:16[169] which, as we argued above, includes infant mortality. בֶּהָלָה appears only three times elsewhere (Lev 26:16; Jer 15:8; Ps 78:33), and in each case the context is judgment, Yahweh is the agent of בֶּהָלָה, and the outcome is decimation.[170] Leviticus 26:16 is the most significant parallel to v. 23,[171] especially given the priority of this term in the covenant curses. The first curse listed in the long catalogue of consequences for disobedience in Lev 26:14–46 is "I will visit you with calamity (בֶּהָלָה), namely, consuming disease and fever." Perhaps v. 23 intentionally alludes to this first curse as representative of covenant

---

167. See Blenkinsopp, *Isaiah 56–66*, 287–88.

168. As Gowan observes, long life is a surprisingly rare motif in prophetic salvation oracles (*Eschatology*, 90), particularly in comparison to the frequency of references to the numerical expansion of the people. Perhaps this is because the prophets are more concerned with the fate of the nation than with individuals. In the case of Isaiah, this may be due to the formative role of the Abrahamic covenant. However, long life may be present implicitly in other blessings such as peace and protection from enemy peoples.

169. See Brueggemann, *Isaiah 40–66*, 249; Koole, *Isaiah III: Isaiah 56–66*, 461. See Steck, "Der neue Himmel," 349–65, who argues that vv. 16–25 as a whole depend upon Gen 1–3.

170. Benedikt Otzen summarizes, "The noun *behelah* denotes simply the terror that is connected with sudden death, and indeed is identical with it" ("בהל," 5).

171. See Blenkinsopp, *Isaiah 56–66*, 289; Koole, *Isaiah III: Isaiah 56–66*, 462; Steck, "Der neue Himmel," 359.

curses in general, implying that such curses will no longer be a threat in the coming age.[172] Parents need no longer live in fear that Yahweh will bereave them of their children in acts of judgment (cf. Ezek 36:12, 14).

This is true because Yahweh's blessing rests on them and on their descendants (cf. 61:9).[173] The juxtaposition of blessing and offspring has already occurred in 44:3–4 and in 61:9.[174] This may refer simply to blessing in general, but in light of 44:3–4 where it consists of the progeny blessing, it is possible that the progeny blessing is primarily in mind here as well. The themes of land (vv. 21–22) and progeny (vv. 20, 23) may again recall the Abrahamic promises and envision their full realization in the future.[175] However, given the likely allusion to Lev 26:16, these promises come about through the eradication of the curses of the Sinai covenant and the renewal of its blessings.

The vision of new heavens and a new earth is not so much about the expansion of God's people as about the full enjoyment of life for existing persons, rooted in God's blessing and resulting in joy. However, such a description strongly implies the multiplication of the people corporately as well as the full experience of Yahweh's blessing of children for parents who need no longer fear infant mortality and bereavement. Wholesale decimation through war, famine, or other curses is now unthinkable. As in Isa 60, the changes in the natural order that differ from present human experience suggest that this text envisions the end of time as we know it, subsequent to the immediate blessing expected upon return to the land. Little more can be said concerning its timing from the perspective of the book of Isaiah.

Isaiah 66:7–9

Yahweh declares in 66:3–6 that he will punish the hypocritical syncretists, continuing the clear separation between the righteous and the wicked

---

172. See Schultz, *Search for Quotation*, 254, for further possible echoes of the covenant curses in vv. 21–23.

173. It is unclear whether זֶרַע בְּרוּכֵי is a genitive of relationship (i.e., the offspring are the children of those who are blessed) or an epexegetical genitive (i.e., the offspring are themselves the blessed ones). Either way, v. 23b describes blessing for multiple generations.

174. Interestingly, of the four texts in which זֶרַע and צֶאֱצָאִים occur as a word pair in Isaiah (44:3; 48:19; 61:9; 65:23), three are employed in the context of the blessing of progeny or the preservation of life.

175. See Brueggemann, *Isaiah 40–66*, 249; Koole, *Isaiah III: Isaiah 56–66*, 462.

in the community (cf. 65:8–16). A hopeful future awaits the righteous (vv. 7–14), described for one last time in the book as his "servants" (v. 14). This final text in Isaiah dealing with the expansion of the people resumes (and concludes) the story of mother Zion and her children as told in Isa 49, 51, and 54. The birth of many children (vv. 7–9) will result in joy for Zion and children alike (v. 10) as Zion nurses them (vv. 11–12). Finally, the maternal imagery is transferred to Yahweh himself who "comforts" (נָחַם 3x; cf. 40:1) them in Jerusalem (v. 13).

The birth itself logically precedes this joyous future:

בְּטֶרֶם תָּחִיל [176] יָלָדָה	7	"Before she was in labor, she gave birth;
בְּטֶרֶם יָבוֹא חֵבֶל לָהּ		before labor pain came upon her,
וְהִמְלִיטָה זָכָר [177]		she delivered a male.
מִי־שָׁמַע כָּזֹאת	8	Who has ever heard something like this?
מִי רָאָה כָּאֵלֶּה		Who has ever seen such things?
הֲיוּחַל אֶרֶץ בְּיוֹם אֶחָד		Can a land be brought forth in one day?
אִם־יִוָּלֵד גּוֹי פַּעַם אֶחָת		Can a nation be born in a moment?
כִּי־חָלָה		But as soon as she was in labor,
גַּם־יָלְדָה צִיּוֹן אֶת־בָּנֶיהָ		Zion gave birth to her sons.
הַאֲנִי אַשְׁבִּיר וְלֹא אוֹלִיד	9	Will I bring to the point of birth but not deliver?"
יֹאמַר יְהוָה		says Yahweh;
אִם־אֲנִי הַמּוֹלִיד וְעָצַרְתִּי		"Will I who delivers then shut the womb?"
אָמַר אֱלֹהָיִךְ		says your God.

At the outset, neither mother nor child is specified, but this is no typical birth. Such a painless delivery is a miraculous occurrence that may recall Edenic conditions in which pain was absent.[178] The following rhetorical questions (v. 8a) suggest that this is unprecedented. Verse 8b then specifies the details of this birth: the mother is (once again) Zion, the child is an entire אֶרֶץ [179] or גּוֹי,[180] and this birth will take place suddenly in a mere day. In an intermingling of metaphor and referent, the miracle of

---

176. יָלַד and חִיל appear to be Leitwörter in vv. 7–9. The former occurs five times (in three different Stems) while the latter forms a word pair with it three times.

177. The Hiphil form of מָלַט occurs elsewhere in the OT only in Isa 31:5. It is probably causative, "to cause to escape," and may retain a double meaning, referring both to childbirth (on the metaphorical level) and to deliverance of the people from exile (on the historical level). See Webster, "Rhetorical Study," 97.

178. See Motyer, *Isaiah*, 536; Oswalt, *Isaiah: Chapters 40–66*, 674.

179. Metonymy for the population of the land (cf. Isa 45:22; Ps 33:8).

180. The Targum interprets v. 7 messianically, replacing "she delivered a male" with "her king will be revealed." However, it is more likely that v. 8b explains the cryptic statement of v. 7 rather than introduces a separate birth altogether.

this astonishing "birth" is the vast number of Zion's children coupled with how quickly they appear. Yahweh abruptly enters the scene, and we learn that he was responsible for this mass birth (v. 9). By means of additional rhetorical questions, he declares that he will bring the birth to full fruition by delivering her children[181] (i.e., by not shutting her womb). In other words, the people need not fear that God will restore them partially, only to abandon them once again.[182]

As in 54:1–3, mother Zion is portrayed as the matriarch.[183] Just as Sarah gave birth (Polel of חִיל in 51:2) to an entire גּוֹי (Gen 12:2), so mother Zion will bear (Qal of חִיל in v. 8) a גּוֹי. Just as Yahweh had once shut the womb of Sarah (עָצַר; Gen 16:2) but later opened it (Gen 21:1–2), so he will personally enable mother Zion to bear children and will not shut her womb. It appears, however, that mother Zion's capacity to give birth transcends that of Sarah since she will deliver without pain and will bear a nation in a single day. This new nation will constitute the realization—perhaps the ultimate realization—of the Abrahamic promise of numerous progeny, offering daring hope to the post-exilic community, which was still quite small.

It is unclear how and when this "birth" will take place. The replenishment of the population through physical reproduction would fit the metaphor itself and would parallel the means by which Sarah became a great nation. However, the language of vv. 7–9 would not require this. Alternatively, it may refer to the return of the people from exile, as in Isa 49.[184] Finally, in light of the reference to "servants" in v. 14, the "birth" of many children may entail the conversion of Gentiles to Yahwism.[185] Perhaps all three options are viable.[186] Clearly, the point is that Zion will have many children rather than the exact means by which this will be accomplished.

181. Although the Hiphil of יָלַד typically refers to causation at the beginning of the birth process (conception), here it appears to be causation at the end (delivery). This is the only place where Yahweh is the subject of יָלַד (but see 1QSa 2:11). See Isa 55:10; 59:4 for a similar meaning for the Hiphil of יָלַד as "cause to bring forth."

182. Verses 7–9 reverse 26:17–18 in which the people endure labor (חִיל) in their own strength only to give birth to wind. Now mother Zion will be fruitful apart from these labor pains because Yahweh himself will act on her behalf (see Darr, *Isaiah's Vision*, 220; Oswalt, *Isaiah: Chapters 40–66*, 676). These verses also recall Hezekiah's statement in 37:3 (see Darr, *Isaiah's Vision*, 221–22).

183. See Blenkinsopp, *Isaiah 56–66*, 305; Koole, *Isaiah III: Isaiah 56–66*, 490, 494.

184. See Webster, "Rhetorical Study," 98; Westermann, *Isaiah 40–66*, 419.

185. See discussion of 60:22, 66:7–9, and the nations in Isaiah below.

186. Koole, *Isaiah III: Isaiah 56–66*, 496; and Oswalt, *Isaiah: Chapters 40–66*, 675, cite return from exile and the influx of the nations as the dual means of growth and appeal to Calvin for this position.

I Will Surely Multiply Your Offspring

Thus far in our analysis of Isaianic texts, dating each text has been unimportant since this would have little effect on our understanding of the realization of the blessing. For example, 49:19–21 and 54:1–3 depict future growth beyond exile regardless of whether they originate in the pre-exilic or exilic period. However, in the case of 66:7–9, the temporal setting matters. If these verses originate in the pre-exilic or exilic period, the "birth" of the new nation is a future event and the perfect verbal forms in vv. 7–8 are best understood as prophetic perfects. Alternatively, if they originate in the mid- to late-sixth century (as most critical scholars believe), then this birth has already partially taken place through return from exile and v. 9 primarily affirms that Yahweh will bring to completion that which has already begun.[187] It is unlikely, though, that the metaphor of a sudden and quick birth would be an accurate representation of such a gradual return. Future fulfillment is thus most likely. Regardless of whether fulfillment has already begun, in light of v. 9 this is primarily a future-oriented hope.

The story of mother Zion is now complete. Despite the diverse terminology and imagery, the four texts that treat her relationship to her children (49:19–21; 51:2–3; 54:1–3; 66:7–9) should be understood as complementary pictures that represent the same reality. Indeed, a number of common threads connect them beyond the imagery of birth and bereavement:

1. Yahweh's compassion is the basis for his action in favor of Zion in 49:13–16 and 54:7–10.

2. Both 49:19–21 and 51:2–3 are accompanied by references to the return (49:12, 22–23; 51:9–11) as the context and prerequisite for blessing.

3. Both 49:19–21 and 54:1–3 are juxtaposed with the personification of Zion as Yahweh's wife (49:14; 50:1–3; 54:4–10).

4. Joy is the result of the restoration of the population in 51:3, 54:1, and 66:10–11.

5. Peopling the land is the remedy for the "waste" (49:19; 51:3) and "desolate" (49:19; 54:1, 3) places.

Moreover, these four texts complement one another even where they differ, presenting a holistic understanding of the restoration of a

---

187. See Webster, "Rhetorical Study," 98; Westermann, *Isaiah 40–66*, 420. In the final form of the book, this may address the post-exilic situation regardless of the date of the oracle.

The Progeny Blessing in the Book of Isaiah

burgeoning population to Zion. Isaiah 49:14–21 resembles a narrative account in which Yahweh, Zion, and her children all speak while in 54:1–3 the prophet then tells Zion how to act in light of Yahweh's work. Although these texts do not employ the same imagery in their personification of Zion (e.g., bereaved vs. barren), 54:1–3 moves beyond 49:19–21 in that Zion must now respond to the imminent cramped condition of her children by expanding her "tent." Furthermore, whereas 49:19–21 highlights the origin of the children, 54:1–3 emphasizes their destination and foresees their spread even beyond the boundaries of Israel.[188] Although 51:2–3 does not personify Zion in the same manner, it makes a significant contribution to these prior texts by citing the patriarchal promise of numerous progeny that, together with God's compassion, provides the ground for the hope that he will "comfort Zion" (51:3) in the future. Isaiah 54:1–3 further develops these patriarchal allusions by portraying mother Zion as a second Sarah, completing the analogy already implicit in 51:2–3. Isaiah 51:17–20 adds to the personification of mother Zion by drawing attention to the bereavement of her children through judgment, interrupting Yahweh's past and future blessing of progeny.

Zion's story had begun in 49:19–21 with the sudden recovery of children of unknown origin. The story concludes climactically in 66:7–9 with a re-telling of this account in which she suddenly recovers countless children. However, this time she will bear them herself as she has in the past (51:18), a more powerful and satisfying maternal conclusion. Whereas 54:1–3 recalls her past and present barren condition but does not state the origin of her future children, 66:8 emphasizes the future in which her womb will be fruitful once again. And although Yahweh's role in this restoration was not noted in 54:1–3, this is emphasized in 66:9. Moreover, 66:7–9 sheds further light on the identity of the children in 49:19–21 and 54:1–3. That 66:14 identifies the children as Yahweh's "servants" verifies that the enhanced definition of God's people in Isa 56–66 as those who obey him regardless of ethnicity applies to the servant-children of Zion in 54:17.[189] Finally, it is clear that the means by which this new "great nation" will arise is not as important as the very fact of its future existence. Nevertheless, the story of Zion as a whole creates a multi-faceted impression

---

188. As Jeppesen notes, "In 49.12 the captives whom the Servant shall bring home will come from all directions; now [in 54:1–3], the new inhabitants of the mother town shall spread in all directions" ("Mother Zion," 122). See also Willey, *Remember*, 232.

189. See Blenkinsopp, who views 66:7–9 as a commentary on 54:1–8 and draws attention to the role that both play in concluding major sections of the book (*Isaiah 56–66*, 304–5).

whereby return to the land, physical reproduction, and possibly even the conversion of the Gentiles all play a role from the perspective of Zion.

The book of Isaiah closes by reiterating that Yahweh will sustain his people. In the final vision of worship in Zion, Yahweh affirms, "'just as the new heavens and new earth that I make will remain before me ... so your offspring and your name will endure (יַעֲמֹד זַרְעֲכֶם וְשִׁמְכֶם)'" (66:22). This simple statement summarizes the message of Isaiah for the זֶרַע of Yahweh as explicated in previous texts relevant to our study (cf. 44:3; 54:3; cf. also 1:4). In particular, this constitutes the grand fulfillment of the wish in 48:18–19 that the people might obey Yahweh and become numerous, the only other text in Isaiah that uses זֶרַע and שֵׁם together.[190] In addition, it ties together the teaching of Isa 65–66 regarding the people of Yahweh. It reaffirms that Yahweh will "bring forth זֶרַע from Jacob" (65:9). Not only does it allude to the new heavens and new earth (65:17–25), but it also summarizes the salient point of this passage, namely, ongoing life for the blessed זֶרַע (v. 23). Finally, 66:22 (as well as 65:9) envisions the end result of Yahweh's delivery of children for Zion in 66:7–9.

The Progeny Blessing and the Salvation of the Nations in Isaiah

Foreign nations play a multifaceted role in the book of Isaiah. Some texts seem to suggest a "nationalistic" or "particularistic" worldview that is solely concerned with the salvation of Israel and has little concern for the fate of the nations. Others appear to reflect a more "universalistic" perspective whereby the fullness of Israel's salvation is extended to the nations as well. These texts are not easily reconcilable and have generated much scholarly discussion, a discussion that impinges upon our understanding of the progeny blessing in Isaiah. In brief, the more weight we give to a universalistic perspective in Isaiah and the more such texts eliminate clear distinctions between Israelites and Gentile proselytes in the people of God, the more likely it is that the corporate progeny blessing includes proselytes and may be realized in part through conversion.

First we must examine the role of the nations in the book as a whole since the book's final form shapes our reading of individual texts. The nations function in almost every way imaginable in Isaiah:[191]

---

190. See Beuken, "Isaiah Chapters LXV–LXVI," 214.

191. See Davies, "Destiny of the Nations," 104–5, for a more comprehensive

1. The nations as recipients of God's judgment (often specifically for their mistreatment of Israel): e.g., 13–23; 41:11–12; 47; 49:25–26; 51:22–23; 54:15–17; 60:12
2. The nations as agents of God's judgment: e.g., 5:26–30; 10:5–19; 39:5–7
3. The nations as witnesses to God's actions: e.g., 12:3–6; 40:5; 41:5; 45:6; 52:10
4. The nations as subservient to Israel. This takes a variety of forms, some of which are harsher expressions of subservience than others, including facilitating the return of the exiles to the land (11:12; 49:22–23; 60:4, 9; 66:20), serving as a ransom for Israel (43:3–4), being possessed by Israel (54:3), bringing their wealth to Zion (18:7; 45:14; 60:6, 11, 13), serving Israel (14:1–2; 61:5–6), bowing before Israel (49:23; 60:14), and coming to them in chains (45:14).
5. The nations as participants in the salvation and blessing God will extend to Israel: 2:2–4; 11:10–12; 19:16–25; 25:7–9; 42:4, 6; 45:22–26; 49:6; 51:4–5; 56:1–8; 66:18–24

Our primary concern is with the relationship between Israel and the nations with respect to the salvation experienced by both parties (i.e., the relationship between categories four and five).

This tension has been explained in various ways.[192] Davies and Melugin consider these two voices to be in conflict and make little attempt to resolve them.[193] Blenkinsopp proposes that universalism was a late development in Isa 40–66 as a result of changing historical and sociological circumstances and that the earlier nationalistic voices have nevertheless been preserved.[194] Croatto eliminates the universalistic voice altogether by proposing that the terms for "nations" are geographical designations that refer to diaspora Jews in contexts in which salvation is extended to

---

summary of the book's treatment of the nations.

192. See Grisanti, "Israel's Mission," 50–57; Van Winkle, "Relationship of the Nations," 446–47; Watts, "Echoes," 282–83, for a more extensive review of previous scholarship. Note that many of these studies treat the tension between nationalism and universalism within Deutero-Isaiah alone. The results of such studies are thus of limited value for our purposes as we seek to understand the book in its final form, since earlier and later texts in the book will shape how we understand Isa 40–55.

193. Davies, "Destiny of the Nations," 106; Melugin, "Israel and the Nations," 262.

194. Blenkinsopp, "Second Isaiah," 83–103.

the "nations"; foreign nations will receive only judgment.[195] Kaminsky and Stewart argue that Deutero-Isaiah is really only concerned with the salvation of Israel and that texts pertaining to the nations serve to underscore Yahweh's sovereignty over them.[196]

Attempts to take both groups of texts seriously and synthesize them in a coherent manner are more satisfying. With respect to Isa 40–55, Gelston, Grisanti, van Winkle, and Watts[197] all arrive at a similar position, namely, that Israel remains Yahweh's special instrument of blessing and thus her restoration is the means by which the nations will themselves experience blessing. The author is concerned with the salvation of the nations, but Israel still enjoys priority over them. Although it remains unclear precisely how this might occur, this conclusion accounts for all the evidence and is consistent with the historical role of Israel derived from Abrahamic traditions that underlie these chapters.

When we consider the entire book and do not treat Deutero-Isaiah in isolation, we find that a similar dynamic exists in so-called First and Third Isaiah as well. However, the "universalistic" voice grows louder, prompting re-evaluation of Isa 40–55. The book begins (2:2–4) and closes (66:18–24) with two of the clearest expressions of international worship of Yahweh that we find in the book, pushing the entire book in a universalistic direction.[198] Isaiah 19:16–25 is one of the most universalistic texts in the first half of the book. When Yahweh refers to Assyria and Egypt as "my people" (v. 25) alongside Israel, it is difficult to conceive of this meaning anything other than complete equality as the people of God.[199] Furthermore, the final section of the book (Isa 56–66) not only closes but also opens with a text concerning Gentile inclusion (56:1–8), this time regarding individuals rather than whole nations. As in 19:16–25, the eunuch and the foreigner who join themselves to Yahweh will enjoy all of the covenantal privileges of Israelite worshipers. Significantly, the foreigner would then be among

---

195. Croatto, "The 'Nations,'" 143–61. See also Hollenberg, "Nationalism," 23–36.

196. Kaminsky and Stewart, "God of All the World," 139–63. See also Gowan, *Prophetic Books*, 157; Whybray, *Isaiah 40–66*, 32.

197. See Gelston, "Universalism," 380–81, 396; Grisanti, "Israel's Mission," 58–59; van Winkle, "Relationship of the Nations," 457; Watts, "Echoes," 506.

198. See Davies, "Destiny of the Nations," 95; Schultz, "Nationalism and Universalism," 129–30.

199. See Begg, "Peoples and Worship," 42; Hagelia, "Crescendo of Universalism," 86. As Wright states, "The identity of Israel will be *merged* with that of Egypt and Assyria" (*Mission of God*, 493).

his "servants" (v. 6), further clarifying the identity of the "servants," the true people of Yahweh within Israel.

The inclusive character of these texts and their pivotal placement in the book raise the question of whether statements regarding the subservience of the nations have converts to Yahwism in mind. Clearly, the relationship between Israel and the nations remains complex since some nations and individuals will accept Yahweh's offer of salvation and others will not. In texts where the attitude of the nations toward Israel and Yahweh is ambiguous, their submission may be forced as a result of continued opposition (e.g., 49:22–23). Or perhaps these texts refer to entire nations who generally remain resistant and not to individual converts. Alternatively, subservience may refer to a transitional period (e.g., 14:1–2; 45:14).[200] Moreover, some forms of submission, such as facilitating the return or bringing wealth to Zion, may not exclude complete inclusion within Israel. Although proselytes may remain subservient to ethnic Israelites in some manner, it is possible that this is not so, given the book's universalistic tenor and these alternative explanations regarding nationalistic texts.

Although it is doubtful that every distinction between Israelites and Gentile proselytes is eliminated, they are to be identified to the extent that they are counted among Yahweh's servants, "entering fully and equally into the privileges of Israel."[201] Thus we might expect that Yahweh-worshippers among the nations would be counted among the recipients of the progeny blessing upon Israel and contribute to the expansion of the nation through their conversion.[202]

Nevertheless, we must express some caution regarding this conclusion since the themes of salvation for the nations and the renewed proliferation of Israel do not appear to intersect clearly in the book. Since we have rejected the "universalistic" interpretation of 44:5 as improbable, none of the progeny texts that we have examined explicitly includes the nations or individual proselytes as participants in the future realization of

---

200. See Oswalt, "The Nations in Isaiah," 50.

201. Begg, "Peoples and Worship," 55. See Wright, *Mission of God*, 489–500, for a more extensive textual argument from Isaiah.

202. Blenkinsopp refers to this as "the re-interpretation of the promise to Abraham to include proselytes" ("Second Isaiah," 92). Although we basically concur, we might argue that "re-interpretation" implies more discontinuity than may truly be the case. Provision for Gentile inclusion in the people of God is not new, although its emphasis and scope in Isaiah are new.

the blessing. However, neither do they draw the boundaries of the blessing along ethnic lines or exclude foreigners.[203]

In giving interpretive priority to Isa 65–66, Schultz rightly comments, "the initial ambiguity [in the book] is progressively clarified as the book unfolds."[204] This appears to be true with respect to the role of the nations in the progeny blessing. In the story of mother Zion, there is no indication in 49:19–21, 51:2–3, or 54:1–3 that her imminent abundance of children would include foreigners. As a result, we assume that they are entirely Israelites. However, in light of the refined definition of God's servants in Isa 56–66 that is restricted along ethical lines and expanded beyond ethnic lines, we have a fuller understanding of the identity of Zion's children in 66:7–9 than we did in these previous depictions of mother Zion. This then shapes our interpretation of these earlier texts, creating a complex picture for 49:14–26 in particular where her children are brought back to the land by the nations (vv. 22–23). It is doubtful, however, that these are converted nations, and they may be coextensive with those who have opposed Israel (vv. 24–26). Thus, even though 49:14–26 distinguishes between Israel and the nations, the destiny of foreign converts is not (yet) addressed. The promise of future proliferation in 60:22 also occurs in the context of the submission of the nations (60:4, 6, 9, 11, 13–14; 61:5–6). But, again, it is doubtful that these statements exclude believing Gentiles.

As we would expect, the relationship between the multiplication of Israel and the multiplication of the nations is similar to the relationship between Israel's experience of salvation and the nations' experience of salvation, generally speaking. Isaiah's immediate concern is with the nation of Israel since it is through Israel (and the related servant figure) that salvation comes to the nations. Accordingly, Isaiah never claims that the nations will themselves experience growth; this is only anticipated for Israel. Yet foreigners will play a part in the growth of Israel through their inclusion. Given the universalistic trajectory of the book as a whole, the inclusion of Gentiles in the people of God often lies beneath the surface when Isaiah anticipates that Israel will again become a great nation. However, the extent to which Zion's children include foreigners remains underdetermined. This is not a new understanding of the progeny blessing in the story of Israel. Foreigners such as those comprising the mixed

---

203. Although we would be on firmer exegetical ground if the two themes did intersect more clearly, perhaps this disconnect is analogous to the parallel stories of the servant and Zion that do not seem to intersect until 54:17.

204. Schultz, "Nationalism and Universalism," 129.

multitude in the exodus or individuals such as Rahab or Ruth had become a part of the nation of Israel in the past. These isolated instances of conversion to Yahwism contributed to the growth of the people and they too enjoyed Yahweh's covenant blessing of children. However, occurrences of the blessing outside the prophets never draw attention to this fact, perhaps because such inclusion was rare. Now, in the universalistic outlook of Isaiah, more Gentiles are expected to proselytize than previously in Israel's history. Thus, the book emphasizes an aspect of the blessing that was previously unvoiced, namely, conversion. As a result, it is clearer in Isaiah than elsewhere in the OT that the corporate blessing upon Israel is not only accomplished by means of Yahweh's bestowal of children but also by means of the conversion of foreigners.

Conclusion: A Summary of the Progeny Blessing in Isaiah

The articulation of the progeny blessing in Isaiah is more diverse than in any other book in the OT. This is hardly surprising since nearly all the Isaianic texts we have reviewed are poetic, whereas the vast majority of the OT references to this motif outside of Isaiah are prose. As we journey through the book, we encounter some familiar expressions such as the common verb רָבָה in 9:2[3] and 51:2 and the hyperbolic sand simile in 10:22 and 48:19. Other expressions are unique or less common, but generally more evocative. Isaiah 27:6 and 44:3-4 compare the growth and prosperity of Israel to fruitful and well-watered trees—although the inherent ambiguity of these images cast some doubt on whether they specifically denote the progeny blessing. Isaiah 60:22 depicts multiple "mighty nations," and 65:20 and 23 imply proliferation by describing longevity and the removal of the curse. Finally, the restoration of Zion is vividly portrayed as a mother's recovery of her children, climactically through the "birth" of a nation (66:7-9). Her children will be so numerous that they will be cramped in the land (49:19-21) and must spread out (54:1-3). Yahweh is often acknowledged as the source of offspring and the creator of the great nation (9:2[3]; 26:15; 44:3-4; 49:19-23; 51:2-3; 66:7-9). However, even when this is not overt, his agency is implied, since life clearly has no other source (cf. 26:17-18 and 66:7-9).[205]

---

205. Note that these different expressions cut across the three "Isaiahs." This is generally the case as we compare the Isaianic progeny texts, although certain emphases are at times distinctive to Isa 40-55 in particular.

As was the case in Deuteronomy, within Isaiah we are able to reconstruct a relatively comprehensive history of Israel's experience of the progeny blessing. Isaiah 45:18 alludes to the universal blessing in Gen 1, one of God's fundamental purposes for humanity. Isaiah 51:2 cites the original promise to Abraham and 26:15 verifies that it was realized. Similarly, 10:22 addresses a pre-exilic audience and probably indicates that the people are (or soon will be) as numerous as the sand. In contrast, 48:19 addresses an exilic audience and, using the same simile, asserts that Israel can no longer view herself as a numerous people because of Yahweh's judgment. However, God will multiply them again in the future (9:2[3]; 44:3–4; 49:19–21; 51:3; 54:1–3; 60:22; 65:20, 23; 66:7–9). This proliferation had not yet begun from the perspective of the book itself. In general, the book defers this expansion to the future. Although the first readers of 9:2[3] may have expected it to come about following Assyrian oppression and the first readers of 49:19–21 may have anticipated its realization by the time of the return initiated by Cyrus, delayed fulfillment does not falsify these texts, since no clear time-frame was given for these events. By the end of the book, the multiplication of the people is pushed into the distant future, indicated by other-worldly language that describes a utopian final state (60:19–22; 65:17–25).

The location for this growth is often just as unclear. Although 9:2[3], 60:22, and 66:7–9 imply that expansion will take place in the land of Israel, 44:3–4, 49:19–21, 51:3, and 54:1–3 do not specify a location. Isaiah 49:19–21 seems to suggest that the exiles will expand greatly in exile prior to return, so this may be the case for 51:3 and 54:1–3 as well. Indeed, this would fit the historical context, since an exilic audience would be interested in present possibilities for blessing.[206] This remains uncertain, however, given the nature of metaphor and since the story of mother Zion is more concerned with Zion as the final destination of her children than it is with their origin. Zion is the destination and focal point for the restored people in 60:22 and 65:20, 23 as well, consistent with the book's fixation on a future glorified Zion, "the source from which all blessings flow"[207] on account of God's presence. However, Zion's restoration is likely representative of the resettling of the entire land of Israel. According to 54:3, this

---

206. Although this distinction could reinforce traditional redaction-critical divisions, it probably owes more to the audience than the author. Growth in exile need not conflict with texts that envision expansion in Israel, but this might imply stages of growth.

207. Gowan, *Eschatology*, 16.

burgeoning population will not necessarily even be confined to the land of Israel—they will possess nations as well.

The identity of those who are promised future growth shifts as we move through the book. The earliest texts in the book appear to pertain primarily to the northern tribes (9:2[3] and 10:22) and to Judah (26:15), although all twelve tribes are probably in view. In Isa 40–55 the entire exilic generation is promised future multiplication. In the final section of the book, this is limited to a righteous remnant. The rebels within Israel are to be excluded from this blessed future. This is clear not only in 60:21–22, which addresses the "righteous," but also in 65:17–25 (cf. 65:8–16) and in 66:7–9 (cf. the "servants" in v. 14). These latter texts lend greater specificity to those in Isa 40–55 (cf. 54:17), so that we understand the true recipients of the future progeny promise to be the righteous remnant within the ethnic nation, potentially including righteous Gentiles as well.

The first texts in the book that envision future multiplication (9:2[3]; 44:3–4) offer little indication that this will transcend or even match prior growth. However, subsequent texts employ various images and typologies in order to portray extravagant growth beyond that which Israel has experienced in the past: they will be too crowded for their former cities (49:19–21); they will spread out even to possess the nations (54:1–3); multiple individuals will, like Abraham, become a great nation (60:22); all will live long (65:20, 23); and a whole nation will be born in a day (66:7–9). Surprisingly, as the book progresses and more time elapses without fulfillment, we do not encounter a diminished hope but rather a greater hope. The exilic and post-exilic audiences are not to doubt God's promise to multiply them once again, but rather to grasp it all the more firmly.

Although the progeny blessing does not typically occur within comprehensive descriptions of blessings in Isaiah, it frequently appears alongside a few related themes.[208] Proliferation accompanies or results in joy (9:2[3]; 51:3; 54:1; 60:5; 65:18; 66:10, 14), underscoring the community's longing for a renewed population. In addition, it is juxtaposed with the return or repossession of the land (26:15; 49:19–21; 54:1–3; 60:21–22; 65:17–25), to be expected given the importance of the Abrahamic traditions in Isaiah's rhetoric. Finally, the destruction of Israel's enemies appears together with the blessing in 9:3–4[4–5]; 26:12–14; 49:17, 23–26. This too is understandable since Israel's enemies threatened and impeded the growth of the nation. Interestingly, human fertility is never correlated

---

208. References to the progeny blessing sometimes do not occur in restoration oracles at all (26:15; 45:18; 48:19).

with fertility of land or animals as in Deuteronomy, although agricultural fertility is employed to describe human fertility (44:3-4; perhaps 27:6).

As the book unfolds, the language of the progeny blessing is used in new, untraditional ways so that multiple factors may be involved in its fulfillment:

1. Many of the texts we have treated, particularly those in the first half of the book, simply denote physical reproduction (9:2[3]; 10:22; 26:15; 45:18; 48:19; 51:2), as expected since this is the standard meaning of the blessing as found in all of the major traditions of the blessing encountered elsewhere in the OT. All the other texts include physical reproduction (49:19-21; 54:1-3; 60:22; 65:20, 23; 66:7-9), but may entail other factors as well.

2. In the story of mother Zion the language of the progeny blessing is employed metaphorically with respect to the return to the land. This is clearly the case in 49:19-21 and may be true in 54:1-3 and 66:7-9 as well. From the perspective of the exilic community, the return need not necessarily entail the multiplication of the people, although we have observed that these texts include it. However, from Zion's frame of reference, if her children are in exile, they do not exist at all. As a result, the return can be described as Yahweh's blessing of children. Thus, *both* material Abrahamic blessings are conflated into this one image wherein the restoration of children denotes both physical reproduction and recovery of the land (as the primary underlying historical referent).

3. Later texts in the book may include the conversion of foreigners as a means toward the creation of a new great nation (60:22; 66:7-9 and perhaps 49:19-21; 54:1-3). All three factors, reproduction, return, and conversion, may be involved in the growth of a multitude of children for mother Zion since all three contribute to her chief concern: a large people restored to the land.

4. Finally, although 65:20 and 23 do not employ the language of the progeny blessing, the vision of the new heavens and new earth introduces an additional avenue through which the corporate blessing may come to fruition, namely, the partial curtailment or postponement of death. In sum, Isaiah uses the progeny motif in a more flexible and original manner than we find elsewhere in the OT.

The diversity that we encounter among Isaianic texts that predict future multiplication begs the question of whether these texts all depict

The Progeny Blessing in the Book of Isaiah

the same growth or whether they describe different fulfillments. For example, does 49:19-21, which appears to correlate the blessing with the imminent return, depict the same historical reality as 60:22 or 65:20, 23, which include cosmic elements that seem to indicate a more distant fulfillment and appear to be unrelated to the exile or return? The poetry and ambiguity in these descriptions resist a conclusive answer. Concrete details regarding time, place, scope, and means are often lacking. Perhaps the best solution lies in the nature of blessing itself. As we have described above, blessing is a state or continuous process rather than a punctiliar event. Some aspects of blessing may have begun during the initial return to the land, but the expectation was that blessing would build and then persist in Zion without end. Therefore, we suggest that, although these texts treating the progeny blessing cannot be harmonized easily as referring to exactly the same circumstances, neither do they describe distinct "events." Rather, they focus on different phases of the continuous process of the growth of Israel following the return. Isaiah 49:19-21 may highlight the beginning of renewed blessing—or it may collapse centuries into one image that begins with the return—while 60:22 and 65:20, 23 may envision a later phase of utopian equilibrium. Furthermore, the progression of the book suggests that later phases of this growth will be accomplished increasingly by Gentile conversions rather than by physical reproduction alone as in earlier stages. However, many details regarding the future of the progeny blessing remain open so that it is difficult to locate our texts along a hypothetical timeline or to claim that they together depict, for example, one, three, or five stages of the blessing. We find different emphases among the Isaianic texts we have examined; however, they are not conflicting or dissonant, but ultimately compatible and complementary.

Among the different progeny traditions that we have identified in the OT, the Abrahamic tradition is the most influential throughout the book of Isaiah.[209] The Abrahamic progeny promise is clearest in 51:2 in which it is explicitly recalled, the only instance in the Latter Prophets where a former progeny tradition is overtly cited. Most of the texts treating the progeny blessing in Isaiah allude to this promise, most evident in Isa 40–55 (10:22; 26:15; 44:3-4; 45:18; 48:19; 49:19-21; 51:2-3; 54:1-3; 60:22; 65:9, 23; 66:7-9).[210] In no case have we found sufficient evidence

---

209. See Anderson, "Exodus Typology," 182-83; Blenkinsopp, *Isaiah 56-66*, 277.

210. The recurrent use of this tradition makes it all the more likely that it underlies those texts in which an Abrahamic allusion would be doubtful if the text were to be treated in isolation (see the "clustering" criterion of Richard B. Hays, *Echoes of Scripture*, 29-33).

to posit dependence on any particular text from Genesis, nor should we necessarily expect this since the promise is frequently repeated throughout Genesis using similar language. However, various textual features recall the Abrahamic blessing in general, including the sand simile (10:22; 48:19), the juxtaposition of recovery of progeny and land, possession (יָרַשׁ) of the land (60:21; 65:9) or the nations (54:3), and other key terms such as זֶרַע (44:3; 48:19; 54:3; 65:9, 23; 66:22), בְּרָכָה/ברך (51:2; 44:3; 65:23), and גּוֹי עָצוּם (60:22). Furthermore, Abraham and Sarah serve as types. Mother Zion is depicted as a second, greater Sarah (54:1–3; 66:7–9) and 51:2–3 and 60:22 allude to the original Abrahamic expansion of the nation as the pattern and precedent for proliferation in the future.

Since 10:22 addresses a pre-exilic audience, the Abrahamic allusion suggests that even this cherished promise would not protect the people from impending judgment. Usually, though, the appeal to Abraham is meant to inspire hope. Particularly in the exilic situation in which the land was lost and the population had been diminished, the community would have questioned whether the Abrahamic promises were still meaningful. Isaiah answers in the affirmative by describing the future using these same Abrahamic categories. Furthermore, not only will these blessings be renewed, but they also will transcend their former realization. This message remained relevant for the post-exilic community as well. In response, Israel should trust and hope in Yahweh, both in his power and in his compassion. If Yahweh first created Israel by making one man into a great nation, how difficult could it be for him to make a small community into a great nation? Abraham may serve as a paradigm for the faith of the community as well: just as Abraham believed that Yahweh could and would keep his promises, so the community ought to believe that Yahweh could fulfill these same promises again.

Although not as prominent, the book of Isaiah exhibits knowledge of other progeny traditions as well:

1. The Solomonic realization of the progeny blessing may have influenced past recollections of the blessing. By alluding to the Solomonic era, and perhaps specifically to 1 Kgs 4, Isa 26:15 and 48:19 (cf. 10:22) verify that the Abrahamic progeny promise was realized in the past.[211]

2. Isaiah 45:18 employs the language of Gen 1–2 and may thus allude to Gen 1:28, the universal progeny blessing (cf. also the reference to Eden in 51:3).

---

211. In addition, 9:1–6[2–7] portrays the future kingdom as a return to Solomonic glory.

The Progeny Blessing in the Book of Isaiah

3. In our analysis, we have not detected any clear allusions to the covenant blessings of Deut 28 or Levi 26, although 65:23 may draw on the covenant curses of Lev 26. This is surprising given the importance of the Sinai covenant and the use of these blessings by other prophets. Perhaps they do play a role in Isaiah's restoration texts, but the poetic presentation masks clear allusions to the covenant blessings of Sinai. And perhaps the Abrahamic blessings are mediated through the covenant blessings, but the fact remains that Isaiah's treatment of the progeny blessing is primarily Abrahamic, probably because this appeal to Abraham is more relevant for his audience.

4. The progeny motif is not an established part of the Zion tradition. However, Isaiah incorporates the progeny blessing into the Zion tradition, most evident in the story of mother Zion. This is unsurprising since Zion is the focal point of Israel's hopes and of Yahweh's blessing in the book of Isaiah.

5. Given the abundance of new exodus typology in Isaiah, we might expect to find allusions to the growth of the people prior to the return as in Exod 1:7. We have explored this as a possibility in 49:19–21, but have not otherwise detected evidence of exilic proliferation. Perhaps this is due to Isaiah's fixation on Zion as the place of blessing to the exclusion of any experience of blessing outside the land. Or perhaps Isaiah does not extend the analogy between Egyptian bondage and the exile as far as the growth of the population since the exile, unlike the sojourn in Egypt, has punitive purposes and thus cannot be the locus of blessing as in Exod 1:7. However, it is inappropriate to make much of the location in which expansion takes place since few of the Isaianic progeny texts do so. The correlation between the multiplication of the people and the return to the land in the story of mother Zion does parallel the correlation between the expansion of the people in Exod 1:7 and the initial entry into the land. Therefore, it remains possible that Isaiah intends for Exod 1:7 to serve as a pattern for the future return, despite the different locations.

The function of the progeny blessing in Isaiah can be summarized by examining its relationship to four primary characters in the book: Zion, the people of Israel, the nations, and Yahweh. Zion had lost both husband and children in the exilic judgment. In Isaiah's personification of Jerusalem, the recovery of her children, together with restoration to Yahweh, is her greatest yearning, encompassing her entire "story" from beginning to end. It could hardly be otherwise since the book's trajectory moves toward a restored and glorified Zion and this would not be possible without an abundant population of Yahweh-worshippers to partake of deliverance and blessing. Her glorification certainly entails more, but the progeny blessing is a necessary prerequisite. Like Abraham, small and without land, the exilic community longed for the same material blessings promised to Abraham, land and progeny, in order to recover their nationhood. The situation still had not greatly improved for the post-exilic community. Isaiah's message is one of hope: Yahweh is not finished with his people but will grant them salvation. Much of the book is devoted to inspiring renewed trust in Yahweh, from the story of the servant and the story of Zion to the appeal to creation, Abrahamic, exodus, and Solomonic traditions. The relationship between the nations and the progeny motif is less clear, but we have suggested that they too may enjoy the benefits of Yahweh's blessing and be incorporated within Israel's population should they "turn to Yahweh and be saved" (45:22). Finally, the progeny blessing functions as one of the most basic expressions of Yahweh's compassion (49:13, 15–16; 54:7–10) toward his people. He delights to multiply his people because in so doing he is glorified (26:15; cf. 37:35; 40:5; 42:10–12; 43:7, 20–21, 25; 48:9–11). Indeed, Yahweh is not simply interested in multiplying people, but rather in multiplying true servants who seek and fear him. Thus Zion, the people, the nations, and Yahweh all benefit from his multiplication of the people and take joy in it.

4

The Progeny Blessing in the Book of Jeremiah

INTRODUCTION TO THE BOOK OF JEREMIAH

Jeremiah's Use of Prior Traditions

THE BOOK OF JEREMIAH shares much language and many theological themes with Deuteronomy and the so-called Deuteronomistic History, particularly with the book of Kings.[1] In *Judgment and Promise*, McConville observes that the restoration oracles of Jeremiah anticipate a return to the land and the implementation of a new covenant initiated by Yahweh following exile, consistent with the perspective of Deut 30:1-10, but different from the Deuteronomistic History which contains neither hope.[2] He therefore concludes that texts such as Jer 24, 30-33, and 37-45 are an

---

1. The development and priority of these three works has long been debated. Some posit that Jeremiah was himself influenced by deuteronomic theology (e.g., McConville, *Judgment and Promise*, 181). J. Philip Hyatt states that "Jeremiah was acquainted with the original edition of Deuteronomy" ("Jeremiah and Deuteronomy," 119) while affirming later deuteronomic editors and Jeremianic influence on the expansion of Deut 28 (113-27). Others attribute deuteronomic influence to a late editor, Jeremiah's disciples, or a "deuteronomic school" (e.g., Kugler, "Deuteronomists," 142-44; Römer, "How Did Jeremiah," 189-99). The important point for our purposes is simply the existence of the correspondences, some of which appear with modification, and their implications for how the book is to be read in its present form.

2. See McConville, *Judgment and Promise*, 20, 55, 82-83.

"extended reflection" on Deut 30:1–6[3] and that Jeremiah stands in much closer relationship to Deut 30 than to DtH,[4] thus undermining the theory of a "deuteronomistic redaction." His study is compelling and justifies reading the hope of Jeremiah in light of Deut 30:1–10.

Furthermore, the book portrays Jeremiah as a Mosaic prophet. The correspondences between these two figures and their messages are striking. For example, Jeremiah's call is similar to that of Moses. Both serve as intercessors for the people (although this privilege is revoked from Jeremiah in 7:16, 11:14, 14:11, and 15:1), the burning of the first scroll (Jer 36) parallels the shattering of the first tablets at Sinai, and Jeremiah is responsible for preparing a new generation for restoration to the land in a "second exodus" (see 16:14–15; 23:7–8).[5]

In an illuminating article, Gary Yates builds on the Moses typology and deuteronomic correspondences in the book by seeking "to demonstrate that the contrast between Jeremiah's promise of new exodus in Israel's restoration (chs. 30–33) and the story of "no exodus" (or exodus unraveled) in the experiences of Jeremiah and the Jews remaining in the land following the exile (chs. 40–43) is a central unifying feature in Jeremiah 26–45."[6] He does so in convincing fashion by identifying parallels between the exodus and new exodus in Jer 30–31 and parallels between Jeremiah and Moses in Jeremiah 40–43.[7] The two groups of Judahites addressed in the book, those who go to Babylon and those who are left in the land, correspond to two "exodus" experiences. Underscored by the sign-act of 32:1–15, the former group will eventually partake of the new exodus of Jer 30–31. In contrast, those left will not only fail to experience the new exodus, but also undergo a reversal of the original exodus by returning to Egypt, the ultimate covenant curse (Deut 28:68).[8] Yates' identification of exodus typology is confirmed by prior texts in Jeremiah that portray return from exile as an event greater than the exodus (16:14–15; 23:7–8). Given these parallels, it should not surprise us if we find that the future

---

3. Ibid., 124.

4. See ibid., 162.

5. See especially Seitz, "Prophet Moses," 3–27, for these correspondences. William L. Holladay, "Background," 153–64; "Jeremiah and Moses," 17–27, also describes the Moses (and second exodus) typology in the book.

6. Yates, "New Exodus," 2–3.

7. See ibid., 6–9. A. J. O. van der Wal identifies multiple allusions to the exodus event in Jer 30–31 as well, although some of his proposed allusions are tenuous ("Themes from Exodus," 559–66).

8. See Yates, "New Exodus," 9, 13.

The Progeny Blessing in the Book of Jeremiah

blessing of progeny corresponds typologically to the growth of Israel in the original exodus (Exod 1:7).

Future Hope in Jeremiah

The proclamation of future hope beyond exile in Jeremiah is concentrated in the "Book of Comfort" in Jer 30–33 (30:3, 7b–11, 16–22; 31:1–40; 32:15, 37–44; 33:6–26). However, portrayals of restoration occur throughout the book, both as extended descriptions (3:14–18; 12:15–16; 16:14–15; 23:3–8; 24:5–7; 29:10–14; 46:27–28; 50:4–5, 19–20) and as brief notes of hope (1:10b; 27:11; 48:47; 49:6, 39; 50:34a; 51:5a, 10).

Just as the book of Jeremiah not only proclaims judgment for Judah but for the nations as well (25:12–38; 27:1–10; 46–51), future prosperity is promised not only for Judah and Israel but also for the nations. However, this hope is relatively undeveloped, and certainly nothing comparable to the description of their future in Isaiah. Jeremiah 27:11 promises a future for nations that submit to Babylon and 3:17 and 16:19 envision a future gathering of the nations to Jerusalem. Using the language of 1:10, in 12:15–16 Yahweh pledges to restore Israel's neighbors to their lands after "uprooting" (נָתַשׁ) them, and will even "build (בָּנָה) them up in the midst of my people" should they turn to him (cf. 4:2). Finally, the oracles against Moab (48:47), Ammon (49:6), and Elam (49:39) conclude with the ubiquitous phrase, "I will restore [their] fortunes" (אָשִׁיב אֶת־שְׁבוּת),[9] affirming that it is not only his own people who have a future (cf. 46:26 regarding Egypt).

Apart from these isolated verses, however, Jeremiah's oracles of salvation are fixated upon Judah and Israel. The physical return is the most consistent promise, missing only in 33:14–26 and 51:5a, 10 among Jeremiah's restoration texts. This is typically described as an act of Yahweh, and often introduces and/or concludes restoration oracles, since this logically precedes enjoyment of blessing in the land. Jeremiah's vision of

---

9. The LXX does not include this clause in 48:47 and 49:6 and is therefore slightly less optimistic regarding the fate of foreign nations. This expression occurs eleven times in Jeremiah, seven of which are in the "Book of Comfort" (30:3, 18; 31:23; 32:44; 33:7, 11, 26) and appears to serve as a refrain. It is unclear whether the phrase refers specifically to return from exile (so Seitz, *Theology in Conflict*, 210 n. 8) or more generally to restoration of well-being (so Holladay, *Jeremiah 2*, 355; Westermann, *Prophetic Oracles*, 258–61). Treating שְׁבוּת as a cognate accusative, John M. Bracke argues persuasively for the latter ("Sûb sebût," 233–44) and concludes that the expression is "a technical term indicating a restoration to an earlier time of well-being" (244).

renewal in the land is not other-worldly, and differs little from portrayals of an ideal society found in the Pentateuch and Former Prophets:[10] cities will be rebuilt (30:18; 31:4), the people will multiply (3:16; 23:3; 30:19; 31:27; 33:22), the land will be fruitful again (31:5, 12), good kings will rule the people (3:15; 23:4–5; 30:9; 33:14–26), they will live in security (23:6; 30:10; 32:37; 33:16; 46:27), enemies will not harm them (30:11, 16), no one will be afraid (23:4; 30:10; 46:27) but rather they will be filled with joy (30:19; 31:12–13; 33:11), and Israel and Judah will be reunited (3:18; 30:3; 50:4). This picture does, however, transcend Israel's previous experiences in that what was formerly merely an ideal will now be realized. For example, kings will truly practice justice and righteousness, resulting in genuine security and joy in the land.

This restoration is rooted in Yahweh's gracious determination to renew his relationship with his people (e.g., 31:20). In isolation, some texts of hope appear to suggest that the return depends solely upon the repentance of the people. However, the full testimony of the book ultimately attributes spiritual restoration to God's initiative.[11] In a "new" (31:31), "everlasting" (32:40; 50:5) covenant, God will bring about inner change in order that the people might repent and respond in obedience (see 3:17; 24:7; 31:31–34; 32:39–40). Grounded in the forgiveness of their sins (31:34; 33:8; 50:20), this inner renewal, perhaps the driving hope in the book, is expressed in various ways: "they will no longer walk after the stubbornness of their own evil heart" (3:17); "I will give them a heart to know me" (24:7); "I will put my law within them and write it on their hearts" (31:33); and "I will put the fear of me in their hearts" (32:40).[12] As a result, Yahweh declares, "they

---

10. Gerhard von Rad rightly states, "Jeremiah has nothing to say of any changes in the natural world of the land where God's chosen people are to dwell; and nothing of any paradise-like fertility" (*Old Testament Theology: Prophetic Traditions*, 212).

11. Jeremiah Unterman argues that there was a "development of Jeremiah's thought on the relationship of repentance to redemption" toward seeing redemption as solely the work of God (31:27–37; 32:37–41; 33:1–26; 50:17–20 and perhaps 23:1–8; *From Repentance to Redemption*, 21). Although there may be some credence to this developmental hypothesis, the overall effect of these texts on the exilic audience is to ground redemption in God's mercy and initiative without negating the personal responsibility to repent, with some texts placing more emphasis on the one than on the other. An alternative explanation for the diversity found in these texts, just as plausible as Unterman's, is that no shift occurred in Jeremiah's thinking, but that he adjusted his emphasis depending on the pedagogical needs of the current audience.

12. McConville rightly states, however, that the new covenant both overcomes "the failure of the human will and preserve[s] the reality of human responsibility" (see 24:7; 29:12–13) (*Judgment and Promise*, 175).

will be my people and I will be their God" (24:7; 30:22; 31:1, 33; 32:38). There is little indication of a distinction among those who return—it appears that all will be granted a new heart. Therefore, Israel's hope beyond exile is different from their experience of life prior to exile in that Yahweh will grant them hearts to love him, thus ensuring a right relationship with God, and resulting in a prosperous society laden with God's blessing.

Following the initial return, the exiles addressed in the book may have guessed that the further promises of social renewal and inner change would follow almost immediately. However, most oracles, introduced by common phrases that simply refer to the future such as "in those days" (בַּיָּמִים הָהֵמָּה),[13] "at that time" (בָּעֵת הַהִיא),[14] and "behold, days are coming" (הִנֵּה־יָמִים בָּאִים)[15] leave the question open. Thus we must conclude that the temporal relationship between the initial return and the further blessings remains ambiguous in Jeremiah's portrayal.

As highlighted by McConville, the future outlook of Jeremiah has a particular affinity to Deut 30:1–10. Both foresee a return to the land following exile that God himself will accomplish (vv. 3–5), rooted in God's compassion (v. 3). Like Jeremiah, Deut 30 envisions the restoration of the ideal society, including the multiplication of the people (vv. 4, 9), agricultural bounty (v. 9), and the elimination of Israel's enemies (v. 7). In addition, it depicts an inner "circumcision of the heart" (v. 6) that enables the people to obey and love Yahweh (vv. 2, 6, 8, 10). As is the case in Jeremiah, this appears to be God's own doing (v. 6), yet does not eliminate human responsibility (v. 10). In addition to these conceptual similarities, common language is employed to describe these realities: Yahweh has "driven them away" (הִדִּיחַ; vv. 1, 4; e.g., Jer 16:5; 23:3, 8); he will "restore (שָׁב) their fortunes (שְׁבוּת)" (v. 3; e.g., Jer 29:14; 30:3); he will "have compassion" (רִחֲמָ) on them (v. 3; e.g., Jer 12:15; 30:18; 33:26); he will "gather" (קִבְּצְךָ; vv. 3, 4; e.g., Jer 23:3; 29:14; 32:37) them and "bring them back" (הֱבִיאֲךָ; v. 5; e.g., Jer 16:15; 23:3; 24:6); he will "multiply" them (הִרְבְּךָ; v. 5; Jer 3:16; 23:3; 29:6; 30:19; 33:22); and the people will "return" (שַׁבְתָּ; vv. 2, 8, 10; Jer 24:7) to Yahweh. Given these parallels, we might expect to find that

---

13. See Jer 3:16, 18; 5:18; 31:29; 33:15, 16; 50:4, 20, all introducing hope.

14. See Jer 3:17; 8:1; 31:1; 32:2; 33:15; 39:10; 50:4; 50:20, all introducing future hope except for 8:1 (judgment) and 32:2 and 39:10 (current events).

15. See Jer 7:32; 9:24[25]; 16:14; 19:6; 23:5, 7; 30:3; 31:27, 31, 38; 33:14; 48:12; 49:2; 51:47, 52. All of these texts refer to the future, but half of them refer to salvation and half to judgment. These three formulas appear to be synonymous expressions and occur alongside one another in the same texts.

Deut 30:1–10 is the primary intertext for the progeny blessing in Jeremiah, although this must be evaluated on a case-by-case basis.

The Progeny Blessing in Jeremiah

Six texts in the MT of Jeremiah cite the progeny blessing (3:16; 23:3; 29:6; 30:19; 31:27; 33:22), all in the context of oracles of hope, with the exception of 29:6. First, we must examine the negation of the blessing, perhaps more evident in Jeremiah than in any other prophetic book.

Population Decimation in Jeremiah

As was the case in Deut 28, the judgment that Yahweh inflicts on his people consists primarily in loss of land and decimation of the population, the undoing of the Abrahamic blessings. Jeremiah describes the coming judgment as the undoing of creation itself, including the removal of humankind (4:23–26), and as the reversal of the three-fold deuteronomic expression of fertility (fruit of the ground, the womb, and animals; 5:17; 7:20). The people will be decimated by means of destruction of cities (2:15; 4:7; 9:9–10[10–11]), wild animals (5:6; 8:17; 15:3), war (6:4, 22–26; 12:12; 20:4; 33:4–5; 39:1–2), bereavement of children (15:7; 18:21),[16] and cannibalism (19:9). However, the most frequent (and typical prosaic) judgment refrain in Jeremiah is that God will destroy his own people by means of sword (חֶרֶב), famine (רָעָב), and pestilence (דֶּבֶר) (14:12; 21:7, 9; 24:10; 27:8, 13; 29:17, 18; 32:24, 36; 34:17; 38:2; 42:17, 22; 44:13).[17] Jeremiah does not avoid graphic descriptions of widespread death (7:32–34; 9:20–21[21–22]; 13:14; 14:16). These decimation themes correspond closely to the covenant curses of Lev 26 (vv. 22, 25, 29, 31–33) and Deut 28 (vv. 21–22, 25–26, 41, 52–57, 62), conceptually if not always verbally.[18]

---

16. Interestingly, the people had already been bereaving themselves of their children through their idolatrous practices of human sacrifice (19:4–5; 32:35).

17. This formula often functions as a summary of God's coming judgment (e.g., 21:3–10; 24:10; 29:17–18; 38:2). In addition to these fifteen occurrences of the full formula, sword and famine occur together an additional nine times (11:22; 14:16, 18; 15:2; 16:4; 18:21; 42:16; 44:12, 27). Outside Jeremiah, these three means of judgment appear together eight times in Ezekiel (5:12, 17; 6:11, 12; 7:15 (2x); 12:16; 14:21). Although the three do not occur together in the curses of Deut 28, all three terms are present (vv. 21, 22, 48). In Lev 26, חֶרֶב and דֶּבֶר appear together in v. 26 but רָעָב is not present in the chapter.

18. Delbert R. Hillers concludes in his study that, "[o]f the prophetic books,

The Progeny Blessing in the Book of Jeremiah

Moreover, Jer 11:1–13 rehearses the history of the broken Sinai covenant, pronouncing the covenant curses upon those in the present generation (vv. 3–5, 9–13) who do not respond to it with obedience (vv. 3, 8), as Yahweh had punished a previous generation (vv. 6–8).[19] Therefore, imminent judgment should be understood as the execution of the covenant curses from the Sinai covenant.

In the midst of a litany of curses yielding death (15:1–9), Yahweh exclaims, "Their widows have become more numerous than the sand of the sea" (עָצְמוּ־לִי אַלְמְנֹתָו מֵחוֹל יַמִּים, v. 8). Used later in Jer 33:22 to refer to multiplication in a positive sense, the "sand of the sea" simile appears to be an ironic play on the progeny blessing. Whereas the "sand" simile was once employed to depict the proliferation of people (e.g., 2 Sam 17:11; 1 Kgs 4:20; Hos 2:1[1:10]), particularly within the context of the Abrahamic promise (see Gen 22:17; 32:13[12]), it now envisions widespread death of spouses. In Jer 16:2, Jeremiah is himself forbidden by Yahweh from begetting children since all offspring will soon be slaughtered (v. 4). Therefore, in the current situation children are hardly a "blessing." Unique in the OT,[20] this command serves as a sign to Jeremiah's contemporaries but will later be reversed in the exilic setting (29:6).

Even after the devastating destruction of Jerusalem (39:1–10), decimation continues for those who remain in the land. Because of their defiant idolatry after fleeing to Egypt (44:15–25), Jeremiah predicts that they will be left "few in number" (מְתֵי מִסְפָּר; 44:28; cf. 44:11–14).

In a return to pre-conquest conditions, exile involved loss of land, prosperity, security, and monarchy. However, exile also prepared the people for God's gracious restoration of these privileges beyond exile. Similarly, the loss of life itself through judgment paves the way for future restoration through proliferation.

Jeremiah contains by far the most numerous and impressive parallels to treaty-curses" (*Treaty-Curses*, 77). Without positing influence, he identifies some particularly strong parallels between Israel's own covenant curses and Jeremiah: death by wild animals in Lev 26:22 and Jer 5:6, 8:17 (55), consuming one's children in Deut 28:53–57, Lev 26:29 and Jer 19:9 (63), and lack of a proper burial in Deut 28:26 and Jer 7:33, 8:2, 9:21[22], 14:16, 16:4, 6, 22:19, 25:33, 34:20, and 36:30 (68–69).

19. See Lundbom, *Jeremiah 1–20*, 623–24.
20. See Thompson, *Jeremiah*, 403.

Jeremiah 3:16

Following a lengthy indictment of Judah and Israel for their many sins (2:1—3:10), Yahweh invites his people to repent (3:11-14, 3:22—4:4). The initial appeal in 3:11-14a precedes the first restoration oracle in the book of Jeremiah in vv. 14b-18. This appeal is directed toward the northern kingdom, and probably serves as a model for Judah's own repentance when Yahweh then addresses them in v. 14a, declaring, "return (שׁוּבוּ), faithless sons."[21] Intriguingly, this call to spiritual return is immediately followed by Yahweh's pledge of physical return: "I will bring you back (וְהֵבֵאתִי) to Zion" (v. 14b).

The relationship between repentance and the return of the Babylonian exiles is not entirely clear. Perhaps repentance is the condition for the return. However, it is more likely that the hope of vv. 14a-18 motivates repentance rather than depends upon it as a condition,[22] since 1) other restoration oracles in Jeremiah do not mention repentance but rather attribute the future return to God's initiative (see throughout Jer 30-33); 2) v. 12a grounds hope in God's character rather than in the people's ability to repent; and 3) vv. 14-18 are closely related to 23:1-8 (see below), which says nothing of repentance. Thus, as Brueggemann claims, "[t]he shift from faithlessness to restoration is accomplished because of Yahweh's resilient fidelity."[23]

First, the renewal of society is described. In contrast to the evil "shepherds" (הָרֹעִים) introduced in 2:8, God will install good "shepherds" (רֹעִים), i.e., kings, who rule "with[24] knowledge and understanding" (v. 15). Furthermore, the people will multiply (v. 16a). Verses 16b-17 then depict new spiritual conditions. All of Jerusalem will replace the ark of the covenant as "the throne of Yahweh,"[25] resulting in the gathering of all nations to Jerusalem and inward transformation (v. 17b), although we are not told how this transformation will occur. The passage ends (v. 18) as it began (v.

---

21. Craigie et al., *Jeremiah 1-25*, 60; McConville, *Judgment and Promise*, 35; McKane, *Jeremiah*, 1:72, recognize a shift to Judah in v. 14a.

22. See Fretheim, *Jeremiah*, 89-90; McConville, *Judgment and Promise*, 35, 40-41. Cf. Jones, *Jeremiah*, 101.

23. Brueggemann, *Jeremiah: Exile and Homecoming*, 47.

24. This is better understood as the manner in which the shepherds feed the people than as the people's "food."

25. Lev 16:2, 13, 2 Kgs 19:15, and Ps 80:2[1] appear to identify the ark as Yahweh's "throne" (see Holladay, *Jeremiah 1*, 121; Jones, *Jeremiah*, 102; Thompson, *Jeremiah*, 203).

14b) with the return, this time cited as the occasion for the reunification of the twelve tribes (cf. Ezek 34 and 37:15–23).

The progeny blessing in v. 16a (וְהָיָה כִּי תִרְבּוּ וּפְרִיתֶם בָּאָרֶץ) uses the two verbs commonly found together in Genesis as hendiadys (Gen 1:22, 28; 8:17; 9:1, 7; 17:20; 28:3; 35:11; 47:27; 48:4) and only in Lev 26:9, Jer 23:3, and Ezek 36:11 elsewhere in the OT. However, v. 16a and Ezek 36:11 are distinctive in that they reverse the two verbs. Perhaps, as Beentjes proposes, "by this deviating model [the author] attains a moment of extra attention in the listener (or reader), because the latter hears something else than the traditional words."[26] Similarly, Talmon suggests that the inversion of synonymous elements draws attention to the presence of a quotation.[27]

The relationship between multiplication and the surrounding clauses hinges on the meaning of וְהָיָה כִּי. It could present a condition (cf. LXX?), but this would place primary responsibility for multiplication on the people and would call its realization into doubt, which does not fit the present context of promises. Some treat it as a clarifying כִּי ("and it will happen that ...").[28] However, the occurrences of וְהָיָה כִּי elsewhere in Jeremiah (5:19; 15:2; 16:10; 25:28) consistently introduce temporal statements (cf. LXX renderings), with the possible exception of 25:28 which may be conditional. Furthermore, in each of these texts this construction provides the temporal context for that which follows in the text rather than for that which precedes. Therefore, v. 16a provides the temporal setting for v. 16b (and likely v. 17 as well), introduced by בַּיָּמִים הָהֵמָּה ("in those days"), a structural marker that introduces a new thought throughout Jeremiah (see 3:16, 18; 5:18; 31:29; 33:15, 16; 50:4, 20). Since the proliferation of the people may be the result of the good shepherds "feeding" the people (see below),[29] v. 16a may then serve as a hinge between the renewal of society in v. 15 and the effects of the new spiritual relationship of God with his people in vv. 16b–17.

It is not entirely clear whether v. 16a denotes a continuous or completed multiplication in the promised land.[30] The former is possible since

---

26. Beentjes, "Inverted Quotations," 523.

27. See Talmon, "Textual Study," 358–78. See also Schultz, *Search for Quotation*, 75–76, 293.

28. So Shields, *Circumscribing the Prostitute*, 101.

29. See McKane, *Jeremiah*, 1:73.

30. Robert P. Carroll appears to understand v. 16a as a reference to the return (i.e., multiplication with respect to the land) rather than to physical reproduction (*Jeremiah*, 149), but this would be inconsistent with the reproductive nature of these verbs throughout the OT.

blessings, ideally, are never complete but are always advancing. Verse 16a would thus be translated, "And when you are multiplying and being fruitful in the land, in those days . . ." However, the latter is possible as well since in the past there had been a point when it could be said that Israel's multiplication had been accomplished (e.g., Exod 1:7; Deut 26:5; 1 Kgs 4:20). Regardless, the ambiguity of this clause leaves the timing of the events of vv. 16–17 open.

Jeremiah 23:3

In Jer 21–22, Jeremiah emphasizes the failures of the contemporary "house of David" (21:12; cf. 22:2), addressing the four kings who preceded the exile of 587. Yahweh commanded them to "administer justice (מִשְׁפָּט)" (21:12) and "practice justice and righteousness (מִשְׁפָּט וּצְדָקָה)" (22:3), but it is clear that they have failed to care for the people as they ought (22:13–17, 21–22, 24–30). The indictment and sentence of the kings concludes with a final woe against the "shepherds" (23:1–2), probably a reference to the aforementioned kings of Judah (cf. 22:22).[31] Yahweh declares, "you have scattered (הֲפִצֹתֶם) my flock, driven them away (וַתַּדִּחוּם),[32] and not attended (פְּקַדְתֶּם) to them." As a result, God will "attend" (פקד) to the shepherds in judgment (v. 2).

However, this is not the end of the Davidic dynasty. Verses 3–8 affirm a future for Davidic kingship, not by sustaining his line, but by reviving it following exile. In this oracle of hope, there is no emphasis on a renewed relationship with Yahweh or a promise of inner change. Rather, vv. 3–8 focus upon the return (vv. 3, 7–8) and the ideal society under good "shepherds" (vv. 4–6), in stark contrast to the kings of Jeremiah's own day. As a result of the care of these new shepherds, the people will no longer be afraid or experience judgment (v. 4). The Davidic king[33] will perform

---

31. See Fretheim, *Jeremiah*, 324; Klein, "Jeremiah 23:1–8," 168.

32. Throughout the book it is Yahweh who will "scatter" (הֵפִיץ; 9:15[16]; 13:24; 18:17; 30:11) and "drive away" (הִדִּיחַ; 8:3; 16:15; 23:3, 8; 24:9; 27:10, 15; 29:14, 18; 32:37; 46:29; 49:5) the people through exile. Furthermore, Assyria and Babylon have "driven away" the people in 50:17. As Fretheim states, "God and Babylon become subjects of the scattering only because of the prior activity on the part of the shepherds; and, in an even more complex way, the Babylonians become involved because God uses them to mediate the judgment" (Fretheim, *Jeremiah*, 330; see also Klein, *Israel in Exile*, 62).

33. The relationship between the plurality of shepherds in v. 4 and the single Davidic king in vv. 5–6 is not entirely clear. Either the individual king comes from a line

The Progeny Blessing in the Book of Jeremiah

justice and righteousness (מִשְׁפָּט וּצְדָקָה, v. 5; cf. 22:3), and as a result "Judah will be saved and Israel will dwell in security" (v. 6), implying the reunification of the nation.[34]

The shift from judgment to hope begins by depicting Yahweh as the true shepherd in v. 3:

| וַאֲנִי אֲקַבֵּץ אֶת־שְׁאֵרִית צֹאנִי מִכֹּל הָאֲרָצוֹת אֲשֶׁר־הִדַּחְתִּי אֹתָם שָׁם וַהֲשִׁבֹתִי אֶתְהֶן עַל־נְוֵהֶן וּפָרוּ וְרָבוּ | But I will gather the remnant of my flock out of all the countries where I have driven them, and I will bring them back to their pasture, and they will be fruitful and multiply. |

Apart from 3:16, this is the only occurrence of פָּרָה in Jeremiah, one of many links between 3:14-18 and 23:3-8[35] that indicate that they are mutually interpreting. As in 3:16, the progeny blessing is expressed in the middle voice, although Yahweh's agency is probably implied. And as return to the land precedes multiplication in 3:16, return to "their pasture"

---

of many shepherds or each of the shepherds fits the description of vv. 5-6. Fretheim is probably right to opt for the latter in light of the similar text in 33:14-26 (*Jeremiah*, 326).

34. Scholars have rightly noted that this text is similar to Isa 11:1-16 in its language and motifs (see Sweeney, "Jeremiah's Reflection," 310, 317-18) and that Jer 23:1-3 in particular bears a close resemblance to Ezek 34:1-16 (see Block, *Ezekiel: Chapters 25-48*, 275-76; Mendecki, "Sammlung," 99-103), although the progeny blessing is not overtly present there.

35. Unterman identifies many of these parallels, some of which even occur in the same sequence:

> a promise to ingather the remnant back to their land—3.14; 23.3; the people will then be ruled by divinely ordained rulers—3.15; 23.4; the new spiritual situation will be indicated by a new name given to a focal point of the people's life—3.17 (Jerusalem); 23.6 (David's descendant); the reiteration of the promise of return from the land of the North to the homeland—3.18; 23.8. Another point of contact is that the events associated with the exodus will be superseded by the new reality—3.16-17 (the ark will be forgotten); 23.7-8 (the exodus will be forgotten); cp. 31.31-34. (*From Repentance to Redemption*, 127-28)

Interestingly, he fails to cite the progeny blessing among the parallels, perhaps because he deems it an insignificant theme. (Weinfeld, "Jeremiah and the Spiritual Metamorphosis," 41-43, does, however, include the progeny blessing in his similar list of parallels.) In addition, only in 3:15 and 23:4 do we encounter good "shepherds" in Jeremiah, contrasted with the bad "shepherds" of Jeremiah's day (2:8; 10:21; 12:10; 22:22; 23:1, 2; 25:34, 35, 36; 50:5). Given these parallels, perhaps these two texts represent the same basic speech given by Jeremiah at different times for different contexts.

precedes growth in 23:3. In both cases, the land is first filled as a result of the return, and then further filled by means of physical reproduction.

In both Jer 3:16 and 23:3, the progeny blessing is juxtaposed with God's promise to raise up good kings. In neither case are these kings said to be directly responsible for the growth of the people. However, these texts may imply a relationship between the two promises. Jeremiah holds the kings culpable for the impending exile, and thus culpable for the ensuing population decimation as well (cf. 21:4–10, one of the starkest descriptions of decimation in the book). Furthermore, their exploitation of the people resulted in the death of some (22:17). If bad shepherds both prompt Yahweh's judgment and themselves harm their subjects, it stands to reason that good shepherds will bring about Yahweh's blessing on the people and righteous rule will result in the betterment and expansion of the people. Indeed, the results of righteous rule in vv. 4–6 (no more judgment, salvation from enemies, security) are part and parcel of population proliferation. Yahweh is responsible for the multiplication of the people, but the experience of blessing depends in some measure upon the conduct of the kings who represent the people.

The question remains whether the progeny blessing in 3:16 and 23:3 clearly alludes to one of its primary articulations elsewhere in the OT, whether it assumes all the previous articulations, or whether this is a new understanding of it.[36] Many tie the promise of Jer 23:3 to creational texts such as Gen 1:28 and 9:1.[37] Others, however, link it to the patriarchal promises,[38] Exod 1:7,[39] or Deut 28:4.[40] The most compelling evidence is simply the terminology employed here that echoes the creation blessings of Genesis. As we have noted before, such language does not necessarily imply that this will be the fulfillment of the creational blessing, but it does portray the return as a new creation in accordance with God's purposes

---

36. Commentators cite a variety of texts as cross-references to these verses, although it is unclear at times whether they intend to identify specific parallel texts to which Jeremiah alludes or whether they are simply noting the progeny texts with which they are most familiar.

37. See Craigie et al., *Jeremiah 1–25*, 327; Fretheim, *Jeremiah*, 325; Huey, Jr., *Jeremiah, Lamentations*, 211; Jones, *Jeremiah*, 299; Lundbom, *Jeremiah 21–36*, 168–69; Mendecki, "Sammlung," 102; Mulzac, "'Remnant of My Sheep,'" 140.

38. See Fretheim, *Jeremiah*, 325; Holladay, *Jeremiah 1*, 615.

39. See Craigie et al., *Jeremiah 1–25*, 327; Mendecki, "Sammlung," 102; Mulzac, "'Remnant of My Sheep,'" 140. Fretheim lists Exod 1:7 as the primary allusion for Jer 3:16 (*Jeremiah*, 83).

40. See Huey, Jr., *Jeremiah*, 211.

for creation. Furthermore, since vv. 7-8 compare the return to the original exodus, this proliferation of Israel in v. 3 may mirror the initial expansion documented in Exod 1:7. However, the future multiplication of Israel takes place following the return, a crucial difference (but see Jer 29:6 below). In addition, although nothing is said explicitly regarding the patriarchal promises, the gifts of land and progeny are juxtaposed at the outset of both texts, sufficient to allude to the patriarchal promises, the core of God's commitment to his people. Although Jer 3:16 and 23:3 do not appear to be linked to the covenant blessings of Deut 28:4, 11 either in terminology or in their contingency on obedience, Jer 23:3 shares language with Deut 30:3-5 (אֲקַבֵּץ, הִדַּחְתִּי, וַהֲשִׁבֹתִי, וְרָבוּ). Finally, 1 Kgs 4:20 attests that, historically, the pinnacle of just kingship corresponded to the pinnacle of the expansiveness of the people of Israel. Jeremiah 23:3 shares this perspective. In sum, the progeny blessing in Jer 3:16 and 23:3 fits comfortably within the whole spectrum of the complementary progeny texts in the OT and does not appear to stress one manifestation of it over or against others.

Jeremiah 29:6

Jeremiah 29:4-23 includes the text of a letter Jeremiah sent to the exiles in Babylon sometime after the first exile of 597, but prior to the second exile of 587 (vv. 1-3).[41] Continuing the theme of Jer 27-29, which record Jeremiah's conflict with the prophets regarding whether the return will be immediate or distant, the purpose of the letter is to encourage the exiles to prepare for a long stay, contrary to the false claims of their resident prophets (vv. 8-9). First he instructs the exiles to re-establish their lives while in Babylon. However, he does not leave them without hope. Yahweh has promised (vv. 10-14) that at the conclusion of the seventy years of Babylonian domination,[42] he will bring them back to the land (vv. 10, 14) and prosper them (v. 11), although the details remain unspecified. Prior to this return, the people will call upon Yahweh and he will hear their call (vv. 12-13).[43] This hope of vv. 10-14 serves as the rationale and motivation for obedience to Jeremiah's instructions in vv. 5-7.

---

41. The letter is probably best dated to 594, following an attempted revolt that may have prompted Jeremiah's letter (see Clements, *Jeremiah*, 170; Holladay, *Jeremiah 2*, 140).

42. Lundbom suggests that the seventy years refer not to the length of Israel's exile but rather to the length of Babylon's world domination (*Jeremiah 21-36*, 353).

43. Again, there is debate regarding whether this cry to Yahweh is a promise from

Interestingly, the progeny blessing does not appear in vv. 10–14, but rather among the instructions of vv. 5–7, making v. 6 the only progeny text in the book that does not occur in the context of a proclamation of hope. Jeremiah's instructions comprise three basic commands, all indicating a lengthy stay in Babylon: build houses and plant gardens (v. 5), multiply (v. 6), and seek the peace of the city (v. 7). In the present form of the book addressed to the exiles not only of 597 but of 587 as well, these counterintuitive instructions function as the community's "torah" tailored to their unique situation and are without parallel in the book.[44] Furthermore, Carroll claims that this description of approved domestic living in a foreign land is "virtually unique" in the OT.[45] Although it may be difficult for the exilic community to accept that Yahweh's will for them is to carry on life apart from all that they hold dear, such as the land, the temple, and the monarchy, the parable of the good and bad figs (24:4–10) and the second half of Jeremiah's letter (29:16–19) underscore that Yahweh's favor rests upon the exiles, not upon those who avoided exile. Nevertheless, to abide by these instructions will require great faith.

Elsewhere in the book, it is either Jeremiah who is told to "build and plant" (1:10) or Yahweh's own work (18:9; 24:6; 31:28; 42:10; 45:4). It can hardly be coincidental that here (and only here and in v. 28) the people themselves are instructed to do the same (בְּנוּ and וְנִטְעוּ).[46] From the perspective of the final form of the book, to build and to plant would involve the Babylonian exiles in the very activities of Yahweh and his prophet, Jeremiah, which may imply that these activities are in accord with Yahweh's will and that he will enable the people to accomplish them. Moreover, we see here that Jeremiah's figurative building and planting entails in part the literal building and planting of the exiles in Babylon.[47]

God (Fretheim, *Jeremiah*, 403, 411; Lundbom, *Jeremiah 21–36*, 354; Smelik, "Letters to the Exiles," 288; cf. Deut 4:29) or a requirement/condition placed on the people (Brueggemann, *Jeremiah: Exile and Homecoming*, 259; Unterman, *From Repentance to Redemption*, 86–87; Yates, "New Exodus," 22). Fretheim rightly observes that the emphasis in vv. 12–14 appears to be on God's new inclination to hear his people rather than on Israel's efforts (411). This "search" for Yahweh while still in Babylon (cf. Deut 30:2; 1 Kgs 8:33–34) is to be distinguished from the new heart God grants his people *following* their return to the land (cf. Deut 30:6).

44. Brueggemann refers to vv. 5–9 and 10–14 as the "core convictions of the Jeremiah tradition" (*Jeremiah: Exile and Homecoming*, 260).

45. See Carroll, *Jeremiah*, 556. Israel's prior sojourn in Egypt may be a close parallel (see below).

46. See Seitz, *Theology in Conflict*, 210.

47. On the basis of the appearance of the same sequence of build-plant-marry-seek

The Progeny Blessing in the Book of Jeremiah

The instructions of v. 6 employ four different expressions that underscore the proliferation of progeny:

קְחוּ נָשִׁים וְהוֹלִידוּ בָּנִים וּבָנוֹת	1) Take wives [in order to] bear sons and daughters.
וּקְחוּ לִבְנֵיכֶם נָשִׁים וְאֶת־בְּנוֹתֵיכֶם תְּנוּ לַאֲנָשִׁים וְתֵלַדְנָה בָּנִים וּבָנוֹת	2) Then take wives for your sons and give your daughters to men in order that they might bear sons and daughters.[48]
וּרְבוּ־שָׁם	3) Multiply there,
וְאַל־תִּמְעָטוּ	4) And do not decrease.

It appears that the very purpose of marriage in the first two lines is childbearing, summarized by the final two lines, a common perspective in the ancient Near East, but explicit only here in the OT.

Reproduction is rarely expressed in the imperative mood.[49] We have argued above that all other imperative occurrences of פָּרָה and/or רָבָה (Gen 1:22, 28; 9:1, 7; 35:11) are not to be construed as commands but rather as permissive imperatives that express God's desire and imply his enabling.[50] Therefore, we should consider whether this is the case here as well. Holladay sees v. 6 as an expansion on the Priestly tradition of Gen 1:28, concluding that "as such [v. 6 is] an affirmation of Yahweh's promise."[51] However, there is good reason in this text to view these imperatives as commands: 1) Unlike the creation blessings, vv. 5–7 are not referred to as a "blessing" from Yahweh. 2) If Jeremiah wished to emphasize Yahweh's agency or that this was a promise in vv. 5–6, he likely would have used second masculine plural imperfects or third masculine singular causative Hiphil forms, as

---

the peace of the city in Deut 20:5–10, Adele Berlin argues that, "in addition to encouraging settlement, Jeremiah is also subtly counseling against revolt. Do these things, he tells the exiles, for which Deuteronomy permits a man to refrain from going to war" ("Jeremiah 29:5–7," 4). This proposal may have some credence, but the command in v. 7 to seek the peace of the city already includes this idea anyway. Her theory aside, the presence of these elements together in Deut 20:5–10 indicates that these are the primary and stereotypical activities of domestic life. She further notes that the sequence build-plant-marry/children also occurs in Deut 28:30–32; Isa 65:21–23; and Ps 107:36–38 (5–6).

48. The LXX lacks the final clause of this line, reading only, καὶ λάβετε τοῖς υἱοῖς ὑμῶν γυναῖκας καὶ τὰς θυγατέρας ὑμῶν ἀνδράσιν δότε. The LXX thus includes only three progeny expressions and envisions only two generations rather than three, perhaps anticipating a shorter stay in Babylon.

49. This is the only imperative form of יָלַד (regardless of stem) in the OT.

50. See discussion of Gen 1:28 above.

51. Holladay, *Jeremiah 2*, 138.

we encounter elsewhere. 3) "Do not decrease," the negative articulation of "multiply there" (litotes), employs a אַל + imperfect construction which can denote prohibition, warning, negative desires, or negative requests, none of which fit particularly well if "multiply there" is permissive or promissory.[52] 4) Finally, to command marriage and childbirth is appropriate for the exilic context. Unlike the creational context, the exiles are now faced with a situation in which multiplication is not desirable. As Lundbom surmises, "[s]ome of the exiles may be refusing to marry and have children, which goes with unsettled times."[53] "Permission" or "promise" is only appropriate when the recipients desire to bear children. As with other commands from Yahweh, obedience requires faith, in this case faith that Babylon will not be their end and that Yahweh plans for them "a future and a hope" (v. 11). In light of these considerations, v. 6 appears to be the only instance in the OT in which child-bearing is truly a command.

This does not imply, however, that Yahweh is uninvolved in these processes. Yahweh must still enable childbirth, and the very fact that Yahweh issues this command implies that he has withdrawn the curses of decimation and now intends to bless the people once again,[54] even prior to their return to the land, since God would hardly command the "good figs" to work against his own purposes. Yet, as in Egypt, his provision will once again be "behind the scenes,"[55] since texts of hope in the book (such as vv. 10–14) portray Yahweh as absent until he springs into action by gathering and returning the people to the land. The people are told to build, plant, and multiply in Babylon in preparation for Yahweh's future building, planting, and multiplying (30:19; 31:27) on behalf of the people.

In contrast to 3:16 and 23:3, it appears that the progeny motif in 29:6 does allude to a specific aspect of the progeny blessing in the OT, namely, the proliferation of the people of Israel while in Egypt prior to the exodus.[56]

---

52. See Arnold and Choi, *Syntax*, 4.2.3; §GKC 109c, 152f.

53. Lundbom, *Jeremiah 21–36*, 351. See Novak, "Be Fruitful," 13–14, who argues that child-bearing constitutes "a conscious act of faith" (13) among suffering communities and is not a natural desire.

54. See Keown et al., *Jeremiah 26–52*, 66, 72; Holladay, *Jeremiah 2*, 138. This command reverses the command issued to Jeremiah in 16:2 not to bear children, again indicating the change in situation (see McConville, *Judgment and Promise*, 90).

55. See Fretheim, *Jeremiah*, 409.

56. This connection is noted by a number of commentators, including Brueggemann, *Jeremiah: Exile and Homecoming*, 257; Fretheim, *Jeremiah*, 409; Keown et al., *Jeremiah 26–52*, 71; Lundbom, *Jeremiah 21–36*, 351; Klein, *Israel in Exile*, 131–32. In terms of thematic correspondences, exile also functions similarly to the wilderness wanderings in that in both instances enough time elapses as a result of judgment that

Although not highlighted by Yates, vv. 5–7 support his recognition of exodus themes in the second half of the book of Jeremiah. Prior to Jacob's descent to Egypt, Yahweh instructs him, "Do not be afraid to go down to Egypt, for there I will make you into a great nation. I myself will go down with you to Egypt, and I will also bring you up again" (Gen 46:3–4). Later, it is recorded that "Israel lived in the land of Egypt, in the land of Goshen, and they acquired property in it (וַיֵּאָחֲזוּ בָהּ) and were fruitful and multiplied greatly" (Gen 47:27). Exod 1:7 then expands on the magnitude of their multiplication. Yahweh's instructions in Gen 46:3–4 (and the subsequent sojourn in Egypt and population explosion) are not unlike the instructions Yahweh gives the Babylonian exiles. Both situations are even accompanied by the promise that God will bring them back (Gen 46:4; Jer 29:10, 14), the latter reflecting, yet transcending, the former according to Jer 16:14–15 and 23:7–8. Despite the different purposes for Egypt and Babylon, the Babylonian exiles should view themselves as similar to the original Israelite "exiles" in Egypt, providing hope that Yahweh would restore them as he once restored the people to the land in the first exodus. Furthermore, it is their duty to multiply even as Israel multiplied while in Egypt in preparation for the return as a "great nation."[57] Only while they were in Egypt did Israel previously in her history multiply outside the land.[58] God desires this to take place for the exiles as well.

Given the correspondences to Deuteronomy that we already have seen in Jeremiah's letter,[59] it is possible that the allusions in Deuteronomy to the proliferation of Israel in Egypt (Deut 1:10; 10:22; 26:5) provide the closest textual parallel to the duty of the exiles in Jer 29:6. However, Exod 1:7 is similar to v. 6 in one particularly intriguing way: God is not cited as the agent of multiplication in either instance. Just as Yahweh is portrayed as distant and uninvolved until he "hears their cry" (וְאֶת־צַעֲקָתָם שָׁמָעְתִּי; Exod 3:7) and acts to deliver his people in Exodus, so here he is seemingly uninvolved in life in Babylon until he "hears" (וְשָׁמַעְתִּי)

---

an entirely new generation arises for entry into the land (Seitz, "Prophet Moses," 13).

57. See Smelik, "Letters to the Exiles," 290. It is questionable, however, whether their proliferation in Babylon would achieve the scope of that in Egypt. Therefore, it is possible that Yahweh's expansion of the people following the return continues to transform the people into a "great nation" as in Exod 1:7.

58. Once they left Egypt, the population declined slightly during the wilderness wanderings.

59. Karl Friedrich Pohlmann identifies correspondences between vv. 5–7 and Deut 28:30, 32, 33, 39–41 ("Das 'Heil' des Landes," 144–64).

when they "call" (וּקְרָאתֶם; Jer 29:12) and then responds.[60] Despite adverse external circumstances, God's people appear to multiply naturally.

Jeremiah 30:19

Following the record of Jeremiah's correspondence with the Babylonian exiles (Jer 29), the so-called "Book of Comfort" (Jer 30–33)[61] offers hope to the exiles by focusing primarily (though not solely) on the good future Yahweh has for them. The three remaining occurrences of the progeny blessing in the MT are found in these chapters. Jeremiah 30–31 consists of six poems introduced by the messenger formula that oscillate between masculine and feminine address (30:5–11, 12–17, 18—31:1, 31:2–6, 7–14, 15–22), followed by a largely prosaic conclusion (31:23–40).[62]

The third poem (30:18—31:1) consists of two stanzas (vv. 18–22, 23—31:1), both of which begin with "behold" (הִנֵּה) and conclude with the covenant formula (30:22[63] and 31:1),[64] which "functions as a kind of summary of this new situation for Israel and anticipates the new covenant passage in 31:31–34."[65] The first stanza treats the restoration of Israelite society, grounded in Yahweh's compassion (v. 18a).[66] Generally speaking, he will "restore the fortunes (שָׁב שְׁבוּת) of the tents of Jacob" (v. 18a), a reference to reunification in light of 30:3, 7, 10 and 31:1. Specifically, cities[67] will be rebuilt (v. 18b), resulting in thanksgiving (v. 19a), the people

---

60. Alternatively, some tie Jer 29:6 to Gen 1:28 since vv. 5–7 depict the establishment of civilization, as is the case in Gen 1:28, and since the Babylonian community may be portrayed here as a "new creation" (Holladay, *Jeremiah 2*, 138; Keown et al., *Jeremiah 26–52*, 71; Stulman, *Jeremiah*, 251). Perhaps it is best to affirm this connection, but only because Exod 1:7 itself points back to Gen 1:28, portraying the original Israelite nation as a "new creation."

61. In the view of some scholars, due to structural markers and/or the belief that Jer 32–33 are later expansions, only Jer 30–31 constitutes the Book of Comfort (e.g., Becking, *Between Fear and Freedom*, 50–52; Carroll, *Jeremiah*, 568; Holladay, *Jeremiah 2*, 148; Keown et al., *Jeremiah 26–52*, 82).

62. For 30:1—31:22, we adopt the structure of Barbara A. Bozak (*Life "Anew,"* 19–20), followed by Becking (*Between Fear and Freedom*, 70).

63. This verse is not present in the LXX.

64. See Bozak, *Life "Anew,"* 22.

65. Fretheim, *Jeremiah*, 424.

66. This restoration oracle is directly from Yahweh, employing six first-person verbal declarations.

67. Although this may refer primarily to Jerusalem, it is probably a collective reference (see Bright, *Jeremiah*, 279; Jones, *Jeremiah*, 382; Lundbom, *Jeremiah 21–36*,

will multiply (v. 19b), enemies will be punished (v. 20b), and a king[68] will rule them once again (v. 21). However, there is no mention here of inner change.

The returned people will be blessed not only with rebuilt cities but also with progeny and status (v. 19b):

וְהִרְבִּתִים וְלֹא יִמְעָטוּ   I will multiply them, and they will not be few;
וְהִכְבַּדְתִּים וְלֹא יִצְעָרוּ   I will honor them, and they will not be insignificant.

In this tight structure, the first verb in each line has Yahweh as subject and the people as object, while the second verb expresses a parallel thought by negating the antonym of the first verb (litotes) with the people as the subject. Jeremiah 30:19 uses the same verbs as 29:6 (וּרְבוּ־שָׁם וְאַל־תִּמְעָטוּ). In both texts, the use of the antonym of רָבָה indicates that the time of judgment and "tearing down" (1:10) is now over. Since מָעַט is rarely employed to refer to decrease in human population in the OT (Lev 26:22; Jer 29:6; 30:19; Ezek 29:15; Ps 107:39; Eccl 12:3; and perhaps Jer 10:24) and since nowhere else are these two verbs used together to denote the progeny blessing,[69] it is probable that 30:19 recalls 29:6, a point underscored by their close textual proximity. This draws attention to the shift that takes place between these two texts. The temporal setting has shifted from present to future. The spatial setting has moved from Babylon to the promised land. What was once commanded is now promised. Responsibility for childbirth has shifted from the people to Yahweh. The mood has shifted from despairing, yet hopeful, to celebratory.

It is not immediately evident whether the final line of v. 19[70] denotes quantitative greatness, expressing the same idea as the previous line, or qualitative greatness, stating an additional benefit. Kselman argues that the roots רָבָה and כָּבֵד are a poetic word pair and cites Gen 18:20, 1 Kgs 3:8–9, Jer 30:19, and Nah 3:3, 15b–16 as evidence (in addition to Akka-

---

405–6; Thompson *Jeremiah*, 561).

68. Although this individual is not referred to as a מֶלֶךְ, the terms used (מֹשֵׁל, אַדִּיר) can be accounted for by the poetic context and Jeremiah's aversion to using מֶלֶךְ given the negative connotations it carries in his historical context. In light of 30:9, this individual may be the Davidic king (see Holladay, *Jeremiah 2*, 179; Jones, *Jeremiah*, 382; Lundbom, *Jeremiah 21–36*, 408; Thompson, *Jeremiah*, 562).

69. They do appear together in Ps 107:38–39, but there מָעַט is not negated.

70. This line is not included in the LXX. Perhaps the LXX unintentionally omitted it through haplography (see Lundbom, *Jeremiah 21–36*, 407). Alternatively, the MT may have added this parallel line to complement the multiplication clause (see McKane *Jeremiah*, 2:775). Neither explanation is clearly preferable.

dian parallels).⁷¹ In Gen 18:20 both terms appear to denote qualitative greatness, whereas in the other cases both seem to refer to quantitative greatness, thus indicating that they do function together as equivalent terms. However, the Hiphil form of כָּבֵד, which occurs seventeen times, does not refer to quantitative greatness in any other case. Furthermore, the other occurrences of its antonym (צָעַר) in Zech 13:7 and Job 14:21 appear to refer to qualitative insignificance. Therefore, it is unlikely that this line is simply a synonymous parallel to the progeny blessing. Rather, it adds the blessing of honor to that of multiplication, but this honor is inextricably linked to the proliferation of the people. In other words, multiplication results[72] in honor or is the means by which[73] Yahweh conveys honor upon his people. This further goal of honor goes beyond 29:6, where the purpose of multiplying is merely survival and preparation for return.

The following line in v. 20a, "and their children will be as before" then prompts the questions: 1) in what respect(s) will they be as before and 2) to what past time does this refer? With respect to the former question, only in v. 19 are the people themselves the direct objects of Yahweh's actions, so the reference to "their children" (בָּנָיו) likely has v. 19, and thus primarily multiplication, in mind. It is with good reason, then, that the Targum renders this clause, "and their children will multiply as formerly" (ויסגון בניהון כיד מלקדמין), and that McKane translates, "they will have as many sons as once they had."[74] If this is indeed a reference to a time of former (כְּקֶדֶם) numerical greatness, the primary candidates are the conquest generation, the united monarchy under Solomon, and their pre-exilic size. The hope of rebuilt cities and a reinstated king seems to point to the united monarchy[75] since the divided kingdom was never the ideal. This renewal is merely "as before," not "greater than before," and thus does not portray conditions that transcend those previously experienced.

---

71. See Kselman, "RB//KBD," 110–14. Holladay, *Jeremiah 2*, 177–78; Keown et al., *Jeremiah 26–52*, 104; and Lundbom, *Jeremiah 21–36*, 407, acknowledge this word pair on the basis of Kselman's article, but do not discuss its significance.

72. So Bozak, *Life "Anew,"* 62.

73. So Holladay, *Jeremiah 2*, 177–78. His translation, "I will make them impressive and they shall not be beneath notice," (151) is attractive in that it includes the connotation of size.

74. McKane, *Jeremiah*, 2:771. See also Bozak, *Life "Anew,"* 133; Keown et al., *Jeremiah 26–52*, 105.

75. See Bright, *Jeremiah*, 280; Huey, *Jeremiah*, 267. Contra Lundbom, *Jeremiah 21–36*, 407.

As in Jer 3 and 23, 30:18–22 includes both the promise of progeny and the promise of a future good king. In this case, a direct relationship between the two is uncertain since the two promises are separated by v. 20 and not immediately juxtaposed. Nevertheless, the two will coincide in the future restoration.[76]

Jeremiah 31:27[77]

The prosaic unit in 31:23–40 exhibits a chiastic structure, based on content, key words, and structural markers, summarized by Lundbom:[78]

    A Rebuilding the holy Jerusalem (23–26)
        B Sowing seed of Israel and Judah (27–30)
            C New covenant with Israel and Judah (31–34)
        B1 Preserving seed of Israel and Judah (35–37)
    A1 Rebuilding holy Jerusalem (38–40)

The second unit (vv. 27–30) opens with the promise of progeny (v. 27):

הִנֵּה יָמִים בָּאִים נְאֻם־יְהוָה וְזָרַעְתִּי אֶת־בֵּית יִשְׂרָאֵל וְאֶת־בֵּית יְהוּדָה זֶרַע אָדָם וְזֶרַע בְּהֵמָה	"Look, days are coming"—oracle of Yahweh—"when I will sow the house of Israel and the house of Judah with the seed of humans and with the seed of animals."

This statement is a partial remedy for the despair of 31:15 and is unique to Jeremiah both in its formulation and in its scope.

---

76. There are no clear indications that 30:19 alludes to one particular manifestation of the progeny blessing. Its possible typological correspondence to the exodus motif will be treated below with 31:27.

77. Bernhard W. Anderson argues that Jer 31:22 may contain a reference to the progeny blessing as well ("Something New," 367–80), translating the enigmatic line נְקֵבָה תְּסוֹבֵב גָּבֶר as "the woman will enfold a man," referring to the recovery of Virgin Israel's progeny (380). This is quite possible in light of v. 15, and vv. 15–22 would then present a metaphorical promise similar to that of Isa 49:14–21. However, we will not treat this text at length since נְקֵבָה תְּסוֹבֵב גָּבֶר remains obscure and because this language is never used elsewhere to denote the progeny blessing. Furthermore, this metaphor would likely denote the return to the land rather than the physical proliferation of the people, as in Isa 49:14–21.

78. See Lundbom, *Jeremiah 21–36*, 454–55, also adopted by Keown et al., *Jeremiah 26–52*, 126.

I Will Surely Multiply Your Offspring

The image of Yahweh "sowing" (זָרַע) people is rare, occurring elsewhere in Hos 2:25[23], Nah 1:14, and Zech 10:9. Most scholars see Hos 2:25[23] as the closest parallel (וּזְרַעְתִּיהָ לִּי בָּאָרֶץ), and possibly the source for Jeremiah's imagery.[79] Hosea 2:25[23] (as a parallel to Hos 2:1[1:10]) provides the best indication that this language does not refer merely to a return to the land but to proliferation of the people (see below on this text).[80] The image is natural, given the common metaphorical use of זֶרַע to denote human offspring, frequent throughout Jeremiah and in Jer 30–33 in particular (30:10; 31:27, 36, 37; 33:22, 26 [3x]). Verse 27 thus combines the literal and metaphorical senses of זֶרַע by speaking of Yahweh sowing Israel and Judah with "seed." Rather than baldly stating that the people will multiply, Jeremiah graphically compares this act to the filling of the land with crops.

The proliferation not only of humans but of animals as well is rare (cf. Ezek 36:11). The fate of אָדָם and בְּהֵמָה is linked elsewhere in Jeremiah,[81] indicating that both judgment and blessing affect the entire created order.[82] Both were created by Yahweh (27:5), both are subject to his judgment (7:20; 21:6), and the land lacks both as a result (32:43; 33:10, 12). However, in the future, both will be sown again in the land (31:27) and, as a result, both will again dwell in the land (33:10–13).[83] Scalise[84] and McKane[85] rightly observe that the expansion of cattle is a means by which the people themselves proliferate since this contributes to food production, but that does not appear to be the point here. Rather, this refers to a creational multiplication more comprehensive in scope than merely humans.[86]

---

79. See, e.g., Carroll, *Jeremiah*, 607; Clements, *Jeremiah*, 188; Holladay, *Jeremiah 2*, 196; Keown et al., *Jeremiah 26–52*, 129; Lundbom, *Jeremiah 21–36*, 374; Unterman, *From Repentance To Redemption*, 92.

80. Note also Lev 12:2 and Num 5:28 where זֶרַע describes impregnation.

81. These two terms appear to be a fixed pair since אָדָם appears alongside בְּהֵמָה in ten out of eighteen of the occurrences of the latter. Both are collective and appear predominantly in prose.

82. See Fretheim, *Jeremiah*, 439.

83. However, (wild) animals also function as agents of God's judgment in 7:33, 15:3, 16:4, 19:7, and 34:20.

84. Keown et al., *Jeremiah 26–52*, 129.

85. McKane, *Jeremiah*, 2:813.

86. Bozak proposes that this is a merism, thus referring to an even broader scope encompassing all creatures (*Life "Anew,"* 115 n. 461). This is possible given its frequency, but may be difficult to demonstrate.

Here the progeny blessing serves as a means of accomplishing the new general purpose of Yahweh to "build and plant" (v. 28), one of many references to Jeremiah's original commission in 1:10.[87] It may not be coincidental that "sowing" and "planting" are similar activities at the literal level, providing a possible explanation for the choice of the sowing metaphor in this context.[88] Furthermore, this connection between the progeny blessing and God's overall purpose suggests that this blessing constitutes "the foundations of the rehabilitation of Israel and Judah."[89]

Highlighted by the chiastic structure of vv. 23–40, v. 27 corresponds thematically and lexically (זֶרַע in vv. 36, 37) to vv. 35–37.

כֹּה אָמַר יְהוָה	35	Thus says Yahweh,
נֹתֵן שֶׁמֶשׁ לְאוֹר יוֹמָם		the one who gives the sun for light by day
חֻקֹּת יָרֵחַ וְכוֹכָבִים		and the fixed order of the moon and the stars
לְאוֹר לָיְלָה		for light by night,
רֹגַע הַיָּם וַיֶּהֱמוּ גַלָּיו		the one who stirs up the sea so that its waves roar,
יְהוָה צְבָאוֹת שְׁמוֹ		Yahweh of armies is his name:
אִם־יָמֻשׁוּ הַחֻקִּים הָאֵלֶּה	36	"If this fixed order departs
מִלְּפָנַי נְאֻם־יְהוָה		from before me," declares Yahweh,
גַּם זֶרַע יִשְׂרָאֵל יִשְׁבְּתוּ		then the offspring of Israel will also cease
מִהְיוֹת גּוֹי לְפָנַי כָּל־הַיָּמִים		from being a nation before me forever."
כֹּה אָמַר יְהוָה	37	Thus says Yahweh,
אִם־יִמַּדּוּ שָׁמַיִם מִלְמַעְלָה		"If the heavens above are able to be measured,
וְיֵחָקְרוּ מוֹסְדֵי־אֶרֶץ לְמָטָּה		and the foundations of the earth below are able to be explored,
גַּם־אֲנִי אֶמְאַס בְּכָל־זֶרַע יִשְׂרָאֵל		then I will also reject all the offspring of Israel
עַל־כָּל־אֲשֶׁר עָשׂוּ		because of all that they have done."
נְאֻם־יְהוָה		declares Yahweh.

Here we have a slightly different, yet complementary, promise regarding progeny. The first conditional statement (vv. 35–36) compares the created order to Yahweh's fidelity to "the offspring of Israel" (זֶרַע יִשְׂרָאֵל), implying that since the fixed order of creation will never cease, Israel as a nation will never cease. The second condition (v. 37) makes a similar assertion, implying that, since creation cannot be measured, Yahweh will never reject (אֶמְאַס) Israel as a people. Thus it is not expansion of progeny that is at

---

87. Jeremiah's mission is "to uproot and to break down, to destroy and to overthrow, to build and to plant" (לִנְתוֹשׁ וְלִנְתוֹץ וּלְהַאֲבִיד וְלַהֲרוֹס לִבְנוֹת וְלִנְטוֹעַ; 1:10), language that reverberates throughout the book, tying it together (12:14–17; 18:7–10; 24:4–7; 29:5, 28; 31:28; 42:9–12; 45:4).

88. See Fretheim, *Jeremiah*, 439; Keown et al., *Jeremiah 26–52*, 129.

89. McKane, *Jeremiah*, 2:813.

stake, but the survival of the people as a whole. Whereas v. 27 is a spatial guarantee regarding great size, this is a temporal guarantee of eternal longevity, adding a dimension to the progeny blessing. Yahweh's commitment to "sow" the people in the land will never end.

This commitment to grant physical life to Israel is grounded in his renewed covenant commitment to Israel. The making of a "new covenant" (vv. 31–34) that results in a restored relationship (v. 33b) is based on Yahweh's resolve to forgive the sins of the people (v. 34b; cf. 33:8; 50:20) and Yahweh's own initiative to change the hearts of his people (vv. 33b–34a; cf. 24:7; 32:39–40).

The promise of progeny in Jer 31:27 appears to correspond to multiple aspects of the progeny blessing in the OT. First, the multiplication of animals alongside people recalls the creational blessings of Gen 8:17 and 9:1, 7. In addition, the creation language of vv. 35–37 that alludes to Yahweh's pledge to sustain creation in Gen 8:22 makes the reference to creation in v. 27 more likely. Thus the repopulation of a reunited Israel and Judah is depicted as a new creation.[90]

However, with the exception of Ezek 36:11, the tripartite fertility formula in Deuteronomy is the only place in the OT where the fertility of humans and the fertility of animals are juxtaposed. Although the language is different, there may be a connection between v. 27 and Deut 30:9 in particular, given Jeremiah's general indebtedness to the thought of Deut 30:1–10.

The metaphorical use of זֶרַע recalls the Abrahamic promises,[91] where the use of זֶרַע to refer to descendants is common (e.g., Gen 12:7; 13:15, 16; 15:5; 22:17). Furthermore, Yahweh's commitment to sustain the "offspring of Israel" (vv. 36–37) is likely rooted in the Abrahamic covenant.[92] Thus, in this covenant-rich text, a change in the operation of the Sinai covenant (vv. 31–34) secures the continuity of the Abrahamic covenant, including the blessings of land (vv. 23–24, 38–40) and progeny (vv. 27, 36–37), which is as fixed as Yahweh's pledge in Gen 8:22 that accompanies the covenant with Noah and creation (vv. 35–36). Although v. 27 most likely corresponds primarily to the Abrahamic promises, we must conclude as

---

90. See Jones, *Jeremiah*, 398. Cf. McKane, *Jeremiah*, 2:813.

91. See Bozak, *Life "Anew,"* 115; Jones, *Jeremiah*, 398; Keown et al., *Jeremiah 26–52*, 129.

92. Fretheim observes that the Book of Comfort opens with a reference to the patriarchal promises (30:3) and closes with a reference to the patriarchs (33:26), suggesting that "the entire unit should be read in terms of the covenant with Abraham" (*Jeremiah*, 414).

we did for Jer 3:16 and 23:3 that 31:27 may encompass multiple progeny traditions.[93]

Jeremiah 33:22[94]

Thus far the Book of Comfort has had little to say regarding the leaders of Israel (but see 30:9, 20), a prominent concern throughout Jeremiah. Finally, at the conclusion of the Book of Comfort (33:14–26), we learn that the future new conditions rooted in the new covenant (31:31–34) do indeed have a place for both the royal and priestly offices. Jeremiah 33:1–13 pertains to the entire nation and concludes with a description of the repopulation of the land as a result of the return (vv. 10–13). Like 31:27, these verses anticipate the reversal of the desolation of the land that lacks both אָדָם and בְּהֵמָה (vv. 10, 12), although multiplication does not appear to be in view.

Verses 14–26 then shift to Jerusalem and the leadership. Yahweh will fulfill his "good word" to a reunited Judah and Israel (v. 14) by causing a good Davidic "branch" to "sprout" (vv. 15–16). This promise is guaranteed and expanded by Yahweh's declaration that "David will never lack a man to sit on the throne of the house of Israel" (v. 17), a promise extended to the Levitical priests (לַכֹּהֲנִים הַלְוִיִּם) as well (v. 18).[95] Verses 19–26 support these claims by affirming Yahweh's fidelity to his covenants. In an argument nearly identical to that of Jer 31:35–37, vv. 21–22 assert that since "my covenant with the day and my covenant with the night" (אֶת־בְּרִיתִי הַיּוֹם וְאֶת־בְּרִיתִי הַלָּיְלָה) can never be broken (v. 20), neither can "my covenant" (בְּרִיתִי) with "David my servant" (אֶת־דָּוִד עַבְדִּי) or Levi ever be broken (cf. vv. 25–26).[96]

Earlier texts in the book of Jeremiah are employed to express these new ideas.[97] Scalise therefore correctly states that "[t]his chapter is a de-

---

93. In addition, the multiplication of Judah and Israel in the land as described in Jer 30:19 and 31:27 fits the new exodus motif (see below).

94. Jeremiah 33:14–26 is missing from the LXX. See LXX section below regarding possible explanations for this difference from the MT.

95. The Levites appear only here (33:18, 21, 22) in Jeremiah.

96. See Gen 8:22 for the creation covenant, 2 Sam 7:12–16 for the Davidic covenant, and Num 25:10–13; Neh 13:29; and Mal 2:4–9 for Yahweh's commitment to the Levites (specifically Phinehas) as his priests.

97. In fact, nearly every verse in vv. 14–26 echoes previous texts: v. 14 from 29:10, vv. 15–16 from 23:5–6, vv. 19–26 from 31:35–37. In addition, vv. 17–18 use the same formulation as 1 Kgs 2:4; 8:25; 9:5 (see Holladay, *Jeremiah 2*, 228–29).

velopment, elaboration, and explanation of earlier promise themes."[98] Interestingly, two of the texts used (23:5–6 in vv. 15–16 and 31:35–37 in vv. 19–26) are in the general proximity of the promise of progeny. Indeed, we find the progeny blessing in v. 22 of the present text, but its application is surprising and unlike any other articulation of it in the OT.

Both as evidence of his unshakable commitment to his covenants with David and Levi and as the means of keeping them, Yahweh will multiply their offspring (v. 22):

אֲשֶׁר לֹא־יִסָּפֵר צְבָא[99] הַשָּׁמַיִם	As the host of heaven cannot be counted
וְלֹא יִמַּד חוֹל הַיָּם	and the sand of the sea cannot be measured,
כֵּן אַרְבֶּה אֶת־זֶרַע דָּוִד עַבְדִּי	so I will multiply the seed of David, my servant,
וְאֶת־הַלְוִיִּם מְשָׁרְתֵי אֹתִי	and the Levitical priests who minister to me.

The "stars of heaven" and "sand of the sea" metaphors recall the Abrahamic promise of progeny (Gen 15:5; 26:4; 32:13[12]),[100] particularly Gen 22:17, the only place where both images are employed (although using כּוֹכָב rather than צְבָא). However, here they are employed in the context of the promise of progeny to two particular lineages within the nation of Israel, not to the people of Israel as a whole. Furthermore, the argument does not appear to be that Yahweh will multiply their offspring so that they number *as many as* the stars and sand, but rather that the *certainty* with which Yahweh will multiply them is comparable to the impossibility of counting the stars and sand.[101] Thus an image traditionally used to denote the *extent* to which God will multiply the people is here used in an entirely different way—and in a way similar to the arguments in vv. 20, 25. Nevertheless, the choice of the imagery of the Abrahamic progeny promise is certainly intentional, and suggests that the expansion of the Davidic and Levitical lines are as assured as God's past expansion of Abraham's line.[102]

Within the entire OT, this is the only text in which the human recipients of the progeny blessing are any group other than all of humanity (as in Gen 1–11) or the people of Israel (Gen 12ff.). The wide-scale proliferation

---

98. Keown et al., *Jeremiah 26–52*, 169.

99. Although typically כַּאֲשֶׁר, אֲשֶׁר here denotes a comparison (cf. Exod 10:6; Isa 54:9; Jer 48:8).

100. See Brueggemann, *Jeremiah: Exile and Homecoming*, 320; Carroll, *Jeremiah*, 638; Jones, *Jeremiah*, 424; Lundbom, *Jeremiah 21–36*, 544.

101. See Fretheim, *Jeremiah*, 479.

102. Contra Johan Lust, this allusion does not "[imply] a transfer of the Davidic promise from the individual king to the collective people" ("Messianism," 107).

of their offspring per se was not part of the original covenants with David and Levi, although succession was guaranteed for both. Yet in Jer 33:14–26 Yahweh's covenant commitments to them entail the blessing of progeny in the same way that his commitment to Abraham does and thus goes beyond the prior articulations of mere succession or survival, expanding their genealogies horizontally as well as vertically. Therefore, based on this novel text, it is clear that the progeny blessing is a significant element not only in the creation blessings, the Abrahamic covenant, the Sinai covenant, and the new covenant, but in the covenants with David and Levi as well. The complete evidence of the OT thus indicates that Yahweh's covenants always include the promise of progeny, a blessing that can only come from Yahweh himself. This is perhaps not surprising since a covenantal relationship requires beneficiaries of the relationship and, in Yahweh's purposes for humanity and his own people, the more the better.

The connection between Yahweh's covenant commitments and the blessing of progeny is especially clear in Jer 30–33 where, arguably, five different covenants are in play. Just as the future proliferation of Israel (31:27) is based on Yahweh's fidelity to his covenant with Abraham (31:35–37), so the future multiplication of the Davidic and Levitical lines (33:22) is inextricably linked to his fidelity to the covenants he previously made with David and Phinehas (33:17–26). Yahweh's faithfulness to these covenants is compared to his covenant with creation in both cases (31:35–37; 33:20, 25), and both progeny promises appear to be grounded in his gracious enactment of a "new" covenant (31:31–34).[103] In both texts, the expansion of the people and their longevity are intertwined.

Situated at the close of the Book of Comfort, Jer 33:14–26 underscores the importance of the royal and priestly lines for the future of Israel and indicates that these traditional elements of Israel's past (including the temple, implicitly) will also be part of her future. These offices are not indispensable, contrary to what one may be led to believe, based on Jeremiah's harsh critique of both in his own day. For Jeremiah's exilic audience, who had recently suffered the loss of monarchy, temple, and priesthood, the promises of vv. 14–26 require faith—a faith based not on wishful thinking but rather on Yahweh's ancient commitments to Israel, David, and Levi, as sure as the constancy of creation.

---

103. See Jones, *Jeremiah*, 424.

I Will Surely Multiply Your Offspring

The Progeny Blessing in the LXX Text of Jeremiah

The LXX text of Jeremiah differs from the MT in significant respects. Most notably, the LXX text is approximately one-seventh shorter, lacking texts found in the MT, the most substantial of which are 10:6–8; 17:1–4; 29:16–20; 33:14–26; 39:4–13 and 51:45–48.[104] Furthermore, the oracles against the nations occur in a different order and are placed not at the end of the book but following 25:13 just prior to the "cup of wrath" against the nations. It is unlikely that these differences are to be accounted for by positing a common *Vorlage* that was altered. Rather, it appears that the MT, Targums, Syriac, and Vulgate represent one text tradition and the LXX, 4QJer[b] and 4QJer[d] represent another. Perhaps the most viable hypothesis, defended by Tov and followed by Archer, is that the LXX was translated from a "first edition" of the book, and that the MT reflects a "second edition,"[105] perhaps even compiled by Baruch.[106] Ultimately, we favor the MT tradition as the more "finished" work that represents the completion of the process of redaction and editing.[107] However, the LXX text is still worthy of attention and may be deemed authoritative in its own right. In general, the presentation of the progeny blessing is the same in the LXX text. However, there are two key differences in the Book of Comfort (which appears later in the book as Jer 37–40).

In Jer 31:8 (LXX 38:8), the LXX includes the expansion of the people where the MT does not:

MT	LXX	LXX translation

---

104. See Gleason L. Archer, "Relationship," 144–46, for these and other divergences.

105. See ibid., 141; Tov, *Textual Criticism*, 321. See also Blenkinsopp, *History of Prophecy*, 130.

106. See Archer, "Relationship," 141; Dillard and Longman III, *Introduction*, 293. Alternatively, Baruch may be responsible for the LXX edition, compiled in Egypt, and Seraiah for the MT edition, compiled in Babylon (see Lundbom, *Jeremiah 1–20*, 100–101).

107. See Waltke, "Aims," 93–108, who summarizes five different text-critical aims for reconstruction. The second position that aims for the final redacted text is adopted here (see Brotzman, *Textual Criticism*, 124, 129–32; Wegner, *Student's Guide*, 137; Würthwein, *Text of the Old Testament*, 109, for other adherents to this position).

הִנְנִי מֵבִיא אוֹתָם מֵאֶרֶץ צָפוֹן	ἰδοὺ ἐγὼ ἄγω αὐτοὺς	Look, I myself am bring-
וְקִבַּצְתִּים מִיַּרְכְּתֵי־אָרֶץ בָּם	ἀπὸ βορρᾶ καὶ συνάξω	ing them from the north,
עִוֵּר וּפִסֵּחַ הָרָה וְיֹלֶדֶת יַחְדָּו	αὐτοὺς ἀπ' ἐσχάτου τῆς	and I will gather them
קָהָל גָּדוֹל יָשׁוּבוּ הֵנָּה	γῆς ἐν ἑορτῇ φασεκ· καὶ	from the end of the earth
	τεκνοποιήσῃ ὄχλον πολύν,	at the Passover festival,
	καὶ ἀποστρέψουσιν ὧδε	and you will bear a large crowd, and they will return here.

This difference in v. 8b is not the result of a different *Vorlage* or textual corruption. Rather, the LXX translator understood the Hebrew text differently and rendered it paraphrastically. In the MT, הָרָה and יֹלֶדֶת are nominal terms, two of the categories of people whom Yahweh will "gather," and in apposition to "a large crowd." In the LXX, however, ילדת is treated as a Qal Perfect second masculine singular verb with "a large crowd" as its object and הָרָה appears to be ignored (or treated together with יֹלֶדֶת as hendiadys). As a result, in the LXX, we have a unique expression for the progeny blessing not seen elsewhere. It is not entirely clear whether this proliferation would occur prior to the return or after it, but the latter would be more likely and would make this text similar to 23:3 or 30:19. However, this would be a very unusual expression and does not appear to account well for הָרָה. Therefore, the appearance of the progeny motif in 31:8 (LXX 38:8) is due to poor translation and thus should not be taken into account within our examination of the LXX.

The other significant difference is the absence of 33:14–26 in the LXX. Some believe this text existed in the original edition of Jeremiah and was subsequently removed from the book either by haplography[108] or intentionally due to its irrelevance (or embarrassment) to the Jewish community in the diaspora.[109] However, this would be a surprisingly large piece of text to be lost through a copying error, making the first option unlikely. Regarding the second option, it is difficult to explain why the Davidic hope would be removed here, but still included elsewhere in the LXX where a deletion would have been less noticeable (e.g., 23:5–6; 30:9). Nor is there reason to believe that this promise would not have been

---

108. See Lundbom, *Jeremiah 21–36*, 537–39.

109. Jonathan F. Grothe argues on the basis of second-century changes to the text of Sirach that it is reasonable to assert that a second-century LXX translator would have deleted a text such as Jer 33:14–26 on account of its irrelevance to his community ("Argument," 188–91). See a summary of similar theories in Lust, "Messianism," 100–102.

welcomed.¹¹⁰ More likely, it was absent in the first edition and added in the second.¹¹¹ This does not necessarily mean, however, that this text is "inauthentic" to Jeremiah since both editions may ultimately derive from him.¹¹² As a result of this omission, the LXX text of the progeny blessing nowhere applies the blessing to a subgroup within Israel as does 33:22 in the MT, and it thus does not support or expand upon Yahweh's abiding commitments to David and Levi.

Conclusion: A Summary of the Progeny Blessing in the MT of Jeremiah

In the book of Jeremiah, the progeny blessing is generally articulated in terms familiar from other prosaic formulations in the OT.¹¹³ With the exception of Jer 31:27, each occurrence of the blessing employs רָבָה. Jeremiah 3:16 and 23:3 juxtapose this word with פָּרָה, and 29:6 and 30:19 share the similar formulation, מְעַט + לֹא/אַל. Given this common language to denote proliferation, there is little doubt that reproduction is in view.

Although it may not have been intended by the final editor(s) of the book, a progression can be discerned within the six progeny texts with respect to the active agents of multiplication, reflected in the person and mood of the verbs. By using intransitive verbs with the people as the subject in 3:16 and 23:3, the agent is left unspecified. Perhaps this further emphasizes the responsibility placed on the people themselves in 29:6 where childbearing is commanded. In the remaining texts, the verbs are transitive with Yahweh as subject and the people as object. Thus it is clear that Yahweh will himself build, plant, and multiply the people (30:19; 31:27-28) just as the people have built, planted, and multiplied in exile. Thus human responsibility and divine action with respect to reproduction are both affirmed as we have seen elsewhere in the OT, although in this

---

110. See Archer, "Relationship," 145.

111. See Bright, *Jeremiah*, 298; Carroll, *Jeremiah*, 639; Clements, *Jeremiah*, 199; Holladay, *Jeremiah 2*, 228-29; Lust, "Messianism," 101. Nearly all of these scholars believe, however, that this text was added centuries after the lifetime of Jeremiah.

112. According to Archer, "Perhaps we may surmise that this particular oracle was not revealed to the prophet until after the original Egyptian edition was out, but prior to his decease" ("Relationship," 145). See also Dillard and Longman III, *Introduction*, 293.

113. Although the line between prose and poetry is a fluid one, particularly in Jeremiah, only 30:19 appears to occur in a poetic context.

case the former precedes the latter both chronologically and in the textual sequence.

With respect to time and place, 29:6 envisions multiplication during the exile in Babylon. The other progeny texts in Jeremiah describe a proliferation that will take place following return from exile back in the land of promise, God's chosen location for blessing. No more than this is clearly specified, but the juxtaposition of some texts with the reunification of Israel and Judah (3:16; 23:3; especially 31:27) may indicate that not all elements of the projected restoration, including multiplication, are expected to occur immediately following the return after the seventy years of Babylonian dominance. Nor is it clear for how long God will continue to multiply his people, although 31:35–37 emphasizes that he will do so insofar as it ensures that they will never cease to be a people.

In Jer 29:6, the blessing is confined to the Judahite exilic audience in Babylon. However, in the restoration oracles, the scope encompasses both Israel and Judah, implicit (as argued above) in 3:16, 23:3, and 30:19, but explicit in 31:27. The three texts in the Book of Comfort nuance the scope of the progeny blessing in additional ways. Whereas other texts do not define the extent of Israel's multiplication, 30:19–20 anticipates a people as large as, but not necessarily greater than, before. Jeremiah 31:27 applies the blessing not only to the human but also to the animal realm. Finally, 33:22 applies the blessing to a specific subgroup within Israel, namely, the offspring of David and Levi, while emphasizing the eternality of their lines as well on the basis of Yahweh's fidelity to covenants. Within Jeremiah's parochial worldview, concern for the proliferation of peoples outside of Israel is lacking.

The progeny blessing typically occurs in the context of descriptions of the restoration of Israelite society following return to the land. The multiplication of the people plays a foundational role in such renewal since one cannot have a thriving society without a thriving population. As we have seen, effective kingship is the most common feature of this future society that appears alongside the progeny blessing, appearing in the immediate context of 3:16, 23:3, 30:19, and 33:22.[114] This juxtaposition indicates that, as was the case in the past (1 Kgs 4:20), there will be a correlation between the flourishing of the life of the people and just and righteous kingship. Although Yahweh's new relationship with the people is not addressed in

---

114. This pairing first appears in the patriarchal blessings in Gen 17:6, 16; 35:11. See Gross, "Israel's Hope," 101–33, who examines the motif of the renewal of kingship in Jeremiah, Ezekiel, and the priestly writer in Genesis and observes that the progeny blessing is often juxtaposed with it.

all of the oracles of hope containing the progeny blessing (but see 3:16–17; 30:22), 31:31–37 grounds all future restoration of society in Yahweh's gracious resolve to forgive sins in enacting a new covenant with the people, based on his fidelity to his prior covenant commitments.

We have found it difficult to locate each progeny text in Jeremiah within a specific progeny tradition elsewhere in the OT. Rather, many of the texts could be identified with various manifestations of the blessing, which should not be surprising given the complementary nature of the blessing in the OT. Correspondences with the creation blessing can be discerned in 3:16, 23:3, and 31:27, portraying this future event as a new creation. The blessing appears to be understood as a realization of the Abrahamic promises in the Book of Comfort in particular (30:19; 31:27; 33:22). Given the shared perspective between Jeremiah and Deut 30:1–10, we might see a correlation with Deut 30:6 in 3:16, 23:3, and 31:27 (and perhaps in 30:19 as well). Furthermore, the relationship of multiplication to good kingship links 3:16, 23:3, and 30:19 to 1 Kgs 4:20. In the final analysis, we conclude that the author(s) of Jeremiah were familiar with the progeny traditions from creation, the Abrahamic covenant, Deut 30:1–10, the Davidic covenant, and perhaps a Levitical tradition.

It appears, however, that the progeny motif in Jeremiah fits particularly well within the framework of new exodus typology. As argued above, the instructions of Jer 29:5–7 suggest that the Babylonian exile is comparable to Israel's ancient stay in Egypt, with multiplication in Babylon mirroring the proliferation documented in Exod 1:7. Yates demonstrates that Jer 30–31 contains a good deal of exodus imagery, portraying Jeremiah as a new Moses, the return from Babylon as a new exodus, and the new covenant in 31:31–34 as an improved version of the Sinai covenant.[115] Bernard Gosse extends this theme to other texts of hope and argues that 3:14–18, 23:7–8, and 31:31–34 are part of "a family of texts interpreting the return from exile as the equivalent, in the new covenant, of the journey up from Egypt in the covenant with the fathers (cf. Jer 31:32)."[116] Based on common links such as the phrase "it will no longer be said" (3:16; 31:29; 23:7–8) which denotes a shift from the old covenant to the new, he claims that both 3:14–18 and 23:3–8 depict new covenant realities rooted in 31:31–34.[117] Although he fails to take note of the progeny blessing, it is

---

115. See Yates, "New Exodus," 4–8. See also van der Wal, "Themes from Exodus," 559–66.

116. Gosse, "L'ouverture," 385, my translation.

117. See ibid., 387–89.

significant that three of the four progeny texts in Jeremiah that depict a future proliferation of the nation occur in these contexts (and the fourth, 30:19, is in the new exodus context of Jer 30–31). Thus it appears that multiplication is a significant component of the new exodus typology. This new multiplication of the nation does not have an exact typological correspondence to multiplication in the first exodus since expansion of the nation occurred in Egypt prior to the exodus and since proliferation within the land was conditional upon obedience according to the covenant blessings. However, Yahweh's commitment to bless Israel with progeny in Israel's re-creation remains as firm as his original commitment to multiply the people when creating the nation in the first place, so the progeny blessing strengthens the correspondence in Jeremiah between Moses/exodus/Sinai covenant and Jeremiah/new exodus/new covenant.

The function of the progeny blessing in the book of Jeremiah is multifaceted. The command to bear children in 29:6 ensures the survival of the exilic community and prepares them for the promised return. In 30:19, Yahweh pledges to multiply the people in order to honor them. More generally, the blessing of progeny is an aspect of Yahweh's "building and planting" project (see 31:27–28), a reversal of the population decimation that occurred during the "tearing down and uprooting" phase. Furthermore, the promise of future restoration, of which proliferation is a part, motivates the exiles to seek God and repent (e.g., 3:14–16).

Perhaps the most crucial function of the progeny blessing within Jeremiah lies in its relation to the covenants. Jeremiah 3:16, 23:3, 30:19, and 31:27 indicate that the progeny blessing is a key component of the new covenant, but allusions in these texts to previous covenants suggest that it is a renewal of the Abrahamic and Sinai covenants as well, and even the covenants with David and Levi (33:22). In the face of exilic judgment that appeared to indicate otherwise, Yahweh's adherence to his covenants (cf. 31:27–37; 33:14–26) is the bedrock of the faith and hope for the exilic addressees of the book, who doubtless felt abandoned by God and despaired. Within the covenants, the progeny blessing serves a vital theological role in that it is the primary physical means by which he will sustain Israel and her kingly and priestly lines. At the same time, Yahweh's covenant faithfulness remains the basis for the promise of progeny. As with the covenants themselves, the future blessing of progeny is in substantial continuity with the past, although 33:22 is a new expression of it that surpasses the previous commitment to David and Levi.

5

The Progeny Blessing in the Book of Ezekiel

INTRODUCTION TO THE BOOK OF EZEKIEL

Ezekiel's Use of Prior Traditions

THAT THERE IS A literary relationship between the books of Jeremiah and Ezekiel is clear given the many lexical and thematic parallels between them.[1] Furthermore, Ezekiel contains some Deuteronomic motifs.[2] However, Ezekiel is undeniably most indebted to the priestly tradition. Specifically, a close relationship exists between Ezekiel and the Holiness Code of Lev 17–26.[3] As is often the case, it is difficult to prove the direction of dependence, resulting in advocates of every possible view: the priority of Ezekiel, the priority of Leviticus, Ezekielian authorship of Leviticus, a common source or tradition, or mutual influence over a long period of growth.[4] In the estimation of Zimmerli, "It is above all Lev 26

---

1. See, for example, Boadt, "Common View," 14–31; Leene, "Ezekiel and Jeremiah," 150–75; Lust, "Gathering and Return," 119–42; Raitt, *Theology of Exile*, 128–230.

2. See Patton, "Pan-Deuteronomism," 200–15, who argues that deuteronomistic influence can be detected in Ezekiel, but denies that there is enough evidence to posit a deuteronomistic redaction of the book as a whole. Indeed, it appears that much of the "deuteronomistic" influence could be attributed to Jeremiah's influence on Ezekiel.

3. See Lyons, *From Law to Prophecy*. See Zimmerli, *Ezekiel 1*, 48–52, for a summary of these correspondences.

4. See Lyons, *From Law to Prophecy*, 35–46, for a summary of these views. Lyons argues throughout his work that Ezekiel uses the Holiness Code. In contrast, Zimmerli favors a very complex relationship whereby both are indebted to a common priestly tradition (*Ezekiel 1*, 52).

which made one consider seriously the similarity of authorship of [the Holiness Code] and Ezekiel," although they exhibit "striking independence of formulation." In an examination of the relationship between Lev 26 and Ezekiel, Milgrom identifies nine clear parallels, including the use of Lev 26:3-13 in Ezek 34:24-28, 36:9-11, and 37:26-27, and concludes that in each case it appears that Lev 26 was prior,[5] leading him to conclude boldly that "[Ezekiel] probably had the entire text of Lev 26:3-39 (as is now preserved in the MT) before him."[6] Accordingly, Lev 26:3-13 may be the primary intertext for understanding future blessing in Ezekiel.[7]

As was the case in Jeremiah, Ezekiel exhibits strong conceptual and linguistic parallels with Deut 30:1-10 as well.[8] Since both of these texts from the Pentateuch contain the progeny blessing, intertexts for Ezekiel's use of the blessing are readily at hand. Part of our task will be to attempt to discern, if possible, whether Ezekiel's own articulation of the blessing best fits its portrayal in Deut 30, Lev 26, Jeremiah, a combination of these, or is novel, in order to best understand its function within the book as a whole.

Future Hope in Ezekiel

The restoration oracles of Ezekiel do not envision an other-worldly experience previously unknown to God's people, but rather the reinstatement within an enhanced covenant relationship of all that was lost in the judgments imposed upon them. Thus the salvation themes are the positive counterparts of the judgment themes. Although Ezek 1-24 consist mainly of pronouncements of judgment against Jerusalem, intermittent projections of hope beyond exile (11:14-21; 14:11; 16:53-63; 17:22-24; 20:32-44; and 28:24-26) underscore that this will not bring about the complete end of God's people and that restoration is his ultimate will for them. These texts tend to treat future blessings following return succinctly and do not elaborate upon them, similar to the character of the restoration oracles of Jeremiah. In contrast, in the hope-filled latter portion of the book (Ezek 34-48) that follows news of the fall of Jerusalem (see 33:21)

---

5. See Milgrom, "Leviticus 26 and Ezekiel," 57-62.

6. Ibid., 61.

7. In addition, it is clear that Ezek 16:59-63 has a strong affinity with Lev 26:40-45.

8. See Joyce, *Divine Initiative*, 119-21; Lust, "Gathering and Return," 122-25.

historically, theologically, and literarily, Ezekiel develops aspects of this restoration in greater depth.[9]

Unlike Isaiah, Ezekiel is not concerned with the salvation of the nations, confining the scope of his oracles of hope solely to Israel. Rather, Yahweh's desire for the nations is their acknowledgement of him based on what he does for Israel, often expressed in the recognition formula.[10] Ezekiel 29:13–16 is the sole exception where, following the dispersal of Egypt among the lands, Yahweh will restore them to their own land, but only as "the lowest of the kingdoms . . . so small (וְהִמְעַטְתִּים) that they will not rule over the nations" (v. 15), a paltry hope given their proud history. They may survive as a people, but Yahweh apparently does not intend to bless them with progeny to the extent that they multiply as a people.[11]

Yahweh's most fundamental promise to the exiles is that he will himself orchestrate their return (11:17–18; 16:53; 20:34, 41, 42; 28:25; 34:12–13; 36:8, 24; 37:1–14, 21; 39:27–28), typically expressed, as in 34:12–13, as "gathering" (וְקִבַּצְתִּים) them and "bringing" them out from the nations (וְהוֹצֵאתִים) and into their own land (וַהֲבִיאֹתִים). The resulting restoration of society is a muted hope in Ezek 1–24, where glimpses of it can be discerned only in 16:55 and 17:22–24 since Ezekiel is more concerned with the future renewal of the relationship between the covenant partners. Thereafter, however, Ezekiel describes a full-blown reconstitution of Israel's former ideal way of life: security in the land (28:26; 34:25, 27, 28; 38:8, 11, 14; 39:26) apart from fear (34:28; 39:26), protection from enemy peoples (28:24–26; 34:28–29; 38–39), agricultural fertility (34:26–27; 36:29–30, 35; 47:9–12), the proliferation of the people (36:10–14, 37–38; 37:26), and rebuilt cities (28:26; 36:10, 33–36). A reunified people (37:16–22) will enjoy these benefits under divine (34:11–16) and Davidic (17:22–24; 34:23–24; 37:22, 24–25) rule and a renewed cultic system (40–46).

Yahweh's determination to restore his people and mend the covenant relationship is grounded in his concern for his reputation (36:22–23, 32) as well as in his resolve to "remember" (וְזָכַרְתִּי; 16:60) and "uphold" (וַהֲקִמוֹתִי; 16:60) the "everlasting covenant" (בְּרִית עוֹלָם; 16:60; see 37:26), also referred to as the "covenant of peace" (34:25; 37:26). Yahweh will

---

9. Gowan states that "[Ezekiel] contains a virtual plan for the restoration, unlike the piecemeal promises that appear in the other prophetic books" (*Prophetic Books*, 134).

10. See Ackroyd, *Exile and Restoration*, 115–17.

11. Most likely it is "because Egypt did not exploit or rejoice over Israel's defeat" as did the other nations that they alone among the nations receive this promise (Greenberg, *Ezekiel 21–37*, 611; cf. Block, *Ezekiel: Chapters 25–48*, 145).

enable his people to obey and serve him (11:20; 14:11; 20:39-41; 36:27; 37:24; 43:7-8) by giving them a "new heart" and a "new spirit" (11:19; 36:26-27; cf. 37:14 and 39:29). This inner transformation coincides with Yahweh's acts of "cleansing" (טָהֵר; 36:25, 29, 33; 37:23) and making atonement for their sins (כִּפֶּר; 16:63). As a result, Yahweh's favor will remain upon them (36:9; 39:25, 29) and he will dwell in their midst (37:26-28; 43:1-9; 48:35), a harmonious relationship summarized by the "covenant formula" (11:20; 14:11; 34:30-31; 36:28; 37:23, 27). It appears that this unparalleled divine work on the heart will take place following return to the land (see 11:17-19; 36:24-26) and in conjunction with the restoration of society (see 36:33).[12]

In the book's presentation of coming salvation, Ezek 34-48 describe the restoration progressively. The description commences with the re-establishment of society under divine and, to a lesser extent, Davidic kingship (34), followed by the renewal of the land itself through purification, rebuilding, and repopulation (35:1—36:15). Ezekiel then treats the restoration of Yahweh's honor through the cleansing of the people (36:16-38) and the return and reunification of the people of Israel (37). The defeat of Gog and Magog once Israel is again secure in the land underscores Yahweh's protection of his people, indicating that a disaster like that of 587 BCE will never occur again (38-39).[13] Finally, Ezek 40-48 describe the restoration of the temple, the sacrificial system, the cultic ordinances, and the tribal boundaries within the fertile land.[14]

There are crucial differences between the visions of hope in Ezekiel and Jeremiah. For example, 1) Yahweh's motivation for bringing about the restoration in Jeremiah is compassion, whereas it is concern for his own name in Ezekiel; 2) in Ezekiel the return is designed to bring about remorse (6:9; 16:54, 61, 63; 20:43; 36:31), but this motivation is absent from Jeremiah; and 3) Ezekiel foresees an intermediate "wilderness" period (20:35-38) between delivering the people from the nations and their re-entry into the land, also missing from Jeremiah. Nevertheless, the similarities are so striking that von Rad asserts that "one feels that Ezekiel must somehow have had Jeremiah's prophecies in front of him."[15] Both stress

12. Renz observes that it is never clear whether spiritual or societal restoration takes place first (*Rhetorical Function of Ezekiel*, 229).

13. See Block, "Gog and Magog," 115-16; Renz, *Rhetorical Function of Ezekiel*, 117-18.

14. See Boadt, "Salvation Oracles," 1-21, for the best discussion of the coherence and progression of these chapters.

15. Von Rad, *Old Testament Theology: Prophetic Traditions*, 235.

that the hope of Israel lies with the Babylonian exiles rather than with those left in the land. Both employ the second exodus motif in descriptions of the return (see Ezek 20:33–44). Both envision societal restoration as a return to the past ideal under a Davidic ruler. Both emphasize that the people are themselves unable to repent apart from a work of Yahweh to transform them, described in similar terms as a work on their heart.[16] The blessing of progeny is one of the many features common to these two depictions of the future, and we will entertain the possibility that this may be the result of the influence of one prophet upon the other.[17]

THE PROGENY BLESSING IN EZEKIEL

The progeny blessing explicitly occurs in the book of Ezekiel in three places (36:10–14; 36:37–38; and 37:26), all in close proximity in the context of oracles of hope. Prior to our treatment of these texts, we will examine the frustration of the progeny blessing in Ezekiel.

Population Decimation in Ezekiel

As in Isaiah and Jeremiah, the proliferation of the people in the future restoration is the reversal of the decimation that Yahweh imposes during the judgment that precipitates exile. Since Ezekiel's ministry follows the first exile of 597 BCE, his oracles of judgment pertain specifically to the fall of Jerusalem in 587 BCE. The dominant agent of depopulation in Ezekiel is the sword (חֶרֶב), mentioned ninety-one times in the book, including an extended judgment oracle that proclaims that Yahweh's own sword will fall upon Jerusalem (21:1–17) through "the sword of the king of Babylon" (21:19). It also occurs in the tripartite decimation formula, sword (חֶרֶב), famine (רָעָב), and pestilence (דֶּבֶר), which summarizes the fate of the people (see 5:12, 17; 6:11, 12; 7:15 [2x]; 12:16; 14:21), most prevalent in Jeremiah but common in Ezekiel as well. In addition, Yahweh will destroy his people through cannibalism (5:10), wild beasts (5:17; 14:21; 33:27), bereavement of children (5:17) and fire (23:25). In the culminating sign-act

---

16. Joyce plausibly suggests that Ezekiel was influenced by both Deuteronomic theology and the Jeremiah tradition while in Jerusalem, and that this dual influence best accounts for his use of some shared elements such as the heart motif (*Divine Initiative*, 118–24).

17. See Zimmerli, *Ezekiel 1*, 44–46, for a summary of correspondences between Jeremiah and Ezekiel in general.

of Ezekiel's ministry, Yahweh takes Ezekiel's own wife (24:16–18) in order to show the exiles that in the fall of Jerusalem "your sons and daughters you left behind will fall by the sword" (24:21). Yahweh's sentence on the people for their sin is clearly widespread loss of life, not simply loss of land and possessions.[18]

Furthermore, the rebellious people have already been depopulating themselves through their sinful and idolatrous practices. Yahweh indicts the leaders of Jerusalem for their corrupt rule, claiming, "you have multiplied (הִרְבֵּיתֶם) your slain in this city, and you have filled the streets with the slain" (11:6). Since רָבָה is later used to refer to Yahweh's multiplication of the people (36:10, 11, 37; 37:26), perhaps the use of רָבָה here is intentional, contrasting the purposes of God with those of the wicked leaders. Whereas Yahweh's ultimate desire is to multiply life in the land, the leaders counter his purposes by multiplying death, an indictment further developed in Ezek 34 in which these leaders are accused of devouring and abusing the populace (34:2–8). Moreover, the people had slaughtered their own children by sacrificing them to idols (16:20–21; 23:37–39). With good reason, Yahweh describes Jerusalem as "the bloody city" (22:1–12), a charge that refers to more than murderous crimes, but certainly includes it.

Ezekiel 34:25–30

Prior to news of the fall of Jerusalem in Ezek 33, the salvation oracles in the book tend to emphasize the future return, inner transformation, and renewed relationship rather than the restoration of a prosperous society, perhaps because this message was more pertinent to the pre-fall situation. Therefore, it is not surprising that the progeny blessing does not appear in oracles of hope in Ezek 1–33.[19]

---

18. Given the close relationship between Ezekiel and the Holiness Code, and Lev 26 in particular, these curses of decimation ought to be understood as the execution of the covenant curses of Lev 26:14–39 (see Lyons, *From Law to Prophecy*, 117–22, 181–84, for a summary of these parallels).

19. A possible reference to Yahweh's blessing of progeny appears in 16:7 where the history of Jerusalem is allegorically portrayed as the birth and growth of a woman. Assuming the originality of the MT reading (since the LXX likely attempts to paraphrase an awkward, yet readable, phrase), Yahweh says of her, "I made her רְבָבָה like (a) plant(s) of the field." Among the seventeen other occurrences of רְבָבָה in the OT, it serves as a quantitative qualifier of great size, typically 10,000. Thus, the phrase could denote "an intrusion of the reality behind the metaphor (the great increase of Israel in Egypt?)" (Greenberg, *Ezekiel 1–20*, 276), assuming Jerusalem represents the whole

However, it is surprising that the blessing is not mentioned in 34:25–30, the book's first explication of the restoration of Israel's society. As Milgrom ably argues, this text is dependent upon the covenant blessings of Lev 26:4–13 which include the progeny blessing (v. 9).[20] Perhaps the progeny blessing is not cited here because the concern of this text, via Lev 26, is to emphasize the reversal of specific curses of decimation prominent in Ezek 1–24. Wild animals will be removed (vv. 25, 28), the land will be fertile so there will be no more famine (vv. 26–27a, 29a), and the inhabitants will no longer need to fear enemy attacks (vv. 27b–28, 29b), three out of the four elements from the decimation formula in 14:21 (sword, famine, wild beasts, pestilence), each being mentioned twice. Thus, the progeny blessing is indirectly present, since the reversal of decimation curses naturally results in the proliferation of the people. However, the positive articulation of the blessing awaits Ezek 36.

Ezekiel 36:10–14

The theme of the rehabilitation of the land continues in 35:1—36:15. Here, the current fortunes of Edom and Israel are reversed and contrasted. Ezekiel first addresses Mount Seir (הַר שֵׂעִיר; v. 2) in 35:1–15, an oracle of judgment that indicts Edom, representative of Israel's enemies,[21] for their exploitation of Israel in her day of distress (vv. 5, 10–13). As a result, he will make Edom a desolation (שְׁמָמָה)[22] and a waste (vv. 3–4, 7, 9, 14–15)

---

people of Israel. However, it is more likely that רְבָבָה functions here as a cognate noun based on the qualitative meaning of רָבָה and thus serves as a qualitative qualifier representing the child's development (so Block, *Ezekiel: Chapters 1–24*, 481; Greenberg, *Ezekiel 1–20*, 276) since quantitative expansion makes little sense in the context of the allegorical description of a single individual and since no biblical tradition exists concerning the proliferation of Jerusalem's population, the reference to the whole nation here being doubtful. Therefore, the best reading is, "I made her grow/flourish like a plant of the field." See also Malul, "Adoption of Foundlings," 13, who argues that this phrase may refer to adoption due to the use of רְבָבָה in adoption contexts in cognate languages.

20. See Milgrom, "Leviticus 26 and Ezekiel," 57–62. See also Block, *Ezekiel: Chapters 25–48*, 303. See his comparison of these two texts on p 304. In addition, it appears that Ezek 34 as a whole is dependent on Jer 23:1–6, which contains the progeny blessing in v. 3 (see Block, *Ezekiel: Chapters 25–48*, 275–76).

21. See Woudstra, "Edom and Israel," 21–35, for a summary of the history of Edom-Israel relations as recorded in the OT, Edom's representative role among the nations, and the role of Edom within Ezekiel.

22. This term functions as a *Leitwort* within Ezek 35, appearing seven times as well as twice more in its verbal form (שָׁמֵם).

just as Israel is currently desolate and waste (vv. 12, 15). Their land will be filled with the slain (v. 8) just as Israel's has been.

Ezekiel then addresses the "mountains of Israel" (הָרֵי יִשְׂרָאֵל; v. 1) in 36:1–15. However, the first half of the address (v. 1–7) continues to judge Edom (see v. 5) and Israel's other enemies (vv. 3, 5–7), indicating that the renewal of Israel's own land (vv. 8–15) will occur within the context of the judgment of her enemies, which implies her own salvation. These two addresses to the opposing mountains are intimately related, and both recall the prior address of judgment against the "mountains of Israel" (הָרֵי יִשְׂרָאֵל) in Ezek 6.[23] In all three texts, the land rather than the people is primarily in view, and the primary themes of blessing and curse relate to the population and their dwelling places: Edom, once prosperous, will be decimated and desolate (Ezek 35); Israel, once desolate and decimated from Yahweh's judgment (Ezek 6), will be rebuilt and repopulated (36:8–15). The decimation and desolation once imposed upon Israel (Ezek 6) are now imputed to Edom (Ezek 35). The contrasts could hardly be sharper.

Verses 8–15 continue to address the personified mountains of Israel (v. 8) and are dominated by Yahweh's own declarations concerning what he will do on behalf of the land and, implicitly, the people. Block appropriately summarizes this text as envisioning "the complete restoration of the deity-nation-land relationship,"[24] although the focus here is on the renewal of a thriving society in the land, reserving treatment of the new relationship between Yahweh and the people for later in the chapter. First, Yahweh promises renewed fertility for the land (vv. 8a, 9b)[25] in anticipation of Israel's imminent return (v. 8b) and declares his favor toward the land in general (v. 9a). What follows is arguably the most extensive meditation on the progeny blessing in the OT, depicting the repopulation of the land both positively (vv. 10–12a) and negatively (vv. 12b–14).

Verses 10 and 11 contain multiple progeny blessing expressions:

23. See Block, *Ezekiel: Chapters 25–48*, 309–11; and Greenberg, *Ezekiel 21–37*, 723, for a summary of the parallels between Ezek 6, 35, and 36. See especially Bernard Gosse regarding the transfer of the curses of Ezek 6 from Israel to Edom in Ezek 35 ("Ézéchiel 35–36, 1–15 et Ézéchiel 6," 511–17).

24. Block, *Ezekiel: Chapters 25–48*, 333.

25. It is tempting to see v. 9b (וְנֶעֱבַדְתֶּם וְנִזְרַעְתֶּם: "you will be tilled and sown") as an introductory reference to the sowing of the land with people since זֶרַע is used elsewhere metaphorically to refer to filling the land with people (see Jer 31:27; Hos 2:25[23]; Zech 10:9). However, it is more likely that agriculture is in mind here since 1) זֶרַע more commonly denotes sowing the seed of plant life, 2) עָבַד is never employed metaphorically elsewhere to refer to the progeny blessing, and 3) v. 8 appears to refer to the fertility of plant life (cf. עָבַד in v. 34).

I Will Surely Multiply Your Offspring

וְהִרְבֵּיתִי עֲלֵיכֶם אָדָם	10	I will multiply people on you,
כָּל־בֵּית יִשְׂרָאֵל כֻּלֹּה		all the house of Israel, the whole thing.
וְנֹשְׁבוּ הֶעָרִים		The cities will be inhabited
וְהֶחֳרָבוֹת תִּבָּנֶינָה		and the waste places will be rebuilt.
וְהִרְבֵּיתִי עֲלֵיכֶם אָדָם וּבְהֵמָה	11	I will multiply people and animals on you,
וְרָבוּ וּפָרוּ		and they will multiply and be fruitful.
וְהוֹשַׁבְתִּי אֶתְכֶם כְּקַדְמוֹתֵיכֶם		And I will cause you to be inhabited as formerly,
וְהֵטִבֹתִי מֵרִאשֹׁתֵיכֶם		and I will do more good to you than before.
וִידַעְתֶּם כִּי־אֲנִי יְהוָה		Then you will know that I am Yahweh

In v. 10, Yahweh is responsible for multiplication, a proliferation that will take place on the mountains,[26] synecdoche for the whole land of Israel. The object of multiplication is אָדָם, defined as "all the house of Israel, the whole thing."[27] In light of 11:15–17 and 35:10, this likely refers not merely to the Judahite exiles but to all twelve tribes, transcending what may have seemed possible to Ezekiel's audience. As a result of repopulation, "the cities will be inhabited and the waste places will be rebuilt" (cf. 6:6; 34:5), overturning decimation and desolation at once.

Verse 10 contains little that is not also in v. 11, repeating much of the same content (i.e., multiplication and inhabiting the land), particularly, the first three words concerning multiplication which are repeated verbatim. As a result, many reject v. 10 as a late and unnecessary insertion,[28] although no manuscript evidence supports this judgment. However, if we accept the MT, v. 11 expands upon v. 10 in crucial respects, an acceptable literary technique (but see below for what may be a more satisfactory explanation).[29]

---

26. Here עֲלֵיכֶם is probably a locative use of the preposition, and the second masculine plural suffix refers to the הָרִים.

27. Both expressions allude to Edom in the wider literary context. The repetition of אָדָם in vv. 10, 11, 12, 13, and 14 is likely a wordplay on אֱדוֹם (see Allen, *Ezekiel 20–48*, 171; Johan Lust, "Edom—Adam," 394), and the unusual modifier "all of it" (כֻּלֹּה) mirrors similar expressions with respect to Edom in 35:15 and 36:5.

28. E.g., Cooke, *Ezekiel*, 388; Eichrodt, *Ezekiel*, 489; Zimmerli, *Ezekiel 2*, 233. With respect to vv. 8–15, Westermann states that "[t]hese motifs have been brought together mechanically, with repetitions, and with no logical connection" (*Prophetic Oracles*, 170).

29. With the exception of פָּרָה in v. 11, each articulation of the progeny blessing in the book of Ezekiel (36:10–11, 37; 37:26) employs the verb רָבָה. The twenty occurrences of רָבָה in Ezekiel are the most among the Latter Prophets, typically employed in a quantitative sense. In Ezek 34–38, all seven uses are found in Ezek 36–37 (six in Ezek 36 alone), all positive fertility assertions concerning the multiplication either of people (36:10, 11, 11, 37; 37:26) or of grain, fruit, and produce (36:29–30). All seven of these occurrences are transitive Hiphil verbs with God as subject except for the second

The Progeny Blessing in the Book of Ezekiel

First, Yahweh's multiplying work is extended to the animal realm as well, reversing the decimation of אָדָם וּבְהֵמָה in 14:13, 17, 19, 21, 25:13, and 29:8.

Second, this clause is complemented by "and they will multiply and be fruitful" (וְרָבוּ וּפָרוּ),[30] a phrase missing in the LXX (although included in Aquila and Theodotian). Due to this minus in the LXX, the redundant nature of the phrase, and a supposed awkward shift from first person speech to third person speech, most commentators reject this phrase as a late gloss.[31] However, the phrase should be retained for several reasons. First, the phrase may have existed in the *Vorlage* of the LXX but either the original translator or subsequent LXX copyists/editors may have removed it as repetitive or awkward, as modern commentators also are inclined to do. Second, this may not be a text-critical problem that arose in the transmission process but rather a matter of literary development between the first edition of the book, represented by the LXX translation, and the second, fuller edition of the book, represented by the MT. The inclusion of the phrase then depends on the aims of the text-critical enterprise. Since in our judgment its proper goal is to recover the text at the end of literary formation and at the start of the transmission process (though acknowledging that this transition is not always clear and that the two processes may overlap), even "glosses" or "insertions" that are firmly established by external evidence (apart from the earlier edition of the LXX) are to be retained. Finally, this phrase is neither superfluous nor awkward; on the contrary, it makes a meaningful contribution to the passage (see below).

Third, the scale of Yahweh's action is specified. Verse 11 and perhaps all of vv. 8–11 are summarized in the statement, "I will do more good to you than before" (וְהֵטִבֹתִי מֵרִאשֹׁתֵיכֶם). Yahweh will not merely reinstate the size of the population but will expand it beyond their previous experience.

Finally, v. 11 concludes with the "recognition" formula, "then you (i.e., the mountains) will know that I am Yahweh," the ultimate purpose of Yahweh's actions. Since this formula routinely concludes oracles in Ezekiel, this is the rationale not only for the previous clause, but also for all

---

occurrence in 36:11, which is a Qal intransitive verb with the people as subject.

30. As in Jer 3:16, this reversal "exemplifies late Biblical Hebrew's penchant for reversing traditional pairs" (Greenberg, *Ezekiel 21–37*, 720) and may draw attention to the presence of an inner-biblical allusion or quotation (see Talmon, "Textual Study," 358–78; Schultz, *Search for Quotation*, 75–76, 293).

31. E.g., Allen, *Ezekiel 20–48*, 169; Cooke, *Ezekiel*, 388; Eichrodt, *Ezekiel*, 489; Gross, "Israel's Hope," 118; Zimmerli, *Ezekiel 2*, 230.

his actions on behalf of the land in vv. 8–11 (and perhaps including vv. 1–7 as well).

Perhaps vv. 10–11 are repetitive because they draw on multiple texts. Clearly, Lev 26 is one source for vv. 8–15, based on the following conceptual and linguistic parallels:

Ezekiel 36	Leviticus 26
Mountains yielding fruit (v. 8)	Trees yielding fruit (v. 4)
וּפָנִיתִי אֲלֵיכֶם (v. 9)	וּפָנִיתִי אֲלֵיכֶם (v. 9)
וְהִרְבֵּיתִי עֲלֵיכֶם (vv. 10, 11)	וְהִרְבֵּיתִי אֶתְכֶם (v. 9)
לְשַׁכְּלָם (vv. 12–14)	וְשִׁכְּלָה אֶתְכֶם (v. 22)
Israel's land devouring people (vv. 13–14)	Enemies' land devouring people (v. 38)

Ezekiel 36:9–11 employs two phrases from Lev 26:9, merely altering אֶת to עַל in the multiplication clause in order to address the mountains rather than the people.[32] Leviticus 26 describes the blessings that Israel would continue to experience in the land after the exodus contingent upon their obedience (v. 3), with the threat of curse if disobedient (vv. 14–15). By using this text, Ezekiel underscores that Israel will again experience the same kinds of blessings they were always intended to enjoy in the land following the new exodus. However, in a significant shift, Ezekiel eliminates contingency, proclaiming unconditional hope without the threat of curse.

In addition, Deut 30:1–10 appears to be a key intertext for Ezek 36. In v. 24 Ezekiel employs the same three verbs to refer to the return (וְלָקַחְתִּי, וְהֵבֵאתִי, וְקִבַּצְתִּי) found in Deut 30:3–5, verbs found together only here and in 37:21 in the book. Conceptually, circumcision of the heart yielding obedience (Deut 30:6, 8) parallels the thought of Ezek 36:25–27. In our immediate text, Ezek 36:11 corresponds closely to Deut 30:5: 1) Both contain the unconditional promise of multiplication beyond exile, expressed with the Hiphil of רָבָה. 2) Both contain the construction Hiphil of יָטַב + comparative מִן that is present elsewhere in the OT only in Nah 3:8 and Ruth 3:10. In these latter two texts the expression does not refer to God's actions toward Israel, unlike the former two texts.[33] According to Deut 30:5 Yahweh will do more good to the returnees than to their "fathers" (מֵאֲבֹתֶיךָ), whereas according to Ezek 36:11 he will do more good to them

---

32. See Milgrom, "Leviticus 26 and Ezekiel," 59.

33. Furthermore, this is the only occurrence of יָטַב in Ezekiel other than in 33:32 where it functions adverbially.

than he had in the past (מֵרִאשֹׁתֵיכֶם). These phrases are thus roughly synonymous.³⁴ 3) In Deut 30:9, Yahweh reaffirms his desire to do good (טוֹב) toward his people while promising fertility not only to humans but also to animals (בְּהֵמָה), as in Ezek 36:11.

Therefore, the repetitive nature of vv. 10–11 may be accounted for by proposing that Ezekiel here appeals to multiple progeny blessing traditions with which he is familiar, first to the blessings of Lev 26, from which he often draws, and then to the fullest tradition regarding postexilic restoration outside the Latter Prophets (Deut 30:1–10). This thesis is further buttressed by the inclusion of וְרָבוּ וּפָרוּ in v. 11, where the inversion of the traditional verb order may suggest an allusion to a prior tradition. Although these two verbs occur together in Lev 26:9, this is probably an allusion to the creation blessings of Gen 1:28 and 9:1, 7 since they share third common plural Qal forms, absent from the rest of Ezekiel and Lev 26:9.³⁵ Thus, this phrase may be included in order to refer to a third progeny tradition. Just as NT authors or modern-day exegetes may cite various biblical texts that make a similar point, Ezekiel may here allude to and conflate three separate traditions pertaining to the progeny blessing in order to emphasize Yahweh's gracious work of blessing Israel with progeny. Or perhaps he alludes to the richness of the progeny tradition in the OT to indicate that this is at once a realization of the blessings of creation and the Sinai covenant.

Ezekiel 36:12 is transitional between the progeny blessing in vv. 10–11 and the promise in vv. 13–15 that the land will no longer decimate the people. Verse 12 begins in a manner similar to vv. 10 and 11, imitating their syntactical structure and stressing the proliferation of Israel on the land, yet now using the image of Yahweh "leading" or "causing them to walk" on the land (וְהוֹלַכְתִּי עֲלֵיכֶם אָדָם אֶת־עַמִּי יִשְׂרָאֵל), resulting in their possession of the land (וִירֵשׁוּךָ וְהָיִיתָ לָהֶם לְנַחֲלָה), perhaps drawing on legal imagery for land ownership (see Gen 13:17; Josh 24:3).³⁶

---

34. Deuteronomy 30:5 itself is a reply to Deut 28:63 where the same two verbs (רָבָה and יָטַב) are used to describe pre-judgment blessing.

35. See Greenberg, *Ezekiel 21–37*, 719; and Lapsley, *Can These Bones Live?* 161–62, for further possible creation imagery in vv. 8–11.

36. The LXX continues the theme of the progeny blessing, reading, "I will beget people on you" (γεννήσω ἐφ' ὑμᾶς ἀνθρώπους). However, this reading of Yahweh "begetting" is strange and almost certainly resulted from the confusion of consonants כ and ד in the *Vorlage* of the LXX which may have appeared to read וְהוֹלַדְתִּי. The Targum continues the progeny theme as well and begins in the same way as do vv. 10 and 11, using the Aramaic equivalent of רָבָה: "I will multiply people on you" (ואסגי עליכון אנשא), perhaps an assimilation to the prior context.

I Will Surely Multiply Your Offspring

The further comment in v. 12b, "and you (i.e., the land) will no longer bereave them of their children" (וְלֹא־תוֹסִף עוֹד לְשַׁכְּלָם), leads to the reversal of a popular saying concerning the treatment of the land toward God's people. Although in the past it had been recognized that "you devour (אֹכֶלֶת) people[37] and have been bereaving your nation(s)[38] of their children (וּמְשַׁכֶּלֶת)" (v. 13), this will no longer be the case (v. 14).[39] The verb שָׁכַל occurs twice previously in Ezekiel and denotes the result of the decimation curses of wild animals (5:17; 14:15) and famine (5:17). Leviticus 26:22 is likely the source of Ezekiel's use of this motif, including the resulting desolation of the land: "I will send wild animals against you, and they will bereave you of your children (וְשִׁכְּלָה) and destroy your animals so that you are few in number (וְהִמְעִיטָה) and your roads will be desolate (וְנָשַׁמּוּ)." Although שָׁכַל often refers to the loss of young children in particular, in the present context where the nation of Israel is addressed and the phrase is juxtaposed with the devouring of אָדָם, it probably refers to the loss of Israelites in general. This promise that the land will no longer decimate the people complements and logically precedes the growth of the population positively articulated in the previous verses. The land will now provide a positive environment that fosters rather than hinders life—the relationship between Yahweh and the land and between the people and the land is restored to health.

As a result of the new positive disposition of the land toward the people, it will no longer be subject to the insults or reproach (כְּלִמָּה //

---

37. See Lev 26:38 and Num 13:32, where the land similarly devours.

38. Each of the three occurrences of גוֹי in vv. 13–15 appears as a *Kethiv-Qere* in the MT, written in the singular but to be read as plural. Despite the fact that all Versions read the singular, the *Qere* suggests that at some point at least one of these occurrences was plural but perhaps changed to the singular to agree with the others or because Israel is typically referred to as a single nation (so Barthélemy, ed., *Ézéchiel, Daniel et les 12 Prophètes*, 295). However, the northern and southern kingdoms are together referred to as "nations" in 35:10 and 37:22. Therefore, if "nations" is the correct reading here, vv. 13–15 underscore that all twelve tribes are in view, not merely Judah. (All three occurrences are rendered as plurals by NEB, KJV, and Greenberg, *Ezekiel 21–37*, 711–12.)

39. In both v. 14b and v. 15b, different texts read either שָׁכַל ("bereave") or כָּשַׁל ("stumble"). Clearly, either accidental metathesis or deliberate assimilation (based upon the perception of accidental metathesis in the *Vorlage*) accounts for these variants. In agreement with Barthélemy it seems most likely that the variant in v. 14b ought to read שָׁכַל (with *Qere*, Versions, and many Hebrew Mss) to form a parallel with v. 13 and was wrongly assimilated to the following verse. However, v. 15b should read כָּשַׁל (with LXX and many Hebrew Mss), assuming that the alternative reading was wrongly assimilated to vv. 13–14 (*Ézéchiel, Daniel et les 12 Prophètes*, 295).

חֶרְפָּה) of surrounding nations (cf. v. 6). It is now these nations themselves who will bear insults (כְּלִמָּה; v. 7).

In most cases in the OT, it is clear that Yahweh's multiplication of the people refers to physical reproduction and the numerical expansion of the population. However, in Ezek 36:10-11, the people multiply not relative to the current size of the population but relative to the current population of Israelites in the land since the land is addressed rather than the people. From this we may conclude that vv. 10-11 refer to filling the land as a result of the return to the land rather than to the proliferation of the people themselves.[40] Indeed, the imagery of habitation, rebuilding, and possession in v. 12a suggests a shift not from some people to more people but rather from no people to many people, supporting this interpretation. However, there are indications that the numerical expansion of the population itself must be included as well: 1) It is unlikely that Ezekiel would employ three separate traditions that refer to reproductive fertility as a metaphor for the return alone. 2) Specifically, the phrase וְרָבוּ וּפָרוּ probably should not be construed as referring to anything other than physical reproduction due to its rooting in the creation blessings. In addition, the abrupt shift in person briefly changes the frame of reference from the land to the people themselves. In fact, perhaps this phrase was included to clarify the nature of multiplication in vv. 10-11. 3) Verses 12b-14 pertain to physical decimation, not simply exile from the land. It is thus likely that the same is the case for the positive articulation in vv. 10-12. It is best to conclude that both senses of multiplication are in mind in vv. 10-14 since both the return and reproduction fill the desolate land, the hope of the text.

Ezekiel 36:37-38

The citation formula in v. 16 begins a new textual unit that extends to the end of the chapter in v. 38. Although this unit is primarily concerned with the vindication of Yahweh's name, the emphasis on the rehabilitation of the land continues, especially in vv. 33-38, so that Ezek 36:16-38 remains closely tied to 35:1—36:15.[41]

40. This seems to be the interpretation adopted by Baruch J. Schwartz, who sees no concern for the well-being of the people: "[Yahweh] resolves to console the land by giving it back its population—not to console his people by giving them back their land!—and to confer security upon its inhabitants (36:1-15)" ("Ezekiel's Dim View," 61).

41. See Odell, *Ezekiel*, 436.

The compositional history of this unit has been the subject of much debate in recent decades because vv. 23b–38 are not present in the oldest known LXX manuscript, Chester Beatty papyrus 967 (approximately second-third century CE). Although some had attributed this omission to parablepsis, Johan Lust has argued that an omission of this size could hardly be accidental.[42] On the basis of the presence of rare or different language in the MT as well as in the LXX within this section, he proposes that these verses were absent from the *Vorlage* of P967 and that this papyrus represents an earlier stage in the composition of the book of Ezekiel.[43] He suggests that this section "is to a large extent an anthology of expressions found elsewhere in Ezekiel and Jeremiah . . . assembled so as to introduce chap. 37."[44] Some have accepted Lust's conclusion,[45] but others have not found him persuasive and have challenged his theory.[46] Perhaps the most significant consideration is that we must be cautious in basing a theory regarding the literary growth of a book on the basis of one manuscript, albeit an early one, given the many unknown factors that could account for the omission of vv. 23b–38. For example, the translator of P967 may have deliberately altered this section of his *Vorlage* (or the scribe altered his base manuscript) for some unknown (theological?) reason, a page may have been lost,[47] or perhaps his *Vorlage* was simply inferior. The recent discovery of a Hebrew manuscript of Ezekiel at Masada dating no later than the first century CE that does include these verses[48] casts further doubt on Lust's thesis. Furthermore, even if it could be proven that vv. 23b–38 are, in fact, a late addition, in our judgment they should still be retained within the book since their addition precedes the establishment of the final form of the text, even in the LXX.

In the new unit, Yahweh raises a theological problem: not only has Israel's disobedience defiled the land (v. 17), but also as a result of his

---

42. See Lust, "Ezekiel 36–40," 518–20.

43. See ibid., 520–25.

44. Ibid., 525.

45. See, e.g., Crane, *Israel's Restoration*, 207–64; Tov, "Recensional Differences," 100–101. See also Lust, "Textual Criticism," 29–30, where Lust addresses issues raised by Block's critique.

46. See especially the critique of Block, *Ezekiel: Chapters 25–48*, 339–43. See also Greenberg, *Ezekiel 21–37*, 739; van der Meer, "New Spirit," 147–58. Hector M. Patmore argues that P967 represents a "different," not necessarily earlier, text tradition ("Shorter and Longer Texts," 231–42).

47. See Spottorno, "La omission," 93–98.

48. See Greenberg, *Ezekiel 21–37*, 740; Patmore, "Shorter and Longer Texts," 236.

The Progeny Blessing in the Book of Ezekiel

punishment they have profaned his "holy name" (שֵׁם קָדְשִׁי; v. 20; cf. vv. 21, 22, 23). Therefore, out of deep concern for his own reputation (v. 21) among the nations (vv. 20–23), Yahweh declares that he will act for his own sake rather than for Israel's sake in both v. 22 and v. 32, forming an inclusio around vv. 23–31, which outline the actions he will undertake for Israel's benefit and for his own vindication. This encompasses the return (v. 24), inner transformation (vv. 25–29a), and the fertility of the land, promising the "multiplication" (וְהִרְבֵּיתִי) of their grain, fruit, and crops (vv. 29b–30). The exposition of inner transformation is significant, the most comprehensive description in Ezekiel of Yahweh's work within the people (cf. 11:18–20). He will cleanse (וְטִהַרְתֶּם) his people (v. 25) and give them a new heart and a new spirit (v. 26) that enable them to obey (v. 27; cf. Jer 31:31–33), resulting in a restored relationship (v. 28), not out of compassion, as in Jeremiah, but in order to restore his own reputation.

Yahweh's concern for the vindication of his honor continues in vv. 33–38.[49] Nearly all commentators treat this section as two appendices (vv. 33–36 and vv. 37–38)[50] that reiterate previous themes, possibly designed to tie the material together. Since these do appear to be two short, self-contained units, both beginning with כֹּה אָמַר אֲדֹנָי יְהוִה and concluding with the recognition formula, this hypothesis seems likely, although this in no way renders these verses less valuable or "authentic." The theme of the first unit (vv. 33–36) is the reversal of the desolation of the land, summarized as "rebuilding" (בָּנִיתִי; cf. v. 10) and "replanting" (נָטָעְתִּי) in v. 36 (cf. Jer 1:10). This unit thus returns to a theme of vv. 8–15, particularly vv. 10–11, the only other text in Ezekiel that anticipates the re-emergence of inhabited (vv. 10, 11, 33, 35) cities in the land.[51] The purpose of Yahweh's action on behalf of the land is that the nations may see it and acknowledge him as God (v. 36a), realizing his stated goal in v. 23. All of this will take place "on the day that I cleanse you from all your iniquities" (v. 33a), further linking this text literarily to vv. 22–32 (cf. v. 25) and implying that the physical restoration of the land will take place concurrently with the spiritual transformation of the people.

The second appendix (vv. 37–38) pertains to the repopulation of the cities, continuing the concern of vv. 33–36, while returning to the themes

---

49. See Block, *Ezekiel: Chapters 25–48*, 343.

50. See, e.g., Blenkinsopp, *Ezekiel*, 164; Cooke, *Ezekiel*, 386; Greenberg, *Ezekiel 21–37*, 733; Zimmerli, *Ezekiel 2*, 244–45.

51. Note that the *Leitwort* שָׁמֵם (in its verbal and nominal uses) that occurs 9x in Ezek 35 occurs 5x in vv. 34–36, providing closure to the unit that begins in 35:1.

I Will Surely Multiply Your Offspring

previously treated in vv. 8–15 (as in vv. 33–36). Earlier in the book, Yahweh refuses to listen to the requests or pleas of the people (14:3; 20:3, 31) on account of their idolatry. Now, in a "radical transformation in his disposition" that displays "the personal, sensitive side of Yahweh,"[52] he proclaims,

עוֹד זֹאת אִדָּרֵשׁ לְבֵית־יִשְׂרָאֵל [53]	37	Also, this I will allow the house of Israel to ask me to do for them:
לַעֲשׂוֹת לָהֶם		
אַרְבֶּה אֹתָם כַּצֹּאן[54] אָדָם		I will multiply their people like flocks.
כְּצֹאן קָדָשִׁים	38	Like flocks for sacrifices,
כְּצֹאן יְרוּשָׁלַם בְּמוֹעֲדֶיהָ		like flocks at Jerusalem during her appointed feasts,
כֵּן תִּהְיֶינָה הֶעָרִים הֶחֳרֵבוֹת מְלֵאוֹת צֹאן אָדָם		so the waste cities will be filled with flocks of people.
וְיָדְעוּ כִּי־אֲנִי יְהוָה		Then they will know that I am Yahweh.

The use of the "flocks" (צֹאן) metaphor (cf. 34:1–31) to denote the progeny blessing is unique in the OT, as is the expression "flocks of people" (צֹאן אָדָם). Some have suggested that this extended simile indicates the holiness of this renewed people since the most spotless lambs were reserved for sacrificial and festival purposes.[55] This may indeed be a secondary significance, but the primary point throughout is that the future people will be numerous just as the Jerusalem streets were clogged with numerous sacrificial animals during the feasts (cf. 1 Chr 29:21; 2 Chr 7:4; 29:33; 35:7–9).

That this is the one request that Ezekiel records that Yahweh will answer does not necessarily imply that this was their only request or even their greatest plea. However, v. 37 indicates that the replenishment of the population was one of the most urgent requests of the nation in exile. Yahweh's renewed favor toward his people by pledging to bless them with progeny once again was no doubt the source of great hope. The immediate goal of multiplication is filling the "waste cities" (הֶעָרִים הֶחֳרֵבוֹת), a term used elsewhere in Ezekiel only in v. 35, linking the two appendices with this common concern. As in vv. 33–36, the ultimate goal is the revitalization of Yahweh's reputation, yet this time it is the "house of Israel" who will

---

52. Block, *Ezekiel: Chapters 25–48*, 364.

53. אִדָּרֵשׁ likely denotes permission here (see Arnold and Choi, *Syntax*, 40).

54. אָדָם probably functions as an appositional clarifier for אֹתָם rather than as the material genitive of כַּצֹּאן.

55. E.g., Block, *Ezekiel: Chapters 25–48*, 365; Lapsley, *Can These Bones Live?* 169; Zimmerli, *Ezekiel 2*, 251.

acknowledge Yahweh's greatness when they witness his response to their prayer and experience the rebirth of the nation through his life-giving work as Creator.

Since the two additions in vv. 33–38 recapitulate previous themes, the progeny motif in vv. 37–38 complements its presentation in vv. 10–14. But whereas the mountains of Israel were addressed in vv. 8–15, here the people themselves are addressed. As a result, it is clear that this is not a metaphor for the return but rather refers to the multiplication of the population itself. Together, these two texts convey that both the land and the people have a vested interest in the multiplication of the people—the land yearns to be filled and the people long to be a great nation again. Land and people enjoy a symbiotic relationship as Yahweh blesses both. Unlike v. 11, in vv. 37–38 there is no clear indication that future proliferation will exceed that which was previously experienced by the nation, but the Edenic reference in v. 35 may hint at this.[56] The object of multiplication is the same, namely, the "house of Israel" (cf. v. 10), but this time there is no accompanying proliferation of animals. Since the filling of the "waste cities" links the two appendices temporally, vv. 33–38 indicate that multiplication will accompany the events of vv. 25–32 following the return, including the fertility of the fruit of the ground (vv. 29–30), so that Ezek 36 includes all three aspects of the tripartite fertility formula found in Deuteronomy. Unlike vv. 10–14, it is difficult to identify clear allusions to other OT texts or progeny traditions, although the Abrahamic promises are a possibility (see below). Since vv. 33–38 appear to be an expansion and reiteration of previous themes in Ezek 36, perhaps vv. 37–38 simply allude to vv. 10–14.

Both progeny texts in Ezek 36 include the rebuilding and filling of the ruined cities of Israel. In both texts the proliferation of the people (both through the return and reproduction) logically precedes and serves as the means by which the once-desolate cities are inhabited. In vv. 8–15 the purpose is simply to avoid insults from the nations. However, in light of vv. 16–32, vv. 33–38 teach that the rehabilitation of the cities and the resulting rehabilitation of the land are for the greater purpose of restoring honor to the name of Yahweh. Interestingly, rebuilding the cities vindicates Yahweh among the nations, and multiplication vindicates him among his own people. Although this distinction should not be pressed too far since the recognition formula is sometimes directed toward Israel and the nations for similar actions, this may be significant (see below).

---

56. See Eichrodt, *Ezekiel*, 503.

The literary units of 35:1—36:15 and 36:16-38 both conclude with the promise that God will again multiply the people. This underscores the importance of the theme and, from an editorial standpoint, may reflect that vv. 33-38 were written to bring together the hope-filled themes of 35:1—36:15 and 36:16-32. Furthermore, the sheep imagery in vv. 37-38 recalls the comparison of people to flocks in Ezek 34 (cf. 34:31), combining the most prominent motif in Ezek 34 with the repopulation motif of Ezek 36 and thus uniting all of Ezek 34–36.[57] In addition, these well-placed verses serve as a fitting introduction to Ezek 37 since God as Creator continues to grant life, now by resurrecting the nation itself (37:1-14), depicted as "an exceedingly great army" (חַיִל גָּדוֹל מְאֹד־מְאֹד; v. 10).

Ezekiel 37:26

This dramatic vision of the revival of all twelve tribes of Israel (cf. 37:11) is followed by a sign-act depicting the reunification of the tribes (37:15-20), the only place in the book that develops this theme. The divine interpretation of the sign-act (vv. 21-28) unfolds in two sections.[58] In vv. 21-23 Yahweh promises to bring back all twelve tribes from exile in order to make them "one" (אֶחָד) kingdom in the land under "one" (אֶחָד) king. Verse 24a serves as a transitional verse by concluding this emphasis on unity under "one" (אֶחָד) shepherd while naming David as the future king, one of the themes of vv. 24b-28.

This final unit in Ezek 37 stresses the perpetuity of the new ideal conditions.[59] "Forever" (לְעוֹלָם) serves as a Leitwort in these verses, occurring five times in vv. 24-28, but only four times elsewhere in the book in restoration contexts (16:60; 43:7, 9; 46:14). Four of Israel's most cherished blessings from Yahweh will endure לְעוֹלָם: possession of the land (v. 25), Davidic rule (v. 25), the covenant (v. 26), and Yahweh's presence among his people in the land (vv. 26, 28).[60] Furthermore, vv. 24-28 serve a crucial

---

57. This sheep imagery emphasizes the passivity of the people throughout these chapters of hope in contrast to God's active work on their behalf, including their proliferation (Lapsley, *Can These Bones Live?*, 168-69).

58. The prophetic word formulas in 37:15 and 38:1 demarcate the unit and tie vv. 24-28 to the prior sign-act.

59. Block rightly notes that this text still pertains to unity, but the focus has shifted since here "Yahweh unites the unified nation with himself in a permanent covenant relationship" (*Ezekiel: Chapters 25–48*, 395).

60. In each case, the clause that includes לְעוֹלָם repeats a clause found elsewhere in vv. 24-28, making the same basic assertion, yet adding the element of eternality, thus

The Progeny Blessing in the Book of Ezekiel

literary purpose, concluding the restoration texts of Ezek 34–37 by combining prominent themes from these chapters in summary fashion.[61] The final theme of the abiding sanctuary (מִקְדָּשׁ) of Yahweh among the people (vv. 26b–28) is the climactic blessing of vv. 24–28. It has not been treated previously, but in this case it anticipates the expansion of this theme in Ezek 40–48 (cf. 43:7, 9). The goal of the passage is once again recognition of Yahweh, tied specifically to his dwelling presence: "Then the nations will know that I am Yahweh who sanctifies Israel when my sanctuary is in their midst forever" (v. 28). Having promised Israel a return to their homeland, political restoration, and a renewed relationship with Yahweh based on the transformation of their hearts, it is fitting that the presentation concludes with the promise that these conditions will endure and that the threat of exile has been abolished.[62]

The "covenant of peace" (בְּרִית שָׁלוֹם) is the basis for the conditions described in vv. 24–25: this new relationship between Yahweh and Israel enables obedience which results in living in the land under David forever (cf. 36:27–28). The content of the covenant likely continues through the covenant formula in v. 27 since this often marks the conclusion of covenantal speech:

וְכָרַתִּי לָהֶם בְּרִית שָׁלוֹם	26	I will make with them a covenant of peace.
בְּרִית עוֹלָם יִהְיֶה אוֹתָם		An everlasting covenant it will be with them.
וּנְתַתִּים		I will place/join them [together],
וְהִרְבֵּיתִי אוֹתָם		and I will multiply them,
וְנָתַתִּי אֶת־מִקְדָּשִׁי בְּתוֹכָם לְעוֹלָם		and I will place my sanctuary in their midst forever.
וְהָיָה מִשְׁכָּנִי עֲלֵיהֶם	27	My dwelling will be over them,
וְהָיִיתִי לָהֶם לֵאלֹהִים		and I will be their God,
וְהֵמָּה יִהְיוּ־לִי לְעָם		and they will be my people.

The phrase אוֹתָם וְהִרְבֵּיתִי וּנְתַתִּים is missing in the oldest LXX tradition. Some reject its originality, attributing this minus to the earlier, shorter edition of Ezekiel, subsequently added to the MT.[63] However, most rightly

---

further underscoring the unshakable nature of these four promises.

61. Nearly every phrase in vv. 24–26 has occurred previously in the book: v. 24: 34:23–24; 36:27; v. 25: 28:25–26; 34:24–25; 36:28; v. 26: 16:60; 34:25; 36:10–11, 37. Accordingly, these verses are commonly thought to represent one of the latest stages in the composition of the book (e.g., Zimmerli, *Ezekiel 2*, 273). See Block, *Ezekiel: Chapters 25–48*, 394 n. 6.

62. See Zimmerli, *Ezekiel 2*, 276.

63. See Eichrodt, *Ezekiel*, 512.

retain at least the multiplication clause since it is more likely that the LXX is the result of scribal error. The fact that אוֹתָם brackets this phrase suggests parablepsis by homoeoteleuton, or possibly homoeoarchton from the repetition of וְנָתַתִּי.

Many scholars do, however, doubt the originality of וּנְתַתִּים given the semantic and syntactical difficulties it presents.[64] The third masculine plural pronoun certainly refers to the people of Israel, but the expression seems to lack either an indirect object or a locative prepositional phrase. However, the UBS Committee for the Textual Analysis of the Hebrew Old Testament points out that "to employ the verb נתן in the sense of 'to establish in a position and a place well chosen' was characteristic of the book of Ezekiel," citing 17:22 and 34:26.[65] They further point out that LXX recensions (including Aquila, Theodotian, and the Lucian recension) include both the multiplication clause and וּנְתַתִּים, and thus assign a "B" rating in favor of the MT.[66] Indeed, this phrase ought to be retained given the paucity of external evidence against it and since it is comprehensible in context. With respect to its meaning, the Targum (followed by the NRSV) understood this to be a shorthand parallel to 34:26 (וְנָתַתִּי אוֹתָם וּסְבִיבוֹת גִּבְעָתִי בְּרָכָה), rendering it "I will bless them." Alternatively, given the use of נָתַן in the context of the gift of the land and the prevalence of this theme, this may be shorthand for "I will place them in the land."[67] But the best indicator of meaning may be the preceding context in v. 19. There Yahweh declares that he will place the stick of Ephraim onto the stick of Judah: וְנָתַתִּי אוֹתָם עָלָיו אֶת־עֵץ יְהוּדָה. Thus וּנְתַתִּים may recall וְנָתַתִּי אוֹתָם in v. 19 as shorthand for reunification, providing a link between the summary of vv. 24–28 and the immediately preceding theme.

---

64. E.g., Allen, *Ezekiel 20–48*, 189; Cooke, *Ezekiel*, 403; and Zimmerli, *Ezekiel 2*, 270; accept the multiplication clause but reject this word. The theory of D. Johannes Herrmann that וּנְתַתִּים was a marginal note to mark the insertion of the lost multiplication clause that then found its way into the text itself (*Ezechiel*, 234) has been deemed plausible by each of these commentators, giving further weight to the rejection of the term. Although this is possible, no manuscript evidence exists to support either the presence of a marginal note or the inclusion of the multiplication clause but the absence of וּנְתַתִּים.

65. Barthélemy, *Ézéchiel, Daniel et les 12 Prophétes*, 301.

66. See ibid., 300–301.

67. See ESV. However, the people are usually the indirect object of the verb. Block proposes that the third common plural suffix is a "dative suffix" and that the phrase is thus shorthand for the land grant formula: "I will give to them [the land of Israel]" (cf. 11:17) (*Ezekiel: Chapters 25–48*, 408 n. 86). Although possible, dative suffixes are rare (e.g., Gen 17:6; Zech 7:5; see *IBHS* 304–5), making this option less likely.

The Progeny Blessing in the Book of Ezekiel

If וּנְתַתִּים does indeed refer to reunification, it would naturally complement the multiplication clause since both would pertain to the renewal of the population of the nation, first by recovering the ten lost tribes, then by reproduction. Thus, its juxtaposition with multiplication here might add a dimension of significance to reunification not mentioned earlier.

The multiplication clause itself (וְהִרְבֵּיתִי אוֹתָם) is succinct, more like its articulation in Jeremiah than in its previous appearances in Ezekiel that entail greater development. This proliferation will take place back in the land (v. 25) at some undefined point in the future beyond exile.[68] Clearly, it pertains to all twelve tribes, regardless of the meaning of the preceding clause. The ultimate purpose of multiplication is the same as that of the passage as a whole: for the sake of Yahweh's reputation among the nations (v. 28). This goal is tied most directly to his presence among the people in the sanctuary, but this presence is expressed and displayed in part by means of the proliferation of Israel.

Furthermore, multiplication occurs here under Davidic rule, a correlation that we observed in Jeremiah, but has been absent thus far in Ezekiel (unless 34:23–31 is taken into account). In general, the idyllic picture of vv. 24–28 resembles the golden years of the United Monarchy when Yahweh had richly blessed Israel with progeny (see 1 Kgs 4:20). Thus, at the very least, the people will probably be as numerous as they were in the days of David and Solomon. Perhaps they will even transcend these proportions since the covenant is inviolable and perpetual and therefore this blessing will never cease.

We should note that the progeny blessing is not one of the four emphasized eternal blessings of vv. 24–28, so its role in the present passage should not be overemphasized. Nevertheless, its inclusion here in the climactic collection of the great themes of restoration does imply that it is a significant blessing for Ezekiel. In fact, it is one of only three explicit benefits of the covenant of peace alongside reunification (assuming our interpretation of וּנְתַתִּים) and God's presence with the people.

Ezekiel 34:23–31 and Lev 26:4–13 shed further light on the role of the progeny blessing in 37:26. We have already summarized the former text, the only other place in Ezekiel that mentions a "covenant of peace" (בְּרִית שָׁלוֹם; v. 25), implying that these two texts are mutually interpreting. Ezekiel 34:23–31 and 37:24–28 share a number of themes, including the

---

68. Block notes that this portrays "not so much the consummation, the end of history, as its climax" (*Ezekiel: Chapters 25–48*, 417). It is not indicated whether these events will take place in the near or distant future, but they will be final.

restoration of Davidic leadership (34:23–24; 37:24–25), Yahweh's presence with his people (34:30; 37:26–28), the permanence of the new conditions (34:28–29; 37:25–28), and a form of the covenant formula in conclusion (34:30; 37:27).[69] But much of the content appears to be different. Ezekiel 34:25–29 describes the removal of the decimation curses of sword, famine, and wild animals at length whereas 37:26–27 has nothing explicit to say on the matter. We suggest, however, that this emphasis is summarized in 37:26 in the simple and succinct statement, "I will multiply them." The difference in presentation can be accounted for by the differing literary (and perhaps historical) contexts in which these two texts appear. Ezekiel 34 reflects on the judgment that they have experienced from Yahweh and the abuse that they have endured at the hands of corrupt "shepherds." Therefore, Ezekiel paints a hopeful future by anticipating the removal of the pain of the past. In contrast, 37:26–27 is entirely forward-looking, employing only positive language to describe the glorious future, including its articulation of the progeny blessing. Thus 37:26–27 confirms our earlier judgment that the progeny blessing is indeed present in 34:25–30 as well, and therefore the progeny blessing is a prominent component of the future covenant of peace in Ezekiel.

As was the case for Ezek 34:25–30, it appears that 37:24–28 is dependent on Lev 26. In particular, "Ezekiel 37:26–27 is an expansion and reworking of Lev 26:9, 11a, 12:"[70]

Leviticus 26	Ezekiel 37
(v. 9) וְהִפְרֵיתִי אֶתְכֶם וְהִרְבֵּיתִי אֶתְכֶם	(v. 26) וְהִרְבֵּיתִי אוֹתָם
(v. 9) וַהֲקִימֹתִי אֶת־בְּרִיתִי אִתְּכֶם	(v. 26) וְכָרַתִּי לָהֶם בְּרִית שָׁלוֹם
(v. 11) וְנָתַתִּי מִשְׁכָּנִי בְּתוֹכְכֶם	(v. 26) וְנָתַתִּי אֶת־מִקְדָּשִׁי בְּתוֹכָם[71]
(v. 12) וְהָיִיתִי לָכֶם לֵאלֹהִים	(v. 27) וְהָיִיתִי לָהֶם לֵאלֹהִים
(v. 12) וְאַתֶּם תִּהְיוּ־לִי לְעָם	(v. 27) וְהֵמָּה יִהְיוּ־לִי לְעָם

---

69. Furthermore, it is clear that there is a relationship between these two texts since the following phrases occur only here in Ezekiel: עַבְדִּי דָוִד (34:23; 37:24); רוֹעֶה אֶחָד (34:23; 37:24); David as נָשִׂיא (34:24; 37:25); וְכָרַתִּי לָהֶם בְּרִית שָׁלוֹם (34:25; 37:26).

70. Milgrom, "Leviticus 26 and Ezekiel," 60. He further claims that the clauses in vv. 9–12 not employed by Ezekiel (vv. 10, 11b) would be irrelevant in this new context (60). See also Allen, *Ezekiel 20–48*, 192, 194; Greenberg, *Ezekiel 21–37*, 760. Dieter Baltzer combines the parallels to Lev 26:4–13 from both Ezek 34 and 37 and demonstrates that they draw from different verses but together incorporate most of the content of Lev 26:4–13 (*Ezechiel und Deuterojesaja*, 156–57).

71. Note that מִשְׁכָּנִי is used in the next clause in v. 27a.

It is precisely the content of the covenant of peace in Ezek 37:26-27 that draws from Lev 26:9-12, indicating that Lev 26:9 is the source for the progeny blessing in v. 26. However, Ezekiel does not use the entire formula, perhaps because he deemed this Priestly formula to be redundant. As was the case in Ezekiel's previous adaptations of Leviticus, the primary shift lies in the fact that these promises are no longer contingent but are guaranteed "forever." Living in the land is still contingent upon obedience (Lev 26:3f; Ezek 37:24-25), but obedience is now assured.[72]

Finally, we must consider the nature of this covenant and its relationship to previous covenants. Both descriptions of the covenant of peace focus on the material benefits[73] following the return rather than on inner transformation (although Yahweh's presence is a key component). Based on the components of the covenant, שָׁלוֹם likely denotes holistic well-being and entails the cessation of Yahweh's wrath against the people, resulting in a harmonious relationship with Yahweh, with the nations, and with the land,[74] a peace previously absent (13:10, 16). Ezekiel 37:26 equates this covenant with the "everlasting covenant" (בְּרִית עוֹלָם)[75] previously mentioned in 16:60-63, where Yahweh promises to "remember" (וְזָכַרְתִּי; 16:60) and "uphold" (וַהֲקִמוֹתִי; 16:60, 62)[76] what is most likely the Abrahamic covenant.[77] Indeed, the blessings mentioned in Ezek 37:24-28 correspond closely to those of the Abrahamic covenant: land (v. 25), progeny (v. 26) and presence (vv. 26-28). Furthermore, it is clear that the content of the covenant of peace is continuous with the blessings of the Sinai covenant since they correspond to Lev 26. Therefore, vv. 24-28 probably allude to the original promise to the patriarchs, mediated through the blessings of the Sinai covenant, and now permanently enacted for the sake of Yahweh's

---

72. It appears that both 34:25-30 and 37:24-28 are dependent on Lev 26 rather than on each other (see Allen, *Ezekiel 20-48*, 192), although the Davidic content could be due to borrowing between them.

73. Bernard Gosse states that these verses describe "the paradisical character of the era" ("La nouvelle alliance," 426).

74. See Polan, "Ezekiel's Covenant," 20; Block, *Ezekiel: Chapters 25-48*, 422.

75. בְּרִית עוֹלָם is used to describe various covenants throughout the OT, including the Noachic (Gen 9:16), Abrahamic (Gen 9:16; 17:7, 13, 19; Ps 105:10), and Davidic (Isa 55:3) covenants.

76. This verb does not denote the establishment of a new covenant but rather the maintenance of an existing covenant (e.g., Gen 6:18; 17:7; Lev 26:9). See Block, *Ezekiel: Chapters 1-24*, 516; Boadt, "Salvation Oracles," 14; Dumbrell, *Covenant and Creation*, 190.

77. See Block, *Ezekiel: Chapters 1-24*, 516-17; Schwartz, "Ezekiel's Dim View," 48. Note also the reference to Jacob in 37:25.

name. Thus, the covenant of peace is both new and not new. Yahweh's previous covenants made with Abraham, Israel, and David[78] are all affirmed and realized in the context of this final covenant. With respect to the progeny blessing, there is nothing fundamentally new about its inclusion in the covenant of peace since it has been present in all previous covenants, but its guarantee and perpetuity are an improvement upon previous covenants.

Conclusion: A Summary of the Progeny Blessing in Ezekiel

The contours of the progeny blessing in Ezekiel are more monolithic than was the case in either Isaiah or Jeremiah. The blessing is consistently expressed with רָבָה in its Hiphil form with Yahweh as the agent (36:10, 11, 37; 37:26). The only exception is in 36:11, which includes the phrase וְרָבוּ וּפָרוּ. Typical of Ezekiel's style, he develops this theme beyond this simple verb. In 36:12–14, he includes the reversal of bereavement, personifying the land and implying that, in order for the people to multiply in the future, both Yahweh and the land must be favorably disposed toward them. In 36:37–38, the imagery of flocks of sheep depicts the extent of future proliferation. While Ezek 36:37–38 and 37:26 address the people themselves, 36:10–14 addresses the land. That not only the people but also the land benefit from the multiplication of the population (cf. also 36:37–38) indicates the close relationship between the people and the land with respect to Yahweh's blessing.[79]

According to Ezekiel, the multiplication of the people will occur in the land promised to the fathers following the imminent (cf. 36:8) return. Ezekiel 36:33a indicates that this will coincide with the cleansing of their sin, while 37:24–28 claims that Yahweh's blessing will be abiding and final. All twelve tribes will experience proliferation, expressed in all three primary texts either by means of the phrase "the house of Israel" (36:10, 37) or through the reunification theme (37:14–28). Ezekiel 36:11 extends the progeny promise to the animal realm, but there is no indication that the nations will experience it. Based on 36:11 and 37:24–28, it appears that Ezekiel anticipates an expansion of the nation exceeding anything previously experienced in the nation's history.

---

78. Block shows that vv. 24–25 are dependent on 2 Sam 7 and that these verses therefore reaffirm the Davidic covenant (*Ezekiel: Chapters 25–48*, 418).

79. See Block, *Gods of the Nations*, 110–11.

The Progeny Blessing in the Book of Ezekiel

If we include 34:23-31, the progeny blessing surfaces twice in the context of the covenant of peace under Davidic rule (34:23-31; 37:24-28) and twice in the context of the rebuilding and reinhabiting of cities in the land (36:10-14, 33-38). Thus the progeny blessing is one facet of the social rehabilitation of the nation. Although it is juxtaposed with Yahweh's presence in the land in 37:26-28, it does not occur in the context of the spiritual rehabilitation of the people. As we read synchronically, these related themes occur chiastically in these four texts (covenant-rebuilding-rebuilding-covenant). However, it seems unlikely that this chiasm is intentional. Rather, the two central occurrences are united by their common content in Ezek 36 and the two expositions of the covenant of peace are intentionally placed in order to introduce and conclude the words of hope in Ezek 34-37.

The exposition of covenant blessings in Lev 26:4-13 clearly serves as the primary source for the progeny blessing as it appears in Ezek 34:25-30, 36:10-11, and 37:26 (as well as 36:27-28 via 36:10-14). These three texts exhibit the clearest uses of Lev 26:4-13 in the book, which suggests that the progeny theme was worthy of mention whenever this text was employed (though indirectly in 34:25-30).[80] By using this text, Ezekiel indicates that Israel's future prosperity in the land will entail many of the same blessings that she was to experience under the Sinai covenant. However, under the "covenant of peace," their enjoyment will be assured and irrevocable due to Yahweh's gift of a new heart and spirit.

However, Lev 26:9 is not the sole progeny text that corresponds to the progeny texts of Ezekiel. The restoration blessings of Deut 30:5, 9 and the creation blessing of Gen 1:28; 9:1, 7 are both reflected in Ezek 36:11. In addition, Ezek 37:26 may be associated with 1 Kgs 4:20 given their common depiction of the golden age of the United Monarchy. Ezekiel is also similar to Jeremiah with respect to the progeny blessing. For example, 1) both books include it as a key element in their portrayal of the future covenant (Jer 31:27; Ezek 37:26);[81] 2) both include the proliferation of animals alongside people (Jer 31:27; Ezek 36:11); and 3) both reverse the common וּפָרוּ וְרָבוּ expression (Jer 3:16; Ezek 36:11). Such correspondences may have arisen independently or from a common source, although there is no clear evidence that Jeremiah made use of Lev 26:9. More likely, the

---

80. Furthermore, this may verify common authorship of our progeny texts (see Allen, *Ezekiel 20-48*, 171).

81. Note as well that the progeny blessing in Ezek 36:10-14 and 37:38 encloses the "new heart and new spirit" text of vv. 26-27.

two are interdependent, but it is the similarities themselves that are most crucial to note.

The Abrahamic promise of progeny has been largely absent from our discussion thus far. Ezekiel seldom refers explicitly to the patriarchal promises in the course of the book,[82] and his references to the progeny blessing do not clearly allude to the Abrahamic promise. Nevertheless, there is reason to believe that he may have had it in mind. In Ezek 36, the repossession of the land and the multiplication of the people go hand-in-hand (36:10–14, 33–38). This is perhaps most transparent in the two additions at the end of the chapter where the first (vv. 33–36) pertains to land and the second (vv. 37–38) pertains to progeny.[83] Clearly, there is a logical relationship between the two, but this juxtaposition may allude to Yahweh's material blessings in his covenant commitment to Abraham in order to affirm that Yahweh would uphold it. Perhaps the request for multiplication (v. 37) was grounded in doubts concerning Yahweh's fidelity to this covenant. Moreover, this hypothesis would make sense of Yahweh's positive response, revealing him as Yahweh to Israel in particular (v. 38). It is also striking that the only other text promising the proliferation of the people (37:26) immediately follows one of the few references in the book to the patriarchal land promise: "they will dwell in the land I gave to my servant Jacob" (v. 25).[84] Once again, the progeny blessing is juxtaposed with recovery of the land. Therefore, even though the covenant blessings of Lev 26:4–13 appear to have been the primary source for Ezekiel's use of the progeny blessing, it is likely that, in his view, the blessing furthers the Abrahamic progeny promise, as is likely with the covenant blessings in Leviticus and Deuteronomy themselves, as argued above. This must remain a tentative conclusion since one would expect this connection to be more explicit if Yahweh's fidelity to the Abrahamic covenant is indeed one of Ezekiel's theological concerns. Nevertheless, it remains a "subtext" that his exilic audience may have detected.

In both 36:10–14 and 36:33–38, the immediate purpose of multiplication is that the desolate cities might be rebuilt and inhabited once again. However, significantly, each textual unit including the progeny blessing

---

82. The only mention of Abraham in the book occurs in 33:24 with respect to his possession of the land. The gift of the land to Jacob is noted in 28:25 and 37:25.

83. See Allen, *Ezekiel 20–48*, 179. Similarly, Block states that the promises of 36:8–15 are in response to the question of whether or not Yahweh had remembered the Abrahamic commitment (*Ezekiel: Chapters 25–48*, 336).

84. Accordingly, Block asserts that the multiplication clause here alludes to the Abrahamic promise (*Ezekiel: Chapters 25–48*, 420).

concludes with a form of the recognition formula. As Yahweh explains to his people, his actions on behalf of Israel (including the progeny blessing) are "for the sake of my holy name" (36:22). Thus, the ultimate purpose of Yahweh's act of multiplying the people is that he might be vindicated and acknowledged as Yahweh by the world. His blessing results in knowledge of him among the mountains of Israel in 36:11, among Israel herself in 36:38 (see also 34:30), and among the nations in 37:28 (although here it is explicitly tied to his presence, not the progeny blessing). The explosion of the population will reveal Yahweh to be the covenant-keeping God of their fathers, in continuity with the Abrahamic covenant and the covenant blessings of Sinai, now permanently guaranteed.

6

The Progeny Blessing in the Book of the Twelve

Reading the Book of the Twelve

IN RECENT YEARS, A number of scholars have argued that the twelve minor prophets ought to be read together as one coherent book.[1] Historical, literary, and theological arguments have been proffered to justify this claim:

1. All the available evidence from 200 BCE to 400 CE indicates that the Twelve were preserved together on one scroll and counted as one book.[2]

2. The individual books are linked to one another at the seams by means of "catchwords" or *Stichwörter*. Some of the proposed catchwords may be merely coincidental. In some cases they may have dictated the organization of the twelve prophetic books within the larger collection. In other cases these links may be the result of intentional redaction.[3] Overall, these catchwords create a literary unity that may indicate that the Twelve are to be read together.

---

1. See Collins, *Mantle of Elijah*, 59–87; House, *Unity of the Twelve*; House and Watts, eds., *Forming Prophetic Literature*; Nogalski, *Literary Precursors*; Nogalski, *Redactional Processes*; Nogalski and Sweeney, eds., *Reading and Hearing*; Redditt and Schart, eds., *Thematic Threads*; Seitz, *Prophecy*; and the articles in *Interpretation* 61 (2007): 115–97.

2. See 4QXIIa–b; 8HevXIIgr; MurXII; Sir 49:10; 4 *Ezra* 14:41; *Ag. Ap.* I.40; *B. Bat.* 13b–15a; LXX.

3. Nogalski entertains all three possibilities on a case-by-case basis in his thorough study in *Literary Precursors* and *Redactional Processes* (see *Literary Precursors*, 13–16).

The Progeny Blessing in the Book of the Twelve

3. Several prominent motifs reappear in many or most of the twelve prophets, creating thematic coherence. The Day of Yahweh (יוֹם יְהוָה) concept is perhaps the clearest such example since this theme plays a minor role in Isaiah, Jeremiah, and Ezekiel, but is common in the Twelve.[4] The multi-dimensional שׁוּב motif is present in nearly every minor prophet as well.[5] In addition, themes such as the fertility of the land, the character of God as revealed in Exod 34:6–7, and theodicy unite these works.[6]

4. Some of the individual books in the Twelve are lacking one or more of the major prophetic themes that we encounter in each of the major prophets. However, reading the twelve works together creates a theologically-rich blend of all these themes comparable to that of the other major prophets.

5. It is clear that both the MT and LXX (which contain slightly different arrangements) have ordered the Twelve in a meaningful way so as to create flow from one book to the next and from the beginning of the Twelve to the end. This ordering is mostly chronological, but thematic factors, the length of each work, and catchwords at the seams may have played a role as well.[7] Given these considerations, there is clearly more to the joining of the Twelve than the claim of *Pesah* 87b that they were combined to prevent the individual books from being lost since they are small.

However, we must not read the Twelve as one book in the same manner as we read Isaiah, Jeremiah, or Ezekiel:[8]

1. The most important (and most obvious) consideration is that the Twelve preserve twelve different headings citing twelve different prophets and maintain literary divisions between the different works. Furthermore, no title or introduction exists prior to Hosea to indicate that the Twelve ought to be read as one book. Although

---

4. See Rendtorff, "How to Read," 75–87; and the detailed studies, Beck, *Der "Tag YHWHs"*; Schwesig, *Die Rolle*.

5. See Bowman, "Reading the Twelve," 54.

6. See Collins, *Mantle of Elijah*, 65; Nogalski, "Recurring Themes," 125–46.

7. See Jones, *Formation*; Seitz, *Prophecy*, 204–16; Sweeney, "Sequence and Interpretation," 49–64, for explanations for the growth and present order of the Twelve. See Schart, "Reconstructing," 34–48, for a review of scholarly reconstructions of the redactional and compositional history of the Twelve as a whole.

8. See ben Zvi, "Twelve Prophetic Books," 125–56, for the most comprehensive argument against reading the Twelve as one book.

some have compared the book of the Twelve to Isaiah (assuming the critical view that the latter was written by many hands over 300 years or more), Isaiah presents itself as one book whereas the Book of the Twelve does not.

2. The collection of the twelve prophets on one scroll, the presence of catchwords at the seams, and the intentional organization of the Twelve do not necessitate a reading strategy that treats the Twelve as one book with a developing plot.[9]

3. Moreover, attempts to read the Twelve as one work with a developing plot are not compelling. For example, House proposes that the Twelve exhibit a comedic plot from sin (Hosea–Micah) to judgment (Nahum–Zephaniah) to restoration (Haggai–Malachi).[10] However, this is probably due to the chronological arrangement of the books and the historical situation underlying each work rather than the result of a conscious effort to construct a coherent plotline. Furthermore, such a generalization is reductionistic to the point of being misleading altogether. For example, Zechariah contains more oracles of restoration than any other book in the Twelve, but Hosea is a close second, followed by Micah.

4. The difference in sequence in the LXX and MT is an additional difficulty for those wishing to treat the Twelve as a coherent work.

5. Finally, each of the twelve prophets has it own structure, language, and themes.[11]

The total evidence leads us to a mediating position regarding the viability of reading the Twelve as one book. On the one hand, each of the twelve books retains a distinct voice so that a literary unit within Hosea (for example) should be understood primarily within the context of Hosea. On the other hand, it appears that we are invited to read the twelve works together as mutually interpreting and complementary voices. Even if we do not treat the Twelve as a "book" but simply as a carefully organized collection or anthology, the whole is greater than and somewhat different from the sum of the parts. Inevitably, interpreting Hosea within the context of the Twelve will affect how it is understood. Moreover, different emphases will emerge when the Book of the Twelve is read as a whole. In

9. See ibid., 130–42.

10. See House, *Unity of the Twelve*, 109, 161. Similarly, see Redditt, *Introduction*, 204–5.

11. See ben Zvi, "Twelve Prophetic Books," 151–54.

The Progeny Blessing in the Book of the Twelve

sum, we will read the Twelve both as individual books and as one work.[12] As a result, our examination of the progeny blessing in the book of the Twelve will entail a synthesis of the progeny motif in the context of each individual prophet in which it appears, as well as a brief synthesis of the progeny blessing in the entire book (or rather, collection) of the Twelve.

Scholars have observed that fertility/infertility of the land is one of the themes that unifies the twelve prophets.[13] Fertility is the mark of God's blessing (Hos 2:17[15], 23–24[21–22]; 14:6–8[5–7]; Joel 2:19, 22–26; 4:18; Amos 9:13–14; Hag 2:19; Zech 8:12; 9:17–10:1; Mal 3:10–11), and infertility is the sign of his displeasure (Hos 8:7; 9:2; Joel 1; Amos 4:6–9; Hab 3:17; Hag 1:10–11). We might expect the "fertility of the womb" to be just as pervasive since these two themes are commonly combined in Deuteronomy (see 7:13–14; 28:4, 11; 30:9). However, we do not find this to be the case, since the progeny blessing occurs only in Hosea and Zechariah among the Twelve. Accordingly, we will study only these two prophets.[14]

Introduction to the Book of Hosea

Hosea's Use of Prior Traditions

Perhaps more than any other writing prophet, Hosea's oracles are thoroughly grounded in Israel's prior traditions. On multiple occasions, Hosea alludes to the patriarchal narratives (2:1[1:10]; 11:8–9; 12:2–6[1–5], 12–13) and the wilderness traditions (2:16–17[14–15]; 9:10; 11:3; 12:10[9]; 13:5). Like other prophets, he uses the exodus motif both to remind the people of Yahweh's grace in the past (11:1–4; 12:10[9], 14[13]; 13:4–5) and as a type for future restoration (11:10–11). Furthermore, the reversal of the exodus serves as an image for exile (8:13; 9:3; 11:5). In his view, "[t]he present community can only understand its dilemma in the context of these historical traditions."[15] Hosea's indictment of Israel is based on

---

12. See Petersen, *The Prophetic Literature*, 176; Rendtorff, *Canonical Hebrew Bible*, 266; Sweeney, *Twelve Prophets: Volume One*, xxxix; who maintain a similar balance.

13. See Collins, *Mantle of Elijah*, 65. See the extended treatment of this theme by Nogalski in "Intertextuality," 113–16 and "Joel as 'Literary Anchor,'" 98, 101–4.

14. This is not to say that nothing could be said regarding the progeny blessing elsewhere in the Twelve since some of the other prophets attest to population decimation. However, the contribution of these other books toward a synthesis of the blessing in the Twelve is negligible since any positive articulation of the progeny motif is absent.

15. Brueggemann, *Tradition*, 36. See 26–36 for a summary of Hosea's use of historical traditions.

235

their breach of the Sinai "covenant" (6:7; 8:1) and their rejection of Yahweh's תּוֹרָה (4:1–3, 6; 8:1, 12). As both Stuart and Brueggemann argue, the sentence for violation of the covenant stipulations is based on the curses of Lev 26 and Deut 28. Moreover, Israel's future restoration is rooted in the covenant blessings found in these same chapters.[16] In sum, Hosea is hardly an innovator, functioning as a covenant mediator after the pattern of Moses.[17]

Future Hope in Hosea

In the end, Israel will be restored simply because Yahweh loves them. Yahweh's emotional descriptions of his tender care and unconditional compassion for his people (1:7; 2:16–25[14–23]; 11:1–4, 8–11; 13:5; 14:5[4], 9[8]) are unmatched in the prophets.[18] Accordingly, Yahweh will renew the "marriage" and the covenant with Israel (2:18–22[16–20]) and will again declare them to be "his people" (2:1[1:10]; 2:3[1], 25[23]).

This rejuvenated relationship will accompany the complete restoration of Israel to the land, described in 2:1–3[1:10–2:1], 2:16–25[14–23], 3:5, 6:11—7:1, 11:8–11, and 14:5–9[4–8]. The return to the land itself is explicit only in 11:10–11, where it is portrayed as a second exodus, but 2:2[1:11] and 2:25[2:23] may allude to it as well (see below). A reunified nation of Israel will be restored to the land under one (Davidic) leader (2:2[1:11]; 3:5). The population will expand (2:1[1:10]; 2:25[23]) and the land will be fruitful (2:17[15], 24[22]; 14:8[7]). Yahweh will heal his people (6:11; 7:1) and peace and safety will prevail (2:20[18]). Nearly all the restoration blessings found in other prophetic books are present in Hosea's portrayal of the future. The only missing typical blessing is power over and protection from enemy peoples. This is unsurprising since Hosea only expresses interest in God's own people and has nothing to say concerning the positive or negative futures of the nations.

---

16. See ibid., 76–78; Stuart, *Hosea–Jonah*, 6–7.

17. See Brueggemann, *Tradition*, 98–100.

18. Yahweh expresses his compassion for his people elsewhere in the Twelve in Joel 2:18; Mic 7:18–20; Zech 1:16–17; 10:6.

The Progeny Blessing in Hosea

Population Decimation in Hosea

With respect to judgment, as we find in the Sinai covenant curses and in the Major Prophets, one of Yahweh's principle means of disciplining his people in Hosea is the decimation of their population. Yahweh will kill (וַהֲמִתִּיהָ) the personified land of Israel (2:5[3]), rip the people in pieces as a lion (5:14; 6:5; 13:8), and send the sword against them (7:16; 11:6; 14:1[13:16]). In 9:10–17 we encounter a direct reversal of the blessing of progeny. Ephraim will be cursed with "no birth, no pregnancy, no conception" (מִלֵּדָה וּמִבֶּטֶן וּמֵהֵרָיוֹן; v. 11). Even if they manage to raise children, Yahweh declares, "I will bereave them" (וְשִׁכַּלְתִּים; v. 12) and "kill" (וְהֵמַתִּי) their offspring (v. 16) so that now they "bring out their children for slaughter" (לְהוֹצִיא אֶל־הֹרֵג בָּנָיו; v. 13). The prophet affirms this judgment[19] by praying that God will "give them a miscarrying womb and dry breasts" (תֵּן־לָהֶם רֶחֶם מַשְׁכִּיל וְשָׁדַיִם צֹמְקִים; v. 14), a reversal of the blessing on Joseph in Gen 49:25.[20] Ironically, Ephraim, the "fruitful one," will no longer bear fruit (בְּלִי־יַעֲשׂוּן פֶּרִי; v. 16). Similarly, in the concluding (and perhaps summarizing) judgment sentence in the book, Ephraim will be rendered fruitless (13:15) and children and pregnant women alike will be slaughtered (14:1[13:16]; cf. 10:14).

The Fertility Motif in Hosea

The curse of human infertility is one aspect of the fertility motif that pervades the book of Hosea. Hosea identifies Baal as the primary god with whom the people have committed adultery against Yahweh. Since Baal (along with his consort, Anath) served as the Canaanite fertility god of agriculture, animals, and the human womb,[21] Yahweh's (and Hosea's) confrontation with Baal concerns who is the true source of fertility, particularly with respect to agricultural yields. Accordingly, both ensuing judgment and distant restoration pertain to fertility to a greater extent than we typically find in the prophets. This theme is most prominent in

---

19. Deborah Krause rightly argues that this is an "ironic and judgmental" assent to the death sentence ("Blessing," 191–94).

20. See ibid., 196–97; Beal, "Blessings Lost," 23.

21. See Albright, *Archaeology*, 73–79; Blenkinsopp, *History of Prophecy*, 88–89; Wolff, *Hosea*, 38–39.

the book's introductory lawsuit (2:4[2]) in Hos 2. All along, food and drink have been supplied by Yahweh (2:10[8]). However, because Israel attributed her sustenance to her new "lovers" and did not acknowledge Yahweh as the source, Yahweh will demonstrate that he is the only God of fertility by rescinding grain, wine, flax, wool, figs, and Israel's joyous festivals (Hos 2:7–17[5–15]; cf. 8:7; 9:2).[22] Nevertheless, when Yahweh restores his relationship with his bride in the future, he will again provide grain, wine, and oil for Israel (2:16[14], 23–24[21–22]). In addition, Hosea employs fertility language metaphorically to represent Israel (9:16; 10:1) and to depict Yahweh's judgment (9:16; 13:15) or favor (6:3; 14:6–8[5–7]) toward the people. In Yahweh's final word in the book (14:9[8]) just prior to the concluding note to the reader (14:10[9]), he reaffirms that he is Israel's sole provider: "from me comes your fruit" (מִמֶּנִּי פֶּרְיְךָ נִמְצָא).[23] Although Hosea does not connect the Baal cult to human fertility as clearly as he does for the fertility of the land in Hos 2:7–17[5–15], the book's treatment of the progeny blessing reveals a similar polemical thrust.

Hosea 2:1–3 [1:10—2:1]

The first literary unit in Hosea (1:2—2:3[1]) is programmatic in that it summarizes Hosea's key themes and provides a pattern for the rest of the book, moving from indictment (1:2) to sentence (1:4–9) to restoration (2:1–3[1:10—2:1]).[24] Hosea's three "children of harlotry" (יַלְדֵי זְנוּנִים) conceived with his "wife of harlotry" (אֵשֶׁת זְנוּנִים; v. 2) represent the people of the northern kingdom of Israel and signify both their sin and their punishment. With the birth of each child, the gravity of the coming judgment increases.[25] "Jezreel" (יִזְרְעֶאל) has ambiguous connotations, referring to the city in v. 4 and the valley in v. 5, while the accompanying judgment focuses on the royal house of Jehu for his deeds as recorded in 2 Kgs 9–10. The seriousness of the judgment for the whole northern kingdom becomes more clear with the birth of "No Compassion" (לֹא רֻחָמָה; literally,

---

22. This corresponds to the covenant curses on the land in Lev 26:16, 20 and Deut 28:38–40, although these Pentateuchal texts do not have the same polemical twist (cf. Deut 7:13; 11:8–17).

23. See Braaten, "God Sows," 104–32, on the role of the land and fertility themes in Hosea.

24. See Silva, "Literary Structure," 190; Wolff, *Hosea*, 26.

25. See Wolff, *Hosea*, 23.

"not having obtained compassion"),[26] but even more severe with the birth of "Not My People" (לֹא עַמִּי), the negation of the ubiquitous "covenant formula," indicating that the covenant relationship between Yahweh and Israel has been severed (v. 9).

Shockingly, without any transition or explanation concerning how this might still be possible, 2:1–3[1:10—2:1] then proclaims future blessing and the restoration of the relationship. This word of hope begins with the blessing of progeny:

וְהָיָה מִסְפַּר בְּנֵי־יִשְׂרָאֵל כְּחוֹל הַיָּם אֲשֶׁר לֹא־יִמַּד וְלֹא יִסָּפֵר וְהָיָה בִּמְקוֹם אֲשֶׁר־יֵאָמֵר לָהֶם לֹא־עַמִּי אַתֶּם יֵאָמֵר לָהֶם בְּנֵי אֵל־חָי	1	However,[27] the number of the children of Israel will be like the sand of the sea, which cannot be measured or numbered. And in the place where it was said to them, "You are not my people," it will be said to them "Children of the living God."
וְנִקְבְּצוּ בְּנֵי־יְהוּדָה וּבְנֵי־יִשְׂרָאֵל יַחְדָּו וְשָׂמוּ לָהֶם רֹאשׁ אֶחָד וְעָלוּ מִן־הָאָרֶץ כִּי גָדוֹל יוֹם יִזְרְעֶאל	2	The children of Judah and children of Israel will be gathered together and will appoint for themselves one head, and they will go up from the land, for great will be the day of Jezreel.
אִמְרוּ לַאֲחֵיכֶם עַמִּי וְלַאֲחוֹתֵיכֶם רֻחָמָה	3	Say to your brothers, "My People" and to your sisters, "Compassion."

We have already encountered the sand simile in other prophetic texts (Isa 10:22; 48:19; Jer 15:8; 33:22). Although this is a stock phrase denoting great numbers, there is little question that its biblical articulation denoting the expansion of the people of Israel alludes to the Abrahamic promises (Gen 22:17; 32:13[12]; cf. 1 Kgs 4:20).[28] This is all the more likely given patriarchal references elsewhere in the book, as noted above. The additional

---

26. The רחם root occurs nine times in Hos 1–2, only once elsewhere in Hosea, and only seven times in the rest of the Twelve. It thus appears to be a unifying concept/Leitwort. Apart from the name of Hosea's daughter (1:6, 8; 2:25[23]), it conveys that Yahweh will no longer have compassion on Israel in the near future (1:6; 2:6[4]), although he does have compassion on Judah for the immediate future (1:7). However, in the end, he will once again have compassion on Israel (2:3[1], 21[19], 25[23]; 14:4[3]).

27. The converted perfect constructions in vv. 1–3 signal a clear shift to the future (see Joüon, Grammar, §119c). The LXX renders this first line in the past tense (Καὶ ἦν ὁ ἀριθμὸς . . .), but this does not fit contextually and lacks other external manuscript support.

28. See Ben Zvi, Hosea, 46; Mays, Hosea, 31; McComiskey, "Hosea," 29; Silva, "Literary Structure," 190 n. 38; Sweeney, Twelve Prophets: Volume One, 23; Wolff, Hosea, 26.

phrase, אֲשֶׁר (לֹא־יִמַּד) וְלֹא יִסָּפֵר, appears in the context of the progeny blessing in Gen 15:5, 16:10, 32:13[12], 1 Kgs 3:8, and Jer 33:22, and accompanies the sand metaphor in Gen 32:13[12] and Jer 33:22. Again, since this is part of a standard formula for innumerability, this does not mean that Hosea alludes to any one text in particular. However, it may reinforce the claim that v. 1 recalls the patriarchal promises. As we suggested for Isa 10:22 and 48:19, Hos 2:1[1:10] may allude to the Abrahamic promise via its realization during Solomon's reign (1 Kgs 3:8; 4:20).[29] The reunification of Judah and Israel under one "head" (רֹאשׁ)[30] in 2:2[1:11] recalls this golden age in Israel's past when the people were "as numerous as the sand on the seashore."

Typically, the progeny blessing applies to the entire people of God, but that may not be the case here where the "children of Israel" (בְּנֵי־יִשְׂרָאֵל) will multiply. In the preceding context, the northern יִשְׂרָאֵל בֵּית (1:4, 6) is distinguished from the southern בְּנֵי־יְהוּדָה (1:7). Similarly, elsewhere in Hosea בְּנֵי־יִשְׂרָאֵל appears to refer to the northern kingdom alone (2:2[1:11]; 3:1, 4, 5; 4:1), nowhere more clearly than in the following verse where the בְּנֵי־יְהוּדָה and בְּנֵי־יִשְׂרָאֵל will be reunited. This seems to indicate that v. 1 addresses only the ten northern tribes.[31] Nevertheless, some have argued that בְּנֵי־יִשְׂרָאֵל in v. 1 refers to both kingdoms.[32] Stuart argues that the reunification of the nation in 2:2[1:11] indicates that both north and south together will enjoy all future restoration blessings.[33] This being the case, Judah may rightly anticipate that Yahweh will bless them with a vast population as well. However, the northern kingdom remains the primary addressee in v. 1, not because Judah is excluded from this promise, but rather because judgment is imminent for the northern kingdom,

---

29. Andersen and Freedman, *Hosea*, 202–3; and Hubbard, *Hosea*, 66, similarly argue that v. 1 refers to both Abrahamic and Solomonic traditions. Perhaps v. 1 is a conflation of the two articulations of the realization of the blessing in Solomon's day in 1 Kgs 3:8 and 4:20. However, it is uncertain whether Hosea would have had access to the Solomon narrative or tradition in a form that contained both of these texts or articulations.

30. This may refer to a Davidic king (see 3:5 and 1 Sam 15:7; Job 29:25; Ps 18:44[43]) without using the tainted term מֶלֶךְ.

31. So Abma, *Bonds of Love*, 162; Kelle, *Hosea 2*, 213; Mays, *Hosea*, 32; Sweeney, *Twelve Prophets: Volume One*, 23.

32. See Andersen and Freedman, *Hosea*, 202; Ben Zvi, *Hosea*, 57; Davies, *Hosea*, 60; Stuart, *Hosea-Jonah*, 38.

33. Stuart, *Hosea-Jonah*, 38.

The Progeny Blessing in the Book of the Twelve

and thus it is the north that is especially in need of this promise of future restoration.[34]

The rest of 2:1–3[1:10—2:1] emphasizes the reversal of Israel's fate through the reversal of the names of Hosea's children. Surprisingly, "Not My People" does not become "My People" in v. 1 (although this appears in v. 3), but rather "Children of the living God." This seldom-used phrase (see Josh 3:10; Ps 42:3; 84:3 for "the living God") may contrast the future generation with the "children of harlotry" in 1:2. It may also reinforce that Yahweh is the source of all life, explaining the expansion of the people and anticipating Baal's rival claim to be the god of fertility.[35] At the conclusion of the unit, the unified people affirm the reversal of two of the names of the children by declaring to one another, "My People" and "Compassion" (2:3[1]). The name "Jezreel" is not changed but redefined due to the name's inherent ambiguity. No longer is it associated with a place of bloodshed. The "day of Jezreel" (יוֹם יִזְרְעֶאל) now suggests that "God sows" in deliverance and blessing.

The order and nature of these events depend on the meaning of the cryptic phrase, וְעָלוּ מִן־הָאָרֶץ. Among the various proposed solutions, two stand out as most plausible:[36] 1) This could refer to the northern kingdom's return to the land of Israel from exile in Assyria.[37] This would temporally precede and facilitate the reunification of Judah and Israel under one head and Jezreel may then refer to Yahweh "sowing" them back in the land by means of the return. Contextually, this interpretation fits well since the return is often stated or presupposed in prophetic salvation

---

34. Although this promise is specifically for the northern tribes, it may be fitting for Judah to appropriate these same promises in light of their own exile given the ideal unity of the people of God and in light of the fact that other prophets make the same promises to Judah. Paul and Peter expand the scope of this promise even further, identifying "Not My People" with Gentiles who are now included within the people of God through faith in Christ (see Paul's use of Hos 2:1[1:10] and 2:25[23] in Rom 9:25–26 and Peter's use of Hos 2:3[1], 25[23] in 1 Pet 2:10). Accordingly, Stuart (*Hosea-Jonah*, 37) and McComiskey ("Hosea," 29) assert that the progeny blessing in Hos 2:1[1:10] includes Gentile proselytes. While this may be a valid understanding of Hosea from a NT perspective, there is no hint of this in the book of Hosea.

35. See Macintosh, *Hosea*, 36; Wolff, *Hosea*, 27.

36. For a review of these and other proposals, see Abma, *Bonds of Love*, 163–65; Kelle, *Hosea 2*, 219–24; Macintosh, *Hosea*, 31–33.

37. The Targum explicitly identifies this phrase with the return and a number of modern commentators continue to adopt this interpretation as well (see Abma, *Bonds of Love*, 164–65; Andersen and Freedman, *Hosea*, 209; Ben Zvi, *Hosea*, 50; Stuart, *Hosea-Jonah*, 39).

oracles, including Hos 11:8–11. Furthermore, עָלָה is employed in 2:17[15] (כְּיוֹם עֲלֹתָהּ מֵאֶרֶץ־מִצְרָיִם) and 12:14[13] to refer to the original exodus from Egypt.[38] Since Hosea depicts the return as a second exodus in 11:10–11, he may be doing the same here by using this language. However, some find this view problematic since אֶרֶץ is always qualified by "of Egypt" or "of Assyria" in Hosea when referring to any land other than Israel. 2) וְעָלוּ מִן־הָאָרֶץ may be a fertility metaphor for the growth of the population similar to the metaphors found in 14:6–8[5–7].[39] According to this interpretation, הָאָרֶץ refers to the ground (in Israel, presumably) and עָלָה refers to the people "springing up" from it as a plant. However, this option is unlikely since these meanings of עָלָה and הָאָרֶץ are uncommon. In addition, unlike other uses of עָלָה to denote growth (10:8; Gen 41:5, 22; Deut 29:22[23]; Isa 52:3; 55:13), there is insufficient contextual information to indicate that this is a fertility metaphor.[40] In our judgment, it is more likely that וְעָלוּ מִן־הָאָרֶץ refers to the return from exile since the use of הָאָרֶץ to refer to a land other than Israel is not an insuperable difficulty. There is no reason why it cannot be used to denote an unspecified land, even if this is the only such instance in the book. Furthermore, this is just one more example of ambiguity in the language of this verse (e.g., רֹאשׁ, יִזְרְעֶאל), and may even be intentional in order to recall the original exodus from Egypt as well as to predict the new exodus from Assyria.[41] Therefore, here "Jezreel" connotes the sowing of God's people in the land of promise both through multiplying the people and through bringing them back to the land, summarizing the content of 2:1–2[1:10–11].

The function of the progeny blessing in 2:1[1:10] is multifaceted:

1. The message of 1:2–9 that Yahweh's covenant relationship with Israel built on the Abrahamic covenant was no longer valid would have caused the people to question whether there was any hope for the relationship. By alluding to the Abrahamic promises in 2:1[1:10], Hosea assures them that they are still meaningful since Yahweh intends to maintain his commitment to Abraham, although much remains

---

38. See also Exod 1:10; 3:8, 17; 12:38; 13:18; 17:3; 32:1, 4, 7, 8, 23; 33:1, where the exodus narratives use עָלָה to refer to the exodus.

39. Originally proposed by Vriezen (*Hosea*, 13, 22), this interpretation has won support from Davies, *Hosea*, 62–63; Garrett, *Hosea, Joel*, 73; Macintosh, *Hosea*, 32–33; McComiskey, "Hosea," 30.

40. See Abma, *Bonds of Love*, 164, for additional considerations that call this interpretation into question.

41. So Ben Zvi, *Hosea*, 51.

unexplained between 1:9 and 2:1[1:10].⁴² Shockingly, right after saying that they are not his people, Hosea states, in effect, "but you will be his people again!"

2. If this is an allusion to conditions under Solomon as well, the progeny promise here affirms that Yahweh will restore the unified nation to the population size that they attained during their heyday under Solomon. Despite this break in the relationship, Yahweh will bless the people again in the future in the same way that he has in the past, reinstating this golden age.⁴³

3. The progeny promise addresses what already may have been a growing concern⁴⁴ and stresses that the decimation of exile will only be temporary.

4. Finally, in the context of the fertility showdown between Baal and Yahweh, Yahweh asserts at the outset in accordance with Israel's prior traditions that he is the source of Israel's offspring. Yahweh, the "living God," not Baal, "sows."⁴⁵

In Hos 1–3, the ruptured covenant relationship, signified by "Not My People" and "No Compassion" and described as divorce proceedings, results in the removal of fertility and decimation of the population. The renewed relationship, signified by "My People" and "Compassion," and described as a marriage ceremony, results in renewed fertility and, as we see in 2:1[1:10], the proliferation of the population. Although 2:1[1:10] is the only clear reference to the progeny blessing in Hosea, we will briefly treat 2:25[23], 4:7, 10, and 14:6–8[5–7], since these texts have some relevance for our study as well.

---

42. McComiskey, "Hosea," 29.

43. See Hubbard, *Hosea*, 66.

44. Assyria had already begun to deport the population by 733 (see Macintosh, *Hosea*, 35). Furthermore, the population of Israel was relatively small at this time (Stuart, *Hosea–Jonah*, 37; Wolff, *Hosea*, 26).

45. Although the text does not cite Yahweh as the facilitator of the events of 2:1–3[1:10—2:1], his agency is clearly implied, particularly in the name Jezreel. His absence in this text of hope contrasts with the next (2:16–25[14–23]), which is filled with Yahweh's first-person speech.

Hosea 2:25[23]

Following Yahweh's indictment of his people for attributing the fertility of the land to Baal and the corresponding judgment of infertility (2:4-15[2-13]), Yahweh again suddenly promises restoration (2:16-25[14-23]). Yahweh will initiate a new marriage relationship in which he alone will be Israel's husband and they will know him fully (2:18-22[16-20]). Within this new relationship, Yahweh will be the true fertility God,[46] described through a chain reaction of "answering" (vv. 23-25a[21-23a]):

וְהָיָה בַּיּוֹם הַהוּא אֶעֱנֶה נְאֻם־יְהוָה	23[21]	"In that day I will answer," declares Yahweh
אֶעֱנֶה אֶת־הַשָּׁמָיִם		"I will answer the heavens,
וְהֵם יַעֲנוּ אֶת־הָאָרֶץ		and they will answer the earth,
וְהָאָרֶץ תַּעֲנֶה אֶת־הַדָּגָן וְאֶת־הַתִּירוֹשׁ וְאֶת־הַיִּצְהָר	24[22]	and the earth will answer the grain, wine, and oil,
וְהֵם יַעֲנוּ אֶת־יִזְרְעֶאל		and they will answer Jezreel,
וּזְרַעְתִּיהָ לִּי בָּאָרֶץ[47]	25a[23a]	and I will sow her for myself in the land."

The final link, Jezreel, recalls the name of Hosea's first child and provides a transition into the conclusion of the restoration oracle in which all three names are once again reversed (v. 25[23]), parallel to the message of 2:1-3[1:10—2:1]. In this context, it is clear that the first line of v. 25[23] represents the positive significance of the name "God sows."

However, the meaning of v. 25a[23a] is unclear. Some have suggested that this line is a continuation of the emphasis on agricultural fertility, referring to God sowing the land with produce.[48] This also could denote Israel's return to the land.[49] More likely, this refers to Yahweh "sowing" the people of Israel in the land by multiplying their numbers:[50]

1. In the progression of one thing "answering" another, each element is the prerequisite or agent for the next. Therefore, it is significant that

---

46. The terms הַדָּגָן, הַתִּירוֹשׁ, and הַיִּצְהָר in v. 24[22] (cf. Deut 7:13; 11:14) may be deliberately polemical, attributing to Yahweh agricultural blessings often associated with pagan deities (see Block, "Other Religions," 50-51).

47. Apart from the name Jezreel, this is the only occurrence of זָרַע in the book.

48. So Ben Zvi, *Hosea*, 68; Stuart, *Hosea-Jonah*, 61.

49. So Wolff, *Hosea*, 54, although he applies this phrase specifically to the return of the population of the Jezreel valley.

50. So Davies, *Hosea*, 90; Macintosh, *Hosea*, 89; Mays, *Hosea*, 53; McComiskey, "Hosea," 48.

the grain, wine, and oil are not equated with Jezreel, but "answer" Jezreel, implying that food is necessary to produce whatever Jezreel connotes. Logically, Jezreel would then represent the maintenance and expansion of the population.[51]

2. As already noted, elsewhere "sowing" (זָרַע) people refers to the progeny blessing (Jer 31:27).

3. In this highly polemical chapter pitting Yahweh against Baal, it is more likely that the promise of restoration concludes with the affirmation that Yahweh is the God of all manner of fertility, of both land and womb, than with a reference to the return to the land.

4. The prior positive articulation of Jezreel in 2:2[1:11] connoted the progeny blessing, so the same is likely the case here.

However, the agricultural metaphor of "sowing" involves not only locating the "seed" but also the growth of the "seed." We thus conclude for both of these texts that, although the progeny blessing is central to the notion of Jezreel as "God sows," the return from exile is probably included in this concept as well.

The juxtaposition of הַדָּגָן, הַתִּירוֹשׁ, and הַיִּצְהָר is especially common in Deuteronomy (7:13; 11:14; 12:17; 14:23; 18:4; 28:51; see also Jer 31:12; Hos 2:10[8]; Joel 2:19, 24), and is combined with the progeny blessing in Deut 7:13. Since these themes converge in Hos 2:24[22], perhaps this verse alludes to the covenant blessings of Deuteronomy. Furthermore, 2:16–25[14–23] abounds with allusions to the original exodus and covenant relationship sealed at Sinai, depicting this future day as a re-creation of the nation. Therefore, such growth may correspond typologically to the original realization of the Abrahamic promise, namely, the expansion of the nation in Exod 1:7 in preparation for entry into the land (although this new expansion will take place in the land itself). As in 2:1–3[1:10—2:1], proliferation is a by-product of Yahweh's compassion and covenant relationship with his people.

Hosea 4:7, 10

After indicting the people of Israel for their persistent violation of the law of Yahweh (4:1–3), blame falls on the high priest (4:4–6), culminating in the sentence, "I will forget your children" (v. 6). Yahweh most likely refers

---

51. See Macintosh, *Hosea*, 90.

to these children when he then laments, כְּרֻבָּם כֵּן חָטְאוּ־לִי[52] (v. 7). Some suggest that this indicates an increase in the wealth or influence of the priestly class,[53] a possibility given the historical circumstances (cf. 10:1). Alternatively, this may refer to quantitative growth, best translated, "the more they multiplied, the more they sinned against me."[54] Although this could be seen as a specific manifestation of the progeny blessing for the priestly class, it may not refer to the expansion of the priesthood by means of increased birthrates but rather to the successful recruitment of more volunteers for this office, given its possibilities for wealth and power.[55] Furthermore, even if this does indicate that the priestly class enjoyed abundant fertility, the rhetorical point of this statement is hardly that God has blessed them. Rather, this is a further indictment of the extent of their sin.

The scope of the punishment expands in vv. 9–10 to address not only the priests but also the people of Israel. Since they have left Yahweh, "they will eat, but not be satisfied; they will act like a harlot, but not spread out (הִזְנוּ וְלֹא יִפְרֹצוּ)" (v. 10). As in Gen 28:14, Exod 1:12, and Isa 54:3, פָּרַץ probably denotes spreading out through the growth of the population.[56] Alluding once again to the pagan fertility cult, Yahweh declares that their expectation that Baal will give them a fruitful land and a fruitful womb will go unrealized. As in 2:23–25[21–23], where the fertility of land and humanity are juxtaposed, they appear together in v. 10 as that which Yahweh will withhold in judgment due to their reliance on false fertility gods. Furthermore, if v. 7 refers to the progeny blessing, this judgment overturns the former growth of the priesthood in fulfillment of v. 6b.[57]

---

52. A comparative clause such as this indicates that the severity of their sin corresponds to their numbers or wealth (see *IBHS* 641).

53. See Targum; Andersen and Freedman, *Hosea*, 354; Macintosh, *Hosea*, 141; McComiskey, "Hosea," 63; Stuart, *Hosea-Jonah*, 78.

54. See Hubbard, *Hosea*, 102; Mays, *Hosea*, 70. The pointing of כְּרֻבָּם is ambiguous. The first option would be derived from the noun רֹב, which can denote either quantity or quality. Alternatively, if כְּרֻבָּם is a Qal Infinitive Construct from רָבַב, only the quantitative option is a possibility.

55. See Garrett, *Hosea, Joel*, 118–19.

56. See Andersen and Freedman, *Hosea*, 263; Davies, *Hosea*, 121; Macintosh, *Hosea*, 149; Mays, *Hosea*, 71; McComiskey, "Hosea," 64; Stuart, *Hosea-Jonah*, 80; Wolff, *Hosea*, 82. פָּרַץ occurs in Hosea in 4:2, but with respect to "breaking out" in transgression.

57. See Hubbard, *Hosea*, 103.

Hosea 14:6–8[5–7]

The book of Hosea closes with a final call to repentance (14:2–4[1–3]) and a concluding restoration oracle (14:5–8[4–7]). In this last word of hope, Yahweh pledges to heal and love them (14:5[4]). Metaphorically, Israel will blossom and sprout and flourish as a flower or a tree as a result of Yahweh's favor toward the nation (14:6–8[5–7]), language quite similar to that of Isa 27:6.[58] Given Hosea's thematic emphasis on fertility and its true source, it is fitting that the book concludes with fertility language. However, the referent(s) of this metaphor remain ambiguous. The Targum interprets the phrase "his shoots will spread out" (יֵלְכוּ יֹנְקוֹתָיו; v. 7[6]) as a reference to the multiplication of Israel's children, but nowhere else is similar language employed to denote the progeny blessing. Perhaps the clearest hint that this imagery involves the progeny blessing lies in the clause, "he will take root like [the trees of?] Lebanon" (וְיַךְ שָׁרָשָׁיו כַּלְּבָנוֹן; v. 6[5]). Since the only other occurrence of the root שָׁרַשׁ in Hosea, the drying up of Ephraim's שֹׁרֶשׁ, results in the barrenness of the womb (9:16), the spreading of roots may indicate a reversal of this prior curse and depict human fruitfulness here. Nevertheless, when we consider the vegetation metaphors of vv. 6–8[5–7] as a whole, it is unlikely that human fertility is the primary or sole referent. As we concluded for Isa 27:6, the progeny blessing is almost certainly included, but the scope of this imagery is much broader, encompassing health, fecundity, prosperity, security, and holistic well-being.[59] In v. 9[8], which may serve as a summary for the prior unit and, indeed, for the message of the entire book,[60] Yahweh states, "from *me* comes your fruit" (מִמֶּנִּי פֶּרְיְךָ נִמְצָא), another play on "Ephraim" (אֶפְרַיִם; v. 9a[8a]). This concluding polemic against the Canaanite fertility deities probably encompasses all forms of fertility (human, cattle, land).[61] Thus, the first and last words of hope in the book of Hosea pertain to Yahweh's multiplication of the people of Israel, attributing the gift of fecundity to him alone.

---

58. See our treatment of this text above. Isaiah 27:6 may be dependent on this text (see Day, "Inner Scriptural Interpretation," 309–19).

59. See Garrett, *Hosea, Joel*, 274; Macintosh, *Hosea*, 579; McComiskey, "Hosea," 233; Stuart, *Hosea-Jonah*, 216; Wolff, *Hosea*, 238.

60. So Garrett, *Hosea, Joel*, 278.

61. See Davies, *Hosea*, 309. McComiskey suggests that this refers specifically to the Abrahamic promise of abundant offspring ("Hosea," 236), but there are no good intertextual parallels within Hosea or elsewhere that indicate that the simple reference to פְּרִי in connection with Ephraim would denote the blessing of progeny in particular.

I Will Surely Multiply Your Offspring

Introduction to the Book of Zechariah

Zechariah's Use of Prior Traditions

Whereas Hosea addresses a pre-exilic audience during the infancy of classical written prophecy, Zechariah addresses a post-exilic audience when the prophetic word was waning. Perhaps more than any other prophetic book, Zechariah is indebted to earlier canonical writings since these "texts were so much part of his textual worldview."[62] Zechariah appears to be far more dependent on the pre-exilic and exilic prophets than on the traditions that they used.[63] For example, Tuell concludes from the parallels in form and style between Ezekiel and Zech 1–8 that Zechariah likely modeled his work on that of Ezekiel.[64] Furthermore the hopes expressed in Zech 9–14 appear to be heavily indebted to the restoration program of Ezek 34–48. Jeremiah and the related deuteronomic tradition were also formative influences on both halves of the book of Zechariah.[65] Concluding his study of the use of prior materials in Zechariah, Risto Nurmela declares, "In summary, both of the main parts of Zechariah are significantly dependent on the same books, Isaiah, Jeremiah and Ezekiel, at a similar redactional stage, and are also mutually dependent on one another."[66] This comes as little surprise since Zechariah himself refers to the "former prophets" (הַנְּבִיאִים הָרִאשֹׁנִים; 1:4; 7:7, 12), underscoring the importance of their message.

---

62. Stead, "Sustained Allusion," 170. According to Meyers and Meyers, "[i]t may not be an exaggeration to suggest that Zechariah 9–14 surpasses any other biblical work in the way it draws from existing traditions" (*Zechariah 9–14*, 35).

63. However, Larkin identifies allusions to each of the five books of Moses within Zech 9–14 (*Eschatology*). Zechariah is ultimately dependent on the Pentateuch, but through earlier prophetic voices.

64. See Tuell, "Haggai–Zechariah," 273-91.

65. See Person, *Second Zechariah*; Sweeney, *Twelve Prophets: Volume Two*, 563-64.

66. Nurmela, *Prophets in Dialogue*, 235. See Larkin, *Eschatology*, for a similar conclusion with respect to Zech 9–14. Tai, *Prophetie als Schriftauslegung*, primarily recognizes the influences of Jeremiah and Ezekiel on Zech 9–14. Although Nurmela accepts the prevailing source-critical division between Zech 1–8 and 9–14, this conclusion contributes to the argument for the unity of the book. Most studies of intertextuality in Zechariah treat only First or Second Zechariah, but there does not appear to be any clear distinction between the two halves of the book with respect to their use of prior texts.

The Progeny Blessing in the Book of the Twelve

Future Hope in Zechariah

Although the return from exile has begun, from the standpoint of the book of Zechariah it is not an accomplished event since Yahweh pledges that he will bring far more Israelites back to the land (2:10–11[6–7]; 8:7–8; 10:6–12). However, since fulfillment is beginning, Zechariah appropriately emphasizes the restoration of the nation more than any other prophet in the Twelve. This restoration revolves around the rebuilding of the temple (1:16; 4:9; 8:9) and around the priestly and royal leadership, the present seed from which renewal will flourish. The exaltation of this leadership foreshadows a future "branch" (3:8; 6:12; cf. Jer 23:5) and king (9:9). The details of Israel's hopes are familiar from other prophetic salvation oracles: the restoration of a large population (2:8[4]; 8:4–5; 10:8, 10), agricultural fertility (8:12; 9:17–10:1), the destruction or subjugation of enemy peoples (2:4[1:21]; 2:12–13[8–9]; 6:8; 9:8, 10; 12:4–9; 14:12–15), peace (9:10), security (3:10; 14:11), and joy (2:14[10]; 8:19; 9:9; 10:7). Ultimately, Yahweh himself will be king (14:9; cf. 4:14; 6:5). The curse will be gone (14:11) and Israel will again serve her purpose as a blessing among the nations (8:13).

As in the other prophetic books, and most like Hosea within the Twelve, the resurrection of the nation is based on the renewal of Israel's covenant relationship with Yahweh (see 8:8; 13:9), rooted in his compassion for them (1:16–17; 10:6; cf. Deut 4:31). He will again "return" (שַׁבְתִּי) to Zion (8:3) and "bring good" (לְהֵיטִיב) to her (8:15). In light of the temple reconstruction, Zechariah emphasizes that Yahweh will dwell among them again (2:9[5], 14–15[10–11]; 8:2, 23). Furthermore, he will remove iniquity from the land (3:9), associated with the "branch" figure and portrayed in the seventh vision (see also 13:1). As a result, in the future the people will walk in the name of Yahweh (10:12), call upon him (13:9), and confess that he is their God (13:9).

The Nations in Zechariah

As in Isaiah, the nations play a significant, but complex, role in the book of Zechariah. In Zech 12–14 they are primarily enemies of Israel who will persist in coming against Jerusalem in battle, but will face destruction in the end since Yahweh will defend his people (12:1–9; 14:1–3, 12–15; cf. Mic 4:11–13). Similarly, the first (1:7–17), second (2:1–4[1:18–21]), third (2:5–9[1–5]), and eighth (6:1–8) night visions anticipate doom for Israel's enemies. However, Zechariah also expresses hope for the nations, more so, in fact, than the rest of the Twelve combined.[67] Foreigners will recognize that Yahweh is God and that his people are blessed and seek his favor at Jerusalem (8:20–23). There is a glimmer of hope even for the Philistines (9:6b–7). The coming king will "speak peace to the nations" (9:10). The commentary on the third night vision (2:10–17[6–13]) may serve as a summary of Zechariah's treatment of the nations since it involves both hope and judgment for them, indicating that there will be a division among the nations between friends and foes of Israel. Foes will become plunder (vv. 12–13[8–9]), but other nations will "join themselves to Yahweh . . . and will be my people" (v. 15[11]). Similarly, the conclusion of the book envisions judgment for those who oppose God's people (14:12–15), a potential second chance for remaining foreigners to serve Yahweh (v. 16), and an enduring curse for those who continue to refuse (vv. 17–19).

The Progeny Blessing in Zechariah

Population Decimation in Zechariah

Since the exilic judgment is largely past, Zechariah speaks of this theme and the motif of population decimation far less than the other prophets (but see 11:6, 9, 16; 13:8). However, the Abrahamic promise that Yahweh would make of him a great nation had been reversed. Zechariah addresses a diminutive community that had suffered the effects of this judgment.[68] As a result, the rejuvenation of the population of Jerusalem and of Judah was doubtless one of the chief concerns of the post-exilic community. It is fitting, then, that Zechariah addresses this corporate despair by promising the renewal of a vast people in the land in 2:5–9[1–5], 8:4–5, and 10:8, 10.

Zechariah 2:5–9[1–5]

The first two night visions pave the way for the third night vision concerning the restoration of the city of Jerusalem. The first vision (1:7–17) culminates in Yahweh's resolve to "return to Jerusalem with compassion" (שַׁבְתִּי לִירוּשָׁלַם בְּרַחֲמִים; 1:16) and grant her prosperity once again (1:16–17). The third night vision in 2:5–9[1–5] (and its expansion in

---

67. This theme is found only in Mic 4:1–3 and, possibly, in Hag 2:6–9.

68. According to Ezra 2:64 and Neh 7:66, 42,360 individuals respond to the edict of Cyrus and return to the land. See excursus in chapter 2 regarding the size of Israel's population.

2:10-17[6-13]) depicts the result of Yahweh's compassion and a development of 1:16-17, employing similar language and concepts. The second vision (2:1-4[1:18-21]), which portrays Yahweh's judgment of Judah's enemies, then anticipates and coincides with the renewal of Zion's peace and prosperity in the third vision.

The details of the third vision are not entirely clear, particularly the identities and roles of the four characters involved, but the message and significance of the vision are apparent. A man departs to measure (cf. Ezek 40–48) the walls of Jerusalem (or perhaps to plan for the rebuilding of the walls as a surveyor[69]), but a messenger is sent to stop him (vv. 5–7[1–3]). In v. 8[4], the messenger is instructed to inform him that his task will be futile (or is misguided) since:

פְּרָזוֹת תֵּשֵׁב יְרוּשָׁלָ͏ִם   Jerusalem will be inhabited like[69] villages without walls
מֵרֹב אָדָם וּבְהֵמָה בְּתוֹכָהּ   because of the abundance of people and cattle within it.

The lexeme פְּרָזוֹת, which occurs only in the plural, appears elsewhere only in Ezek 38:11, where these dwellings are specifically noted to be "without walls" (אֵין חוֹמָה), and in Esth 9:19. In each of these instances, the inhabitants of the פְּרָזוֹת are vulnerable to enemy attacks, but in each case Yahweh protects them. The gentilic, פְּרָזִי, occurs only three times in the OT. In Deut 3:5 and 1 Sam 6:18 it is contrasted with fortified cities and in Esth 9:19 it simply identifies the inhabitants of the פְּרָזוֹת. Therefore, פְּרָזוֹת designate smaller villages, often near cities, that had neither the population nor the means to protect themselves with walls.[71] Therefore, v. 8[4] indicates that Jerusalem will be without walls and open to attack. However, Jerusalem will be vulnerable not because she lacks the population or ability to create walls (as in the current post-exilic situation), but rather because the city will be so full of both people and animals that walls would be unable to contain them!

In light of the general use of רֹב in Zechariah (cf. 8:4; 14:14), its use in similar expressions that denote great numbers of people (Gen 16:10; 32:13[12]; 48:16; Deut 1:10; 10:22; 28:62; Josh 11:4; Judg 6:5; 7:12; 1 Sam 13:5; 2 Sam 17:11; 1 Kgs 3:8; 4:20), and the present literary context, the expression מֵרֹב אָדָם וּבְהֵמָה clearly denotes quantity. However,

---

69. See Webb, *Zechariah*, 80.

70. פְּרָזוֹת functions here as an adverbial accusative of comparison (see GKC §118r; Joüon, *Grammar*, §126e) or state (cf. Isa 21:8; 22:18; Ps 11:1; 144:12). It may be frontloaded for emphasis.

71. See Grisanti, "פְּרָזוֹן," 682.

this growth probably reflects a general restoration of well-being, already evident in the accompanying abundance of cattle.[72] In Zech 1:17 Yahweh promised, "my cities will once again overflow with prosperity" (עוֹד תְּפוּצֶינָה עָרַי מִטּוֹב), singling out Jerusalem in particular. Since Zech 2:5-17[1-13] seems to be an expansion of 1:16-17, perhaps the literal overflow of the population in vision three demonstrates the metaphorical overflow of the cities with good.[73] Furthermore, v. 16[12] indicates that Yahweh is not ultimately concerned with the city of Jerusalem alone but with all the cities of the land. This may suggest similar population growth in other cities as well.

A Jerusalem without walls raises the obvious question concerning the source of the city's protection. Yahweh addresses this concern in the concluding verse of the vision proper (v. 9[5]) by promising that he himself will protect the city by acting as a "wall of fire" (חוֹמַת אֵשׁ)[74] around her and by filling her with his glory (כָּבוֹד). In so doing, Yahweh promises to dwell within Zion, one aspect of the significance of the temple-building project that provides the occasion for the night visions.

Although the following verses (vv. 10-17[6-13]) have commonly been deemed a later addition unrelated to the visions themselves, Sweeney rightly notes that they are included in the text as the continuation of the messenger's speech in vv. 8-9[4-5] and should be read as such.[75] These verses consist of a triad of exhortations that elaborate on vv. 8-9[4-5] and delineate the proper response to the vision. First, Yahweh commands those still exiled to return to the land of promise since their plunderers will now themselves be plundered (vv. 10-13[6-9]). Yahweh then exhorts daughter Zion to rejoice since he is coming to dwell among the people (vv. 14-16[10-12]) upon completion of the temple (1:16). Finally, in what may be a transitional exhortation to the fourth night vision, all flesh is commanded to be silent since Yahweh has roused himself from his heavenly temple (v. 17[13]). We find here not only three appropriate responses to Yahweh's activity, but also the means by which he intends to accomplish Jerusalem's restoration as outlined in the third vision and first described

---

72. It appears that the fate of אָדָם and בְּהֵמָה are linked in Zechariah since they are also juxtaposed in 8:10 and 14:15. As Petersen notes (*Haggai and Zechariah 1–8*, 170) and as we have seen in two previous texts we have treated (Jer 31:27; Ezek 36:11), this may be a stereotypical phrase for all living creatures.

73. See Conrad, *Zechariah*, 79.

74. Cf. Exod 3:2; 13:21; 2 Kgs 2:11 where fire similarly symbolizes Yahweh's presence.

75. See Sweeney, *Twelve Prophets: Volume Two*, 587.

in 1:16–17. First, the positive response to the call to the dispersed exiles to return home will contribute to the realization of an overflowing population in Jerusalem so that the third vision motivates the return and the return accomplishes the vision.

Second, although it is not the primary thrust of the second exhortation, the influx of the nations may contribute to the growth of the population as well. In an elaboration of the announcement that Yahweh will dwell among his people and protect Jerusalem (v. 9[5]), Yahweh and the messenger announce the following in vv. 14b–15a[10b–11a] as the basis for the exhortation to rejoice:

וְשָׁכַנְתִּי בְתוֹכֵךְ נְאֻם־יְהוָה	14[10]	"I will dwell in your midst," declares Yahweh.
וְנִלְווּ גוֹיִם רַבִּים אֶל־יְהוָה בַּיּוֹם הַהוּא	15[11]	Many nations will join themselves to Yahweh in that day;
וְהָיוּ לִי לְעָם		"They will become My people,
וְשָׁכַנְתִּי בְתוֹכֵךְ		and I will dwell in your midst."[76]

The implicit logic appears to be as follows: the nations will recognize Yahweh's presence with his people upon temple completion and the blessing and protection that this entails and as a result will "join themselves" to Yahweh in order to become his people, reminiscent of Isa 14:1–2 and 56:3–8.[77] The citation of the "covenant formula" that indicates a renewed relationship between Yahweh and his people is not unusual in such a restoration oracle, as we have seen in previous prophetic texts. Surprisingly, however, it is cited here not with respect to Israelites but rather with respect to the גּוֹיִם.[78] Nothing less than full inclusion within the people

---

76. Although it seems out of place, the first person language may identify the covenant formula as a quotation, since this formula typically comes from the mouth of Yahweh himself, including later in the book (cf. 8:8; 13:9). See Barthélemy, *Ézéchiel, Daniel et les 12 Prophètes*, 941–43; Meyers, and Meyers, *Haggai, Zechariah 1–8*, 162.

77. The Niphal of לָוָה is also employed in Isa 14:1 and 56:3, 6 with respect to the nations joining themselves to Yahweh and in Jer 50:5 with respect to Israelites. On the basis of four linguistic and two thematic parallels, Nurmela rightly deems this a "sure allusion" to Isa 14:1–2 (*Prophets in Dialogue*, 61–62) despite the fact that in Isa 14:1 they attach themselves to Israel, not Yahweh. Mark J. Boda argues for this allusion as well, since in the wider context of both Isa 14:1–2 and Zech 2:15[11] this influx follows the destruction of Babylon ("Hoy, Hoy," 178, 188). Although the parallels to Isa 14:1–2 appear to be stronger, Petersen (*Haggai and Zechariah 1–8*, 181) and Sweeney (*Twelve Prophets: Volume Two*, 590) correctly recognize similarities to Isa 56:3–8 as well. There is little doubt that Zechariah corresponds closely here to the Isaianic tradition.

78. In part this is surprising because the first two night visions as well as the immediately preceding verses (vv. 12–13[8–9]) predict not salvation but judgment for

of God is envisioned. It is not clear whether the inclusion of the nations implies that they will stream to Jerusalem (cf. Isa 2:2-4; Mic 4:1-3) and dwell there so that they contribute to the overflow of Jerusalem itself.[79] However, if this is indeed an expansion of vv. 8-9[4-5] and if Zechariah has in mind Isaianic texts such as 14:1-2 and 56:3-8, where converts do come to dwell in the land, this remains a possibility.[80] Nevertheless, even if the nations remain in their own lands, they may now be included among God's growing people.

As is generally the case in Zechariah, the third vision appears to be indebted to a wide variety of prior prophetic traditions, particularly Isa 12-14, Jer 25, 50-51, and Ezek 38-48.[81] The thematic parallels between Zech 2:5-17[1-13] and the summary of Ezekiel's restoration program in 37:24-28 are particularly striking, including return to the land, the progeny blessing, the covenant formula, a form of the recognition formula, a role for the nations, and a special emphasis on the presence of Yahweh among them.[82] However, the correspondences between Zech 1:16-17; 2:8-14[4-10] and Isa 49:13-26 (and its supplementation in 54:1-10) are even stronger.[83] It is especially significant that both texts treat these common themes in roughly the same order, first depicting repopulation of the land and then explaining the means by which this will be accomplished, namely, return from exile and the subjugation of enemies, the reverse of the logical order of events:

---

the nations.

79. So McComiskey, "Zechariah," 1064-65.

80. Conrad, *Zechariah*, 84; and Kline, *Glory*, 76; express less caution and believe that v. 15[11] indicates that converts from the nations will fill Jerusalem.

81. See Boda, "Hoy, Hoy," 171-90; Nurmela, *Prophets in Dialogue*, 49-63; Tuell, "Haggai-Zechariah," 273-91.

82. See Tuell, "Haggai-Zechariah," 277.

83. Kline, *Glory*, 84; Petersen, *Haggai and Zechariah 1-8*, 170-71; Stead, "Sustained Allusion," 160-65; also recognize some of the following parallels.

Theme	Zechariah	Isaiah 49	Isaiah 54
Yahweh's compassion for Zion (רחם)	1:16	vv. 13, 15–16	vv. 7–8
Zion comforted (נָחַם) by Yahweh	1:17	v. 13	
Jerusalem (and other cities) filled with people	2:8[4]	vv. 19–21	vv. 1–3
Physical return from exile	2:10–11[6–7]	vv. 12, 22–23	
Subjugation of enemies	2:12–13[8–9]	vv. 19, 22–26	
Recognition formula ("then you will know...")	2:13[9]	v. 23	
Zion exhorted to rejoice (רָנִּי)	2:14[10]		v. 1
Personification of Zion	2:11–14[7–10]	vv. 14–26	vv. 1–17[84]
Hope for the nations	2:15[11]	vv. 22–23?	

The parallels between these texts are especially close with respect to their treatment of the progeny blessing. Apart from the book of Zechariah, only in Isa 49:19–21 and 54:1–3 is Jerusalem the focal point of the proliferation of the people in the land, although unlike Zech 2:8[4] Isaiah has the wider land in mind as well. Moreover, these texts do not merely state the refilling of the city, but they graphically depict the inability of the city or land to hold the multitudes: the land is too cramped (Isa 49:19–21), Zion is a tent that must be spread out further (Isa 54:1–3), and it must now exist without walls (Zech 2:8[4]). The chapter as a whole is likely a conflation of various prophetic texts of restoration, but, in light of these cumulative considerations, the proliferation of people and animals in Jerusalem in Zech 2:8[4] is probably indebted to Isa 49:19–21 and 54:1–3. By alluding to this Isaianic tradition, Zechariah indicates to a despairing post-exilic community that Yahweh's promises of restoration for the city remain valid. Furthermore, Zechariah seems to bring together the Isaianic themes of the proliferation of the people in the land and the inclusion of proselytes within the people of Israel. We observed above that the relationship between these themes remains ambiguous in Isaiah since they are never clearly brought together there. However, by drawing on Isa 14:1–2 in v. 15[11], Zechariah suggests that Gentile inclusion within the people of God is one means by which the population in the land is restored.

---

84. It is also noteworthy that Zech 2:10–17[6–13] mirrors Isa 54:1–8 structurally: both consist of three imperatives followed by the rationale behind each imperative, introduced with כִּי-clauses.

I Will Surely Multiply Your Offspring

Zechariah ministered within a small community living in a dilapidated city without a completed temple. His third night vision simultaneously addresses all three of these concerns. Although the vision only specifies that the population in the city of Jerusalem will be greater than before, Jerusalem may represent a similar proliferation in other cities across the land since "Yahweh will inherit Judah as his portion in the holy land" (v. 16[12]). Indeed, it would be odd and a paltry hope if the city will be expansive only because all those who return will be willing to reside only at Jerusalem. Therefore, the people will probably be more numerous than before and perhaps ever-growing, since walls appear to be useless altogether. The return of further exiles and possibly the influx of many nations will yield this great multitude. There is no explicit indication that the progeny blessing as typically understood, namely, as physical reproduction, will play a part. Nevertheless, in light of 8:4–5, perhaps this contributes to the expansion of the people in the land as well.

Zechariah 8:4–5

In response to the question from the Bethel delegation regarding fasting (7:1–3), Zechariah not only calls the people to repentance (7:4–10) but also offers hope of a future day of blessing for Jerusalem (8:1–23). The parallels between the third night vision and Zech 8 are striking and probably address the same future period of well-being. From a synchronic perspective, Zech 8 expands on the restoration of Jerusalem that Zechariah saw in the night vision two years earlier:

The Progeny Blessing in the Book of the Twelve

Theme	Zechariah 1–2	Zechariah 8
Yahweh's return to Zion (שַׁבְתִּי)	1:16	8:3
Jerusalem replenished with people	2:8[4]	8:4–5, 8
בְּהֵמָה and אָדָם	2:8[4]	8:10
Physical return of exiles to Jerusalem	2:10–11[6–7]	8:7–8
Yahweh's dwelling (שָׁכַן) in the midst of Jerusalem	2:14–15[10–11]	8:3[85]
A form of the covenant formula	2:15[11]	8:8
Inclusion of the nations	2:15[11]	8:20–23

In light of these numerous parallels, we must examine how 8:4–5 complements the restoration of the population in 2:8[4], how 8:20–23 enhances our understanding of the inclusion of the nations in 2:15[11], and whether Zech 8 provides further warrant for seeing the latter theme as a means to accomplishing the former.

Verses 4–5 summarize the benefits for Yahweh's people resulting from his passionate "jealousy" (קִנְאָתִי, twice in v. 2) for Zion and his return to Zion (v. 3; cf. v. 8):

כֹּה אָמַר יְהוָה צְבָאוֹת	4	Thus says Yahweh of hosts,
עֹד יֵשְׁבוּ זְקֵנִים וּזְקֵנוֹת בִּרְחֹבוֹת יְרוּשָׁלָ͏ִם		"Once again old men and women will sit in the plazas of Jerusalem,
וְאִישׁ מִשְׁעַנְתּוֹ בְּיָדוֹ מֵרֹב יָמִים		each with staff in hand because of great age.
וּרְחֹבוֹת הָעִיר יִמָּלְאוּ יְלָדִים וִילָדוֹת		And the plazas of the city will be filled with
מְשַׂחֲקִים בִּרְחֹבֹתֶיהָ	5	boys and girls playing[86] in its plazas."

This is an idyllic picture of tranquility in which people of all ages[87] enjoy life together. We may deduce the following from this portrait: 1) Yahweh will grant long life in the restored Jerusalem. As in the third night vision, this multitude is largely the result of the return from exile (vv. 7–8). However, since elderly folks needing a staff would scarcely have made the journey back to Jerusalem from exile, vv. 4–5 probably do not describe Jerusalem immediately after the return but rather at a later time when those who have returned have experienced prolonged life.[88] 2) Therefore,

---

85. Together with 8:8 where the people will "dwell" in the land, these are the only four uses of שָׁכַן in Zechariah.

86. The Piel of שָׂחַק can refer to playing (see Ps 104:26; Job 40:20) or celebrating (see 2 Sam 6:5, 21; Jer 30:19; 31:4), but it always connotes joy.

87. Verses 4–5 clearly function as a merism whereby totality is expressed through contrasting elements.

88. See Baldwin, *Haggai, Zechariah, Malachi*, 150.

the abundance of children in the city is probably not primarily the result of the return but rather the result of Yahweh's blessing on the wombs of those within the post-exilic community at Jerusalem.[89] 3) Altogether, the Jerusalem population is large and thriving. Even the city squares[90] will be filled with children, in stark contrast to the relatively desolate plazas in Zechariah's day as a result of Yahweh's judgment (cf. 7:14).[91]

Although this description differs somewhat from that of 2:8[4], it complements it. In 8:4–5 we catch a glimpse of the quality of life for Jerusalem's inhabitants as a result of Yahweh's protecting presence in 2:9[5], echoed in 8:3. Zechariah 2:8[4] focuses on the physical extent of the city and 8:4–5 focuses on the inhabitants within it, but both are concerned with the repopulation of the city of Jerusalem in particular, a rare theme in the prophets. Although both texts cite the return from exile as the primary means by which Zion will be fully reinhabited, 8:5 suggests that the reproductive blessing of progeny will be a factor as well.[92]

Whereas Zech 2:8[4] corresponds closely to Isa 49:19–21 and 54:1–3, Zech 8:4–5 reflects Isa 65:17–25, the recreation of a new Jerusalem within a new heavens and new earth. Like Zech 8:4–5, Isa 65:17–25 describes a time of joy, tranquility, and the absence of sorrow. Furthermore, it similarly depicts the universal enjoyment of long life by guaranteeing that the old man (זָקֵן) will live out his days (יָמָיו; v. 20) and implies the presence of a multitude of children by eradicating infant mortality and premature death (vv. 20, 23).[93] Therefore, Zech 8:4–5 is best understood as an elaboration of 2:8[4], based on Isa 65:17–25, underscoring the abiding importance of this Isaianic text for the future.[94]

89. See Webb, *Zechariah*, 122.

90. Although רְחֹב may occasionally refer to a street, it seems that it typically denotes a public place in the city where people gather both formally and informally (see Ezra 10:9; Neh 8:1, 3, 16; 2 Chr 29:4; 32:6 for other post-exilic usages), as appears to be the case here (see Meyers and Meyers, *Haggai, Zechariah 1–8*, 415–16; Price, "רְחֹב," 1092–93).

91. Moreover, that the elderly are "sitting" (יֵשְׁבוּ) in the plazas and the children are "playing" (מְשַׂחֲקִים) there indicates not only peace and safety but also economic prosperity since, evidently, these demographics need not participate in work (see Meyers and Meyers, *Haggai, Zechariah 1–8*, 415–17).

92. Both 2:8[4] and 8:4 share the verb יָשַׁב and the construction מִן + רֹב. Although these terms are not used in the same way in these verses, מֵרֹב is a rare construction, occurring only twenty-two times in the OT and only in Nah 3:4 elsewhere in the Twelve and thus provides an additional linguistic link between these texts.

93. See Sweeney, *Twelve Prophets: Volume Two*, 648.

94. Zechariah's correspondences to Isaiah and the parallels between Zech

Zechariah 8's comprehensive description of Jerusalem's restoration culminates in the nations' pilgrimage to Jerusalem (vv. 20–23). Verses 22–23 summarize the reaction of the nations to Yahweh's universal kingship (cf. 14:9):

וּבָאוּ עַמִּים רַבִּים וְגוֹיִם עֲצוּמִים לְבַקֵּשׁ אֶת־יְהוָה צְבָאוֹת בִּירוּשָׁלָם וּלְחַלּוֹת אֶת־פְּנֵי יְהוָה	22	So many peoples and mighty nations will come to seek Yahweh of hosts at Jerusalem and to entreat the favor of Yahweh.
כֹּה אָמַר יְהוָה צְבָאוֹת בַּיָּמִים הָהֵמָּה אֲשֶׁר יַחֲזִיקוּ עֲשָׂרָה אֲנָשִׁים מִכֹּל לְשֹׁנוֹת הַגּוֹיִם וְהֶחֱזִיקוּ בִּכְנַף אִישׁ יְהוּדִי לֵאמֹר נֵלְכָה עִמָּכֶם כִּי שָׁמַעְנוּ אֱלֹהִים עִמָּכֶם	23	Thus says Yahweh of hosts: in those days ten men from every language and nation will grasp, they will grasp the garment of a Jew, saying, "Let us go with you, for we have heard that God is with you."

The correspondences between the third night vision and Zech 8 and the common theme of foreign recognition of Yahweh's kingship suggest 8:20–23 is an expansion of 2:15[11][95] where it is simply said that "many nations will join themselves to Yahweh in that day" and thus become his people.[96] Zechariah 8:20–23 enhances our understanding of the inclusion of foreigners within the people of God in several respects: 1) Zechariah 8:20–23 confirms that "joining themselves to Yahweh" involves coming to Jerusalem, the place of God's presence. Accordingly, this text provides further warrant for the possibility that the nations in 2:15[11] contribute to an overflowing Jerusalem. Although 8:20–23 is somewhat further removed textually from 8:4–5 than 2:15[11] is from 2:8[4], within Zech 8 it may likewise be the case that the pilgrimage of the nations to Jerusalem contributes to the city's population.[97] Once again, Zechariah brings together population growth in Israel and the influx of the nations. 2) The ten-to-one ratio of foreigners to "Jews" underscores that it is not merely a few foreigners making this pilgrimage, but vast throngs. 3) Although for-

---

2:5–17[1–13] and Zech 8 may have the effect of bringing together Isa 49, 54, and 65 as portraying the same era.

95. See Baldwin, *Haggai, Zechariah, Malachi*, 155.

96. Zech 8:20–23 corresponds quite closely both linguistically and conceptually to Isa 2:2–4 and Mic 4:1–3, and to Micah's version in particular (see Rudman, "Zechariah 8:20–22," 50–54; Sweeney, *Twelve Prophets: Volume Two*, 654–56; see also Nurmela, *Prophets in Dialogue*, 87–90, who deems this a "sure allusion" (90) to Isa 2:2–4).

97. It is uncertain whether the nations who come to seek Yahweh will stay at Jerusalem, but perhaps it is assumed that they would have no desire to leave.

eigners will be included fully within the people of God (2:15[11]), ethnic Israelites retain a special role as mediators of the knowledge and presence of Yahweh, in accordance with their ideal relationship to the nations as stated in Gen 12:3 (cf. Zech 8:13) and Exod 19:6.

Building on 2:5–17[1–13], Zech 8 envisions a restored population in Jerusalem and suggests that this will be accomplished by the three primary channels that we have encountered in the prophets: through physical reproduction, through the return of the exiles, and through Gentile inclusion. In addition, long life will contribute to this end.

Zechariah 10:8–10

In the present form of the book, the two "burdens" in Zech 9–11 and 12–14 expand on Zech 7–8 by describing how the hopes of Zech 8 (and the night visions) will be realized.[98] The first "burden" contrasts the coming good king (9:9–10) with the present poor leadership (Zech 10–11). Since the "shepherds" who have been entrusted with the "sheep" have failed to care for them (10:2b), Yahweh will punish them (10:3a) and will care for the people himself (10:3b). Because Yahweh is with them, Judah will be renewed with vigor (vv. 3b–5), summarized in the concluding statement, "I will strengthen the house of Judah" (וְגִבַּרְתִּי אֶת־בֵּית יְהוּדָה; v. 6a). With the next clause, "I will save the house of Joseph," the focus shifts to the restoration of the long-lost northern kingdom (vv. 6b–12).[99] Although some argue that these verses pertain to a unified kingdom,[100] this hope pertains to the northern kingdom in particular because this text refers to Ephraim (v. 7), it identifies Assyria as the place of exile (vv. 10, 11), and it envisions return to the northern territories of Gilead and Lebanon. As with the prior unit concerning Judah, v. 12a concludes, "I will strengthen them in Yahweh" (וְגִבַּרְתִּים בַּיהוָה), thus summarizing the foregoing description of restoration.

Because of his compassion for them (רִחַמְתִּים), Yahweh will restore them so that "they will be as if I had not rejected them" (v. 6). The specifics

---

98. See Kline, *Glory*, 246–47; Sweeney, *Twelve Prophets: Volume Two*, 567; Webb, *Zechariah*, 31.

99. So Conrad, *Zechariah*, 169; Gowan, *Prophetic Books*, 170. Baldwin, *Haggai, Zechariah, Malachi*, 175; Meyers and Meyers, *Zechariah 9–14*, 207; Redditt, *Haggai, Zechariah, Malachi*, 119; Sweeney, *Twelve Prophets: Volume Two*, 673; assert that only vv. 7–12 address the northern kingdom since v. 6 pertains to either Judah or both kingdoms as a transitional verse.

100. See McComiskey, "Zechariah," 1180–85; Webb, *Zechariah*, 140.

of this restoration revolve around the return to the land and the proliferation of the people (vv. 8–10), resulting in joy (v. 7):

אֶשְׁרְקָה לָהֶם וַאֲקַבְּצֵם	8	I will whistle for them and gather them,
כִּי פְדִיתִים		for I have redeemed them,
וְרָבוּ כְּמוֹ רָבוּ		and they will multiply as they multiplied before.
וְאֶזְרָעֵם בָּעַמִּים	9	I will sow them among the peoples;
וּבַמֶּרְחַקִּים יִזְכְּרוּנִי		in distant places they will remember me,
וְחָיוּ אֶת־בְּנֵיהֶם וָשָׁבוּ		and they will live/recover with their children and return.
וַהֲשִׁיבוֹתִים מֵאֶרֶץ מִצְרַיִם	10	Then I will cause them to return from the land of Egypt,
וּמֵאַשּׁוּר אֲקַבְּצֵם		and from Assyria I will gather them,
וְאֶל־אֶרֶץ גִּלְעָד וּלְבָנוֹן אֲבִיאֵם		and I will bring them to the land of Gilead and Lebanon,
וְלֹא יִמָּצֵא לָהֶם		since no room will be found for them.

Verse 8 may summarize that which is described in greater detail in vv. 9–11 by stating that Yahweh will "gather" (וַאֲקַבְּצֵם)[101] them to the land and multiply them, the two material expressions of Yahweh's favor toward his people that stretch back to the Abrahamic promises. The most common verb denoting the multiplication of the people in the OT, רָבָה, occurs only here in the Book of the Twelve with respect to the progeny blessing. Given the pervasive use of prior OT texts in Zechariah, this term recalls not a single text, but the entire trajectory of Israel's predicted and realized growth.[102] It is not clear whether the expression וְרָבוּ כְּמוֹ רָבוּ indicates that they will again begin to multiply in the same manner as they had in the past or that they will become as numerous as they once were. The latter is more likely since the former idea is best expressed simply with "וְרָבוּ."

Verse 9 then describes the first stage of restoration prior to the physical return (vv. 10–11). Most translations and commentators struggle with the initial phrase, וְאֶזְרָעֵם בָּעַמִּים. Typically, וְאֶזְרָעֵם is understood as a negative reference to Yahweh's "scattering" of his people in exilic judgment and is rendered as a past concessive ("although I scattered them among the nations..."). However, a converted imperfect verbal form would best denote the past. Moreover, a consonantal emendation is often suggested since זָרָה (usually in the Piel stem) describes exilic scattering elsewhere (Lev 26:33;

---

101. Although the Piel of קָבַץ is used only in vv. 8, 10 in Zechariah, it is employed elsewhere in the prophets to denote the return (e.g., Isa 11:12; 43:5; Jer 23:3; 29:14; 31:8; Ezek 20:34; 34:13; 36:24). Note especially the parallel verb וַהֲשִׁיבוֹתִים in v. 10.

102. Cf. Meyers and Meyers, *Zechariah 9–14*, 215.

1 Kgs 14:15; Jer 15:7; 31:10; Ezek 5:2, 10, 12; 12:14–15; 20:23; 36:19; Zech 2:2, 4[1:19, 21]), but זֶרַע does not. Rather, זֶרַע nearly always refers to the literal sowing of seed. However, when people are the object of the sowing, we have seen that it is employed in a metaphorical sense to refer to the growth of the population (see Jer 31:27; Hos 2:25[23]). Therefore, there is no reason to emend the text here, and the MT ought to be retained as a reference to the progeny blessing.[103] Having just announced that the exiles of the northern kingdom will multiply to their former extent (v. 8b), v. 9 identifies the time and place in which this will occur, namely, prior to the return among the lands to which they have been exiled.

The increase of the people in exile will be accompanied by (and perhaps result in) their remembrance of Yahweh (v. 9). This results in the return to the land of promise (vv. 10–11). Curiously, Yahweh does not bring them back to the northern heartland, but rather to Gilead and Lebanon, the marginal regions to the east and north of Samaria that formerly had remained relatively uninhabited. The following phrase, וְלֹא יִמָּצֵא לָהֶם, further explains this unusual destination. In Josh 17:16–17 the same phrase appears to refer to the lack of space because the people are too numerous, a meaning that fits the present context as well.[104] The logic between the two clauses is also unclear. It may be that Yahweh brings them to Gilead and Lebanon until no room is found for them, indicating that even these regions will be filled. Alternatively, God may bring them there because no room is found for them in their expected destination in Samaria. Or God may bring them there but no room will be found because these regions will be full, suggesting that they will have to overflow even these regions. The extent to which the land will be filled is at stake in this decision. Nevertheless, each alternative makes the same point: since even the fringe regions will be filled, the population of the northern kingdom clearly will eclipse its former numbers.[105]

Given the more general terminology employed and the various textual influences that can be discerned within Zech 10, it is difficult to identify any single intertext for the progeny motif in 10:8–10. Most agree that much of the content of Zech 10 derives from Jer 23:1–8 on the basis of conceptual parallels, including the critique of "bad shepherds," the

---

103. See McComiskey, "Zechariah," 1183. This reading appears to be uncontested among the LXX (καὶ σπερῶ αὐτοὺς) and the versions.

104. See Isa 49:19–20 for the same concept but without this expression. See Num 11:22 and Judg 21:14 for the same phrase, best translated "it is not enough."

105. See Conrad, *Zechariah*, 170; Meyers and Meyers, *Zechariah 9–14*, 222–23; Petersen, *Zechariah 9–14*, 77; Redditt, *Haggai, Zechariah, Malachi*, 122.

The Progeny Blessing in the Book of the Twelve

progeny blessing, the return to the land with the promise "I will gather" (אֲקַבֵּץ; v. 3), and the comparison of this return to the exodus from Egypt, all in roughly the same order.[106] The simple phrase "they will be fruitful and multiply" (וּפָרוּ וְרָבוּ; Jer 23:3) may thus be the initial inspiration for the introduction of the progeny motif in Zech 10:8.[107] In addition, the parallels between Zech 9–10 and Jeremiah[108] suggest the use of זֶרַע to denote the progeny blessing in Jer 31:27 may parallel its use in Zech 10:9.

With respect to the progeny blessing in particular, however, Zech 10:8–10 corresponds more closely to Hosea, since Hosea anticipates restoration and multiplication specifically for the northern kingdom (Hos 2:1[1:10]), including their "gathering" (וְנִקְבְּצוּ; Hos 2:2[1:11]; cf. Zech 10:8, 10), all due to Yahweh's compassion for them (Hos 2:3[1]; cf. Zech 10:6). Furthermore, in Hos 2:25[23] Yahweh "sows" (וּזְרַעְתִּיהָ) the people[109] and, as in Zech 10:6, Yahweh's compassion is juxtaposed with his claim to be their God. Finally, Hosea compares the Assyrian exile to a return to Egypt (8:13; 9:3; 11:5), the same analogy drawn in Zech 10:10–11. Thus centuries after Hosea's prediction, Zechariah affirms a restored northern population despite the contemporary evidence that may render it extremely unlikely.[110]

Zechariah 10:6–12 also contains several exodus allusions. In addition to the implicit analogy between the return from Assyria and the exodus from Egypt (10:10–11), Yahweh declares that he has "redeemed" them (פְּדִיתִים; v. 8), a term used in Deut 7:8, 15:15, 21:8, and 24:18 to refer to the original exodus (and also in Isa 1:27, 35:10, 51:11, and Jer 31:11 with respect to return from exile). Furthermore, v. 11 compares the return to

---

106. See Larkin, *Eschatology*, 98; Mason, "Earlier Biblical Material," 74; Nurmela, *Prophets in Dialogue*, 120–21; Person, *Second Zechariah*, 110, 122; Sweeney, *Twelve Prophets: Volume Two*, 668–69, 674.

107. Nurmela regards the progeny blessing clause in Zech 10:8 as a "sure allusion" to Jer 23:3 (*Prophets in Dialogue*, 125). See also Tai, *Prophetie*, 103–5.

108. See Tai, *Prophetie als Schriftauslegung*, 280–82, who argues that Zech 9:1–11:3 is dependent on Jeremiah 5:20–25; 25:34–38; 21–23; 31. See also Mendecki, "Deuterojesajanischer und Ezechielischer Einfluss," 340–44, who identifies a number of parallels between vv. 8–10 and other prophetic books but does not argue for the dominance of any particular intertext. In addition, Larkin, *Eschatology*, 100; and Mason "Use of Earlier," 73, identify resemblances between Zech 10 and Jer 3:15–18, yet another text in Jeremiah that includes the progeny blessing.

109. Tai argues that Zech 10:6 is dependent here on the prior "sowing" tradition of both Jer 31:27 and Hos 2:25[23] (*Prophetie als Schriftauslegung*, 105–6).

110. See Sweeney, *Twelve Prophets: Volume Two*, 672–73. Isaiah 9:2[3] and 10:22 are the only other texts in the prophets that specifically envision the future expansion of the northern tribes.

passing through the sea as in the first exodus (although here regarding the Nile). Given these allusions, the reference to the expansion of the people in v. 9a adds to the exodus typology.[111] Aside from v. 9a, only two other occurrences of the progeny blessing clearly depict the multiplication of the people of Israel outside of the land, in both cases in preparation for entry into the land, as here. The first is Exod 1:7, the initial realization of the Abrahamic promise prior to the exodus event. The other is Jer 29:6 which itself employs exodus typology from Exod 1:7 in order to encourage the growth of the exilic community while in Babylon in preparation for the return (cf. Isa 49:19–23). The parallels between Zechariah and Jeremiah suggest v. 9a presents the northern counterpart to proliferation prior to return in Jer 29:6.

Zechariah 10:6–10 also echoes prior progeny texts in Zechariah. For example, the lack of room and resulting overflow within Jerusalem (2:8[4]) is similar to the crowded land when the northern tribes return. Furthermore, joy (2:14[10]; cf. 10:7), the return (2:10–11[6–7]; 8:7–8; cf. 10:6, 8–11), and the covenant formula (2:15[11]; 8:8; 10:6) are common themes in these texts. Nevertheless, it appears that 10:8–10 corresponds more closely to other prophetic texts than it does to these prior occurrences of the progeny blessing in Zechariah. Zechariah clearly had an abundance of progeny texts and traditions at his disposal. In Zech 10 alone we see correspondences to the progeny texts of Hosea, Jeremiah, and the multiplication of Israel related to the exodus tradition. Zechariah 10:8–10 is a rich conflation and blending of these complementary traditions. The result is a progeny promise unlike any other in the OT.

Verse 8 envisions the growth of the northern tribes to their former size.[112] The use of רָבָה suggests this is not simply another way of describing the magnitude of the return but rather Yahweh's actual blessing of progeny. In this summary statement, how, when, and where this will take place remain unstated, but vv. 9–10 provide these details. They will multiply in foreign lands prior to the return to the extent that they will be too numerous for their former habitations upon return, thus going beyond the implications of v. 8 with respect to the scope of this growth.

---

111. McComiskey recognizes the contribution of the progeny blessing to the exodus typology here, connecting it to Exod 1:7, yet fails to recognize that the multiplication clause in v. 9a creates perhaps the strongest parallel since they are still in exile ("Zechariah," 1183).

112. This probably refers to the size of the north during the zenith of the united monarchy under Solomon. However, it is possible given the exodus typology that it refers to the size of the people at the time of the exodus.

The primary contribution of 10:6–12 lies in its affirmation that the entire people of God, not just Judah, will be restored and reunited (cf. 9:10, 13). Perhaps the post-exilic community was not as concerned with the ten northern tribes as with their own brothers still in exile in Babylon, but Yahweh's compassion for them was no less.[113] Just as Yahweh would continue to fulfill the Abrahamic promises of land and progeny for the southern kingdom, so he would reinstate them for the northern tribes as well. Just as he would bless Judah with progeny even in exile in preparation for the exodus-like return (Jer 29:6), so would he bless the northern tribes even in exile prior to their own return. Just as Jerusalem would overflow due to the abundance of people returning, so the northern lands would overflow their previous borders.

Conclusion: A Summary of the Progeny Blessing in Zechariah

Each of the three texts in Zechariah that cites Yahweh's blessing of progeny (2:8[4]; 8:4–5; 10:8–10) uses different language to describe it. The three are, however, similar in that they depict the filling of specific places, whether Jerusalem (2:8[4]; 8:4–5) or the northern territories (10:8–10). In Zechariah's day, the return from Babylonian exile had begun, but the prophetic promises of restoration had hardly been realized. Zechariah 2:8[4] and 8:4–5 envision a far greater return and filling of Jerusalem in the future accompanying Yahweh's dwelling with the people in the city, underscoring the importance of the current temple-building project. However, it is clear that Jerusalem is not full and overflowing by the time of the completion of the temple in 516 BCE, since even in Nehemiah's day it was necessary to draft people to live in the city (Neh 11:1–2). In contrast, 10:8–10 describes the future return of the northern tribes and indicates that the multiplication of the people will occur in the land of exile prior to return. In this case, there is no stated connection to the temple project.

With respect to the scope of the promises, 2:8[4] and 8:4–5 address exiles from the southern kingdom and 10:8–10 addresses exiles from the northern kingdom, thus encompassing the entire people of Israel and implying their reunification and joint restoration. In its own way, each text depicts a multiplication of the nation that transcends the previous experience of the nation.

---

113. Perhaps this hope addresses the northern delegation from Bethel (see 7:1–3) and others like them who may have been awaiting the northern return.

In Zech 2 and 8 the fullness of the return from exile appears to be the primary means by which the land's population is to be restored, but in both cases the inclusion of Gentile proselytes may contribute to this as well. Multiplication through reproduction is clearest in 10:8-10, but it may lie beneath the surface in 8:4-5 as well. Finally, as in Isa 65:17-25, the experience of long life in Zech 8:4 is a fourth factor contributing to the creation of a numerous people.

Interestingly, the themes of return to the land (2:10-11[6-7]; 8:7-8; 10:6-12) and the restoration of the population are inseparable in Zechariah, appearing together three times, but never alone. It appears that from the perspective of Zechariah the significance of the return lies in its ability to address one of the greatest needs of the post-exilic community, namely, to increase as a people so as to be a "great nation" once again. Although not forgotten, there is less emphasis on regaining the land itself than in other prophetic books since 2:10-11[6-7] and 8:7-8 are primarily concerned with Jerusalem alone and since in all three cases the land is mentioned only as a point of reference to describe the extent of the growth of the population.

Logically, the recovery of land and the population go hand-in-hand. However, these two material blessings are also inseparable theologically as the manifestation of Yahweh's blessing upon his people as promised to the patriarchs. The three texts that we have explored in Zechariah contain no clear references to the Abrahamic promises. Nevertheless, since the themes of land and progeny coincide in the book and since Zechariah is steeped in previous prophetic texts that do refer to the Abrahamic promises, this ancient basis for Israel's hopes may serve as an underlying framework for the restoration of the nation.[114] We have concluded that Zechariah is not directly dependent on Pentateuchal articulations of the progeny blessing at all. Rather, the book echoes other prophetic predictions of growth beyond exile that draw from the Pentateuch: Zech 2:8[4] and 8:4-5 parallel Isaiah (49:13-26 and 65:17-25, respectively) while 10:8-10 corresponds to Jer 23:1-8 (and possibly 29:6 and 31:27) and Hos 2:1[1:10], 25[23]. This is entirely consistent with the book's typical use of prior prophetic texts. Zechariah stands on the shoulders of the prophets before him and reaffirms the authority of their message (cf. 1:4; 7:7, 12).

---

114. Given the common language for the progeny blessing found in 10:8, some commentators propose that this text in particular may recall the Abrahamic promises (see McComiskey, "Zechariah," 1185; Meyers and Meyers, *Zechariah 9-14*, 236).

The Progeny Blessing in the Book of the Twelve

These hopes for future proliferation serve multiple purposes in the book of Zechariah: 1) Historically, the post-exilic community had begun to experience the reinstatement of Yahweh's blessings revoked in the exilic judgment, but there appears to have been a prevailing attitude of despondency due to the delay of fuller blessing. One of the predominant concerns was the paucity of exiles who had returned to the land thus far. Zechariah addresses this concern by describing a future day in which the expectations for the return and a thriving population will be realized. However, Zechariah maintains that repentance is necessary if the community wishes to see this day (see 1:3-6; 8:16–17, 19). The progeny blessing thus contributes to the perlocutionary effect of the book, namely, to motivate and encourage repentance, by providing this hope. 2) Through his treatment of the blessing, Zechariah also addresses the apparent failure of the prophetic restoration promises to materialize by alluding to these prior promises, thus reaffirming their validity. At the same time, Zechariah corrects any misperception that the anticipated restoration would come about in a sudden and complete manner and indicates that its fullness will be deferred into the future on account of lingering sin in the community. 3) The flourishing of the population in the land also serves as visible evidence of Yahweh's compassion toward them (1:16; 10:6) and that he is again "their God" (8:8; 10:6) and they are again "his people" (2:15[11]; 8:8). 4) Finally, 10:6–12 indicates that all twelve tribes will experience restoration to the fullest.

Apart from the introduction to the book (1:1–6), the progeny motif occurs in each of the major divisions within Zechariah (Zech 1–6, 7–8, 9–14). Since this is a consistent concern of the entire book, the progeny blessing is one of many themes that spans so-called "First Zechariah" and "Second Zechariah" and lends credence to the book's literary unity. Although 10:8–10 differs from 2:8[4] and 8:4–5 in that it addresses the north, this does not put it at odds with these preceding texts; rather, it complements them within the book's final form.

A Summary of the Progeny Blessing in the Twelve

Since the Twelve prophets exist together as one collection with a coherent message, we should consider the effect of reading Hosea and Zechariah together as the combined witness to the progeny theme in the Twelve. The two portraits differ in some key respects. Hosea primarily addresses those in the northern kingdom prior to their exile and treats the progeny blessing in a polemical context in which Yahweh and Baal make rival claims regarding bestowing fertility. In contrast, Zechariah addresses the postexilic community from Babylon nearly 200 years later and predicts the restoration of the population in order to address despair within the community. Nevertheless, there are a number of commonalities between the two portrayals. Hosea describes the blessing as "sowing" people (2:2[1:11], 25[23]), as an expression of Yahweh's compassion (2:3[1], 25[23]), as a result of the covenant formula (2:3[1]), and as an event that accompanies the return from exile (2:2[1:11]), all echoed later in Zechariah's depiction of the progeny motif (see 1:16; 2:10–11[6–7], 14–15[10–11]; 8:7–8; 10:6, 8–10).

Interestingly, if we discount the texts in Hosea in which the progeny blessing is unclear or doubtful (4:7, 10; 14:6–8[5–7]), the remaining texts in the Twelve appear to form a chiasm:

Israel (Hos 2:1–3[1:10–2:1], 25[23])
    Judah (Zech 2:8[4])
    Judah (Zech 8:4–5)
Israel (Zech 10:8–10)

The most obvious parallels pertain to the immediate addressees, the first and last texts anticipating the multiplication of the northern kingdom and the middle texts predicting the same for the southern kingdom. However, we have argued above that there are stronger organic connections between these parallel texts, such that Zech 8:4–5 builds upon Zech 2:8[4] while Zech 10:8–10 corresponds more closely to Hos 2:1–3[1:10–2:1], 25[23] than to any other prophetic text that treats the progeny blessing. It may be unlikely that Zechariah or any later editor intentionally created such a pattern. Nevertheless, when we read the Twelve holistically with an eye for the progeny blessing, these relationships create cohesion among these texts. The echoes of Hos 2:1–3[1:10–2:1], 25[23] in Zech 10:8–10 are particularly significant since the multiplication of the northern ten tribes is a rare theme and since this links two different works within the Twelve. In effect, Zech 10:8–10 affirms that the earlier Hosean hope remains valid for the future. Not only must its realization be nearer in Zechariah's day, but he also appears to magnify the extent of the proliferation and return beyond what is discernible from Hosea.

Although four primary texts is a small "sample size," this divided attention between the northern and southern kingdoms makes a special contribution to the prophetic treatment of the progeny blessing since the major prophets focus solely (or predominantly in the case of Isaiah) on the multiplication of the Babylonian Judean exiles. Thus, the Twelve is concerned with the return, proliferation, and renewed covenant relationship of all twelve tribes.

7

A Synthesis of the Progeny Blessing in the Latter Prophets

ACCORDING TO THE OT, Yahweh is the fountainhead of all life, enabling conception, birth, and growth as well as the survival and expansion of the human race. In his common grace, he curtails the debilitating effects of the Fall by blessing all of humankind with progeny, but particularly delights in blessing his own people with children. Having examined all the texts in the Latter Prophets that treat this theme, we will synthesize our results into a prophetic theology of the progeny blessing. First, we will describe the prominence and diverse articulations of the blessing in the Latter Prophets. Second, we will compare and contrast how each prophetic book envisions the operation of the progeny blessing, including its agent, time, place, scope, relationship to other restoration themes, and means of realization. Third, we will synthesize the indebtedness of the prophets to other OT texts and traditions that pertain to the progeny motif. Finally, we will explore the biblical-theological significance of the blessing in the Latter Prophets and compare this with its significance in the rest of the OT.

The Prominence and Articulation of the Progeny Blessing in the Latter Prophets

Apart from Genesis and Deuteronomy, the progeny blessing occurs more frequently in the books of the Latter Prophets than anywhere else in the OT (see Appendix A). The blessing is especially prominent in Isaiah, where the story of mother Zion is primarily concerned with the recovery of her children, perhaps because the restoration of the Abrahamic promises underlies the hopes of Isa 40–66. The progeny motif is less frequent in

A Synthesis of the Progeny Blessing in the Latter Prophets

Jeremiah, but it still occurs in five different restoration oracles. In Ezekiel it only occurs in Ezek 36–37, but the blessing is developed more fully there than any other place in the Latter Prophets. Since the majority of the restoration oracles in the Book of the Twelve occur in Hosea and Zechariah, it is appropriate that the progeny theme appears only in these books. It is, however, an important theme in both works. The progeny blessing plays a crucial role in the restoration oracles of each of these books not only because prosperity is inherently dependent upon a large population, but also because each author was familiar with prior Israelite traditions of creation, the Abrahamic covenant, and the Sinai covenant that include it among Yahweh's fundamental blessings.

Outside the Latter Prophets, verbs such as רָבָה and פָּרָה and similes comparing the innumerability of people to the innumerability of sand, dust, and the stars commonly denote the progeny blessing. Each prophet employs some of these expressions, with Jeremiah and Ezekiel in particular favoring familiar terms, employing רָבָה in nearly every context in which they refer to the blessing (see Jer 3:16; 23:3; 29:6; 30:19; 33:22; Ezek 36:10, 11, 37; 37:26; cf. Isa 9:2[3]; 51:2; Zech 10:8). They are also the only two prophets who employ פָּרָה, always juxtaposed with רָבָה (Jer 3:16; 23:3; Ezek 36:11). In addition, Isa 10:22, 48:19, and Hos 2:1[1:10] use the prevalent sand simile.

In contrast, Isaiah and Zechariah tend to describe proliferation, generating unique articulations of the blessing. As a result, these are some of the most evocative and powerful progeny expressions, but also some of the most ambiguous. Isaiah portrays multiplication through the extended Zion metaphor, the imagery of plant growth (44:3–4), the transformation of "the smallest" (60:22), and long life (65:20). Like Isa 49:19–21, Zechariah simply describes the filling of specific places. Interestingly, even though the image is not found elsewhere, three different prophets promise that Yahweh will "sow" (זָרַע; see Jer 31:27; Hos 2:25[23]; Zech 10:9) the people, denoting numerical growth.

The Major Prophets also employ negative expressions or imagery to describe the progeny blessing (cf. Exod 23:26): premature death will be eradicated (Isa 65:23), the people will not "diminish" (מָעַט; Jer 29:6; 30:19), the decimation curses will be abolished (Ezek 34:25–31), and the land will no longer bereave the nation of their children (Ezek 36:12–14).

I Will Surely Multiply Your Offspring

The Dimensions of the Progeny Blessing in the Latter Prophets

Agent

With one voice, the prophets declare that Yahweh is ultimately responsible for the numerical growth of his people, often expressed with causative Hiphil forms of רָבָה (e.g., Isa 51:2; Jer 30:19; Ezek 36:10). Even when this is not explicit or when the language of the progeny blessing likely denotes the return, the broader literary context indicates that Israel's recovery of her population is Yahweh's work. We have argued that in Jer 29:6 the people are seemingly responsible for procreation, since God is hidden while they are in exile, awaiting *his* return when he will initiate *their* return to the land. However, even in this case, Yahweh is silently at work, blessing his people as in Exod 1:7. Furthermore, Israel bears some responsibility for her own growth since Yahweh's blessing is tied to her covenant loyalty.[1]

Time and Place

Yahweh first multiplied his people in Egypt prior to the exodus. By the time of Solomon, Israel had achieved even greater numbers as a result of God's blessing in the promised land. Only Isaiah acknowledges these past realizations of the blessing. Whereas Isa 51:2 refers to the multiplication of Abraham's seed, 26:15 and 48:19 likely allude to the expansion of the nation under Solomon. In addition, Isa 10:22 claims that Israel was or soon would be as numerous as the sand in Isaiah's own day.

The rest of the prophetic references to the progeny blessing address future proliferation. Nearly all of these texts anticipate the multiplication of the people following the return to the land, Yahweh's chosen setting for blessing in the Sinai covenant. Little more can be said concerning the timing of the blessing, although Zechariah indicates that even though the return had begun in his day, the restoration of the population is still future (Zech 2:8[4]; 8:5). Its juxtaposition with other aspects of restoration, such as the reign of the Davidic king (e.g., Isa 9:5–6[6–7]; Jer 23:4–6; Ezek 37:22, 24–25) or the cleansing of the sin of the people (Ezek 36:33), may suggest that proliferation will take place at this time. However, it is evident that restoration blessings appearing together in prophetic oracles will not

---

1. See chapter 2 conclusion for a fuller explanation of the dynamic between divine and human responsibility in the progeny blessing in the OT.

A Synthesis of the Progeny Blessing in the Latter Prophets

necessarily coincide temporally in their realization.[2] Therefore, from the perspective of the OT, when this will occur remains ambiguous and open-ended. Some texts do, however, indicate that this proliferation will be final and permanent (Isa 60:22; 65:20–23; Jer 31:35–37; Ezek 37:24–28), unlike previous realizations. Typically, the entire land of Canaan is the location of multiplication. However, Zechariah is interested in the numerical growth of Jerusalem in particular (2:8[4]; 8:4–5). Similarly, the Isaianic story of mother Zion emphasizes growth within Zion. This is natural since Zion is the focal point of the restoration hopes of Isaiah and Zechariah. We have argued, however, that in each case the blessing experienced at Jerusalem probably represents blessing across the land (cf. Isa 54:3).

In a few texts, proliferation precedes the return. This is clearest in Jer 29:6 where the exilic community is instructed to multiply in preparation for the return. Isaiah 49:19–21 may indicate growth while in exile as well. Zechariah 10:8–10 predicts that the exiled northern tribes will multiply prior to return to the expanded northern territories. Israel's great hope for her proliferation as a nation awaits the return to the land and the mending of her relationships to Yahweh and the land (cf. Ezek 36:9–14). Nevertheless, this minority voice indicates that the grace and compassion of Yahweh reaches even to the lands of exile as he prepares his people for the return, similar to the blessing and preparation of his people for the exodus in Exod 1:7.

Scope

In God's common grace, the nations of the earth continue to experience Yahweh's blessing of progeny. However, following the Primeval History, the OT is almost solely concerned with the proliferation of Abraham and his descendants, a special manifestation of the universal blessing. This remains true in the Latter Prophets, although some texts may include converted foreigners within the corporate expansion of the people of Israel.

Typically, in Jeremiah and Ezekiel a united Israel and Judah is the object of the progeny blessing.[3] In keeping with their parochialism, neither prophet exhibits any concern for the multiplication of foreign nations or considers their inclusion within Israel. In contrast, Isaiah and the Book of the Twelve present a more diverse and complex picture. Sometimes Isa-

---

2. Note in particular the perspectives of Zechariah and the NT writers.

3. The exceptions are Jer 29:6 which addresses the Judahite exiles, and Jer 33:22 which addresses the lines of David and Levi.

iah focuses on the proliferation of the northern tribes (9:2[3]; 10:22) and sometimes he emphasizes the multiplication of Judah (26:15; 49:19–21; 54:1–3). In Isa 56–66 those who will be blessed are defined ethically rather than ethnically. As a result, there is greater openness to the inclusion of foreigners in the people of God and non-Israelites may be the recipients of the blessing as well (see, e.g. 2:2–4; 19:16–25; 42:4, 6; 56:1–8; 66:18–24). The Book of the Twelve is similar in that Hos 2:1[1:10] and Zech 10:8–10 envision the multiplication of the north and Zech 2:8[4] and 8:4–5 anticipate the expansion of Judah, together depicting the proliferation of all twelve tribes without asserting it in any one place. Furthermore, like Isaiah, Zech 2:15[11] and 8:20–23 may indicate that foreigners will contribute to the multiplication of God's people.[4] In sum, the prophets agree that all twelve tribes will someday experience the fullness of the progeny blessing. Isaiah and Zechariah exhibit hope for the nations as well, consistent with the broader scope of these books.

Extent

The population of Israel continues to grow following entry into the promised land on the basis of the covenant blessings, culminating in the reign of Solomon when, according to Kings, Israel attains the greatest size in her history. Although the Latter Prophets sometimes allude to the size of the people at the time of the exodus and Solomon in their portrayals of future proliferation, they never explicitly compare the future size of the nation to her size at these times.[5] Rarely do they indicate the future extent of growth. This is especially the case in Jeremiah, where only 30:19–20 states that they will be "as before" (כְּקֶדֶם).

However, other prophets anticipate multiplication that surpasses Israel's growth in the past. The Mosaic vision of restoration beyond exile in Deut 30:1–10 provides the Pentateuchal paradigm for such unprecedented growth, promising that Yahweh will prosper and multiply them "more than your fathers" (וְהֵיטִבְךָ וְהִרְבְּךָ מֵאֲבֹתֶיךָ; v. 5). In the context of the multiplication of the people on the land, Ezek 36:11, in which Yahweh promises, "I will prosper you more than before" (וְהֵיטִבֹתִי מֵרִאשֹׁתֵיכֶם),

---

4. Interestingly, Jer 31:27, Ezek 36:11, and Zech 2:8[4] extend the scope of proliferation beyond humanity to include the animal realm as well, indicating a more holistic restoration of both land and people.

5. Isaiah 9:2[3], Ezek 37:26, and Hos 2:1[1:10] may come closest, each apparently alluding to conditions under Solomon as a paradigm for the future.

A Synthesis of the Progeny Blessing in the Latter Prophets

corresponds closely to this text. Isaiah 49–66 employs dramatic imagery to describe unprecedented growth: Zion will no longer hold them (49:19-21; 54:1-3), God's people will consist of multiple "mighty nations" (60:22), and the yield of Mother Zion's "delivery" eclipses that of Sarah (66:7-9). Similarly, Zechariah describes a more populous Jerusalem (2:8[4]; 8:4-5) and northern land (10:8-10) than previously.[6] In each of these texts, we may infer that the nation's (or Jerusalem's) pre-exilic size is the primary point of comparison.

Related Blessings

The progeny blessing appears consistently alongside other restoration themes. A renewed relationship with Yahweh, return to the land, and Davidic kingship logically precede the increase of the nation, whereas rebuilt cities and joy result from this increase.

A restored relationship with Yahweh is the foundation and prerequisite for the future proliferation of Israel. Indeed, apart from God's renewed commitment to his people, blessing would be unthinkable. Juxtaposed with the progeny blessing, this favor is expressed in numerous ways. For example, Yahweh's gift of progeny is the result of his renewed compassion toward his people (Isa 49:13, 15; 54:7-10; Jer 30:18; Hos 2:3[1], 25[23]; Zech 1:16-17; 10:6), coincides with the return of God's presence (Jer 3:17; Ezek 37:26-28; Zech 2:9[5], 14-15[10-11]; 8:3), and operates within the context of a renewed covenant (Jer 31:31-34; Ezek 34:25-31; 37:26-28). Appropriately, the multiplication of Israel frequently appears alongside the covenant formula that summarizes the relationship between Yahweh and Israel (Jer 30:22; Ezek 36:28; 37:23, 27; Hos 2:3[1], 25[23]; Zech 8:8). Because of this correlation, rapid multiplication may indicate to the post-exilic community that God's favor has indeed returned to them.

The return to (Isa 48:20-21; 49:12, 22-23; Jer 3:18; 23:3, 7-8; Ezek 36:8-12; Hos 2:2[1:11]; Zech 2:10-11[6-7]; 8:7-8; 10:6, 8-12) or repossession of (Isa 26:15; 54:3; 60:21; 65:17-25; Ezek 36:12; 37:25) the land is juxtaposed with the progeny blessing in each book as well. Sometimes this may be because these are the two material blessings of the Abrahamic covenant. Typically, however, the two probably appear together simply

---

6. In general, it appears that the texts that address a post-exilic audience (i.e., Isa 56–66 and Zechariah) contain the grandest hopes for the extent of multiplication. Interestingly, in Zechariah these hopes have grown rather than shrunk in the face of unfulfilled expectations.

because the people must return to the land prior to the renewal of society, which includes the expansion of the population.[7] This relationship is even more direct in Zechariah where the apparent purpose of the return is the growth of the population of the post-exilic community since the two themes are always juxtaposed. From the perspective of the land, the return is the means by which "multiplication" occurs (see Isa 49:19–21; Ezek 36:9–11). Furthermore, the land must be in harmony with the people for both to thrive (Ezek 34:25–31; 36:12–15).

The growth of the returned exiles often coincides with the restoration of righteous Davidic kingship. Although the divine king is ultimately responsible for the blessing of progeny, the human king bears some responsibility as well. First, under the Sinai covenant, the king is required to model covenant faithfulness (Deut 17:14–20), resulting in blessing. Second, a thriving and expanding population is the natural result of righteous and just rule.[8] Finally, we see in Samuel–Kings that a strong correlation exists between the faithfulness of the king, Israel's representative, and Yahweh's inclination to bless the people. This is most clearly illustrated in Israel's narratives in 1 Kgs 4:20 where Solomon's wise and just rule is accompanied by the greatest realization of the progeny promise. Although the juxtaposition between Davidic kingship and multiplication occurs throughout the Latter Prophets (Isa 9:5–6[6–7]; Ezek 34:23–24; 37:22, 24–25; Hos 2:2[1:11]), it is particularly consistent in Jeremiah (3:15; 23:4–6; 30:9, 21),[9] perhaps due to Jeremiah's close correspondence to deuteronomic thought.[10] Many of these same texts anticipate the reunification of north and south (Jer 3:18; 23:6; Ezek 37:15–23; Hos 2:2[1:11]),[11] a theme

---

7. There are, of course, a few exceptions to this in which it appears that the people will multiply even while in exile.

8. The inverse is true as well: exploitative rule results in decimation (e.g., Ezek 11:6).

9. In addition, these themes coincide in Jer 33:14–26, although here it is not the people who increase as a result of just rule but rather the Davidic line itself that will multiply.

10. Jeremiah discusses a future David only in 23:1–8, 30:1–11, and 33:14–26, while Ezekiel does so in 34:23–31 and 37:15–28. It thus appears that Jeremiah and Ezekiel can hardly conceive of a future David apart from the proliferation that will accompany (and perhaps result from) his rule. In contrast, Zechariah often mentions the Davidic king (3:8; 6:12–15; 9:9–10; 12:6–13:1), but never in connection with the progeny blessing, perhaps because his role in Zechariah does not appear to be as significant as what we find in Jeremiah and Ezekiel.

11. This is especially noteworthy since no prophetic progeny text treats the reunification of the nation without also including future Davidic kingship.

that corresponds both to kingship, since the ideal Davidic king rules all twelve tribes, and to the proliferation of the nation, since reunification produces a larger nation.

In Ezek 36, the immediate goal of the restoration of the population to the land is the rebuilding and resettlement of the cities lying in ruins from the exilic judgment (vv. 10–11, 33–36; see also Isa 54:3; Jer 30:18). Obviously, people are necessary to rebuild the desolate cities and are then the means by which they will eventually be filled, bringing harmony to the personified land (Ezek 36:1–15).

Finally, Yahweh's blessing of progeny contributes to the joy of the people (Isa 9:2[3]; 51:3; 54:1; 60:5; 65:18–19; Jer 30:19; Zech 2:14[10]; 10:7). Moreover, personified Jerusalem, her inhabitants, and "servants" alike will be joyful at the conclusion to the story of mother Zion in Isaiah (66:10–14) as a result of her many children (66:7–9). In light of all that Yahweh has graciously done for them, the people's response could hardly be otherwise.

Interestingly, the progeny blessing rarely appears alongside the fertility of animals (Jer 31:27; Ezek 36:11; Zech 2:8[4]) or the fertility of the land (Isa 65:21–22; Hos 2:23–24[21–22]). Although the covenant blessings of Deuteronomy employ a three-fold formula that includes each of these aspects of fertility (7:13; 28:4, 11; 30:9), these three never appear together in the restoration blessings in the prophets, with the possible exception of Ezek 36 where fertility of humans (vv. 9–14, 37–38), animals (v. 11), and land (vv. 29–30, 35?) occur in the same chapter. Perhaps this is because many restoration oracles containing the progeny blessing are primarily concerned with restoration to the land and with the re-establishment of ideal society under divine and human rule and thus do not emphasize the fertility of animals and the land.

Means of Realization

Outside the Latter Prophets, the language of the progeny blessing in the OT always denotes numerical expansion via biological processes. This is typically true within the Latter Prophets as well. This involves not only the ability to conceive and reproduce, but low infant mortality rates and long life as well since all prophetic texts that anticipate multiplication are concerned with the corporate rather than individual experience of the blessing. These latter themes are rarely treated directly (but see Isa 65:20–23; Ezek 36:12–14; Zech 8:4), but may be implicitly included elsewhere.

I Will Surely Multiply Your Offspring

Physical proliferation is the sole referent in the texts we have examined in Jeremiah, and is the dominant concern in the other prophetic books (except perhaps Zechariah).

Sometimes, however, when the frame of reference is not the people themselves but rather a location, the portrayal of the expansion of the people more accurately denotes the return to the land. In the Isaianic story of mother Zion, the return to the land metaphorically produces an abundance of children (49:19-21; 54:1-3; 66:7-9). Similarly, from the perspective of the "mountains of Israel," the return of the exiles results in the "multiplication" of people on the land (Ezek 36:9-12). Finally, possibly building on these earlier Isaianic texts, Zechariah describes the extravagant growth of the population of Jerusalem (2:8[4]; 8:4-5), accomplished through the pilgrimage of great throngs to Zion. Although each of these texts refers primarily to the return, other contextual factors indicate in each case (except perhaps Zech 2:8[4]) that the numerical expansion of the people is a factor as well. For example, since the size of the population in Isa 49:19-21 and 54:1-3 exceeds the pre-exilic size of the people, we infer that the people have also physically multiplied.

Finally, in some cases the inclusion of the nations within Israel may contribute to the corporate multiplication of Yahweh's people. This perspective may originate with the book of Isaiah, given its more universalistic perspective and since God's people are increasingly defined along ethical rather than ethnic lines. However, it is with caution that we concluded that the salvation of the nations plays a role in Israel's expansion, since these two themes never come together explicitly. Since they are historically situated in the midst of the disaster of the exile, Jeremiah and Ezekiel are almost entirely concerned with the survival of Israel, emphasizing the restoration of the chosen redemptive agent of God's plan rather than the eventual worldwide effects of that redemption. There is certainly no indication in these books that the progeny blessing might include foreigners. Zechariah revives Isaiah's concern for the nations and appears to draw on Isaiah's inclusivist texts. He brings together multiplication and the inclusion of the nations more closely than Isaiah (see 2:8[4], 15[11]; 8:4-5, 20-23), so that it is likely that converted foreigners are among those who fill Jerusalem as God's people.[12] Although little more can be said from the

---

12. In these two texts, the more weight we give to the conversion of Gentiles in contributing to the size of the city, the less we can give to physical reproduction as a factor in this growth.

perspective of the prophets, this question becomes far more significant in the NT, where these prophetic themes are powerfully merged.

Prior Progeny Texts and Traditions Employed by the Latter Prophets

The OT is rich with texts and traditions pertaining to the progeny blessing. Prior to the writings of the Latter Prophets, we can trace a series of progeny promises and fulfillments through Israel's history: the universal blessing at creation, the Abrahamic promise, its initial realization prior to the exodus, further prospects for blessing in the Sinai covenant, a greater realization during Solomon's reign, and the prediction of proliferation beyond exile in Deut 30. Although only in Isa 51:2 do we see an explicit appeal to a prior progeny tradition, sometimes it is clear that a text is indebted to one or more of these traditions. However, sometimes there may be only hints or no indications at all of such dependence. Many of the correspondences we have identified between prophetic texts and other texts or traditions are simply possibilities rather than certainties, given the subjective nature and imprecision of making such identifications. Nevertheless, we have concluded that each of these prior traditions is employed within the Latter Prophets.

Since nearly all prophetic texts containing the progeny blessing are concerned with the seed of Abraham, it is to be expected that the universal blessing plays only a minor role. Yahweh's stated purpose for creation in Isa 45:18 offers the clearest allusion to the creational blessing, and may correspond to Gen 1:28 in particular given other parallels to Gen 1–2 in the immediate context. Jeremiah 3:16, 23:3, and Ezek 36:11 correspond verbally to the universal blessing since פָּרָה and רָבָה are juxtaposed as we find in Gen 1:28 and 9:1, 7, but only in Gen 35:11 elsewhere (see also Jer 31:27).

The Abrahamic promise is the most important and foundational progeny tradition for the Latter Prophets since it underlies subsequent progeny traditions from which the prophets draw. Direct allusions to Abraham are common as well, especially in the book of Isaiah. Abrahamic moorings are clearest in 51:2, 54:1–3, and 60:22, but we detected likely allusions to the Abrahamic blessing in 9:2[3], 10:22, 26:15, 44:3–4, 48:19, 49:19–21, 65:9, 20–23, and 66:7–9 as well. Each of the other prophetic books also depends on the Abrahamic tradition (Jer 30:19; 31:27; Ezek 36:37–38; 37:26; Hos 2:1[1:10]; Zech 10:8). We have identified some of these texts with the Abrahamic promise simply on the basis of the close juxtaposition between the recovery of land and progeny, the two material blessings of the Abrahamic covenant. Although this is not conclusive evidence, it may be sufficient because of the prominence of this tradition in Israel's Scriptures and history. In general, these allusions provide hope that Yahweh has not forgotten his ancient promises and that he can and will act on behalf of the exiles just as he did in the past for their ancestors.

On the basis of thematic parallels and the new exodus motif, we suggested that Jeremiah in particular depicts the exilic (29:6) and post-return (3:16; 23:3, 7–8; 30:19; 31:27) multiplication of the people as a "new multiplication" similar to Exod 1:7 (see also Hos 2:25[23]). Since Exod 1:7 is the only precedent for the increase of the nation outside the land in preparation for a journey to the land of blessing, other instances where it appears that the people will multiply prior to the return (Isa 49:19–21; Zech 10:9) correspond typologically to Exod 1:7 as well.[13]

Consistent with Ezekiel's indebtedness to the priestly tradition and close correspondences to Leviticus in general, Ezekiel's use of the progeny blessing in 34:25–31, 36:10–14, and 37:26 seems to be directly dependent on Lev 26:9 and the larger catalogue of blessings and curses in Lev 26. Since the restoration blessings operate in the context of a renewed covenant analogous to Sinai (34:25; 37:26), and since obedience is still required (although now guaranteed), this tradition fits nicely. Although we have detected prophetic correspondences to Deut 30:1–10, we have not detected any clear parallels to the covenant blessings of Deuteronomy.[14]

Allusions to the tradition of the realization of the Abrahamic progeny promise during the reign of Solomon are not as clear. However, the inclusion of the progeny blessing in restoration oracles that envision a united kingdom under an ideal Davidic king (see Isa 9:2[3]; Jer 3:16; 23:3; Ezek 37:26; Hos 2:1[1:10]) may recall the days of Solomon since the description of 1 Kgs 4:20—5:8[4:20–28] pertains to the only time in Israel's history where these conditions existed together. While these texts ultimately point to another realization of the Abrahamic blessing, their correspondences to Solomon's reign indicate that Israel's glory days will return. Furthermore,

---

13. See below on the biblical-theological significance of this motif.

14. However, we would expect that prophets such as Jeremiah who may have had access to both Deut 28 and 30 would have employed Deut 30:1–10 in descriptions of Israel's future and left the covenant blessings to the side since Deut 30:1–10 describes the very period that the prophets portray. Furthermore, Ezekiel may rely on the covenant blessings of Leviticus in his description of the future simply because Leviticus contains no comparable vision of prosperity beyond exile (cf. Lev 26:40–45).

A Synthesis of the Progeny Blessing in the Latter Prophets

references to the past or present realization of the progeny blessing (Isa 26:15), particularly those that employ the "sand" metaphor (Isa 10:22; 48:19; Hos 2:1[1:10]; cf. 1 Kgs 4:20), may also recall the size of Israel during the days of Solomon.

Three Pentateuchal texts predict hope beyond eventual exile. We have not detected clear parallels to Lev 26:40–45, which focuses on Yahweh's remembrance of the covenant rather than on the restored conditions in the land. Nor have we found solid correspondences to Deut 4:29–31, although the restoration is sometimes grounded in Yahweh's compassion in the texts we have examined (see Isa 49:13, 15; 54:7–10; Jer 30:18; Hos 2:3[1], 25[23]; Zech 1:16–17; 10:6; cf. Deut 4:31). However, we suggested that Jer 23:3, 31:27, and Ezek 36:11 parallel Deut 30:1–10, which includes the progeny blessing (vv. 5, 9). Since this is the lone text outside the Latter Prophets that develops the post-exilic restoration conditions, it is surprising that there are not stronger links between Deut 30:1–10 and the prophetic texts we have treated. However, the prophetic restoration oracles often contain the same logic and motifs. As a result, Deut 30:1–10 may be the most important intertext for the prophetic progeny texts in general, although it is difficult to demonstrate that the prophets are directly dependent on it.

In addition to prior traditions from Israel's history, at times the prophets depend on other prophetic texts, although the direction of dependence may be debated. This is most clearly the case in Zechariah, where we have argued that Zech 1:16–17, 2:8–14[4–10] depends on Isaiah 49:13–26 as well as on Ezek 37:24–28, that Zech 8:4–5 is based on Isa 65:17–25, and that Zech 10:8–10 employs Jer 23:1–8 (and possibly 29:6 and 31:27) as well as Hos 2:1[1:10], 25[23]. Furthermore, we have noted conceptual correspondences between Jeremiah and Ezekiel that may indicate influence, such as the shepherding imagery that Jer 3:15–16, 23:1–4 and Ezek 34, 37:15–28 share alongside the progeny blessing. Finally, the three texts containing the metaphor of "sowing" people (Jer 31:27; Hos 2:25[23]; Zech 10:9, all using זֶרַע) may be interrelated since this metaphor is found only in the OT prophetic literature. In these prophetic appropriations of other prophetic texts, they probably allude to not just one text, but the entire trajectory of the progeny blessing that underlies it.[15]

---

15. We have also identified a number of texts that are closely related to other texts containing the progeny blessing in the same book, owing either to common authorship or thematic development within the book.

In sum, each prophet tends to draw from different traditions. Isaiah emphasizes the Abrahamic blessings and, secondarily, their ultimate realization under Solomon. Ezekiel is indebted to the covenant blessings of Lev 26. Zechariah relies on previous prophetic texts. Jeremiah does not emphasize any particular tradition, but may be most indebted to Deut 30 and the exodus tradition. Thus there is considerable diversity within unity: the prophets attest with one voice that Yahweh will once again bless his people with progeny following the exile, but each prophet grounds this expectation in a different tradition. Within the prophetic corpus as a whole, no major tradition is forgotten as the prophets cull from the rich history of progeny promises and realizations recorded in the OT. We have also seen that each of the four works in the Latter Prophets reflects knowledge of most of the OT progeny traditions. In Ezekiel, for example, proliferation following exile is understood as a manifestation of the universal blessing, the Abrahamic promise, the covenant blessings of Sinai, and as a return to the days of Solomonic glory. Thus, the prophets tend to view future multiplication as the latest episode in the one continuous history of blessing rather than relying on a specific text or tradition. Accordingly, one tradition should not be favored to the complete neglect of the others.

Although the prophets are largely dependent on prior traditions with respect to the progeny blessing, new facets of the blessing emerge in the prophetic literature. Most notably, the story of mother Zion in Isa 49 uses the progeny blessing as a metaphor for the return. Jeremiah 29:6 is unique in that the exiles are commanded to multiply since they are faced with a situation in which doing so is not inherently desirable (cf. 16:1–4). Moreover, Jer 29:6 envisions proliferation even while in exile. Jeremiah 33:22 applies the progeny blessing to the lineage of David and Levi, the most specific application of the blessing in the OT. By addressing the land rather than the people, Ezek 36:9–14 indicates that the land itself benefits from multiplication and thus the language of increase, as in Isa 49, more accurately denotes the return. The incorporation of the nations contributes to the realization of the progeny blessing in Zech 2:8[4], 15[11] and 8:4–5, 20–23, a connection that is already latent in Isaiah. Finally, Zech 10:8–10 announces that even the northern tribes will multiply in exile prior to their return (cf. Jer 29:6). In each of these respects, the prophets expand the expectations for multiplication in the land following the return as stated in Deut 30:1–10. Thus, each prophet relies heavily on previous traditions, yet goes beyond them.

A Synthesis of the Progeny Blessing in the Latter Prophets

The Theological and Biblical-Theological Significance of the Progeny Blessing in the Latter Prophets

The presence of the progeny blessing in prophetic restoration oracles is intended to have various effects on the audience: 1) The promise that Yahweh will multiply the nation, as with other aspects of the restoration, sometimes motivates repentance.[16] It is only the righteous, Yahweh's servants, those who seek God, who will participate in the glorious future. This motivation is most evident in Jeremiah and Zechariah where the theme is particularly prominent, but it is present in the other books as well. 2) Jeremiah commands the exiles to multiply themselves (Jer 29:6) as an act of faith to ensure the survival of the community and to prepare them for the return. 3) The promise of future proliferation gives the people hope for the future and confidence in Yahweh. During the eighth century, Assyrian oppression threatened the population of the land. Babylonian invasion and exile further decimated the population. Even after the exile, Zechariah addresses a small and floundering population in Yehud. The prophets address these concerns by promising Yahweh's favor and multiplication of their numbers once again. Although decimating judgment is severe, it is only temporary. Hope is on the horizon. 4) Allusions to previous texts and traditions that contain the progeny blessing indicate to the people that Yahweh's promises and covenantal commitments are not void but are still valid, fostering further hope. Yahweh remains committed to his people, in continuity with past blessing, yet surpassing it.

The progeny blessing also plays a multifaceted role within Yahweh's purposes in the Latter Prophets: 1) The increase of the nation is fundamental to the restoration of Israel's well-being. The return to the land, agricultural bounty, reunification under one king, and protection from enemy peoples would only be a paltry hope apart from the re-creation of a "great nation." If Israel's population remained smaller than in Solomon's day, the restoration could never be considered the pinnacle of blessing. Moreover, the nation must multiply in order to fill the cities (e.g., Zech 2:8[4]; 8:4–5) and the land (e.g., Zech 10:8–10). Prosperity and joy are thus dependent on Israel's proliferation. 2) The multiplication of Israel is the product of Yahweh's presence with and favor toward the people, rooted in his compassion, faithfulness to his covenant commitments, and concern

---

16. See especially Jer 3:14 and Hos 2:1–4[1:10—2:2], where repentance and the progeny blessing are closely related.

for his own reputation (Ezek 36:22–23, 32). It is a sign for both Israel and the nations that Yahweh is their God and they are his people. The progeny blessing thus plays a key role in the restoration of the relationships among Yahweh, the people, and the land.[17] As a result of the renewal of the relationship between Yahweh and the people and the transformation of their hearts, he multiplies them, resulting in a peopled and "happy" land (e.g., Ezek 36:9–14; Isa 49:19–21).[18] 3) Ultimately, Yahweh blesses his people in order that he might be known and glorified. This is most clearly expressed in Ezekiel where the recognition formula concludes the restoration oracles containing the progeny blessing (36:38 concerning Israel, 37:28 concerning the nations). It is explicitly tied to the progeny blessing in Isa 26:15 as well.[19] Thus, Yahweh, the people, the land, and even the nations all benefit from Yahweh's blessing of offspring upon Israel.

The progress of the progeny blessing in Israel's history is one of promise, fulfillments, and setbacks. The Abrahamic promise was initially realized just prior to the exodus in Egypt, a special realization of the universal progeny blessing. Further proliferation was contingent on obedience within the Sinai covenant, realized in the days of Solomon, also a greater realization of the Abrahamic promise. Thereafter, because of their perpetual disobedience, Israel incurred curse rather than blessing. In the exilic judgment, Israel temporarily forfeited her special guarantee of national growth and Yahweh decimated her as he had decimated many nations before her, reversing the Abrahamic promises. The Latter Prophets document the restoration of her fortunes,[20] and Yahweh's gracious resolve to renew blessing and multiply his people beyond what he had ever done before. With minor exceptions,[21] this remains only a promise within the Latter Prophets, awaiting a grand fulfillment.

---

17. See Block, *Ezekiel: Chapters 1–24*, 7; Wright, *Old Testament Ethics*, 19.

18. The benefit for the land differs somewhat depending on the book. For example, in Isaiah and Zechariah it is primarily the city of Zion that benefits from the renewed population. From mother Zion's perspective, if she has no children, she has no future.

19. In addition, the fertility emphasis in Hosea is intended to identify Yahweh (rather than Baal) as the true source of progeny and fruitfulness.

20. The Latter Prophets are primarily concerned with the corporate blessing rather than with the experience of the individual, such as we find in the Psalms and Wisdom Literature.

21. Texts that envision increase while in exile (Isa 49:19–21; Jer 29:6) suggest that Yahweh is multiplying the people even during the ministry of some of the prophets. In the post-exilic period, the restoration of a thriving population to the land had begun, but clearly not to the proportions that earlier prophets had envisioned.

A Synthesis of the Progeny Blessing in the Latter Prophets

At creation, Yahweh intended to multiply humanity in order to fill the world with his ruling images. Although sin severely corrupted the image, Yahweh's plans for humanity remain the same. The proliferation of Israel enabled them to be Yahweh's redemptive agent among the nations, bringing blessing to them. Although Israel largely failed in their mission (as stated in Gen 12:3 and Exod 19:5–6), the prophetic restoration oracles anticipate the realization of Yahweh's creational purposes more fully than during any other period in Israel's history. The multiplication envisioned at creation (and renewed in Abraham's offspring) was intended not simply to multiply humans, but humans belonging to and fully devoted to Yahweh. In various ways, the prophets assert that the new expanding people of God will consist of those who truly obey Yahweh. Furthermore, by suggesting that righteous foreigners are included on a grander scale than ever before, Isaiah and Zechariah indicate that Israel not only will succeed in her redemptive function among the nations, but also will be redefined as the sum total of the redeemed.[22] The purpose of the progeny blessing in the Latter Prophets thus more accurately mirrors its purpose at creation than previously in the OT, pointing forward to the NT. Yahweh's creational goal in multiplying humanity is not lost in the Latter Prophets but rather underlies their visions, despite the use of different language. Perhaps this abiding concern with the expansion of Yahweh's true images explains the prominence of the progeny blessing in the prophetic books.

The presence of the progeny motif in Yahweh's covenants with his people underscores its importance in Yahweh's purposes for humanity. Significantly, all the major covenants include a progeny promise, including the Noahic, Abrahamic, Sinai, Davidic, and New covenants.[23] Aside from the covenantal benefit of land possession, which itself would be impossible without numerical expansion, the progeny blessing is the sole material blessing common to each of the OT covenants.[24] We see this covenantal connection most clearly in the book of Jeremiah, which indicates that the progeny blessing is included in each of these covenants, and Ezekiel, which literally depends on the progeny blessing in the Sinai covenant and includes it as a key element in the "covenant of peace." On this basis, we conclude that, as in Gen 1:28, the blessing of multiplica-

---

22. Although foreign converts such as Rahab, Ruth, and Caleb had previously been accepted and included within Israel, this appears to have been rare.

23. See the discussion regarding continuity between these covenants in the conclusion to chapter 2.

24. Land possession is not directly promised in the Davidic covenant, but is presupposed.

tion is Yahweh's most fundamental gift to humanity in general and to his people in particular. Furthermore, Yahweh's own purposes cannot be realized apart from expanding and sustaining his people. Thus, the progeny blessing is essential for both Yahweh and Israel, explaining its prevalence in the covenants.

In addition, the presence of the progeny blessing in these covenants helps to demonstrate their continuity. As we have argued throughout, these covenants are not in conflict or isolated from one another but instead are complementary. The possibility of multiplication in the Sinai covenant motivates obedience and thereby maintains and furthers the fulfillment of the Abrahamic promise. The promise of proliferation in the new covenant similarly motivates obedience and reinstates these prior promises to the descendants of Abraham. Such continuity is underscored by the full testimony of the Latter Prophets regarding the increase of the nation under the new covenant. They do not allude solely to the Abrahamic or Sinai covenant or to another progeny tradition. Rather, they employ all of these traditions, indicating that the new expansion of Israel is at least continuous with, if not a manifestation of, each of these prior covenants. To posit that the progeny blessing in the new covenant is a fulfillment of either the Abrahamic or the Sinai covenant is a false dichotomy. However, there is not complete continuity. Although the Abrahamic, Sinai and new covenant promises of multiplication all depend on loyalty and obedience to Yahweh, the new covenant promise differs from these former covenants in that Yahweh will himself enable obedience and redefine his people as those who truly seek him, guaranteeing the realization of the restoration oracles.

Isaiah, Jeremiah, Ezekiel, and Zechariah all employ exodus typology to describe the future restoration to the land. Indeed, there are a number of similarities between the original exodus and this "second exodus": the people are subject to foreign oppression in a foreign land, Yahweh must bring about deliverance, Yahweh promises to lead them to Canaan, and the people will serve Yahweh under a new covenant. The "second multiplication" of the people, mirroring Exod 1:7, may contribute to these typological correspondences. However, whereas Egypt prepared the Israelites for the initial possession of the land, Babylon serves God's punitive purposes. Accordingly, the prophets rarely indicate that the multiplication of the people, a blessing, occurs in this judgmental context. These few texts (e.g., Jer 29:6; Isa 49:19–21; Zech 10:8–10[25]) correspond particularly closely to

---

25. This text is especially interesting since it indicates that the northern kingdom

A Synthesis of the Progeny Blessing in the Latter Prophets

the original exodus, whether intentionally or not, and suggest that God's grace reaches even to Babylon as he prepares his people for national rebirth in a second exodus. Despite the different location, the more common pattern of multiplication upon return may still correspond typologically to the exodus event (albeit more loosely) since this is still a "second multiplication." It is difficult to know whether the prophetic authors recognized this parallel or even at times included the progeny blessing in a restoration oracle in order to accumulate exodus allusions. Nevertheless, the new proliferation of Israel contributes to the exodus-like new beginning of the people in the context of a renewed relationship with Yahweh.

The Latter Prophets display the fullness of the character of Yahweh. He will not leave his people unpunished for their persistent rebellion against him, but his grace and compassion will ultimately prevail. This dynamic unfolds in the progeny motif: he will chasten his people in the immediate future, but his ultimate disposition and intention is to bless them with abundant life, both quantitatively and qualitatively.

Toward the New Testament and Beyond

The progress of the progeny blessing in Israel's history does not end with the prophetic corpus but continues into the NT and beyond. Interestingly, the physical progeny blessing is largely absent from the NT since, as with the blessing of the land, the NT appears to be more concerned with spiritual blessings and realities than with material blessings. In Isaiah and Zechariah, the OT has increasingly redefined the people of Yahweh as the righteous remnant that transcends ethnicity. The NT writers take this further in light of the gospel, perhaps suggesting that the full post-exilic proliferation predicted by the Latter Prophets is primarily accomplished through the conversion of Gentiles through faith in Christ. Apart from a few citations of prophetic texts that predict multiplication (Isa 10:22 and Hos 2:1[1:10] in Rom 9:25–28; Isa 54:1 in Gal 4:21–31), only the book of Acts uses the language of the progeny blessing, where the same two verbs for multiplication in the LXX text of Gen 1:28 (Αὐξάνεσθε καὶ πληθύνεσθε) are employed with respect to the growth of the Word of God (Acts 5:28; 6:7; 12:24; 19:20) and the church (6:1, 7; 9:13). Although Yahweh continues to bless all peoples with progeny under the universal blessing, whether the NT indicates that the particular progeny blessing for God's people

---

will eventually participate in the reenactment of the exodus story already in progress for the southern kingdom.

continues (or will one day resume) at the reproductive level or is wholly transformed into a metaphor for the expansion of the church through conversion merits further study.

In addition, a host of contemporary ethical issues relate to the progeny blessing, although we cannot explore them here. With respect to abortion, biblical ethicists typically cite biblical texts that emphasize the sanctity of life and that imply that personhood begins at conception to argue that abortion is morally wrong. Our study suggests that, if we adopt the pervasive biblical worldview that children are a blessing, abortion should never even be desirable so that the ethical question should never even arise in the first place. Birth control and reproductive and fertility technologies are not treated in the OT since these possibilities have only arisen with modern science. The related creational concepts of the image of God and dominion may have greater relevance for these concerns than our study, but a firm conviction that children are a blessing will inevitably shape attitudes toward these issues. An OT theology of the progeny blessing does not directly address the modern overpopulation debate either. Nevertheless, we have seen that the prophets occasionally depict overcrowding in cities (Isa 49:19–21; Zech 2:8[4]; 8:4–5) or territories (Zech 10:8–10), but always portray this as a positive development. Moreover, proliferation and the filling of the land is always a blessing from Yahweh, never a curse, possibly calling into question the very concept of "overpopulation." However, since an overflowing population is accompanied by ideal societal conditions in these descriptions, it is unclear how much they have to say to modern societies where proliferation is accompanied by broken and corrupt leadership, poverty, and a scarcity of resources.

Yahweh, the God of Israel, continues to bless humanity even today, granting them children, sustaining them, and expanding the human race across the face of the earth. May all nations give thanks and praise to him "from whom all blessings flow."

Appendix A

Progeny Blessing Texts

Blessing Ref	Key phrases[1]
Genesis	
1:22	"Be fruitful, multiply, fill" to birds and fish
1:28	"Be fruitful, multiply, fill, subdue, rule" to humankind
6:1	"... when humans began to multiply on the face of the land ..."
8:17	"be fruitful and multiply on the earth" to Noah
9:1	"Be fruitful, multiply, fill" to Noah
9:7	"be fruitful, multiply, swarm on the earth, multiply" to Noah
12:2–3	"And I will make you into a great nation" to Abraham
13:16	"I will make your descendants as the dust of the earth" to Abraham
15:5	"Count the stars ... so shall your descendants be" to Abraham
16:10	"I will greatly multiply your descendants" to Hagar

1. Translations are my own.

Progeny Blessing Texts

Blessing Ref	Key phrases
17:2–6	"I will multiply you . . . make you fruitful . . ." to Abraham
17:16	"I will bless her, and she will be [a mother of] nations" regarding Sarah
17:20	"I will make him fruitful, multiply him" regarding Ishmael
18:18	"Abraham will surely become a great and mighty nation"
21:13, 18	"I will make a great nation of [Ishmael]"
22:17	"I will greatly multiply your seed . . . as stars, as sand on seashore"
24:60	"May you, our sister, become thousands of ten thousands" to Rebekah
26:4	"I will multiply you as the stars of heaven" to Isaac
26:22–24	Isaac: "We will be fruitful." God: "I will multiply you"
28:3	Isaac: "May God multiply you and make you fruitful"
28:14	"Your descendants will be as the dust of the earth" to Jacob
32:13[12]	"Descendants as the sand of the sea"
35:11	"Be fruitful and multiply" to Jacob
41:52	Joseph names Ephraim because "God has made me fruitful"
46:3	"I will make [Jacob] into a great nation [in Egypt]"
46:27	"all the persons of the house of Jacob . . . were 70"
47:27	Israel "was fruitful and became numerous" in Goshen
48:4	"I will make you fruitful and numerous"
48:16	Jacob: "May they grow into a multitude"
48:19	Ephraim's "descendants shall become a multitude of nations"
49:22	"Joseph is a fruitful bough"
49:25	"Blessings of the breasts and of the womb" in the blessing on Joseph

Progeny Blessing Texts

Blessing Ref	Key phrases
Exodus	
1:7–12	"The people of Israel were fruitful, swarmed, multiplied, grew exceedingly strong and filled the land"
1:20–21	"The people multiplied and became very strong"
5:5	"The people of the land are now many"
23:26	"There will be no one barren in the land"
23:30	"until you become fruitful"
32:10	God: "I will make [Moses] into a great nation"
32:13	Moses: You promised, "I will multiply your offspring as the stars of heaven"
Leviticus	
26:9	"I will multiply you and make you fruitful"
Numbers	
14:12	"I will make [Moses] into a nation greater and mightier"
22:3	"The people [of Israel] were numerous"
23:10	"Who can count the dust of Jacob?"
Deuteronomy	
1:10–11	Moses: "He has multiplied you as the stars . . . may the Lord increase you a thousand times as many as you are"
6:3	"Obey . . . that you might multiply greatly"
7:7	"You were the fewest of all peoples"
7:13–14	"He will multiply you . . . bless the fruit of your womb . . . there will not be male or female barren among you"
8:1	"Obey . . . that you may live and multiply"
9:14	"I will make [Moses] into a nation greater and mightier"
10:22	"God has made you as numerous as the stars of heaven"
13:18[17]	"that you may increase"

Progeny Blessing Texts

Blessing Ref	Key phrases
26:5	In Egypt "[Abraham] became a great, mighty and populous nation"
28:4	"Blessed be the fruit of your womb"
28:11	"Abound . . . in the fruit of your womb"
28:62–63	"You were as the stars of heaven," but now curse
30:5	"He will multiply you more than your fathers"
30:9	"He will prosper you . . . in the fruit of your womb"
30:16	"Obey . . . that you may live and multiply"
33:6	"May Reuben live and not die, nor his men be few"
33:17	". . . the ten thousands of Ephraim . . . the thousands of Manasseh"

Joshua

11:4	Canaanites "as many as the sand on the seashore"
17:14	Tribe of Joseph: "I am a numerous people whom the Lord has . . . blessed"
24:3	God "multiplied his descendants" regarding Abraham

Judges

6:5	"[Midian] and their camels were innumerable"
7:12	Midian and their camels "as numerous as the sand on the seashore"

1 Samuel

2:5	Hannah: "even the barren gives birth to seven"
13:5	Philistines as numerous as "the sand that is on the seashore"

2 Samuel

17:11	All Israel gathered "like the sand that is by the sea in abundance"
24:3	Joab: "May the Lord your God add to the people a hundred times"

Progeny Blessing Texts

Blessing Ref	Key phrases
1 Kings	
3:8	"A great people ... too many to be numbered or counted"
4:20	"Judah and Israel were as numerous as the sand on the seashore"
Isaiah	
9:2[3]	"You have multiplied the nation"
10:22	"Although your people, O Israel, are as many as the sand of the sea ..."
26:15	"You have added to the nation" (2X)
27:6	"Israel will blossom and sprout ... fill the whole world with fruit"
44:3–4	"They will sprout among the grass like willow trees"
45:18	God "formed [the earth] to be inhabited" (Cf. Gen 1:28)
48:19	"Your offspring would have been like the sand"
49:19–21	"the place is too cramped ... who has begotten these for me?"
51:2	"So that I might bless him and multiply him"—historical reference to Abraham
54:1–3	"the children of the desolate one are more numerous ..."
60:22	"the smallest will become a thousand, and the least a mighty nation"
65:9	"I will bring forth offspring from Jacob"
65:20	"There will no longer be there an infant of only a few days ... the youth will die at one hundred years old"
65:23	"they will not ... bear children for calamity"
66:7–9	Zion gives birth to a nation
66:22	"your offspring and your name will remain"
Jeremiah	
3:16	"When you are multiplied and fruitful in the land"

Progeny Blessing Texts

Blessing Ref	Key phrases
23:3	"They will be fruitful and multiply"
29:6	God commands the exiles to "multiply" in Babylon
30:19	"I will multiply them, and they will not be few"
31:27	"I will sow [Israel] with the seed of humans and the seed of beasts"
33:22	"I will multiply the seed of David . . . and the Levites"

Ezekiel

Blessing Ref	Key phrases
34:25–30	Decimation curses reversed
36:10	"I will multiply people on you"
36:11	"I will multiply people and animals on you, and they will multiply and be fruitful"
36:12	"never again bereave them of children"
36:14	"no longer bereave your nation of children"
36:37–38	"I will increase their people like flocks"
37:26	"I will join them [together] and I will multiply them"

Hosea

Blessing Ref	Key phrases
2:1[1:10]	"the number of the children of Israel will be like the sand of the sea"
2:25[23]	"I will sow her for myself in the land"
4:7	"The more they multiplied, the more they sinned against me"
14:6–8[5–7]	He will blossom, take root, shoots sprout, blossom as vine

Zechariah

Blessing Ref	Key phrases
2:8[4]	"Jerusalem . . . without walls because of the abundance of people and cattle"
8:4–5	Jerusalem will be filled with the elderly and with children
10:8	"they will multiply as they multiplied before"
10:9	"I will sow them among the peoples"
10:10	they will come back and "no room will be found for them"

Progeny Blessing Texts

Blessing Ref	Key phrases
Psalms	
105:24	"He caused his people to be very fruitful"
107:38	"He blesses them and they multiply greatly"
107:41	"He makes his families like a flock"
113:9	"He makes the barren woman . . . a joyful mother of children"
127:3–5	Blessed is the man with many children
128:3	"Your wife shall be like a fruitful vine . . ."
Job	
5:25	"Your offspring [will be] as the grass of the earth"
Proverbs	
14:28	"In a multitude of people is a king's glory"
Ecclesiastes	
6:3	"If a man fathers a hundred . . . but is not satisfied . . . better the miscarriage"
Nehemiah	
9:23	"You made their sons as numerous as the stars of heaven"
1 Chronicles	
4:27	"Their family didn't multiply like all the sons of Judah"
5:23	Manasseh "was numerous"
21:3	Joab: "May the Lord add to his people a hundred times . . ."
27:23	"The Lord had said he would multiply Israel like the stars"
2 Chronicles	
1:9	Solomon king over "a people as numerous as the dust"
12:3	The Egyptians who came up "were without number"

Appendix B

The Old Testament Distribution of the Terminology of the Progeny Blessing[1]

	ברה / הרב	פרה	"הרב הרב"	פרץ	מלא	Dust	Stars	Sand	Total
Genesis	15	13	10	1	2	2	3	2	38
Exodus	5	2	1	1	1		1		10
Leviticus	1	1	1						2
Deuteronomy	9						3		12
Joshua	1							1	2
Judges								1	1
Samuel								2	2
Kings								1	1
Isaiah	2		1	1			1	2	6
Jeremiah	6	2	2					1	10
Ezekiel	5	2	1						7
Hosea	1	1						1	3
Zechariah	2								2
Psalms	1	2							3
Nehemiah	1						1		2
Chronicles	3		1		1	1			6

1. For the purposes of this chart, only those expressions employed at least four times with respect to the progeny blessing are included as a separate column. Thus the totals do not reflect rare or unique expressions of the progeny blessing.

Bibliography

Abma, Richtsje. *Bonds of Love: Methodic Studies of Prophetic Texts with Marriage Imagery: Isaiah 50:1-3 and 54:1-10, Hosea 1-3, Jeremiah 2-3*. Studia Semitica Neerlandica 40. Assen, Netherlands: Van Gorcum, 1999.

Ackerman, J. S. "The Literary Context of the Moses Birth Story (Exodus 1-2)." In *Literary Interpretations of Biblical Narratives*, edited by K. R. R. Gros Louis et al., 74-119. Nashville: Abingdon, 1974.

Ackroyd, Peter. *Exile and Restoration: A Study of Hebrew Thought of the Sixth Century B.C.* Philadelphia: Westminster, 1975.

Albertz, Rainer. "Das Motiv für die Sintflut im Atramhasis-Epos." In *Mythos im Alten Testament und seiner Umwelt: Festschrift für Hans-Peter Müller zum 65. Geburtstag*, edited by Armin Lange et al., 3-16, New York: de Gruyter, 1999.

Albright, William F. *Archaeology and the Religion of Israel*. Baltimore: Johns Hopkins, 1953.

Allen, Leslie C. *Ezekiel 20-48*. Word Biblical Commentary 29. Dallas: Word, 1990.

Allen, Ronald B. "Numbers." In *The Expositor's Bible Commentary*, edited by Frank E. Gaebelein, 2:655-1008. Grand Rapids: Zondervan, 1990.

Alt, Albrecht. "Jesaja 8,23—9,6: Befreiungsnacht und Krönungstag." In *Kleine Schriften zur Geschichte des Volkes Israel*, edited by Martin Noth, 2:206-25. Munich: Beck, 1959.

Andersen, Francis I. *The Sentence in Biblical Hebrew*. Paris: Mouton, 1974.

Andersen, Francis I., and David Noel Freedman. *Hosea: A New Translation with Introduction and Commentary*. Anchor Bible Commentary 24. Garden City, NY: Doubleday, 1980.

Anderson, A. A. *2 Samuel*. Word Biblical Commentary 11. Dallas: Word, 1989.

Anderson, Bernhard W. "Exodus Typology in Second Isaiah." In *Israel's Prophetic Heritage: Essays in Honor of James Muilenburg*, edited by Bernhard W. Anderson and W. Harrelson, 177-95. New York: Harper & Row, 1962.

———. "'The Lord Has Created Something New': A Stylistic Study of Jer 31:15-22." In *A Prophet to the Nations: Essays in Jeremiah Studies*, edited by Leo G. Perdue and Brian W. Kovacs, 367-80. Winona Lake, IN: Eisenbrauns, 1984.

Archer, Gleason L. "The Relationship between the Septuagint Translation and the Massoretic Text in Jeremiah." *Trinity Journal* 12 (1991) 139-50.

Arnold, Bill T. and John C. Choi. *A Guide to Biblical Hebrew Syntax*. Cambridge: Cambridge University Press, 2003.

Baker, David W. "Israelite Prophets and Prophecy." In *The Face of Old Testament Studies: A Survey of Contemporary Approaches*, edited by David W. Baker and Bill T. Arnold, 266-94. Grand Rapids: Baker, 1999.

Bibliography

Baldwin, Joyce. *Haggai, Zechariah, Malachi*. Tyndale Old Testament Commentaries. Downers Grove, IL: InterVarsity, 1972.

Baltzer, Dieter. *Ezechiel und Deuterojesaja: Berührungen in der Heilserwartung der beiden großen Exilspropheten*. Berlin: de Gruyter, 1971.

Baltzer, Klaus. *Deutero-Isaiah*. Translated by Margaret Kohl. Hermeneia. Minneapolis: Fortress, 2001.

Barthélemy, Dominique, editor. *Critique textuelle de l'Ancien Testament: Ézéchiel, Daniel et les 12 Prophétes*. Vol. 3 of OBO 50/3. Göttingen: Vandenhoeck & Ruprecht, 1992.

———. *Critique textuelle de l'Ancien Testament: Isaïe, Jérémie, Lamentations*. Vol. 2 of OBO 50/2. Göttingen: Vandenhoeck & Ruprecht, 1986.

Beal, Lissa M. Wray. "Blessings Lost: Intertextual Inversions in Hosea." *Didaskalia* 16.2 (2005) 17–39.

Beale, G. K. *The Temple and the Church's Mission: A Biblical Theology of the Dwelling Place of God*. New Studies in Biblical Theology 17. Downers Grove, IL: InterVarsity, 2004.

Beck, Martin. *Der "Tag YHWHs" im Dodekapropheton: Studien im Spannungsfeld von Traditions- und Redaktionsgeschichte*. BZAW 356. Berlin: de Gruyter, 2005.

Becking, Bob. *Between Fear and Freedom: Essays on the Interpretation of Jeremiah 30–31*. Old Testament Studies 51. Leiden: Brill, 2004.

Beentjes, Pancratius C. "Inverted Quotations in the Bible: A Neglected Stylistic Pattern." *Biblica* 63 (1982) 506–23.

Begg, Christopher T. "The Peoples and the Worship of Yahweh in the Book of Isaiah." In *Worship and the Hebrew Bible*, edited by M. P. Graham et al., 35–55. Journal for the Study of the Old Testament: Supplement Series 284. Sheffield, UK: Sheffield Academic Press, 1999.

Ben Zvi, Ehud. *Hosea*. Forms of the Old Testament Literature. Grand Rapids: Eerdmans, 2005.

———. "Twelve Prophetic Books or 'The Twelve': A Few Preliminary Considerations." In *Forming Prophetic Literature: Essays on Isaiah and the Twelve in Honor of John D. W. Watts*, edited by Paul R. House and James W. Watts, 125–56. Journal for the Study of the Old Testament: Supplement Series 235. Sheffield, UK: Sheffield Academic Press, 1996.

Berlin, Adele. "Jeremiah 29:5–7: A Deuteronomic Allusion." *Hebrew Annual Review* 8 (1984) 3–12.

Beuken, W. A. M. "Isaiah Chapters LXV–LXVI: Trito-Isaiah and the Closure of the Book of Isaiah." In *Congress Volume: Leuven 1989*, edited by J. A. Emerton, 204–21. Leiden: Brill, 1991.

———. "Isaiah LIV: The Multiple Identity of the Person Addressed." In *Language and Meaning: Studies in Hebrew Language and Biblical Exegesis*, 29–70. Old Testament Studies 19. Leiden: Brill, 1974.

———. "The Main Theme of Trito-Isaiah: 'The Servants of Yahweh.'" *Journal for the Study of the Old Testament* 47 (1990) 67–87.

Biddle, M. E. "The 'Endangered Ancestress' and Blessing for the Nations." *Journal of Biblical Literature* 109 (1990) 599–611.

Blenkinsopp, Joseph. *Ezekiel*. Interpretation. Louisville: John Knox, 1990.

———. *A History of Prophecy in Israel*. Rev. ed. Louisville: Westminster John Knox, 1996.

———. *Isaiah 1-39: A New Translation with Introduction and Commentary.* Anchor Bible Commentaries 19. New York: Doubleday, 2000.

———. *Isaiah 40-55: A New Translation with Introduction and Commentary.* Anchor Bible Commentaries 19A. New York: Doubleday, 2000.

———. *Isaiah 56-66: A New Translation with Introduction and Commentary.* Anchor Bible Commentaries 19B. New York: Doubleday, 2003.

———. *The Pentateuch: An Introduction to the First Five Books of the Bible.* New York: Doubleday, 1992.

———. "Second Isaiah: Prophet of Universalism." *Journal for the Study of the Old Testament* 41 (1988) 83-103.

Blocher, Henri. *In the Beginning: The Opening Chapters of Genesis.* Translated by David G. Preston. Downers Grove, IL: InterVarsity, 1984.

Block, Daniel I. *The Book of Ezekiel: Chapters 1-24.* New International Commentary on the Old Testament. Grand Rapids: Eerdmans, 1997.

———. *The Book of Ezekiel: Chapters 25-48.* New International Commentary on the Old Testament. Grand Rapids: Eerdmans, 1998.

———. *Deuteronomy.* NIV Application Commentary. Grand Rapids: Zondervan, 2012.

———. *The Gods of the Nations: Studies in Ancient Near Eastern National Theology.* 2nd ed. ETS Studies. Grand Rapids: Baker, 2000.

———. "Gog and Magog in Ezekiel's Eschatological Vision." In *"The Reader Must Understand": Eschatology in Bible and Theology*, edited by K. E. Brower and M. W. Elliott, 856-116. Downers Grove, IL: InterVarsity, 1997.

———. "Marriage and Family in Ancient Israel." In *Marriage and Family in the Biblical World*, edited by Ken M. Campbell, 33-102. Downers Grove, IL: InterVarsity, 2003.

———. "Other Religions in Old Testament Theology." In *Biblical Faith and Other Religions: An Evangelical Assessment*, edited by David W. Baker, 43-78. Grand Rapids: Kregel, 2004.

———. "Recovering the Voice of Moses: The Genesis of Deuteronomy." *Journal of the Evangelical Theological Society* 44 (2001) 385-408.

Boadt, Lawrence. "Do Jeremiah and Ezekiel Share a Common View of the Exile?" In *Uprooting and Planting: Essays on Jeremiah for Leslie Allen*, edited by John Goldingay, 14-31. London: T. & T. Clark, 2007.

———. "The Function of the Salvation Oracles in Ezekiel 33 to 37." *Hebrew Annual Review* 12 (1990) 1-21.

Boda, Mark J. "Hoy, Hoy: The Prophetic Origins of the Babylonian Tradition in Zechariah 2:10-17." In *Tradition in Transition: Haggai and Zechariah 1-8 in the Trajectory of Hebrew Theology*, edited by M. J. Boda and M. H. Floyd, 171-90. London: T. & T. Clark, 2008.

Bowman, Craig. "Reading the Twelve as One: Hosea 1-3 as an Introduction to Book of the Twelve." *Stone-Campbell Journal* 9 (2006) 41-59.

Bozak, Barbara A. *Life "Anew": A Literary-Theological Study of Jer. 30-31.* Rome: Editrice Pontificio Istituto Biblico, 1991.

Braaten, Laurie J. "God Sows: Hosea's Land Theme in the Book of the Twelve." In *Thematic Threads in the Book of the Twelve*, edited by Paul L. Redditt and Aaron Schart, 104-32. Beihefte zur Zeitschrift für die alttestamentliche Wissenschaft 325. Berlin: de Gruyter, 2003.

Bibliography

Bracke, John M. "Sûb sebût: A Reappraisal." *Zeitschrift für die alttestamentliche Wissenschaft* 97 (1985) 233–44.

Brettler, Marc Zvi. "Predestination in Deuteronomy 30.1–10." In *Those Elusive Deuteronomists: The Phenomenon of Pan-Deuteronomism*, edited by Linda S. Schearing and Steven L. McKenzie, 171–88. Sheffield, UK: Sheffield Academic Press, 1999.

Bright, John. *Jeremiah*. Anchor Bible Commentaries 21. New York: Doubleday, 1965.

Brotzman, Ellis R. *Old Testament Textual Criticism: A Practical Introduction*. Grand Rapids: Eerdmans, 1994.

Brown, Michael L. "ברך." In *New International Dictionary of Old Testament Theology and Exegesis*, edited by Willem A. VanGemeren, 1:757–67. Grand Rapids: Zondervan, 1997.

Brueggemann, Walter. *A Commentary on Jeremiah: Exile and Homecoming*. Grand Rapids: Eerdmans, 1998.

———. *Isaiah 40–66*. Westminster Commentaries. Louisville: Westminster John Knox, 1998.

———. "The Kerygma of the Priestly Writers." *Zeitschrift für die alttestamentliche Wissenschaft* 84 (1972) 397–413.

———. *The Land: Place as Gift, Promise, and Challenge in Biblical Faith*. 2nd ed. Overtures to Biblical Theology. Minneapolis: Fortress, 2002.

———. "A Shape for Old Testament Theology, I: Structure Legitimation." *Catholic Biblical Quarterly* 47 (1985) 28–46.

———. "A Shape for Old Testament Theology, II: Embrace of Pain." *Catholic Biblical Quarterly* 47 (1985) 395–415.

———. *Theology of the Old Testament: Testimony, Dispute, Advocacy*. Minneapolis: Fortress, 1997.

———. *Tradition for Crisis: A Study in Hosea*. Richmond, VA: John Knox, 1968.

Butler, Trent C. *Joshua*. Word Biblical Commentary. Waco, TX: Word, 1983.

Callaway, Mary. *Sing, O Barren One: A Study in Comparative Midrash*. Society of Biblical Literature Dissertation Series 91. Atlanta: Scholars, 1986.

Calvin, John. *Commentaries on the Book of Genesis*. Translated by John King. Vol. 1. Grand Rapids: Baker, 1998.

Carroll R., M. Daniel. "Blessing the Nations: Toward a Biblical Theology of Mission from Genesis." *Bulletin for Biblical Research* 10 (2000) 17–34.

Carroll, Robert P. *Jeremiah: A Commentary*. Old Testament Library. Philadelphia: Westminster, 1986.

———. *When Prophecy Failed: Cognitive Dissonance in the Prophetic Traditions of the Old Testament*. New York: Seabury, 1979.

Carter, Charles E. "Opening Windows onto Biblical Worlds: Applying the Social Sciences to Hebrew Scripture." In *The Face of Old Testament Studies: A Survey of Contemporary Approaches*, edited by David W. Baker and Bill T. Arnold, 421–51. Grand Rapids: Baker, 1999.

Cassuto, Umberto. *A Commentary on the Book of Exodus*. Jerusalem: Magnes, 1967.

Childs, Brevard S. *The Book of Exodus*. Old Testament Library. Philadelphia: Westminster, 1974.

———. "The Canonical Shape of the Prophetic Literature." *Interpretation* 32 (1978) 46–55.

———. *Isaiah*. Old Testament Library. Louisville: Westminster/John Knox, 2001.

Clements, Ronald E. "בן." In *Theological Dictionary of the Old Testament*, edited by G. J. Botterweck and H. Ringgren, 2:426–33. Grand Rapids: Eerdmans, 1975.

———. *Isaiah 1–39*. New Century Bible Commentaries. Grand Rapids: Eerdmans, 1980.

———. *Jeremiah*. Interpretation. Atlanta: John Knox, 1988.

———. *Old Testament Prophecy: From Oracles to Canon*. Louisville, KY: Westminster John Knox, 1996.

———. *Prophecy and Covenant*. Studies in Biblical Theology 43. London: SCM, 1965.

———. *Prophecy and Tradition*. Growing Points in Theology. Atlanta: John Knox, 1975.

Clines, David J. A. *Ezra, Nehemiah, Esther*. New Century Bible Commentary. Grand Rapids: Eerdmans, 1984.

———. "Humanity as the Image of God." In *On the Way to the Postmodern: Old Testament Essays, 1967–1998*, edited by David J. A. Clines, 447–97. Journal for the Study of the Old Testament: Supplement Series 293. Sheffield, UK: Sheffield Academic Press, 1998.

———. *Job 1–20*, Word Biblical Commentary. Dallas: Word, 1989.

———. *The Theme of the Pentateuch*. 2nd ed. Journal for the Study of the Old Testament: Supplement Series 10. Sheffield, UK: JSOT, 1997.

Cohen, Jeremy. *Be Fertile and Increase, Fill the Earth and Master It: The Ancient and Medieval Career of a Biblical Text*. Ithaca, NY: Cornell University Press, 1989.

Cohen, Jeffrey M. "The Fertility of the Early Israelites." *Jewish Bible Quarterly* 27 (1999) 195–98.

Collins, Terence. *The Mantle of Elijah*. Sheffield, UK: JSOT, 1993.

Conrad, Edgar W. *Reading Isaiah*. Overtures to Biblical Theology. Minneapolis: Fortress, 1991.

———. *Reading the Latter Prophets: Towards a New Canonical Criticism*. Journal for the Study of the Old Testament: Supplement Series 376. London: T. & T. Clark, 2003.

———. *Zechariah*. Readings: A New Biblical Commentary. Sheffield, UK: Sheffield Academic, 1999.

Cooke, G. A. *A Critical and Exegetical Commentary on the Book of Ezekiel*. International Critical Commentary. Edinburgh: T. & T. Clark, 1951.

Craigie, Peter C. *The Book of Deuteronomy*. New International Commentary on the Old Testament. Grand Rapids: Eerdmans, 1976.

Craigie, Peter C., et al. *Jeremiah 1–25*. Word Biblical Commentary 26. Dallas: Word, 1991.

Crane, Ashley S. *Israel's Restoration: A Textual-Comparative Exploration of Ezekiel 36–39*. Supplements to Vetus Testamentum 122. Leiden: Brill, 2008.

Crawford, Timothy G. *Blessing and Curse in Syro-Palestinian Inscriptions of the Iron Age*. New York: Lang, 1992.

Croatto, J. Severino. "The 'Nations' in the Salvific Oracles of Isaiah." *Vetus Testamentum* 55 (2005) 143–61.

Darr, Katheryn Pfisterer. *Isaiah's Vision and the Family of God*. Louisville: Westminster/John Knox, 1994.

Daube, David. *The Duty of Procreation*. Edinburgh: Edinburgh University Press, 1977.

Davies, E. W. "A Mathematical Conundrum: The Problem of the Large Numbers in Numbers i and xxvi." *Vetus Testamentum* 45 (1995) 449–69.

Bibliography

Davies, G. F. *Israel in Egypt: Reading Exodus 1-2*. Journal for the Study of the Old Testament: Supplement Series 135. Sheffield, UK: Sheffield Academic, 1992.

Davies, Graham I. "The Destiny of the Nations in the Book of Isaiah." In *The Book of Isaiah: Le livre d'Isaie: les oracles et leurs relecteurs: unité et complexité de l'ouvrage*, edited by Jacques Vermeylen, 93-120. Louvain: Leuven University Press, 1989.

———. *Hosea*. New Century Bible Commentary. Grand Rapids: Eerdmans, 1992.

Day, John. "A Case of Inner Scriptural Interpretation: The Dependence of Isaiah XXVI.13—XXVII.11 on Hosea XIII.4—XIV.10 (Eng. 9) and Its Relevance to Some Theories of the Redaction of the 'Isaiah Apocalypse.'" *Journal of Theological Studies* 31 (1980) 309-19.

Dempster, Stephen G. *Dominion and Dynasty: A Biblical Theology of the Hebrew Bible*. New Studies in Biblical Theology 15. Downers Grove, IL: InterVarsity, 2003.

Dever, William G. *What Did the Biblical Writers Know and When Did They Know It?* Grand Rapids: Eerdmans, 2001.

Dillard, Raymond B. *2 Chronicles*. Word Biblical Commentary 15. Waco, TX: Word, 1987.

Dillard, Raymond B., and Tremper Longman III. *An Introduction to the Old Testament*. Grand Rapids: Zondervan, 1994.

Dumbrell, William J. *Covenant and Creation: A Theology of Old Testament Covenants*. Nashville: Thomas Nelson, 1984.

Durham, John I. *Exodus*. Word Biblical Commentary 3. Waco, TX: Word, 1987.

Eichrodt, Walther. *Ezekiel: A Commentary*. Translated by Cosslett Quin. Old Testament Library. Philadelphia: Westminster, 1970.

Estes, Daniel. "Like Arrows in the Hand of a Warrior (Psalm 127)." *Vetus Testamentum* 41 (1991) 304-11.

Finkelstein, Israel. *The Archaeology of the Israelite Settlement*. Jerusalem: Israel Exploration Society, 1988.

Finkelstein, Israel, and Neil Asher Silberman. *The Bible Unearthed: Archaeology's New Vision of Ancient Israel and the Origin of Its Sacred Texts*. New York: Free, 2001.

Finkelstein, Jacob J. "Bible and Babel: A Comparative Study of the Hebrew and Babylonian Religious Spirit." *Commentary* 26 (1958) 431-44.

Fleming, Daniel. "Psalm 127: Sleep for the Fearful, and Security in Sons." *Zeitschrift für die alttestamentliche Wissenschaft* 107 (1995) 435-44.

Fokkelman, J. P. "Genesis." In *The Literary Guide to the Bible*, edited by Robert Alter and Frank Kermode, 36-55. Cambridge: Belknap, 1987.

Fouts, David M. "A Defense of the Hyperbolic Interpretation of Large Numbers in the Old Testament." *Journal of the Evangelical Theological Society* 40 (1997) 377-87.

Fretheim, Terence E. *Exodus*, Interpretation. Louisville: John Knox, 1991.

———. *First and Second Kings*. Westminster Biblical Commentaries. Louisville: Westminster John Knox, 1999.

———. *Jeremiah*. Smyth & Helwys Biblical Commentaries. Macon, GA: Smyth & Helwys, 2002.

———. *The Pentateuch*. Edited by Gene M. Tucker. Interpreting Biblical Texts. Nashville: Abingdon, 1996.

Friedman, Richard E. *The Bible with Sources Revealed: A New View into the Five Books of Moses*. San Francisco: Harper, 2003.

Frymer-Kensky, Tikva. "The Atrahasis Epic and Its Significance for Our Understanding of Genesis 1-9." *Biblical Archaeologist* 40 (1977) 147-55.

Bibliography

Garrett, Duane A. *Hosea, Joel.* New American Commentary. Nashville: Broadman & Holman, 1997.
Gelston, Anthony. "Universalism in Second Isaiah." *Journal of Theological Studies* 43 (1992) 377-98.
Gibson, J. C. L. *Davidson's Introductory Hebrew Grammar: Syntax.* 4th ed. Edinburgh: T. & T. Clark, 1994.
Gilbert, M. "'Soyez féconds et multipliez' (Gen. 1, 28)." *La nouvelle revue théologique* 96 (1974) 729-42.
Goldingay, John. *The Message of Isaiah 40-55: A Literary-Theological Commentary.* New York: T. & T. Clark, 2005.
———. *Old Testament Theology: Israel's Gospel.* Downers Grove, IL: InterVarsity, 2003.
Goldingay, John, and David Payne. *Isaiah 40-55.* Vol. 2. International Critical Commentary. London: T. & T. Clark, 2006.
Gordis, Robert. "'Be Fruitful and Multiply': Biography of a Mitzvah." *Mid-Stream* 28 (1982) 21-29.
Gosse, Bernard. "Ézéchiel 35-36, 1-15 et Ézéchiel 6: la désolation de la montagne de Séir et le renouveau des montagnes d'Israël." *Revue Biblique* 96 (1989) 511-17.
———. "L'ouverture de la nouvelle alliance aux nations en Jérémie iii 14-18." *Vetus Testamentum* 39 (1989) 385-92.
———. "La nouvelle alliance et les promesses d'avenir se référant à David dans les livres de Jérémie, Ezéchiel et Isaïe." *Vetus Testamentum* 41 (1991) 419-28.
Gowan, Donald E. *Eschatology in the Old Testament.* Edinburgh: T. & T. Clark, 1986.
———. *Theology of the Prophetic Books: The Death and Resurrection of Israel.* Louisville: Westminster John Knox, 1998.
Gray, George B. *A Critical and Exegetical Commentary on the Book of Isaiah: I-XXXIX,* ICC. Edinburgh: T. & T. Clark, 1912.
Greenberg, Moshe. *Ezekiel 1-20.* Anchor Bible Commentaries 22. New York: Doubleday, 1983.
———. *Ezekiel 21-37.* Anchor Bible Commentaries 22A. New York: Doubleday, 1997.
Grisanti, Michael. "פְּרָזוֹן." In *New International Dictionary of Old Testament Theology and Exegesis,* edited by Willem A. VanGemeren, 3:681-83. Grand Rapids: Zondervan, 1997.
———. "Israel's Mission to the Nations in Isaiah 40-55." *Master's Seminary Journal* 9 (1998) 39-61.
———. "The Relationship of Israel and the Nations in Isaiah 40-55." PhD diss., Dallas Theological Seminary, 1993.
Gross, Walter. "Israel's Hope for the Renewal of the State." *Journal of Northwest Semitic Languages* 14 (1988) 101-33.
Grothe, Jonathan F. "An Argument for the Textual Genuineness of Jeremiah 33:14-26." *Concordia Journal* 7 (1981) 188-91.
Grüneberg, Keith. *Abraham, Blessing and the Nations: A Philological and Exegetical Study of Genesis 12:3 in Its Narrative Context.* Beihefte zur Zeitschrift für die alttestamentliche Wissenschaft 332. New York: de Gruyter, 2003.
Hagelia, Hallvard. "A Crescendo of Universalism: An Exegesis of Isa 19:16-25." *Svensk exegetisk arsbok* 70 (2005) 73-88.
Hamilton, James M. "The Seed of the Woman and the Blessing of Abraham." *Tyndale Bulletin* 58 (2007) 253-73.

Bibliography

Hamilton, Victor P. *The Book of Genesis: Chapters 1–17*. New International Commentary on the Old Testament. Grand Rapids: Eerdmans, 1990.

Hanson, Paul D. *Isaiah 40–66*. Interpretation. Louisville: John Knox, 1995.

Hart, Ian. "Genesis 1:1—2:3 as a Prologue to the Book of Genesis." *Tyndale Bulletin* 46 (1995) 315–36.

Hartley, John E. *Leviticus*. Word Biblical Commentary 4. Dallas: Word, 1992.

Hasel, Gerhard F. *The Remnant: The History and Theology of the Remnant Idea from Genesis to Isaiah*. Berrien Springs, MI: Andrews University Press, 1972.

Hays, Richard B. *Echoes of Scripture in the Letters of Paul*. New Haven: Yale University Press, 1989.

Head, Peter M. "The Curse of Covenant Reversal: Deuteronomy 28:58–68 and Israel's Exile." *Churchman* 111 (1997) 218–26.

Herrmann, D. Johannes. *Ezechiel*. Kommentar zum Alten Testament. Leipzig: Dr. Werner Scholl/A. Deichertsche Verlagsbuchhandlung, 1924.

Heyd, David. "Divine Creation and Human Procreation: Reflection on Genesis in Light of Genesis." In *Contingent Future Persons: On the Ethics of Deciding Who Will Live, or Not, in the Future*, edited by Nick Fotion and Jan Heller, 57–70. Dordrecht, Netherlands: Kluwer Academic, 1997.

Hill, Andrew E. "יסף." In *New International Dictionary of Old Testament Theology and Exegesis*, edited by Willem A. VanGemeren, 2:476–79. Grand Rapids: Zondervan, 1997.

Hillers, Delbert R. *Treaty-Curses and the Old Testament Prophets*. Biblica et orientalia 16. Rome: Pontifical Biblical Institute, 1964.

Holladay, William L. "The Background of Jeremiah's Self-Understanding: Moses, Samuel, and Psalm 22." *Journal of Biblical Literature* 83 (1964) 153–64.

———. *Jeremiah 1*. Hermeneia. Philadelphia: Fortress, 1986.

———. *Jeremiah 2*. Hermeneia. Minneapolis: Fortress, 1989.

———. "Jeremiah and Moses: Further Observations." *Journal of Biblical Literature* 85 (1966) 17–27.

Hollenberg, D. E. "Nationalism and 'the Nations' in Isaiah XL–LV." *Vetus Testamentum* 19 (1969) 23–36.

Hopkins, David C. "The First Stories of Genesis and the Rhythm of the Generations." In *The Echoes of Many Texts: Reflections on Jewish and Christian Traditions: Essays in Honor of Lou H. Silberman*, edited by William G. Dever and J. Edward Wright, 25–41. Brown Judaic Studies 313. Atlanta: Scholars, 1997.

House, Paul R. *1, 2 Kings*. New American Commentary. Nashville: Broadman & Holman, 1995.

———. *The Unity of the Twelve*. Journal for the Study of the Old Testament: Supplement Series 97. Sheffield, UK: Almond, 1990.

House, Paul R., and James W. Watts, editors. *Forming Prophetic Literature: Essays on Isaiah and the Twelve in Honor of John D. W. Watts*. Journal for the Study of the Old Testament: Supplement Series 235. Sheffield, UK: Sheffield Academic, 1996.

Houston, Walter. "What Did the Prophets Think They Were Doing? Speech Acts and Prophetic Discourse in the Old Testament." *Biblical Interpretation* 1 (1993) 167–88.

Houtman, Cornelius. *Exodus*. Translated by Johan Rebel and Sierd Woudstra. Vol. 1. Historical Commentary on the Old Testament. Kampen: Kok, 1993.

Bibliography

Howard, David M., Jr. *Joshua*. New American Commentary. Nashville: Broadman & Holman, 1998.
Hubbard, David Allan. *Hosea*. Tyndale Old Testament Commentaries. Downers Grove, IL: InterVarsity, 1989.
Huehnergard, John. "Asseverative *la and Hypothetical *lu/law in Semitic." *Journal of the American Oriental Society* 103 (1983) 569–93.
Huey, F. B., Jr. *Jeremiah, Lamentations*. New American Commentary. Nashville: Broadman, 1993.
Humphreys, C. J. "The Number of People in the Exodus from Egypt: Decoding Mathematically the Very Large Numbers in Numbers i and xxvi." *Vetus Testamentum* 48 (1998) 196–213.
―――. "The Numbers in the Exodus from Egypt: A Further Appraisal." *Vetus Testamentum* 50 (2000) 323–28.
Hyatt, J. Philip. "Jeremiah and Deuteronomy." In *A Prophet to the Nations: Essays in Jeremiah Studies*, edited by Leo G. Perdue and Brian W. Kovacs, 113–27. Winona Lake, IN: Eisenbrauns, 1984.
Jacobi, Harry M. "Peru U'revu: Mitzvah of Procreation in Jewish Tradition and Law." *Journal of Progressive Judaism* 9 (1997) 83–95.
Janzen, J. Gerald. "Rivers in the Desert of Abraham and Sarah and Zion (Isaiah 51:1-3)." *Hebrew Annual Review* 10 (1986) 139–55.
Japhet, Sara. *1 & 2 Chronicles*. Old Testament Library. Louisville: Westminster John Knox, 1993.
Jeppesen, K. "Mother Zion, Father Servant: A Reading of Isaiah 49–55." In *Of Prophets' Visions and the Wisdom of Sages: Essays in Honour of R. Norman Whybray on His Seventieth Birthday*, edited by H. A. McKay and David J. A. Clines, 109–25. Journal for the Study of the Old Testament: Supplement Series 163. Sheffield, UK: JSOT, 1993.
Johnson, Dan G. *From Chaos to Restoration: An Integrative Reading of Isaiah 24–27*. Journal for the Study of the Old Testament: Supplement Series 61. Sheffield, UK: Sheffield Academic, 1988.
Jones, Barry Alan. *The Formation of the Book of the Twelve: A Study in Text and Canon*. Society of Biblical Literature Dissertation Series 149. Atlanta: Scholars, 1995.
Jones, Douglas R. *Jeremiah*. New Century Bible Commentary. Grand Rapids: Eerdmans, 1992.
Jouön, Paul. *A Grammar of Biblical Hebrew*. Translated by T. Muraoka. 2 vols. Rome: Editrice Pontificio Instituto Biblio, 1991.
Joyce, P. *Divine Initiative and Human Response in Ezekiel*. Journal for the Study of the Old Testament: Supplement Series 51. Sheffield, UK: Sheffield Academic Press, 1989.
Kaiser, Otto. *Isaiah 1–12*. Translated by John Bowden. 2nd ed. Old Testament Library. Philadelphia: Westminster, 1983.
―――. *Isaiah 13–39*. Translated by R. A. Wilson. Old Testament Library. Philadelphia: Westminster, 1974.
Kaminski, Carol M. *From Noah to Israel: Realization of the Primaeval Blessing after the Flood*. Journal for the Study of the Old Testament: Supplement Series 413. London: T. & T. Clark, 2004.
Kaminsky, Joel, and Anne Stewart. "God of All the World: Universalism and Developing Monotheism in Isaiah 40–66." *Harvard Theological Review* 99 (2006) 139–63.

Bibliography

Kelle, Brad E. *Hosea 2: Metaphor and Rhetoric in Historical Perspective*. Society of Biblical Literature Academia Biblica 20. Leiden: Brill, 2005.

Keown, Gerald L., et al. *Jeremiah 26–52*. Word Biblical Commentary 27. Dallas: Word, 1995.

Kikawada, Isaac M., and Arthur Quinn. *Before Abraham Was: The Unity of Genesis 1–11*. Nashville: Abingdon, 1985.

Kitchen, K. A. *On the Reliability of the Old Testament*. Grand Rapids: Eerdmans, 2003.

Kilmer, Anne D. "The Mesopotamian Concept of Overpopulation and Its Solution as Reflected in the Mythology." *Orientalia* 41 (1972) 160–77.

Klein, Ralph W. *Israel in Exile: A Theological Interpretation*. Edited by Walter Brueggemann and John R. Donahue. Overtures to Biblical Theology. Philadelphia: Fortress, 1979.

———. "Jeremiah 23:1–8." *Interpretation* 34 (1980) 167–72.

Kline, Meredith G. "Creation in the Image of the Glory-Spirit." *Westminster Theological Journal* 39 (1977) 250–72.

———. *Glory in Our Midst: A Biblical-Theological Reading of Zechariah's Night Visions*. Reprint. Eugene, OR: Wipf and Stock, 2001.

———. *Kingdom Prologue: Genesis Foundations for a Covenantal Worldview*. Overland Park, KS: Two Age, 2000.

———. *Treaty of the Great King: The Covenant Structure of Deuteronomy: Studies and Commentary*. Grand Rapids: Eerdmans, 1963.

Knoppers, Gary N. *1 Chronicles 10–29*. Anchor Bible Commentaries 12A. New York: Doubleday, 2004.

Köhler, Ludwig. *Old Testament Theology*. Translated by A. S. Todd. Philadelphia: Westminster, 1957.

Koole, Jan L. *Isaiah III: Isaiah 49–55*. Vol. 2. Historical Commentary on the Old Testament. Leuven: Peeters, 1998.

———. *Isaiah III: Isaiah 56–66*. Vol. 3. Historical Commentary on the Old Testament. Leuven: Peeters, 2001.

Korpel, Marjo C. A. "The Female Servant of the Lord in Isaiah 54." In *On Reading Prophetic Texts: Gender-Specific and Related Studies in Memory of Fokkelien van Dijk-Hemmes*, edited by B. Becking and Meindert Dijkstra, 153–67. Leiden: Brill, 1996.

Kraus, Hans-Joachim. *Psalms 60–150*. Translated by Hilton C. Oswald. Continental Commentaries. Minneapolis: Fortress, 1993.

Krause, Deborah. "A Blessing Cursed: The Prophet's Prayer for Barren Womb and Dry Breasts in Hosea." In *Reading Between Texts: Intertextuality and the Hebrew Bible*, edited by Danna Nolan Fewell, 191–202. Louisville, KY: Westminster John Knox, 1992.

Kselman, John S. "RB/ /KBD: A New Hebrew-Akkadian Formulaic Pair." *Vetus Testamentum* 29 (1979) 110–14.

Kugler, Robert A. "The Deuteronomists and the Latter Prophets." In *Those Elusive Deuteronomists: The Phenomenon of Pan-Deuteronomism*, edited by Linda S. Schearing and Steven L. McKenzie, 127–44. Journal for the Study of the Old Testament: Supplement Series 268. Sheffield, UK: Sheffield Academic Press, 1999.

Kuntz, J. Kenneth. "The Contribution of Rhetorical Criticism to Understanding Isaiah 51:1–16." In *Art and Meaning: Rhetoric in Biblical Literature*, edited by David J. A.

Bibliography

Clines et al., 140–71. Journal for the Study of the Old Testament: Supplement Series 19. Sheffield, UK: JSOT, 1982.

Lambert, W. G. and A. R. Millard. *Atra-Hasis: The Babylonian Story of the Flood*. Oxford: Clarendon, 1969.

Lapsley, Jacqueline E. *Can These Bones Live? The Problem of the Moral Self in the Book of Ezekiel*. Beihefte zur Zeitschrift für die alttestamentliche Wissenschaft 301. New York: de Gruyter, 2000.

Larkin, Katrina J. A. *The Eschatology of Second Zechariah: A Study of the Formation of a Mantological Wisdom Anthology*. Kampen: Kok Pharos, 1994.

Leene, Hendrik. "Ezekiel and Jeremiah: Promises of Inner Renewal in Diachronic Perspective." In *Past, Present, Future: The Deuteronomic History and the Prophets*, edited by J. C. de Moor and H. F. Van Rooy, 150–75. Boston: Brill, 2000.

Levine, Baruch A. *Numbers 21–36: A New Translation with Introduction and Commentary*. Anchor Bible Commentaries 4A. New York: Doubleday, 2000.

Lohfink, Norbert. *Die Väter Israels im Deuteronomium: Zu einem Buch von Thomas Römer*, Orbis biblicus et orientalis 111. Fribourg: Éditions Universitaires, 1991.

———. "'Seid fruchtbar und füllt die Erde an!': Zwingt die priesterschriftliche Schöpfungsdarstellung in Gen 1 die Christen zum Wachstumsmythos?" *Bibel und Kirche* 30 (1975) 77–82.

———. *Theology of the Pentateuch: Themes of the Priestly Narrative and Deuteronomy*. Translated by Linda M. Maloney. Minneapolis: Fortress, 1994.

Longman III, Tremper. *Literary Approaches to Biblical Interpretation*. Edited by Moisés Silva. Foundations of Contemporary Interpretation 3. Grand Rapids: Zondervan, 1987.

Louth, Andrew, editor. *Genesis 1–11*. Vol. 1 of *Ancient Christian Commentary on Scripture*. Downers Grove, IL: InterVarsity, 2001.

Lundbom, Jack R. *Jeremiah 1–20*. Anchor Bible Commentaries 21A. New York: Doubleday, 1999.

———. *Jeremiah 21–36*. Anchor Bible Commentaries 21B. New York: Doubleday, 2004.

Lust, Johan. "Edom–Adam in Ezekiel, in the MT and LXX." In *Studies in the Hebrew Bible, Qumran, and the Septuagint Presented to Eugene Ulrich*, edited by Peter W. Flint et al., 387–401. Boston: Brill, 2006.

———. "Ezekiel 36–40 in the Oldest Greek Manuscript." *Catholic Biblical Quarterly* 43 (1981) 517–33.

———. "'Gathering and Return' in Jeremiah and Ezekiel." In *Le Livre de Jérémie: Le Prophète et son Milieu les Oracles et leur Transmission*, edited by P.-M. Bogaert, 119–42. Leuven: Leuven University Press, 1997.

———. "Messianism and the Greek Version of Jeremiah." In *VII Congress of the International Organization for Septuagint and Cognate Studies: Leuven 1989*, edited by Claude E. Cox, 87–122. Society of Biblical Literature Septuagint and Cognate Studies 31. Atlanta: Scholars, 1991.

———. "Textual Criticism of the Old and New Testaments: Stepbrothers?" In *New Testament Textual Criticism and Exegesis*, edited by Adelbert Denaux, 15–31. Leuven: Leuven University Press, 2002.

Lyons, Michael A. *From Law to Prophecy: Ezekiel's Use of the Holiness Code*. Library of Hebrew Bible/Old Testament Studies 507. London: T. & T. Clark, 2009.

Bibliography

Macintosh, A. A. *Hosea*. International Critical Commentary. Edinburgh: T. & T. Clark, 1997.

Magnuson, K. T. "Marriage, Procreation and Infertility: Reflections on Genesis." *Southern Baptist Journal of Theology* 4 (2000) 26-42.

Malul, Meir. "Adoption of Foundlings in the Bible and Mesopotamian Documents: A Study of Some Legal Metaphors in Ezekiel 16:1-7." *Journal for the Study of the Old Testament* 46 (1990) 97-126.

Mason, Rex A. "The Use of Earlier Biblical Material in Zechariah 9-14: A Study in Inner Biblical Exegesis." In *Bringing Out the Treasure: Inner Biblical Allusion in Zechariah 9-14*, edited by M. J. Boda and M. H. Floyd, 2-208. Journal for the Study of the Old Testament: Supplement Series 370. Sheffield, UK: Sheffield Academic Press, 2003.

Mays, James Luther. *Hosea: A Commentary*. Old Testament Library. Philadelphia: Westminster, 1969.

———. *Psalms*. Interpretation. Louisville: John Knox, 1994.

McCarter, P. Kyle, Jr. *II Samuel: A New Translation with Introduction, Notes, and Commentary*. Anchor Bible Commentaries 9. New York: Doubleday, 1984.

McComiskey, Thomas. "Hosea." In *The Minor Prophets: An Exegetical and Expository Commentary*, edited by Thomas McComiskey, 1-237. Grand Rapids: Baker, 1992.

———. "Zechariah." In *The Minor Prophets*, edited by Thomas McComiskey, 1003-244. Grand Rapids: Baker, 1998.

McConville, J. G. *Deuteronomy*. Apollos Old Testament Commentary. Downers Grove, IL: InterVarsity, 2002.

———. *Grace in the End: A Study in Deuteronomic Theology*. Studies in Old Testament Biblical Theology. Grand Rapids: Zondervan, 1993.

———. *Judgment and Promise: An Interpretation of the Book of Jeremiah*. Winona Lake, IN: Eisenbrauns, 1993.

McKane, William. *A Critical and Exegetical Commentary on Jeremiah*. Vol. 1. International Critical Commentary. Edinburgh: T. & T. Clark, 1986.

———. *A Critical and Exegetical Commentary on Jeremiah*. Vol. 2. International Critical Commentary. Edinburgh: T. & T. Clark, 1996.

McKeating, H. "Ezekiel the 'Prophet Like Moses.'" *Journal for the Study of the Old Testament* 61 (1994) 97-109.

Meer, Michaël N. van der. "A New Spirit in an Old Corpus? Text-Critical, Literary-Critical and Linguistic Observations regarding Ezekiel 36:16-38." In *The New Things: Eschatology in Old Testament Prophecy*, edited by Ferenc Postma et al., 147-58. Maastricht: Uitgeverij Shaker, 2002.

Melugin, Roy F. "Israel and the Nations in Isaiah 40-55." In *Problems in Biblical Theology: Essays in Honor of Rolf Knierim*, edited by Henry T. C. Sun and Keith L. Eades, 249-64. Grand Rapids: Eerdmans, 1997.

Mendecki, Norbert. "Deuterojesajanischer und Ezechielischer Einfluss auf Sach 10:8-10." *Kairos* 27 (1985) 340-44.

———. "Die Sammlung und die Hineinführung in das Land in Jer 23:3." *Kairos* 25 (1983) 99-103.

Mendenhall, George E. "The Census Lists of Numbers 1 and 26." *Journal of Biblical Literature* 77 (1958) 52-66.

Merrill, Eugene H. "Old Testament History: A Theological Perspective." In *New International Dictionary of Old Testament Theology and Exegesis*, edited by Willem A. VanGemeren, 1:68-85. Grand Rapids: Zondervan, 1997.

Mettinger, Tryggve N. D. *A Farewell to the Servant Songs: A Critical Examination of an Exegetical Axiom*. Lund: Gleerup, 1983.

Meyers, Carol. "עָצַב." In *Theological Dictionary of the Old Testament*, edited by G. J. Botterweck et al., 11:278-80. Grand Rapids: Eerdmans, 2001.

Meyers, Carol L., and Eric M. Meyers. *Haggai, Zechariah 1-8: A New Translation with Introduction and Commentary*. Anchor Bible Commentaries 25B. Garden City, NY: Doubleday, 1987.

———. *Zechariah 9-14: A New Translation with Introduction and Commentary*. Anchor Bible Commentaries 25C. New York: Doubleday, 1993.

Milgrom, Jacob. *Leviticus 23-27: A New Translation with Introduction and Commentary*. Anchor Bible Commentaries 3B. New York: Doubleday, 2000.

———. "Leviticus 26 and Ezekiel." In *The Quest for Context and Meaning: Studies in Biblical Intertextuality in Honor of James A. Sanders*, edited by Craig A. Evans and S. Talmon, 57-62. Leiden: Brill, 1997.

Miller, Patrick D. *Deuteronomy*, Interpretation. Louisville: John Knox, 1990.

———. "Psalm 127: The House that Yahweh Builds." *Journal for the Study of the Old Testament* 22 (1982) 119-32.

Mitchell, Christopher Wright. *The Meaning of BRK "To Bless" in the Old Testament*. Society of Biblical Literature Dissertation Series 95. Atlanta: Scholars, 1987.

Moo, Douglas J. *The Epistle to the Romans*. New International Commentary on the New Testament. Grand Rapids: Eerdmans, 1996.

Moran, William L. "Some Considerations of Form and Interpretation in Atra-hasis." In *Language, Literature, and History: Philological and Historical Studies Presented to Erica Reiner*, edited by Francesca Rochberg-Halton, 245-55. American Oriental Series. New Haven: American Oriental Society, 1987.

Motyer, Alec. *The Prophecy of Isaiah*. Leicester, UK: InterVarsity, 1993.

Mowvley, Harry. "The Concept and Content of 'Blessing' in the Old Testament." *The Bible Translator* 16 (1965) 74-80.

Mulzac, Kenneth D. "'The Remnant of My Sheep': A Study of Jeremiah 23:1-8 in Its Biblical and Theological Contexts." *Journal of the Adventist Theological Society* 13 (2002) 134-49.

Nelson, Richard D. *First and Second Kings*. Interpretation. Louisville: John Knox, 1987.

Nissinen, Martti. *Prophets and Prophecy in the Ancient Near East*. Edited by Peter Machinist. Society of Biblical Literature Writings from the Ancient World 12. Atlanta: Society of Biblical Literature, 2003.

Nogalski, James. "Intertextuality in the Twelve." In *Forming Prophetic Literature: Essays on Isaiah and the Twelve in Honor of John D. W. Watts*, edited by Paul R. House and James W. Watts, 102-24. Journal for the Study of the Old Testament: Supplement Series 235. Sheffield, UK: Sheffield Academic Press, 1996.

———. "Joel as 'Literary Anchor' for the Book of the Twelve." In *Reading and Hearing the Book of the Twelve*, edited by James Nogalski and Marvin A. Sweeney, 91-109. Atlanta: Society of Biblical Literature, 2000.

———. *Literary Precursors to the Book of the Twelve*. Beihefte zur Zeitschrift für die alttestamentliche Wissenschaft 217. Berlin: de Gruyter, 1993.

Bibliography

———. "Recurring Themes in the Book of the Twelve: Creating Points of Contact for a Theological Reading." *Interpretation* 61 (2007) 125-36.

———. *Redactional Processes in the Book of the Twelve*. Beihefte zur Zeitschrift für die alttestamentliche Wissenschaft 218. Berlin: de Gruyter, 1993.

Nogalski, James D., and Marvin A. Sweeney, editors. *Reading and Hearing the Book of the Twelve*. Atlanta: Society of Biblical Literature, 2000.

Noth, Martin. *The Deuteronomistic History*. Translated by Jane Doull. Journal for the Study of the Old Testament: Supplement Series 15. Sheffield, UK: Sheffield Academic Press, 1981.

———. *A History of Pentateuchal Traditions*. Translated by Bernhard W. Anderson. Englewood, Cliffs, NJ: Prentice-Hall, 1972.

Novak, David. "'Be Fruitful and Multiply': Issues Relating to Birth in Judaism." In *Celebration and Renewal: Rites of Passage in Judaism*, edited by Rela M. Geffen, 12-31. Philadelphia: Jewish Publication Society, 1993.

Nurmela, Risto. *Prophets in Dialogue: Inner-Biblical Allusions in Zechariah 1-8 and 9-14*. Abo, Finland: Abo Akademi University Press, 1996.

O'Kane, M. "Isaiah: A Prophet in the Footsteps of Moses." *Journal for the Study of the Old Testament* 69 (1996) 29-51.

Odell, Margaret S. *Ezekiel*. Smyth & Helwys Biblical Commentaries. Macon, GA: Smyth & Helwys, 2005.

Oden, Jr., Robert A. "Divine Aspirations in Atrahasis and in Genesis 1-11." *Zeitschrift für die alttestamentliche Wissenschaft* 93 (1981) 197-216.

Olson, Dennis T. *Deuteronomy and the Death of Moses: A Theological Reading*. Overtures to Biblical Theology. Minneapolis: Fortress, 1994.

———. *Numbers*. Interpretation. Louisville: John Knox, 1996.

Oswalt, John N. *The Book of Isaiah: Chapters 1-39*. New International Commentary on the Old Testament. Grand Rapids: Eerdmans, 1986.

———. *The Book of Isaiah: Chapters 40-66*. New International Commentary on the Old Testament. Grand Rapids: Eerdmans, 1998.

———. "God's Determination to Redeem His People (Isaiah 9:1-7; 11:1-11; 26:1-9; 35:1-10)." *Review and Expositor* 88 (1991) 153-65.

———. "The Nations in Isaiah: Friend or Foe; Servant or Partner." *Bulletin for Biblical Research* 16 (2006) 41-51.

Otzen, Benedikt. "בהל." In *Theological Dictionary of the Old Testament*, edited by G. J. Botterweck and H. Ringgren, 2:3-5. Grand Rapids: Eerdmans, 1975.

Patmore, Hector M. "The Shorter and Longer Texts of Ezekiel: The Implications of the Manuscript Finds from Masada and Qumran." *Journal for the Study of the Old Testament* 32 (2007) 231-42.

Patton, Corrine L. "Pan-Deuteronomism and the Book of Ezekiel." In *Those Elusive Deuteronomists: The Phenomenon of Pan-Deuteronomism*, edited by Linda S. Schearing and Steven L. McKenzie, 200-15. Journal for the Study of the Old Testament: Supplement Series 268. Sheffield, UK: Sheffield Academic, 1999.

Payne, J. Barton. "The Validity of the Numbers in Chronicles." *Bibliotheca Sacra* 136 (1979) 109-28, 206-20.

Pedersen, Johannes. *Israel: Its Life and Culture*. 2 vols. London: Oxford University Press, 1946-47.

Bibliography

Person, Raymond F. *Second Zechariah and the Deuteronomic School*. Journal for the Study of the Old Testament: Supplement Series 167. Sheffield, UK: Sheffield Academic, 1993.

Petersen, David L. "Defining Prophecy and Prophetic Literature." In *Prophecy in Its Ancient Near Eastern Context: Mesopotamian, Biblical, and Arabian Perspectives*, edited by Martti Nissinen, 33–44. Atlanta: SBL, 2000.

———. *Haggai and Zechariah 1–8*. Old Testament Library. Philadelphia: Westminster, 1984.

———. *The Prophetic Literature: An Introduction*. Louisville, KY: Westminster John Knox, 2002.

———. *The Roles of Israel's Prophets*. Journal for the Study of the Old Testament: Supplement Series 17. Sheffield, UK: JSOT, 1981.

———. *Zechariah 9–14 and Malachi*. Old Testament Library. Louisville: Westminster John Knox, 1995.

Pohlmann, Karl Friedrich. "Das 'Heil' des Landes: Erwägungen zu Jer 29:5-7." In *Mythos im Alten Testament und seiner Umwelt: Festschrift für Hans-Peter Müller zum 65. Geburtstag*, edited by Armin Lange et al., 144–64. Berlin: de Gruyter, 1999.

Polan, Gregory J. "Ezekiel's Covenant of Peace." *The Bible Today* 37 (1999) 18–23.

Porten, P. and U. Rappaport. "Poetic Structure in Genesis IX 7." *Vetus Testamentum* 21 (1971) 363–69.

Price, James D. "רחב." In *New International Dictionary of Old Testament Theology and Exegesis*, edited by Willem A. VanGemeren, 3:1092–93. Grand Rapids: Zondervan, 1997.

Provan, Iain. *1 and 2 Kings*. New International Biblical Commentary on the Old Testament. Peabody, MA: Hendrickson, 1995.

Provan, Iain, V. Philips Long, and Tremper Longman III. *A Biblical History of Israel*. Louisville: Westminster John Knox, 2003.

Rad, Gerhard von. *Deuteronomy*. Old Testament Library. Philadelphia: Westminster, 1966.

———. "The Form-Critical Problem of the Hexateuch." In *The Problem of the Hexateuch and Other Essays*, 1–78. Translated by E. W. Trueman Dicken. Edinburgh: Oliver & Boyd, 1966.

———. *Genesis: A Commentary*. Translated by John H. Marks. Rev. ed. Old Testament Library. Philadelphia: Westminster, 1972.

———. *Old Testament Theology: The Theology of Israel's Historical Traditions*. Translated by D. M. G. Stalker. New York: Harper & Row, 1962.

———. *Old Testament Theology: The Theology of Israel's Prophetic Traditions*. Translated by D. M. G. Stalker. Vol. 2. New York: Harper & Row, 1965.

———. "The Promised Land and Yahweh's Land in the Hexateuch." In *The Problem of the Hexateuch and Other Essays*, 79–93. Translated by E. W. Trueman Dicken. Edinburgh: Oliver & Boyd, 1966.

Raitt, Thomas M. *A Theology of Exile: Judgment/Deliverance in Jeremiah and Ezekiel*. Philadelphia: Fortress, 1977.

Redditt, Paul L. *Haggai, Zechariah, Malachi*. New Century Bible Commentary. Grand Rapids: Eerdmans, 1995.

———. *Introduction to the Prophets*. Grand Rapids: Eerdmans, 2008

Bibliography

Redditt, Paul L., and Aaron Schart, editors. *Thematic Threads in the Book of the Twelve.* Beihefte zur Zeitschrift für die alttestamentliche Wissenschaft 325. Berlin: de Gruyter, 2003.

Rendsburg, Gary A. "An Additional Note to Two Recent Articles on the Number of People in the Exodus from Egypt and the Large Numbers in Numbers 1 and 26." *Vetus Testamentum* 51 (2001) 392-95.

Rendtorff, Rolf. *The Canonical Hebrew Bible: A Theology of the Old Testament.* Translated by David E. Orton. Leiden: Deo, 2005.

———. "How to Read the Book of the Twelve as a Theological Unity." In *Reading and Hearing the Book of the Twelve,* edited by James Nogalski and Marvin A. Sweeney, 75-87. Atlanta: Society of Biblical Literature, 2000.

———. *The Old Testament: An Introduction.* Translated by John Bowden. Philadelphia: Fortress, 1986.

Renz, Thomas. *The Rhetorical Function of the Book of Ezekiel.* Supplements to Vetus Testamentum 76. Leiden: Brill, 1999.

Roberts, J. J. M. "Zion in the Theology of the Davidic-Solomonic Empire." In *Studies in the Period of David and Solomon and Other Essays,* edited by Tomoo Ishida, 93-108. Winona Lake, IN: Eisenbrauns, 1982.

Robinson, R. B. "Literary Functions of the Genealogies of Genesis." *Catholic Biblical Quarterly* 48 (1986) 595-608.

Römer, Thomas. "Deuteronomy in Search of Origins." In *Reconsidering Israel and Judah: Recent Studies on the Deuteronomistic History,* edited by Gary N. Knoppers and J. G. McConville, 112-38. Winona Lake, IN: Eisenbrauns, 2000.

———. "How Did Jeremiah Become a Convert to Deuteronomistic Ideology?" In *Those Elusive Deuteronomists: The Phenomenon of Pan-Deuteronomism,* edited by Linda S. Schearing and Steven L. McKenzie, 189-99. Journal for the Study of the Old Testament: Supplement Series 268. Sheffield, UK: Sheffield Academic Press, 1999.

———. *Israels Väter: Untersuchungen zur Väterthematik im Deuteronomium und in der Deuteronomistischen Tradition.* Orbis biblicus et orientalis 99. Göttingen: Vandenhoeck & Ruprecht, 1990.

Rudman, Dominic. "Zechariah 8:20-22 & Isaiah 2:2-4//Micah 4:2-3: A Study in Intertextuality." *Biblische Notizen* 107-8 (2001) 50-54.

Sailhamer, John. *The Pentateuch as Narrative.* Library of Biblical Interpretation. Grand Rapids: Zondervan, 1992.

Sawyer, J. "Daughter of Zion and Servant of the Lord in Isaiah: A Comparison." *Journal for the Study of the Old Testament* 44 (1989) 89-107.

Scalise, Pamela J. "'I Have Produced a Man with the LORD': God as Provider of Offspring in Old Testament Theology." *Review and Expositor* 91 (1994) 577-89.

Scharbert, Josef. "בְּרָכָה; ברך." In *Theological Dictionary of the Old Testament,* edited by G. J. Botterweck and H. Ringgren, 2:279-308. Grand Rapids: Eerdmans, 1975.

Schart, Aaron. "Reconstructing the Redaction History of the Twelve Prophets: Problems and Models." In *Reading and Hearing the Book of the Twelve,* edited by James Nogalski and Marvin A. Sweeney, 34-48. Atlanta: Society of Biblical Literature, 2000.

Schmitt, J. "The Motherhood of God and Zion as Mother." *Revue Biblique* 92 (1985) 557-69.

Bibliography

Schmutzer, Andrew J. *Be Fruitful and Multiply: A Crux of Thematic Repetition in Genesis 1–11*. Eugene, OR: Wipf & Stock, 2009.

Schultz, Richard L. "Integrating Old Testament Theology and Exegesis." In *New International Dictionary of Old Testament Theology and Exegesis*, edited by Willem A. VanGemeren, 1:185–205. Grand Rapids: Zondervan, 1997.

———. "Isaiah." In *Theological Interpretation of the Old Testament: A Book-by-Book Survey*, edited by K. J. Vanhoozer, 194–210. Grand Rapids: Baker, 2008.

———. "Nationalism and Universalism in Isaiah." In *Interpreting Isaiah: Issues and Approaches*, edited by H. G. M. Williamson and David G. Firth, 122–44. Nottingham, UK: InterVarsity, 2009.

———. *The Search for Quotation: Verbal Parallels in the Prophets*. Journal for the Study of the Old Testament: Supplement Series 180. Sheffield, UK: Sheffield Academic, 1999.

Schwartz, Baruch J. "Ezekiel's Dim View of Israel's Restoration." In *The Book of Ezekiel: Theological and Anthropological Perspectives*, edited by Margaret S. Odell and John T. Strong, 43–67. Atlanta: Society of Biblical Literature, 2000.

Schwesig, Paul-Gerhard. *Die Rolle der Tag-JHWHs-Dichtungen im Dodekapropheton*, BZAW 366. Berlin: de Gruyter, 2006.

Seitz, Christopher. *Isaiah 1–39*. Interpretation. Louisville: John Knox, 1993.

———. *Prophecy and Hermeneutics: Toward a New Introduction to the Prophets*. Studies in Theological Interpretation. Grand Rapids: Baker, 2007.

———. "The Prophet Moses and the Canonical Shape of Jeremiah." *Zeitschrift für die alttestamentliche Wissenschaft* 101 (1989) 3–27.

———. *Theology in Conflict: Reactions to the Exile in the Book of Jeremiah*. Beihefte zur Zeitschrift für die alttestamentliche Wissenschaft 176. Berlin: de Gruyter, 1989.

Selman, Martin J. *1 Chronicles*. Tyndale Old Testament Commentaries. Downers Grove, IL: InterVarsity, 1994.

———. *2 Chronicles*. Tyndale Old Testament Commentaries. Downers Grove, IL: InterVarsity, 1994.

Selwyn, William. *Horae Hebraicae: Critical Observations on the Prophecy of Messiah in Isaiah Chapter IX, and on Other Passages of the Holy Scriptures*. Cambridge: Cambridge University Press, 1848.

Shapiro, David S. "Be Fruitful and Multiply." In *Jewish Bioethics*, edited by F. Rosner and J. D. Bleich, 59–79. New York: Sanhedrin, 1979.

Shields, Mary E. *Circumscribing the Prostitute: The Rhetorics of Intertextuality, Metaphor and Gender in Jeremiah 3.1—4.4*. Journal for the Study of the Old Testament: Supplement Series 387. London: T. & T. Clark, 2004.

Siebert-Hommes, Jopie. *Let the Daughters Live! The Literary Architecture of Exodus 1–2 as a Key for Interpretation*. Leiden: Brill, 1998.

Silva, Charles H. "The Literary Structure of Hosea 1–3." *Bibliotheca Sacra* 164 (2007) 181–97.

Smelik, K. A. D. "Letters to the Exiles: Jeremiah 29 in Context." *Scandinavian Journal of the Old Testament* 10 (1996) 282–95.

Smith, Gary V. *The Prophets as Preachers: An Introduction to the Hebrew Prophets*. Nashville: Broadman & Holman, 1994.

Snoek, Jans. "(Dis)continuity between Present and Future in Isaiah 26:7–21." In *The New Things: Eschatology in Old Testament Prophecy: Festschrift for Henk Leene*, edited by Ferenc Postma et al., 211–18. Maastricht: Uitgeverij Shaker, 2002.

Bibliography

Spottorno, M. V. "La omisión de Ez 36,23b-38 y la transposición de capítulos en el papiro 967." *Emérita* 50 (1982) 93-98.

Stead, Michael R. "Sustained Allusion in Zechariah 1-2." In *Tradition in Transition: Haggai and Zechariah 1-8 in the Trajectory of Hebrew Theology*, edited by M. J. Boda and M. H. Floyd, 144-70. London: T. & T. Clark, 2008.

Steck, Odil Hannes. "Der neue Himmel und die neue Erde: Beobachtungen zur Rezeption von Gen 1-3 in Jes 65,16b-25." In *Studies in the Book of Isaiah*, edited by J. T. A. G. M. van Ruiten and Marc Vervenne, 349-65. Louvain: Leuven University Press, 1997.

Steymans, Hans Ulrich. *Deuteronomium 28 und die ade zur Thronfolgeregelung Asarhaddons: Segen und Fluch im Alten Orient und in Israel*. Göttingen: Vandenhoeck & Ruprecht, 1995.

Stuart, Douglas. *Hosea-Jonah*. Word Biblical Commentary 31. Waco, TX: Word, 1987.

Stulman, Louis. *Jeremiah*. Abingdon Old Testament Commentaries. Nashville: Abingdon, 2005.

Sweeney, Marvin A. "Jeremiah's Reflection on the Isaian Royal Promise: Jeremiah 23:1-8 in Context." In *Uprooting and Planting: Essays on Jeremiah for Leslie Allen*, edited by John Goldingay, 308-21. London: T. & T. Clark, 2007.

―――. "New Gleanings from an Old Vineyard: Isaiah 27 Reconsidered." In *Early Jewish and Christian Exegesis*, edited by Craig A. Evans and William F. Stinespring, 51-66. Atlanta: Scholars, 1987.

―――. "Sequence and Interpretation in the Book of the Twelve." In *Reading and Hearing the Book of the Twelve*, edited by James Nogalski and Marvin A. Sweeney, 49-64. Atlanta: Society of Biblical Literature, 2000.

―――. *The Twelve Prophets: Volume One*. Berit Olam. Collegeville, MN: Liturgical, 2000.

―――. *The Twelve Prophets: Volume Two*. Berit Olam. Collegeville, MN: Liturgical, 2000.

Tai, Nicholas Ho Fai. *Prophetie als Schriftauslegung in Sacharja 9-14: Traditions- und kompositionsgeschichtliche Studien*. CTM 17. Stuttgart: Calwer, 1996.

Talmon, Shemaryahu. "The Textual Study of the Bible—A New Outlook." In *Qumran and the History of the Biblical Text*, edited by Frank Moore Cross and Shemaryahu Talmon, 321-400. Cambridge: Harvard University Press, 1975.

Tate, Marvin E. "The Book of Isaiah in Recent Study." In *Forming Prophetic Literature: Essays on Isaiah and the Twelve in Honor of John D. W. Watts*, edited by James W. Watts and Paul R. House, 22-56. Sheffield, UK: Sheffield Academic Press, 1996.

Thompson, J. A. *The Book of Jeremiah*. New International Commentary on the Old Testament. Grand Rapids: Eerdmans, 1980.

Tigay, Jeffrey H. *Deuteronomy*. The JPS Torah Commentary. Philadelphia: The Jewish Publication Society, 1996.

Tov, Emanuel. "Recensional Differences between the MT and LXX of Ezekiel." *Ephemerides theologicae lovanienses* 62 (1986) 89-101.

―――. *Textual Criticism of the Hebrew Bible*. 2nd Rev. ed. Minneapolis: Fortress, 2001.

Tuell, Stephen S. "Haggai-Zechariah: Prophecy after the Manner of Ezekiel." In *Thematic Threads in the Book of the Twelve*, edited by Paul L. Redditt and Aaron Schart, 273-91. Beihefte zur Zeitschrift für die alttestamentliche Wissenschaft 325. Berlin: de Gruyter, 2003.

Bibliography

Turner, Laurence A. *Announcements of Plot in Genesis*. Journal for the Study of the Old Testament: Supplement Series 96. Sheffield, UK: JSOT, 1990.
Unterman, Jeremiah. *From Repentance to Redemption: Jeremiah's Thought in Transition*. Journal for the Study of the Old Testament: Supplement Series 54. Sheffield, UK: JSOT, 1987.
van der Wal, A. J. O. "Themes from Exodus in Jeremiah 30–31." In *Studies in the Book of Exodus*, edited by Marc Vervenne, 559–66. Louvain: Peeters, 1996.
Van Leeuwen, Raymond C. "'Be Fruitful and Multiply': Is this a Command, or a Blessing?" *Christianity Today* 45 (2001) 58–61.
Van Winkle, D. "Proselytes in Isaiah XL–LV?: A Study of Isaiah XLIV 1–5." *Vetus Testamentum* 47 (1997) 341–59.
———. "The Relationship of the Nations to Yahweh and to Israel in Isaiah 40–55." *Vetus Testamentum* 35 (1985) 446–58.
VanGemeren, Willem A. *The Progress of Redemption: The Story of Salvation from Creation to the New Jerusalem*. Grand Rapids: Baker, 1988.
Vollmer, Jochen. "Zur Sprache von Jesaja 9:1–6." *Zeitschrift für die alttestamentliche Wissenschaft* 80 (1968) 343–50.
Volz, D. Paul. *Jesaia II*. Kommentar zum Alten Testament. Leipzig: Scholl, 1932.
Vriezen, Theodorus C. *Hosea: profeet en cultuur*. Groningen: Wolters, 1941.
Waard, Jan de. *A Handbook on Isaiah*. Winona Lake, IN: Eisenbrauns, 1997.
Waltke, Bruce K. "Aims of OT Textual Criticism." *Westminster Theological Journal* 51 (1989) 93–108.
———. *Genesis: A Commentary*. Grand Rapids: Zondervan, 2001.
———. *The Book of Proverbs: Chapters 1–15*. New International Commentary on the Old Testament. Grand Rapids: Eerdmans, 2004.
Walton, John H. *Ancient Israelite Literature in Its Cultural Context*. Grand Rapids: Zondervan, 1989.
———. *Ancient Near Eastern Thought and the Old Testament: Introducing the Conceptual World of the Old Testament*. Grand Rapids: Baker, 2006.
———. *Genesis*. NIV Application Commentary. Grand Rapids: Zondervan, 2001.
Watson, Wilfred G. E. *Classical Hebrew Poetry: A Guide to Its Techniques*. Journal for the Study of the Old Testament: Supplement Series 26. Sheffield, UK: JSOT, 1984.
Watts, John D. W. *Isaiah 1–33*. Word Biblical Commentary 24. Waco, TX: Word, 1985.
———. *Isaiah 34–66*. Word Biblical Commentary 25. Waco, TX: Word, 1987.
Watts, Rikk E. "Echoes from the Past: Israel's Ancient Traditions and the Destiny of the Nations in Isaiah 40–55." *Journal for the Study of the Old Testament* 28 (2004) 481–508.
Webb, Barry G. *The Message of Zechariah*. The Bible Speaks Today. Downers Grove, IL: InterVarsity, 2003.
———. "Zion in Transformation: A Literary Approach to Isaiah." In *The Bible in Three Dimensions: Essays in Celebration of Forty Years of Biblical Studies in the University of Sheffield*, edited by David J. A. Clines et al., 65–84. Journal for the Study of the Old Testament: Supplement Series 87. Sheffield, UK: JSOT, 1990.
Webster, Edwin C. "A Rhetorical Study of Isaiah 66." *Journal for the Study of the Old Testament* 34 (1986) 93–108.
Wegner, Paul D. *An Examination of Kingship and Messianic Expectation in Isaiah 1–35*. Lewiston, NY: Mellen, 1992.
———. "A Re-examination of Isaiah IX 1–6." *Vetus Testamentum* 42 (1992) 103–12.

Bibliography

———. *A Student's Guide to Textual Criticism of the Bible*. Downers Grove, IL: InterVarsity, 2006.

Wehmeier, Gerhard. "ברך pi. to bless." In *Theological Lexicon of the Old Testament*, edited by Ernst Jenni and Claus Westermann, 1:276–82. Peabody, MA: Hendrickson, 1997.

———. "Deliverance and Blessing in the Old and New Testament." *Indian Journal of Theology* 20 (1971) 30–42.

Weinfeld, Moshe. *Deuteronomy 1–11: A New Translation with Introduction and Commentary*. Anchor Bible Commentaries 5. New York: Doubleday, 1991.

———. "The Covenant of Grant in the Old Testament and in the Ancient Near East." *Journal of the American Oriental Society* 90 (1970) 184–203.

———. "Jeremiah and the Spiritual Metamorphosis of Israel." *Zeitschrift für die alttestamentliche Wissenschaft* 88 (1976) 17–56.

Wenham, Gordon J. *The Book of Leviticus*. New International Commentary on the Old Testament. Grand Rapids: Eerdmans, 1979.

———. *Genesis 1–15*. Word Biblical Commentary 1. Waco, TX: Word, 1987.

Wenham, J. W. "Large Numbers in the Old Testament." *Tyndale Bulletin* 19 (1967) 19–53.

Westermann, Claus. *Blessing in the Bible and the Life of the Church*. Translated by Keith Crim. Overtures to Biblical Theology. Philadelphia: Fortress, 1978.

———. *Elements of Old Testament Theology*. Translated by Douglas W. Stott. Atlanta: John Knox, 1982.

———. *Genesis 1–11: A Commentary*. Translated by John J. Scullion. Continental Commentaries. London: SPCK, 1984.

———. *Genesis 12–36*. Translated by John J. Scullion. Continental Commentaries. Minneapolis: Fortress, 1995.

———. *Genesis 37–50: A Commentary*. Translated by John J. Scullion. Continental Commentaries. Minneapolis: Augsburg, 1986.

———. *Isaiah 40–66: A Commentary*. Translated by D. M. G. Stalker. Old Testament Library. Philadelphia: Westminster, 1969.

———. *Prophetic Oracles of Salvation in the Old Testament*. Translated by Keith Crim. Louisville, KY: Westminster John Knox, 1991.

Whybray, R. N. *Isaiah 40–66*. New Century Bible Commentary. Grand Rapids: Eerdmans, 1987.

Wildberger, Hans. *Isaiah 1–12*. Translated by Thomas H. Trapp. Continental Commentaries. Minneapolis: Fortress, 1991.

———. *Isaiah 13–27*. Translated by Thomas H. Trapp. Continental Commentaries. Minneapolis: Fortress, 1997.

Willey, Patricia Tull. *Remember the Former Things: The Recollection of Previous Texts in Second Isaiah*. Society of Biblical Literature Dissertation Series 161. Atlanta: Scholars, 1997.

Williamson, H. G. M. *1 and 2 Chronicles*. New Century Bible Commentaries. Grand Rapids: Eerdmans, 1982.

———. *Ezra, Nehemiah*. Word Biblical Commentary. Waco, TX: Word, 1985.

Williamson, Paul R. *Sealed with an Oath: Covenant in God's Unfolding Purpose*. New Studies in Biblical Theology 23. Downers Grove, IL: InterVarsity, 2007.

Wilshire, L. E. "The Servant-City: A New Interpretation of the 'Servant of the Lord' in the Servant Songs of Deutero-Isaiah." *Journal of Biblical Literature* 94 (1975) 356–67.
Wilson, Andrew. *The Nations in Deutero-Isaiah: A Study on Composition and Structure*. Lewiston: Mellen, 1986.
Wilson, Robert R. *Prophecy and Society in Ancient Israel*. Philadelphia: Fortress, 1980.
Wolff, H. W. *Frieden ohne Ende: Jesaja 7:1–7 und 9:1–6*. Neukirchen, Kreis Moers: Neukirchener Verlag, 1962.
———. *Hosea*. Translated by Gary Stansell. Hermeneia. Philadelphia: Fortress, 1974.
———. "The Kerygma of the Yahwist." In *The Vitality of Old Testament Traditions*, edited by Walter Brueggemann and H. W. Wolff, 41–66. Atlanta: John Knox, 1982.
Woudstra, Marten H. "Edom and Israel in Ezekiel." *Calvin Theological Journal* 3 (1968) 21–35.
Wright, Christopher J. H. *The Mission of God: Unlocking the Bible's Grand Narrative*. Downers Grove, IL: InterVarsity, 2006.
———. *Old Testament Ethics for the People of God*. Leicester, UK: InterVarsity, 2004.
Würthwein, Ernst. *The Text of the Old Testament: An Introduction to the Biblia Hebraica*. Translated by Erroll F. Rhodes. Rev. ed. Grand Rapids: Eerdmans, 1995.
Yates, Gary E. "New Exodus and No Exodus in Jeremiah 26–45: Promise and Warning to the Exiles in Babylon." *Tyndale Bulletin* 57 (2006) 1–22.
Yegerlehner, David Anthony. "'Be Fruitful and Multiply, and Fill the Earth . . .': A History of the Interpretation of Genesis 1:28 and Related Texts in Selected Periods." PhD diss., Boston University Graduate School, 1975.
Youngblood, Ronald. "The Abrahamic Covenant: Conditional or Unconditional?" In *The Living and Active Word of God: Studies in Honor of Samuel J. Schultz*, edited by Morris Inch and Ronald Youngblood, 31–46. Winona Lake, IN: Eisenbrauns, 1983.
Zimmerli, Walther. *Ezekiel 1*. Translated by Ronald E. Clements. Hermeneia. Philadelphia: Fortress, 1979.
———. *Ezekiel 2*. Translated by James D. Martin. Hermeneia. Philadelphia: Fortress, 1983.
———. *The Fiery Throne: The Prophets and Old Testament Theology*. Edited by K. C. Hanson. Fortress Classics in Biblical Studies. Minneapolis: Fortress, 2003.

Ancient Document Index

Ancient Near Eastern Documents

Atrahasis

I.1–4	31
I.189–97	31
I.280–305	31
I.286	31
I.289–92	31
I.299–304	31
I.352–53	44
I.354–59	44
I.360	44
I.364–416	44
II.i.1–2	44–45
II.i.3–8	44
III.iii.11–16	44
III.vii.1–8	44

Enki and Ninmah

10–43	31
39	31

Enuma Elish

VI.23–42	31

Epic of Gilgamesh

XI.21	43–44

Old Testament / Hebrew Bible

Genesis

1–11	22–24, 26, 34, 47–49, 51, 53, 56–57, 92, 102, 196
1–3	152
1–2	130, 168, 279
1	30, 32–34, 43, 164
1:1	32, 130
1:2	130
1:21	130
1:22	2, 13–15, 24–26, 28–29, 42, 48, 51, 58, 141, 178, 185, 289
1:26–30	43
1:26–28	21, 30, 34
1:26	31–33, 101
1:27–28	40
1:27	33, 130
1:28–30	27, 30, 39, 41, 48
1:28	xi, 1–2, 4–5, 13–15, 22–40, 42–43, 46, 48, 51, 53, 55–56, 58, 60–61, 95, 100–104, 106–7, 131, 141, 168, 179, 182, 185, 187–88, 215, 229, 279, 285, 287, 289
2	32–33

Ancient Document Index

Genesis (cont.)

2:1	32, 130
2:3	24, 130
2:4	32, 130
2:7	130
2:8	130
2:15	32
2:17	39
2:18–25	40
2:19–20	33
2:19	130
3	39, 48
3:3	39
3:14–19	39, 49
3:15	39
3:16	4, 39–41, 43, 100, 152
3:17–19	39
3:17	40
3:22	41
4	48
4:1–2	41
4:17–24	42
4:23	42
4:25	41
5:1—6:1	42
5	23, 42, 47–48
5:2	24, 31, 42, 48
5:3–32	42
5:3	31
5:5	42
5:8	42
5:11	42
5:14	42
5:17	42
5:20	42
5:27	42
5:29	40
5:31	42
6–9	48
6:1–8	42
6:1	14, 42, 289
6:5	44
6:7	42
6:9	42
6:11–13	44
6:11	42
6:13	42
6:17	42
6:18	227
7:4	42
7:21–23	42
8:17	2, 13–15, 24, 29, 46, 48, 51, 58, 179, 194, 289
8:21–22	24, 43
8:21	43
8:22	194–95
9:1–7	34, 42, 44, 53, 102
9:1	2, 13–15, 24, 29, 43, 46–48, 51, 53, 56, 58, 60, 100, 103, 107, 141, 179, 182, 185, 194, 215, 229, 279, 289
9:2	43
9:3–4	43
9:5–6	43
9:6	36, 43
9:7	2, 13–16, 24, 29, 36, 43, 46–48, 51, 53, 56, 58, 60, 100, 107, 179, 185, 194, 215, 229, 279, 289
9:8–17	43, 54, 102
9:11	24
9:15	24
9:16	227
9:19	47
10–11	2, 24, 47
10:1—11:9	48
10	23, 46, 56
10:5	46–47
10:18	46–47
10:20	46
10:25	46
10:31	46
10:32	46–47
11	23, 47–48
11:1–9	46
11:1	46
11:4	46–47
11:6–9	46

Genesis (cont.)

11:6	46
11:8	47
11:9	46–47
11:10–32	48
11:10–26	47
11:20	144
11:30	47, 94
12–50	21–23, 48–49, 51, 57, 196
12	48, 53, 102
12:1–4b	49
12:1–4a	23
12:1–3	22, 49–50, 52
12:1	51, 78
12:2	5, 23, 50, 56, 59, 70, 103, 155
12:2–3	21, 23, 47, 105, 141, 289
12:3	55, 78, 260, 285
12:7	51, 194
12:10–20	52
12:16	51
13:2	51
13:6	51
13:14–17	51
13:15	194
13:16	16, 28, 50, 86, 106, 194, 289
13:17	215
14:15	51
14:22–23	51
15:1–7	51
15:1	95
15:3	12, 28, 51
15:4	51, 83
15:5	16, 50–51, 69, 194, 196, 240, 289
15:9–10	51
15:18–21	51, 84
16:1–2	12, 28, 51
16:2	155
16:10	14, 40, 50–51, 240, 251, 289
17:1–8	51
17:1	51
17:2–6	28, 290
17:2	13, 58, 66
17:4–5	51
17:6–7	66
17:6	14–15, 50, 52, 58, 201, 224
17:7	65, 227
17:9–14	51
17:9	65
17:10	51
17:13	227
17:15–21	51
17:15–19	94
17:16	201, 290
17:19	65, 227
17:20	14–15, 50–51, 58, 141, 179, 290
17:21	65
18:10	51
18:14	51
18:18	49–50, 52, 55, 58, 149, 290
18:19	51, 78
18:20–21	45
18:20	189
19:13	45
20:1–18	51–52
20:17–18	12, 28, 42, 55
21:1–2	12, 28, 51, 106, 155
21:13	51, 290
21:18	51, 290
22	51
22:2	51
22:12	51, 142
22:16–18	51
22:16–17	78
22:17–18	51
22:17	14, 16, 28, 40, 50–51, 69, 84, 120, 133, 141, 146, 177, 194, 196, 239, 290
22:18	49, 51–52, 55, 142

Genesis (cont.)

Reference	Pages
24:1	52
24:35	52
24:55	151
24:60	13, 106, 146, 290
25:11	52
25:12–18	51
25:21	12, 28, 52, 94, 106, 144
25:23	22, 52
26:1–11	52
26:3–5	52
26:4–5	51, 142
26:4	13–14, 16, 49–52, 55, 69, 141, 196, 290
26:5	51, 78
26:12–14	52
26:16	15, 58
26:22–24	290
26:22	14–15
26:24	52, 141
26:28–29	52
27:27–29	13, 22
27:29	52, 55
28:3	14–15, 50, 58, 141, 179, 290
28:4	146
28:13–15	52
28:14	15–16, 49–52, 55, 86, 145, 246, 290
29:31	12, 28, 94, 106, 144
30:2	12, 14, 106
30:22	12, 106
30:24	122
30:27–30	52
30:43	52
31:38	65
32:11[10]	52
32:13[12]	16, 50–51, 84, 120, 133, 177, 196, 239–40, 251, 290
32:27–31[26–30]	13
33:11	52
35:11–12	29, 52, 56
35:11	13–15, 29, 50, 52, 56, 58, 179, 185, 201, 279, 290
36:1–43	52
36:10–30	89
36:40–43	89
37:5–11	22
38:8	96
39–40	22
39:2–5	52
40:4	151
41:5	242
41:22	242
41:52	14–15, 290
41:57	52
42:36	65
46–50	57
46:3–4	187
46:3	50, 56, 59, 69–70, 290
46:4	187
46:8–27	56
46:27	52, 290
47	56–57
47:1–12	57
47:6	57
47:11	57
47:12	96
47:13–26	57
47:27	14–15, 24, 50, 57–60, 69, 179, 187, 290
48:3–4	29
48:4	14–15, 28, 50, 58, 179, 290
48:16	16, 251, 290
48:19	290
49:17	237
49:22	14–15, 290
49:25	290
50:1–14	96
50:6	28
50:20	52

Exodus

1	57–60
1:1	57
1:6	57
1:7–12	56–57, 291
1:7	1–3, 5, 15–16, 51, 57–62, 66, 69, 86, 88, 93, 103–6, 124, 139, 169, 173, 180, 182, 187–88, 202, 245, 264, 272–73, 280, 286
1:8–22	58
1:8–21	60
1:8–12	66
1:8	58
1:9	58–59
1:10	58, 242
1:12	15, 58, 145, 246
1:15–21	58
1:15	88
1:20–21	56, 66, 291
1:20	15, 58, 105
1:22	59
2:24–25	58, 60
2:24	78
3:2	252
3:6–8	60
3:6	78
3:7	187
3:8	242
3:16–17	60
3:17	242
4:18	28
5:5	56, 291
6:1–8	60
6:4–5	78
6:4	65
6:8	78
10:6	196
12:12–13	62
12:38	242
12:40	57
13:18	242
13:21–22	62
13:21	252
14	62
14:11–12	62
14:30	62
14:31	62
15:22–25	62
15:24	62
16:2–3	62
16:4	62
16:13–14	62
16:35	62
17:2–3	62
17:3	242
17:6	62
17:8–13	62
18:13–23	69
19:3–6	101, 105
19:5–6	55, 285
19:6	260
20:12	64
20:22—23:33	64
20:22–24	64
23	64–65, 101
23:16	70
23:19	70
23:20–33	64, 72
23:21	65
23:22–23	64
23:22	65
23:24–25	65
23:25–26	64
23:25	65
23:26	44, 65–66, 71–72, 138, 271, 291
23:27–31	65
23:27–29	64
23:29	26
23:30	15, 65–66, 71, 291
23:31	64
23:32–33	65
23:33	65
24:1–8	62
24:7	62
32:1	242
32:4	242

Exodus (cont.)

32:7–14	63
32:7	242
32:8	242
32:10	62, 291
32:13–14	62
32:13	14, 16, 51, 69, 78, 291
32:23	242
32:28	63
32:31–35	63
32:33–35	63
33:1	242
34:6–7	63, 233
34:22	70
34:26	70

Leviticus

11:29	16
11:41	16
12:2	192
16:2	178
16:3	178
17–26	204
19:25	122
23:10	70
23:40	128
26	64–65, 74, 101–2, 110, 169, 176, 204–5, 209–10, 214–15, 226–27, 236, 280, 282
26:3–39	205
26:3–13	64, 66, 205
26:3	65, 214
26:4–13	65, 210, 225–26, 229–30
26:4–5	110
26:4	214
26:5	84
26:6	84
26:9–12	226–27
26:9	13–15, 28, 51, 65–66, 71, 106, 179, 210, 214–15, 226–27, 229, 280, 291
26:10	110, 226
26:11	226
26:12	226
26:14–46	152
26:14–39	209
26:14–15	65, 214
26:15	66
26:16–39	65
26:16	152–53, 238
26:17	65
26:20	238
26:21	65
26:22	65, 176–77, 189, 214, 216
26:23	65
26:24	76
26:25	65–66, 176
26:26	176
26:27	65
26:29	65, 176–77
26:31–33	176
26:33	261
26:38	214, 216
26:39	65
26:40–45	19, 66, 76, 280–81
26:40–41	76
26:42	66, 78
26:44	66
26:45	66, 76

Numbers

1	63, 70, 88, 90, 96
1:1	63
1:3	63
1:20	63
1:21	88
1:22	63
1:46	63, 88
2:32	63
5:28	192
9:15–23	62
10:4	148
11:1	63
11:14–17	69

Numbers (cont.)

11:22	262
11:33	63
13:32	216
14:2	132
14:12	62, 149, 291
14:26–38	63
14:43	63
14:44–45	63
16:31–35	63
17:6[16:41]	63
17:14[16:49]	63
20:3	132
21:1–3	62
21:6–9	63
21:21–35	62
22–24	13, 64
22:3	64, 291
22:5	64
22:6	13
22:11	64
23:5	64
23:7–10	64
23:10	291
23:12	64
25:1–9	63
25:10–13	195
26	63, 70, 87–88, 90, 113
26:1–4	63
26:51	63, 91
26:52–56	63
26:63–65	63
27:17	94
28:26	70
31:7–12	62
32	31
32:22	31
32:29	31
34:2	95
36:3–4	123

Deuteronomy

1:5—4:40	67
1:7	84, 148
1:8–11	77
1:8	67, 69, 76–78
1:9–18	69
1:10–11	12, 71, 105, 291
1:10	14, 16, 59, 69–70, 74, 76, 80, 87, 103, 187, 251
1:11	16, 69, 77, 79, 122–23
1:35	76
3:5	251
4–11	68
4:1	68
4:2	123
4:10	97
4:25–28	74
4:27	47, 74
4:29–31	19, 75–76, 281
4:31	75-76, 249, 281
4:38	53, 146
4:40	68
5:1—28:69[29:1]	67
5:1	132
5:3	77
5:6	132
5:16	64, 68
5:23—6:3	71
5:29	68, 97
5:33	67–68
6:2	68, 97
6:3	13–14, 68, 71, 77, 79, 291
6:10–11	68
6:10	67, 76–77
6:18	68, 76
6:23	76
6:24	68
7:1	70, 87
7:1–2	68
7:7–8	78
7:7	14, 36, 70, 87, 291
7:8	77, 263
7:12–26	72
7:12–16	68, 72, 76, 78
7:12–13	68, 78

327

Deuteronomy (*cont.*)

7:12	76–78
7:13–16	72
7:13–14	12, 68, 78, 101, 235, 291
7:13	13–14, 68, 72–73, 76–77, 105, 141, 244–45, 277
7:14	44, 72, 105, 125
7:15	68, 72, 78
7:16	68, 78
7:17	70
7:22–24	68
8:1	68, 71, 76–77, 101, 291
8:6	97
8:7–10	68
8:13	13, 68
8:18	77
9:1	53, 70, 146
9:5	77
9:12	74
9:14	62, 105, 149, 291
9:16	74
9:23–24	74
10:11	76
10:12—11:32	69
10:12–13	70
10:16	75
10:20	70
10:21	70
10:22	12, 16, 59, 69–70, 74, 76, 80–81, 87, 187, 251, 291
11:1	70
11:8–9	77
11:9–15	68
11:9	67–68, 76
11:14	244–245
11:21	76
11:23–25	68
11:23	53, 70, 146
11:26–28	73
11:26–27	68
12–26	67
12:1	67
12:10	84
12:17	245
12:25	68
12:28	68
13:17–18[16–17]	71
13:17[16]	68
13:18–19[17–18]	77
13:18[17]	71, 77, 79, 291
14:23	245
14:29	68
15:4	67–68
15:6	68
15:10	68
15:15	263
15:18	68
16:9–12	70
16:15	68
16:20	68
17:14–20	276
17:20	68
18:4	245
18:15–22	17
19:8	67, 76–77
19:9	122
20:1	70
20:5–10	184–85
21:8	263
22:7	68
23:20	67–68
24:18	263
24:19	68
25:5–10	96, 105
25:15	68
26:1–11	70
26:3	76
26:5–9	23, 81
26:5b–10a	70
26:5	50, 59, 66, 69–70, 74, 76, 80, 101, 103, 149, 180, 187, 292
26:6–8	70
26:9	70
26:15	76
26:18–19	69

Deuteronomy (cont.)

Reference	Pages
27:3	67–68, 77
27:12–13	73
28	54, 64, 69, 72, 74, 78, 84, 101–2, 110, 113, 169, 171, 176, 236, 280
28:1–14	64, 68, 73, 76, 78, 84
28:1–2	72
28:1	68, 73, 78
28:3–6	69, 72
28:3	72
28:4–5	68, 72, 78, 110
28:4	14, 28, 66, 68, 72, 76, 84, 105, 125, 182–83, 235, 277, 292
28:5	84
28:6	72
28:7–14	72
28:7	68, 73, 78, 84
28:8	67–68, 73, 78, 84, 110
28:9–10	73
28:9	68, 72, 78
28:10	68-69, 73, 78, 84
28:11–12	68, 73, 78, 110
28:11	14, 28, 66–68, 72–73, 76–77, 84, 105, 125, 183, 235, 277, 292
28:12–13	73
28:12	68, 78, 84
28:13–14	72
28:13	72, 84
28:15–68	74
28:15	72–73
28:16–19	69, 72
28:17–18	74
28:18	14
28:20–68	72
28:20–22	105
28:20	74
28:21–22	74, 176
28:21	176
28:22	176
28:25–26	176
28:26	177
28:30–32	185
28:30	187
28:32	105, 187
28:33	187
28:38–40	238
28:39–41	187
28:41	105, 176
28:45	74, 105
28:48	176
28:51	245
28:52–57	74, 176
28:53–57	44, 105, 177
28:53	14
28:58–68	74, 78
28:58	97
28:59–61	105
28:62–63	105, 292
28:62	16, 74, 176, 251
28:63–68	74
28:63	68, 74–75, 215
28:64	47
28:68	74, 172
29–30	7
29:1[29:2]—30:20	67
29:3[4]	74
29:12[13]	68, 77
29:21–28[22–29]	74
29:21–27[22–28]	85
29:22[23]	242
30	172, 205, 279–80, 282
30:1–10	19, 75–76, 78–79, 103, 138, 171–72, 175–76, 194, 202, 205, 214–15, 274, 280–82
30:1–6	172
30:1–2	75
30:1	175
30:2	75, 175, 184
30:3–5	175, 183, 214
30:3	175
30:4–7	75
30:4–5	76
30:4	175

Ancient Document Index

Deuteronomy (cont.)

30:5	1, 12–13, 67–68, 75–78, 84, 87, 105–6, 149, 175, 214–15, 229, 274, 281, 292
30:6	75–76, 175, 184, 202, 214
30:7	76, 78, 175
30:8	75–76, 175, 214
30:9	1, 12, 14, 68, 72, 75–76, 78, 87, 105, 175, 194, 215, 229, 235, 277, 281, 292
30:10	75–76, 175
30:15–20	73, 77
30:16	67–68, 73, 78, 101, 141, 292
30:19	68, 73, 78
30:20	68, 73, 76–78
31:7	76
31:16–21	74
31:20	76
31:29	74
32:13	125
32:29	132
32:47	68
33:6	71, 292
33:17	71, 81, 292
33:18	28
33:20	71
34:4	76-77

Joshua

1–12	80
1:6	80
2:24	81
3:10	241
6:21	81
7–8	89
7	81
7:7	132
8:24–26	81
10:10–11	81
10:28–43	81
11:4	17, 53–54, 92, 120, 251, 292
11:8–14	81
11:16–23	80
13–21	80
13:1–7	80
13:13	80
14:6–15	80
15:13–19	80
16:10	80
17:3–6	80
17:12–13	80
17:14–18	81
17:14	81, 292
17:16–17	262
17:17	81
18	31
18:1	31
20	89
21:43–45	80
21:43	80
21:44	80
21:45	80
22	81
22:21	148
22:30	148
23:5	80
23:14	80
24	67, 81
24:2–13	81
24:3-4	81
24:3	81, 101, 103, 215, 292
24:14–28	81
24:31	81

Judges

2:1	82
2:7–10	82
2:11–19	82
6:5	17, 53, 92, 148, 251, 292
6:15	89, 148
7:12	17, 53, 92, 120, 251, 292
7:19—8:12	55
8:19	132

Judges (cont.)

9:42–49	82
10:8	82
12:6	82
13:2–5	96
13:2–3	94
13:3	145
13:23	132
20:16	151
20:21	82
20:25	82
20:35	82
20:46	82
21:8–12	82
21:14	262

Ruth

3:10	214
4:10	96
4:11–12	106
4:13	40, 106
4:14–15	96

1 Samuel

1–2	94, 105
1:5–6	106
2:1–10	94
2:5	54, 94, 145, 292
2:8	94
4:10	82
6:18	251
6:19	82
9:21	148
10:19	148
12:22	82
13:5	17, 53–54, 92, 120, 251, 292
15:7	240
15:17	148
24:22[21]	96, 105

2 Samuel

4:7	96
5:12	82
6:5	257
6:21	257
6:23	42
7	228
7:12–16	195
7:12	83
7:16	83
8:11	31
12:8	122
13:20	144
17:11	16, 177, 251, 292
18:7	82
18:23	28
24	82
24:1	82
24:3	292
24:9	85, 91
24:10	82
24:15	82

1 Kings

2:4	195
3:6	104
3:8–9	189
3:8	83–84, 86, 240, 251, 293
3:14	104
4–5	120
4	168
4:20—5:14[4:20–34]	117
4:20—5:8[4:20–28]	83–84, 86, 280
4:20—5:1[4:20–21]	84, 118, 124
4:20	3, 5, 16, 84, 86, 92, 103, 117–21, 133, 177, 180, 183, 201–2, 225, 229, 239–40, 251, 276, 281, 293
5:1[4:21]	80, 84, 118
5:2[4:22]	84

1 Kings (cont.)

5:3 [4:23]	84
5:4–5 [4:24–25]	84, 118
5:4 [4:24]	80, 84, 118, 124, 133–34
5:6 [4:26]	84
5:8 [4:28]	84
8:20	83
8:24	83
8:25	195
8:33–34	184
8:56	83
9:3–9	85
9:4	104
9:5	195
10:9	118
11:4	104
11:6	104
11:33–34	104
11:38	104
12:14	123
12:21	85
14:7–20	85
14:8	104
14:15	262
15:3	104
15:5	104
15:11	104
20:15	85
22:12	28
22:17	94

2 Kings

2:11	252
2:17	28
6:1	137
9–10	238
9:7–10	85
13:7	85
16:2	104
17:6–23	85
17:13–15	10
19:15	178
19:32–35	55
22:2	104
24:16	85
25:21	85

1 Chronicles

3:1–9	85
4:27	86, 295
4:38	15
5:17–18	85
5:21	89
5:23	86, 295
7:5	85
7:17	104
12:23–40	85
14:2–7	85
21:3	123, 295
21:5–6	85, 91
21:5	89
22:18	31
23:3	85
27:1–15	85
27:23	16, 295
29:21	220

2 Chronicles

1:9	16, 86, 103, 295
7:4	220
9:25–26	86
11:1	85
11:18–22	85
12:3	17, 53, 92, 295
13:3	85, 89, 91
13:21	85
14:8	85, 89
14:9	89
17:3	104
17:14–19	85, 91
18:16	94
21	85
21:1–13	85
21:6	85
21:18–19	85

2 Chronicles (cont.)

22:10	95
24:25	85
25:5	85, 89, 91
25:27–28	85
26:11–15	89
26:13	85
27	85
27:23–24	85
28:6	85, 89
28:10	31
29:2	104
29:4	258
29:33	220
32:6	258
33:24–25	85
34:2	104
35:7–9	220

Ezra

2:64	92, 250
8:1–20	92
10:9	258

Nehemiah

1:4	151
5:5	31
7:66	92, 250
8:1	258
8:3	258
8:16	258
9:5–31	86
9:8–9	87
9:16–21	87
9:17	86
9:19	86
9:22–25	87
9:23	16, 87, 101, 103, 295
9:24	87
9:27	86
9:31	86
11:1–2	265
13:29	195

Esther

9:19	251

Job

1:2	97
1:18–19	97
3:7	137
4:1—5:27	97
5:17	97
5:18–27	97
5:24	151
5:25	17, 97, 102, 132, 295
5:26	97
14:21	190
15:34	137
18:17–19	96–97, 105
21:8	132
21:10	65
21:33	17
29:25	240
30:3	137
40:20	257
40:22	128
42:13	97
42:16	97

Psalms

1:3	14
8	32
11:1	251
18:44[43]	240
18:48[47]	95
33:8	154
40:6[5]	15
40:13[12]	15
42:3	241
44:12[11]	94
44:23[22]	94
48:11[10]	123
49:15[14]	94
65:6[5]	123
69:5	15
72:16	126

Ancient Document Index

Psalms (cont.)

78:33	152
80:2[1]	178
81:14[13]	133
84:3	241
90:6	126
92:8[7]	126
92:13–14[12–13]	126
103:15	126
104:26	257
105	93
105:10	227
105:11	93
105:12	93
105:16–23	93
105:24	8, 15, 59, 93, 101, 103, 106, 295
105:25–36	93
107	93–94
107:1–32	93
107:33–43	94
107:33–35	94
107:36–38	185
107:37	94
107:38–39	189
107:38	5, 54, 94, 99, 102, 141, 295
107:39	189
107:41	5, 54, 94, 99, 102, 295
113	94
113:7–9	94
113:7	94
113:9	5, 54, 94, 99–100, 102, 106, 145, 295
115:14	123
127	5, 95–96, 99–102
127:1–2	95
127:3–5	27, 95, 105, 295
127:3	14, 54, 72, 95–96
127:4	95
127:5	95
128	96, 102
128:1–4	97
128:1	96
128:2–3	96
128:3	14–15, 96, 99, 295
128:4	96
132:11	14
137:2	128
144:12	251

Proverbs

2:21–22	97–98
3:2	98, 122
3:33	98
4:10	98
8:32–36	98
8:36	151
9:11	98, 122
10:1—22:16	98
10:1	5, 98
10:27	98
11:10–11	98
11:28	126
12:26	98
14:28	98, 295
15:20	98
16:13	98
16:27–29	98
17:6	98
17:21	98
17:25	98
19:2	151
19:13	98
19:23	98
19:26	98
23:15–16	98
23:24–25	98
27:11	98
28:7	98
28:12	98
28:28	98
29:2	98
29:3	98
29:15	98
29:16	13
29:17	98
31:16	14

Ecclesiastes

5:12-16[13-17]	99
6:1-2	99
6:3-6	99-101
6:3	96, 99, 295
9:7-9	27
10:9	40
12:3	189

Song of Songs

5:6	95
6:8	17

Isaiah

1-39	109, 116
1-26	116
1:4	116, 158
1:7	146
1:9	112
1:15	116
1:19-20	113
1:21-26	135
1:25	109
1:26-27	109-10
1:27-28	18, 111
1:27	263
1:28-31	113
2:2-3	3
2:2-4	19, 108-10, 159-60, 254, 259, 274
2:3	108
3:5	124
3:10-11	111
3:16-17	135
4:2-6	108-9
4:2-3	112
4:3-4	111
4:3	109, 111, 117
4:4	109, 135
4:5-6	108, 110
5:1-7	125
5:2	125
5:4	125
5:5-6	125
5:6	125
5:7	125
5:26-30	159
6-12	114
6:5	108
6:8-13	18
6:10	18
6:11-12	138, 146
6:11	138, 146
6:12	123, 138
7:3	117-18
7:14	117
7:17—8:22	114
7:20-25	114
7:22	112
8:1	114
8:3-4	114
8:11-15	114
8:18	108
8:19-20	114
8:21-22	114
8:22	114
8:23—9:6[9:1-7]	109, 114
8:23—9:1[9:1-2]	114
8:23[9:1]	116-17
9	118
9:1-6[2-7]	116-18, 120-21, 168
9:1-2[2-3]	116
9:1[2]	116
9:2[3]	110, 112, 114-18, 121-23, 134, 141, 163-66, 263, 271, 274, 277, 279-80, 293
9:3-6[4-7]	116
9:3-4[4-5]	114, 165
9:3[4]	118
9:5-6[6-7]	108, 110, 114-17, 272, 276
9:5[6]	117-18
9:6[7]	110, 114, 121
9:7[8]—10:4	118

Ancient Document Index

Isaiah (cont.)

10:5–19	159
10:6–34	118
10:6	116
10:19	118
10:20–27	120–21
10:20–23	118, 120
10:20–22	109, 111
10:20	111, 118–19
10:21–22	119
10:21	110, 118, 120
10:22–23	119–20
10:22	16, 108, 112, 118–21, 123, 133, 163–68, 239–40, 263, 271–72, 274, 279, 281, 287, 293
10:23	121
10:24–27	118
10:24	120
10:26–27	118
11	117–18
11:1–16	109, 118, 181
11:1–5	108, 110, 118
11:6–9	108, 110
11:10–12	159
11:10	108
11:11–16	118, 120
11:11–12	110
11:11	117–18
11:12	159, 261
11:14	110
11:16	108, 110, 117–18
12–14	254
12:1	111
12:3–6	159
13–23	121, 159
13:18	14
14:1–3	109
14:1–2	110, 112, 159, 161, 253–55
14:1	3, 111, 253
14:22	118
14:32	109–10
15:7	128
16:5	108–10
16:14	113, 118
17:3	118
17:9	146
18:7	110, 112, 159
19:16–25	112, 159–60, 274
19:17	110
19:17–25	109
19:24–25	3
19:24	128
19:25	160
21:8	251
21:17	118
22:18	251
23:8	124
23:9	124
23:16	116
24–27	121
24:1–23	113
24:5–6	111
24:5	113
24:6	113
24:10	130–31
24:23	108, 110
25:6–9	108–9
25:7–9	112, 159
26:1–6	121
26:1	110, 122–23
26:2	116, 122
26:1–19	109
26:7–21	122
26:11–19	121, 123
26:12–15	122, 124
26:12–14	165
26:12	122, 124
26:13–14	122–23
26:14	123
26:15	16, 116, 121–24, 126, 163–68, 170, 272, 274–75, 279, 281, 284, 293
26:17–18	155, 163
26:19	124
26:20–21	124

Ancient Document Index

Isaiah (*cont.*)

27:1	124
27:2–6	109, 124–25
27:2–5	111
27:3–4	125
27:3	125
27:5	122
27:6	112, 124–27, 163, 166, 247, 293
27:9	109, 111
27:12–13	109–10
27:13	111
28:5	118
28:20	137
29:13	123
29:17–24	109
29:17	110
29:18	110
29:19	110
29:22	108, 141
29:23	111
30:17	112
30:18–26	109
30:18–19	111
30:18	111
30:19–26	108
30:22	111
30:23–25	110
30:26	110
30:33	116
31:1	15
31:5	109–10, 154
31:7	109, 111
32:1–5	109
32:1–2	110
32:1	108
32:12	14
32:15–20	128
32:15–18	109
32:15	110
32:18	110
33:17–24	108
33:17	108
33:19–20	110
33:19–24	109
33:20	110
33:21–22	111
33:22	108
33:23–24	110
33:24	111
34:1–17	113
34:11	130
35:1–10	109
35:1–2	110
35:4	111
35:5-6	110
35:6–7	110
35:8–10	110
35:10	110, 263
36–39	117
36–37	117
36:9	148
36:16	128
37:22	135
37:27	128
37:30	27
37:31–32	112
37:35	111, 170
38:5	123
39:5–7	159
40–66	109, 134–35, 145, 148, 159, 270
40–55	109, 112, 126, 135, 139, 141, 143, 147–48, 159–60, 163, 165, 167
40–48	136
40:1–2	126, 135
40:1	142, 154
40:2	111
40:3–5	108, 110, 139
40:3–4	110
40:3	132
40:5	111, 159, 170
40:6	128
40:7	128
40:8	128
40:10	95
40:26	108

Ancient Document Index

Isaiah (cont.)

40:29	116
41:5	159
41:8–10	108, 126
41:8–9	111
41:8	141
41:11–12	110, 159
41:16	110
41:17–20	108
41:17	111
41:18–20	110
42:1	150
42:4	159, 274
42:5	108
42:6	159, 274
42:10–12	111, 170
42:16	109–10, 139
42:18—45:8	127
42:18–25	111
42:20	145
42:24–25	108
43:1–7	111, 127
43:1–6	109–10, 139
43:3–4	159
43:4	124
43:5–7	132
43:5	261
43:7	111, 170
43:9–11	132
43:10	111
43:14–21	109–10, 139
43:16–19	132
43:17	132
43:18–19	132
43:19–21	108
43:19–20	110
43:20–21	111, 170
43:20	111, 150
43:22–28	126
43:25	111, 126, 170
43:27–28	108
44:1–5	111, 126–27
44:1–4	129
44:1–2	111, 129
44:1	127
44:2	127
44:3–4	110–11, 113, 126–29, 134, 153, 163–65, 167, 271, 279, 293
44:3	127–28, 132, 153, 158, 168
44:4	127–28
44:5	127, 129, 161
44:21–22	111
44:21	111
44:22	111
44:23	110
44:26–28	110, 137
44:26	110
44:34	166
45:1–13	129
45:4	111, 130, 150
45:5	130
45:6	159
45:7	108
45:11	28
45:12	108
45:13	110, 137
45:14–25	129
45:14–19	130
45:14	110, 112, 130, 159, 161
45:15	131
45:18	37, 108, 129–31, 164–68, 279, 293
45:19	131
45:21	130
45:22–26	112, 159
45:22–23	131
45:22	130, 154, 170
46–47	135
46:3	112
46:4	111
46:13	111, 132
47	159
47:8–9	113, 135, 138
48	132
48:1	132

Ancient Document Index

Isaiah (cont.)

48:4-5	132
48:5	129
48:8	132
48:9-11	111, 124, 170
48:10	109
48:12	132
48:14	132
48:16	132
48:17-19	132-34
48:18-19	108, 132-34, 158
48:18	132-33
48:19	3, 16, 112, 120-21, 132-34, 153, 163-68, 239-40, 271-72, 279, 281, 293
48:20-21	109-10, 132-34, 139, 275
48:20	111
48:21	108, 110
48:22	134
49-66	135, 275
49-55	135
49-54	147
49	136, 154-55, 259, 282
49:1-13	136
49:5-6	136
49:5	124
49:6	159
49:7	116, 122
49:8-13	136
49:8-12	109, 139
49:8	144, 146
49:9-11	108
49:10	111, 136
49:12	110, 156-57, 255, 275
49:13-26	254, 266, 281
49:13-16	156
49:13	111, 136, 142, 170, 255, 275, 281
49:14—50:3	19, 113, 140
49:14-26	162, 255
49:14-21	139-40, 142-43, 147, 157, 191
49:14	136, 147, 156
49:15—50:3	136
49:15-23	142
49:15-16	170, 255
49:15	111, 136, 275, 281
49:17-21	136
49:17-19	138
49:17-18	136
49:17	136-37, 165
49:18-21	137
49:18	137
49:19-23	163, 264
49:19-21	5, 108, 110, 113, 128-29, 134-39, 143-44, 149, 156-57, 162-67, 169, 255, 258, 271, 273-76, 278-80, 284, 286, 288, 293
49:19-20	262
49:19	137-38, 142, 144, 146, 156, 255
49:20	113
49:21	113, 135, 138, 144
49:22-26	146, 255
49:22-23	110, 112, 136, 138, 156, 159, 161-62, 255, 275
49:22	108
49:23-26	165
49:23	110, 136, 159, 255
49:24-26	136, 138, 162
49:25-26	159
49:26	136
50:1-3	136, 156
50:4-9	140
50:4-5	140
50:6	140
50:7-9	140
50:10-11	140
50:10	140, 142
50:11	140
51	154
51:1—52:12	140
51:1-8	140

Ancient Document Index

Isaiah (cont.)

51:1–3	136, 140, 143
51:1–2	108, 141–42
51:1	142
51:2–3	110, 113, 140–43, 156–57, 162–63, 167–68
51:2	116, 123, 128, 134, 141, 143–44, 146, 149, 163–64, 166–68, 271–72, 279, 293
51:3	108, 140, 142–43, 156–57, 164–65, 168, 277
51:4–6	140
51:4–5	159
51:4	108
51:6	132
51:7–8	140
51:7	140
51:9–11	109–10, 139, 142, 156
51:11	110, 263
51:12	128, 142
51:16	111
51:17–23	143
51:17–20	157
51:18–20	144
51:18	143, 157
51:20	143
51:22–23	159
52:1–12	143
52:1–10	110
52:3	242
52:7–9	110
52:7	108, 110
52:9	142
52:10	159
52:11–12	109–10, 139
52:13—53:12	111, 143
52:14	145
52:15	145
53–54	147
53:4–6	111
53:6	94
53:10–11	148
53:10	143, 145
53:11–12	111, 143, 145
54	108, 143, 154, 259
54:1–17	113, 255
54:1–10	254
54:1–8	157, 255
54:1–3	110, 123, 128–29, 136, 143–47, 149, 155–57, 162–68, 255, 258, 274–75, 278–79, 293
54:1	3, 113, 135, 143–47, 156, 165, 255, 277, 287
54:2	143, 146, 155
54:3	15, 144–46, 156, 158–59, 168, 246, 273, 275, 277
54:4–10	143–44, 156
54:4	143–44
54:5	145, 147
54:7–10	156, 170, 275, 281
54:7–8	126, 255
54:7	144
54:8	111, 144
54:9–10	108
54:9	196
54:10	111, 144
54:11–17	143
54:13	145, 148
54:14–17	110
54:14	28
54:15–17	159
54:17	111, 145, 147–48, 150, 157, 162, 165
55:3–5	108
55:3–4	19
55:3	111, 227
55:5	111
55:7	111, 116
55:10	155
55:12–13	109, 139
55:12	110
55:13	110, 242
56–66	112, 147–48, 150, 157, 160, 162, 274–75

Isaiah (cont.)

56:1–8	108, 112, 148, 159–60, 274
56:1	132, 148
56:3–8	253–54
56:3	253
56:6–8	3, 112
56:6	111, 150, 161, 253
57:1	148
57:9	116
57:12	148
57:13	112, 150
57:14	110
57:16	108
57:20–21	112
58:2	148
58:8	148
58:12	137
59:4	148, 155
59:6–7	113
59:16	148
59:17	148
59:20	110, 112
59:21	111
60–62	108, 110, 147
60	149, 153
60:3–14	148
60:4–9	110
60:4	159, 162
60:5	110, 165, 277
60:6	112, 159, 162
60:9	111, 159, 162
60:10	110–11, 137
60:11	112, 159, 162
60:12–14	110
60:12	159
60:13–14	112, 162
60:13	159
60:14	108, 159
60:15–22	148–49
60:17–18	110
60:19–22	164
60:19–20	149
60:21–22	148, 165
60:21	148–49, 168, 275
60:22	110, 147–50, 155, 162–68, 271, 273, 275, 279, 293
61:3	110
61:4	110, 137, 144, 146
61:5–6	159, 162
61:6	111
61:7–9	108
61:7	110
61:8	111
61:9	132, 153
61:10	110, 148
62:1	148
62:4–5	147
62:4	144, 146
62:8	110
62:10	110
62:11	95
62:12	111
63:9–13	109
63:17	111, 150
63:16	141
63:19[64:1]	132, 134
64:5[6]	148
64:9[10]	146
65–66	147, 150, 158, 162
65	259
65:1–7	150
65:8–16	111, 150, 154, 165
65:8–9	111, 150
65:8	128, 150
65:9–16	150
65:9	150–53, 158, 167–68, 279, 293
65:10	150
65:13–15	111
65:13–14	110
65:13	150
65:14	150
65:15	150
65:16–25	152

Isaiah (cont.)

65:17–25	110, 151, 158, 164–65, 258, 266, 275, 281
65:18–19	110, 151, 277
65:18	165
65:20–23	273, 277, 279
65:20	110, 147, 150–53, 163–67, 258, 271, 293
65:21–23	153, 185
65:21–22	152–53, 277
65:22	151
65:23	110, 128, 132, 147, 150–53, 158, 163–69, 258, 271, 293
65:24	111
65:25	110
66	19
66:3–24	111
66:3–6	153
66:7–14	154
66:7–9	110, 129, 147, 150, 153–58, 162–66, 168, 275, 277–79, 293
66:7–8	156
66:7	154
66:8	154–55, 157
66:9	155–57
66:10–14	277
66:10–11	156
66:10	154, 165
66:11–12	154
66:13	142, 154
66:14	111, 126, 150, 154–55, 157, 165
66:18–24	159–60, 274
66:18–23	3, 112
66:20	159
66:21	111
66:22	110, 158, 168, 293
66:23	111
66:24	113

Jeremiah

1:4–19	18
1:10	18, 173, 184, 189, 192, 219
2:1—3:10	177
2:2	135
2:8	178, 181
2:15	176
3	190
3:11–14	18, 177–78
3:12	178
3:14–18	173, 178, 181, 202
3:14–16	203
3:14	178, 181, 283
3:15–18	263
3:15–16	281
3:15	174, 178–79, 181, 276
3:16–17	178–81, 201
3:16	15, 116, 174–83, 186, 194, 200–203, 213, 229, 271, 279–80, 293
3:17	173–74, 178–79, 181, 275
3:18	174–75, 178–79, 181, 275–76
3:22—4:4	177
4:2	173
4:7	176
4:23–26	176
4:31	135
5:6	15, 176–77
5:17	176
5:18	175, 179
5:19	179
5:20–25	263
6:4	176
6:22–26	176
7:16	172
7:20	176, 192
7:32–34	176
7:32	175
7:33	177, 192
8:1	175
8:2	177

Jeremiah (cont.)

8:3	180
8:17	176–77
9:9–10[10–11]	176
9:15[16]	180
9:20–21[21–22]	176
9:21[22]	177
9:24[25]	175
10:6–8	197
10:21	181
10:24	189
11:1–13	176
11:3–5	177
11:3	177
11:6–8	177
11:8	177
11:9–13	177
11:14	172
11:22	176
12:3	94
12:10	181
12:12	176
12:14–17	192
12:15–16	173
12:15	175
13:14	176
13:23	18
13:24	180
14:11	172
14:12	176
14:16	176–77
14:18	176
15:1–9	177
15:1	172
15:2	176, 179
15:3	176, 192
15:7	176, 262
15:8	15, 152, 177, 239
16:1–4	282
16:2	177, 186
16:4	176–77, 192
16:5	175
16:6	177
16:10	179
16:13	129
16:14–15	172–73, 187
16:14	175
16:15	175, 180
16:19	173
17:1–4	197
18:7–10	192
18:9	184
18:17	180
18:21	176
19:4–5	176
19:6	175
19:7	192
19:9	176–77
20:4	176
21–23	263
21–22	180
21:3–10	176
21:4–10	182
21:6	192
21:7	176
21:9	176
21:12	180
22:2	180
22:3	180
22:13–17	180
22:17	182
22:19	177
22:21–22	180
22:22	180–81
22:24–30	180
23	190
23:1–8	174, 178, 262, 266, 276, 281
23:1–6	210
23:1–4	281
23:1–3	181
23:1–2	180
23:1	181
23:2	180–81
23:3–8	173, 180–81, 202
23:3	15, 116, 174–76, 179–83, 186, 194, 199–203, 210, 261, 263, 271, 275, 279–81, 294

Jeremiah (cont.)

23:4-6	19, 180, 182, 272, 276
23:4-5	174
23:4	174, 180-81
23:5-6	195, 199
23:5	175, 180, 249
23:6	174, 181, 276
23:7-8	172, 180-82, 187, 202, 275, 280
23:7	175
23:8	175, 180-81
24	171
24:4-10	184
24:4-7	192
24:5-7	173
24:6	175, 184
24:7	174-75, 194
24:9	180
24:10	176
25	254
25:12-38	173
25:13	198
25:28	179
25:33	177
25:34-38	263
25:34	181
25:35	181
25:36	181
26-45	172
27-29	183
27:1-10	173
27:5	192
27:8	176
27:10	180
27:11	173
27:13	176
27:15	180
27:46-51	173
29:1-3	183
29:4-23	183
29:5-9	184
29:5-7	183-87, 202
29:5-6	185
29:5	184, 192
29:6	27-28, 139, 175-77, 182-87, 189, 200-201, 203, 264-66, 271-73, 280-84, 286, 294
29:7	184
29:8-9	183
29:10-14	173, 183-84, 186
29:10	183, 187, 195
29:11	183, 186
29:12-14	183
29:12-13	183
29:12	187
29:14	175, 180, 183, 187, 261
29:16-20	198
29:16-19	184
29:17-18	176
29:17	176
29:18	176, 180
29:28	184, 192
30-33	171-73, 178, 188, 192, 197
30-31	172, 188, 202
30:1—31:22	188
30:1-11	276
30:3	173-75, 188, 194
30:5-11	188
30:7-11	173
30:7	188
30:9	174, 188, 195, 199, 276
30:10	174, 188, 192
30:11	174, 180
30:12-17	188
30:16-22	173
30:16	174
30:18—31:1	188
30:18-22	188, 190
30:18	173-75, 188, 275, 277, 281
30:19-20	201
30:19	116, 174-76, 186, 188-90, 194, 199-203, 257, 271-72, 277, 279-80, 294
30:20	188, 190, 195

Jeremiah (cont.)

30:21	189, 276
30:22	175, 188, 275
30:23—31:1	188
31	135, 263
31:1-40	173
31:1	175, 188
31:2-6	188
31:4	174, 257
31:5	110, 174
31:7-14	188
31:8	198-99, 261
31:10	262
31:11	263
31:12-13	174
31:12	110, 174, 245
31:15-22	188, 191
31:15	191
31:20	174
31:22	191
31:23-40	188, 191, 193
31:23-26	191
31:23-24	194
31:23	173
31:27-37	174, 203
31:27-30	191
31:27-28	200, 203
31:27	174-76, 186, 190-95, 197, 200-203, 211, 229, 245, 262-63, 266, 271, 274, 277, 279-81, 294
31:28	184, 192
31:29	175, 179, 202
31:31-37	201
31:31-34	174, 181, 188, 191, 193-95, 197, 202, 275
31:31-33	219
31:31	174-75
31:32	202
31:33-34	194
31:33	174-75, 193
31:34	174, 193
31:35-37	191, 193-95, 197, 201, 273
31:35-36	193-194
31:36-37	194
31:36	192-93
31:37	192-93
31:38-40	191, 194
31:38	175
32-33	188
32:2	175
32:1-15	172
32:15	173
32:24	176
32:35	176
32:36	176
32:37-44	173
32:37-41	174
32:37	174-75, 180
32:38	175
32:39-40	174, 194
32:40	174
32:43	192
32:44	173
33:1-26	174
33:1-13	195
33:4-5	176
33:6-26	173
33:7	173
33:8	174, 193
33:10-13	192, 195
33:10	192, 195
33:11	173-174
33:12	192, 195
33:14-26	19, 173-74, 180, 195-99, 203, 276
33:14	175, 195
33:15-16	195
33:15	175, 179
33:16	174-75, 179
33:17-26	197
33:17-18	195
33:17	195
33:18	195
33:19-26	195
33:20	195-97
33:21-22	195

Jeremiah (cont.)

33:21	195
33:22	16, 116, 120, 134, 174–77, 192, 195–97, 200–203, 239–40, 271, 273, 282, 294
33:25–26	195
33:25	196–97
33:26	173, 175, 192, 194
34:11	31
34:16	31
34:17	176
34:20	177, 192
36	172
36:30	177
37–45	171
37–40	198
38:2	176
39:1–10	177
39:1–2	176
39:4–13	198
39:10	175
40–43	172
42:9–12	192
42:10	184
42:16	176
42:17	176
42:22	176
44:11–14	177
44:12	176
44:13	176
44:15–25	177
44:15–19	129
44:27	176
44:28	177
45:4	184, 192
46:23	14, 17, 53
46:26	173
46:27–28	173
46:27	174
46:29	180
48:8	196
48:12	175
48:47	173
49:2	175
49:5	180
49:6	173
49:39	173
50–51	254
50:4–5	173
50:4	174–75, 179
50:5	174, 181, 253
50:17–20	174
50:17	180
50:19–20	173
50:20	174–75, 179, 193
50:34	173
51:5	173
51:10	173
51:45–48	198
51:47	175
51:52	175

Lamentations

2:20	14
4:9	125

Ezekiel

1–33	209
1–24	205–6, 210
5:2	262
5:10	208, 262
5:12	176, 208, 262
5:17	176, 208, 216
6	211
6:6	212
6:9	207
6:11	176, 208
6:12	176, 208
7:15	176, 208
11:6	209, 276
11:14–21	205
11:15–17	212
11:17–19	207
11:17–18	206
11:17	224
11:18–20	219

Ezekiel (cont.)

11:19	207
11:20	207
12:14–15	262
12:16	176, 208
13:10	227
13:16	227
14:3	220
14:6	18
14:11	205, 207
14:13	213
14:15	216
14:17	213
14:19	213
14:21	176, 208, 210, 213
16	135
16:7	209
16:20–21	209
16:53–63	205
16:53	206
16:54	207
16:55	206
16:59–63	205
16:60–63	227
16:60	206, 222–23, 227
16:61	207
16:62	227
16:63	207
17:22–24	205–6
17:22	224
19:10	15
19:11	127
20:3	220
20:23	262
20:31	220
20:32–44	205
20:33–44	208
20:34	206, 261
20:35–38	207
20:39–41	207
20:39	129
20:41	206
20:42	206
20:43	207
21:1–17	208
21:19	208
22:1–12	209
23	135
23:25	208
23:37–39	209
24:16–18	209
24:21	209
25:13	213
28:24–26	205–6
28:25–26	223
28:25	206, 230
28:26	206
29:8	213
29:13–16	206
29:15	189, 206
31:10	127
31:14	127
33	209
33:21	205
33:24	230
33:27	208
33:32	214
34–48	205, 207, 248
34–38	212
34–37	110, 223, 229
34–36	222
34	178, 207, 209–10, 222, 226, 281
34:1–31	220
34:1–16	181
34:2–8	209
34:5	212
34:11–16	206
34:12–13	206
34:13	261
34:23–31	225, 229, 276
34:23–24	19, 206, 223, 226, 276
34:23	226
34:24–28	205
34:24–25	223
34:24	226
34:25–31	271, 275–76, 280

Ezekiel (cont.)

34:25–30	209–10, 226–27, 229, 294
34:25–29	226
34:25	206, 210, 223, 225–26, 280
34:26–27	110, 206, 210
34:26	224
34:27–28	210
34:27	206
34:28–29	206, 226
34:28	206, 210
34:29	210
34:30–31	207
34:30	226, 231
34:31	222
35:1—36:15	207, 210, 217, 222
35	210–11, 219
35:1–15	210
35:1	219
35:2	210
35:3–4	210
35:5	210
35:7	210
35:8	211
35:9	210
35:10–13	210
35:10	212, 216
35:12	211
35:14–15	210
35:15	211–12
36–37	212, 271
36	210–12, 214, 221–22, 229–30, 277
36:1–15	211, 217, 277
36:1–7	211, 214
36:1	211
36:3	211
36:5–7	211
36:5	211–12
36:6	217
36:7	217
36:8–15	211–12, 214, 219–21, 230
36:8–12	275
36:8–11	213–14
36:8	206, 211, 214, 228
36:9–14	273, 277, 282, 284
36:9–12	278
36:9–11	205, 214, 276
36:9	207, 211, 214
36:10–14	137, 206, 208, 210–17, 221, 228–30, 280
36:10–12	211, 217
36:10–11	212, 214–15, 217, 219, 223, 229, 277
36:10	206, 209, 211–12, 214–15, 219, 228, 271–72, 294
36:11	14–15, 179, 192, 194, 209, 211–15, 219, 221, 228–29, 231, 271, 274, 277, 279, 281, 294
36:12–15	276
36:12–14	211, 214, 217, 228, 271, 277
36:12	153, 212, 215–17, 275, 294
36:13–15	215–16
36:13–14	214, 216
36:13	212, 216
36:14	153, 212, 216, 294
36:15	216
36:16–38	207, 217, 222
36:16–32	221–22
36:16	217
36:17	218
36:19	262
36:20–23	219
36:20	219
36:21	219
36:22–32	219
36:22–23	206, 284
36:22	219, 231
36:23–31	219

Ezekiel (cont.)

36:23-38	218
36:23	219
36:24-26	207
36:24	206, 214, 219, 261
36:25-32	221
36:25-29	219
36:25-27	214
36:25	207, 219
36:26-27	207
36:26	219
36:27-28	223, 229
36:27	207, 219, 223
36:28	207, 219, 223, 275
36:29-30	110, 206, 212, 219, 221, 277
36:29	13, 207
36:30	125
36:31	207
36:32	206, 219, 284
36:33-38	137, 217, 219, 221-22, 229-30
36:33-36	206, 219-20, 230, 277
36:33	207, 219, 228, 272
36:34-36	219
36:34	211
36:35	206, 219-21, 277
36:36	219
36:37-38	94, 206, 208, 217-22, 228-30, 277, 279, 294
36:37	209, 212, 220, 223, 228, 230, 271
36:38	217, 230-31, 284
37	207, 218, 222, 226
37:1-14	206, 222
37:10	222
37:11	222
37:14-28	228
37:14	207
37:15-28	276, 281
37:15-23	178, 276
37:15-20	222
37:15	222
37:16-22	206
37:19	224
37:21-28	222
37:21-23	222
37:21	206, 214
37:22	206, 216, 272, 276
37:23	207, 275
37:24-28	222-29, 254, 273, 281
37:24-26	223
37:24-25	19, 206, 223, 226-28, 272, 276
37:24	207, 222-23, 226
37:25-28	226
37:25	222-23, 225-27, 230, 275
37:26-28	207, 223, 226-27, 229, 275
37:26-27	205, 226-27
37:26	206, 208-9, 212, 222-30, 271, 274, 279-80, 294
37:27	207, 226, 275
37:28	222-23, 225, 231, 284
38-48	254
38-39	206-7
38:1	222
38:8	206
38:11	206, 251
38:14	206
39:25	207
39:26	206
39:27-28	206
39:29	207
40-48	207, 223, 251
40-46	206
43:1-9	207
43:7-8	207
43:7	222-23
43:9	222-23
46:14	222
47:9-12	206
48:35	207

Ancient Document Index

Daniel

8:27	151

Hosea

1–3	243
1–2	239
1:2—2:3[1]	238
1:2–9	242
1:2	238, 241
1:4–9	238
1:4	238, 240
1:5	238
1:6	239–40
1:7	236, 239–40
1:8	239
1:9	239, 243
2	238
2:1–4[1:10—2:2]	283
2:1–3[1:10—2:1]	236, 238–45, 268
2:1–2[1:10–11]	242
2:1[1:10]	16, 120, 134, 177, 191, 235–36, 240–43, 263, 266, 271, 274, 279–81, 287, 294
2:2[1:11]	236, 240, 245, 263, 268, 275–76
2:3[1]	236, 239, 241, 263, 268, 275, 281
2:4–15[2–13]	244
2:4[2]	238
2:5[3]	237
2:6[4]	239
2:7–17[5–15]	238
2:10[8]	238, 245
2:16–25[14–23]	236, 243–45
2:16–17[14–15]	235
2:16[14]	238
2:17[15]	235–36, 242
2:18–22[16–20]	236, 244
2:21[19]	239
2:20[18]	236
2:23–25[21–23]	244, 246
2:23–24[21–22]	235, 238, 277
2:24[22]	236, 244–45
2:25[23]	191, 211, 236, 239, 241, 243–45, 262–63, 266, 268, 271, 275, 280–81, 294
3:1	240
3:4	240
3:5	236, 240
4:1–3	236, 245
4:1	240
4:2	246
4:4–6	245
4:6	236, 245–46
4:7	14, 243, 245–46, 268, 294
4:9–10	246
4:10	15, 243, 245–46, 268
5:14	237
6:3	238
6:5	237
6:7	236
6:11—7:1	236
6:11	236
7:1	236
7:16	237
8:1	236
8:7	235, 238
8:12	236
8:13	235, 263
9:2	235, 238
9:3	235, 263
9:10–17	237
9:10	235
9:11	40, 237
9:12	237
9:13	237
9:14	237
9:16	237–38, 247
10:1	238, 246
10:8	242
10:14	237
11:1–4	235–36
11:3	235
11:5	235, 263

Hosea (cont.)

11:6	237
11:8–11	236, 242
11:8–9	235
11:10–11	235–36, 242
12:2–6[1–5]	235
12:10[9]	235
12:14[13]	235, 242
13:3–4	235
13:5	235–36
13:8	237
13:15	237–38
14:1[13:6]	237
14:2–4[1–3]	247
14:4[3]	239
14:5–9[4–8]	236
14:5–8[4–7]	247
14:5[4]	236, 247
14:6–8[5–7]	235, 238, 242–43, 247, 294
14:6[5]	126, 247
14:7[6]	247
14:8[7]	126, 236
14:9[8]	236, 238, 247
14:10[9]	238

Joel

1	235
1:6	17, 149
2:18	236
2:19	235, 245
2:22–26	235
2:24	245
4:18	235

Amos

4:6–9	235
7:2	149
7:5	149
9:13–14	235

Jonah

3:1–10	18

Micah

4:1–3	250, 254, 259
4:1–2	3
4:3	149
4:9–10	135
4:11–13	249
5:1[2]	89
6:7	14
7:18–20	236

Nahum

1:14	191
3:3	189
3:4	258
3:8	214
3:15–16	189

Habakkuk

3:17	235

Haggai

1:10–11	235
2:6–9	250
2:19	235

Zechariah

1–8	248
1–6	267
1:1–6	267
1:3–6	267
1:4	248, 266
1:7–17	249–50
1:16–17	236, 249–54, 275, 281
1:16	249–50, 252, 255, 257, 267–68
1:17	252, 255

Zechariah (cont.)

2	266
2:1–4[1:18–21]	249, 251
2:2[1:19]	262
2:4[1:21]	249, 262
2:5–17[1–13]	252, 254, 258–60
2:5–9[1–5]	249–56
2:5–7[1–3]	251
2:8–14[4–10]	254, 281
2:8–9[4–5]	252, 254
2:8[4]	249, 251, 255, 257–59, 264–67, 272–75, 277–78, 282–83, 288, 294
2:9[5]	249, 252–253, 258, 275
2:10–17[6–13]	250–52, 255
2:10–13[6–9]	252
2:10–11[6–7]	249, 255, 257, 264, 266, 268, 275
2:11–14[7–10]	255
2:12–13[8–9]	249–50, 253, 255
2:13[9]	255
2:14–16[10–12]	252
2:14–15[10–11]	249, 253, 257, 268, 275
2:14[10]	249, 255, 264, 277
2:15[11]	3, 250, 253–55, 257, 259–60, 264, 267, 274, 278, 282
2:16[12]	252, 256
2:17[13]	252
3:8	249, 276
3:9	249
3:10	249
4:9	249
4:14	249
6:1–8	248
6:5	249
6:8	249
6:12–15	276
6:12	249
7–8	260, 267
7:1–3	256, 265
7:4–10	256
7:5	224
7:7	248, 266
7:12	248, 266
7:14	258
8	256–57, 259–60, 266
8:1–23	19, 256
8:2	249, 257
8:3	249, 257–58, 275
8:4–5	249–50, 256–60, 265–68, 273–75, 278, 281–83, 288, 294
8:4	251, 258, 266, 277
8:5	258, 272
8:7–8	249, 257, 264, 266, 268, 275
8:8	249, 253, 257, 264, 267, 275
8:9	249
8:10	252, 257
8:12	235, 249
8:13	249, 260
8:15	249
8:16–17	267
8:19	249, 267
8:20–23	3, 250, 257, 259, 274, 278, 282
8:22–23	259
8:22	149
8:23	249
9–14	248, 267
9–11	260
9:1—11:3	263
9–10	263
9:6–7	250
9:8	249
9:9–10	260, 276
9:9	249
9:10	249–50, 265
9:13	265
9:17—10:1	235, 249
10–11	260
10	262–64

Zechariah (cont.)

10:2	94, 260
10:3–5	260
10:3	260
10:6–12	249, 260, 263, 265–67
10:6–10	264
10:6	236, 249, 260, 263–64, 267–68, 275, 281
10:7–12	260
10:7	249, 260–261, 264, 277
10:8–12	275
10:8–11	264
10:8–10	260–68, 273–75, 281–83, 286, 288
10:8	249–50, 261–64, 266, 271, 279, 294
10:9–11	261
10:9–10	264
10:9	191, 211, 261–64, 271, 280–81, 294
10:10–11	261–63
10:10	249–50, 260–61, 294
10:11	260, 263
10:12	249
11:6	250
11:9	250
11:16	250
12–14	249, 260
12:1–9	249
12:4–9	249
12:5–6	89
12:6—13:1	276
13:1	249
13:7	190
13:8	250
13:9	249, 253
14:1–21	19
14:1–3	249
14:9	249, 259
14:11	249
14:12–15	249–50
14:14	251
14:15	252
14:16	3, 250
14:17–19	250

Malachi

2:4–9	195
3:10–11	235

~

Apocrypha

Sirach/Ecclesiasticus

16:1–3	98–99
17:3	32
49:10	232

Wisdom of Solomon

3:10–14	99
4:1	99
4:3	99

~

Pseudepigrapha

4 Ezra

14:41	232

~

New Testament

Acts

3:24	10
5:28	287
6:1	287
6:7	287

Acts (cont.)

9:13	287
12:24	287
19:20	287

Romans

9:25–28	287
9:25–26	241
9:27–28	120

1 Corinthians

7	37

Galatians

4:21–31	144, 287
4:27	145

1 Peter

2:10	241

Dead Sea Scrolls

1QIsaa

9:2[3]	116
44:4	127
49:17	136
51:2	140

1QSa

2:11	155

4QXIIa–b

	232

Mur

XII	232

8Hev

XIIgr	232

Rabbinic Writings

b. Yebamot

61b–66a	35
61b–62a	35
62a	35
62ab	37, 131
63b	36
64a	35–36

b. Sanhedrin

59ab	35
62ab	35

b. Pesahim

87b	233
88b	37, 131

t. Yebamot

8:4	35
8:5	35
8:7	36

m. Yebamot

6:6	35

m. Gittin

4:5	37, 131

Even Ha-ezer

1.1	36
1.5	35

Megillah

27a	37, 131

Hagigah

2b	37, 131

Baba Batra

13a	37, 131
13b–15a	232

'Eduyyot

1:13	37, 131

Genesis Rabbah

24:14	37

GRECO-ROMAN WRITINGS

Josephus

Against Apion

I.40	232

EARLY CHRISTIAN WRITINGS

Augustine

De civitate Dei

14.22	38

On the Literal Interpretation of Genesis

9.3.5–6	38

John of Damascus

On the Orthodox Faith

4.24	38

Eusebius of Caesarea

Demonstratio evangelica

9.3.8	38

www.ingramcontent.com/pod-product-compliance
Lightning Source LLC
Chambersburg PA
CBHW071148300426
44113CB00009B/1125